Developing Early Comprehension

Developing Early Comprehension

Laying the Foundation for Reading Success

edited by

Andrea DeBruin-Parecki, Ph.D.
Educational Testing Service
Early Childhood Research and Assessment Center
Princeton, New Jersey

Anne van Kleeck, Ph.D., CCC-SLP
University of Texas at Dallas
Dallas, Texas

and

Sabra Gear, Ph.D.
Old Dominion University
Norfolk, Virginia

·P A U L·H·
BROOKES
PUBLISHING CO ®

Baltimore • London • Sydney

Paul H. Brookes Publishing Co.
Post Office Box 10624
Baltimore, Maryland 21285-0624

www.brookespublishing.com

Typeset by Scribe Inc., Philadelphia, Pennsylvania.
Manufactured in the United States by
Sheridan Books, Inc., Chelsea, Michigan.

Cover photograph ©istockphoto/MariyaL

Photos are used by permission of the individuals pictured and/or their parents/guardians.

Case studies are real people or composites based on the authors' experiences. Real names and identifying details are used by permission.

Library of Congress Cataloging-in-Publication Data

The Library of Congress has cataloged the printed edition as follows:

Developing early comprehension : laying the foundation for reading success / edited by Andrea DeBruin-Parecki, Ph.D., Educational Testing Service, Early Childhood Research and Assessment Center, Princeton, New Jersey, Anne van Kleeck, Ph.D., CCC-SLP, University of Texas at Dallas, and Sabra Gear, Ph.D., Old Dominion University, Norfolk, Virginia.
       pages   cm
Summary: "Early comprehension is difficult to measure in prereaders. The topic is therefore often overlooked in research, tools, and interventions. This title serves as a remedy by presenting theoretical models of prereader comprehension as well as skill-boosting approaches to building strong foundations for future reading comprehension. Various methods include using play, academic talk, digital texts, and informational texts to promote emergent language comprehension and using vocabulary intervention to build listening comprehension. Contributors address special subpopulations and offer guidance on working with included and multilingual children. The text also addresses the role of parents, teachers, and executive functioning in prereader comprehension as well as assessment methods (existing and desired), challenges, and opportunities. Some chapters translate knowledge for the benefit of parents and practitioners. Others aim to fill gaps in current thinking, practices, and research"—Provided by publisher.
    Includes bibliographical references and index.
    ISBN 978-1-59857-034-2 (paperback)—ISBN 978-1-59857-918-5 (epub e-book)—ISBN 978-1-59857-917-8 (pdf e-book)
    1. Reading (Early childhood)—United States.   2. Reading comprehension—United States.
I. DeBruin-Parecki, Andrea.

LB1139.5.R43D48 2015
372.40973—dc23   2014040090

British Library Cataloguing in Publication data are available from the British Library.

2019   2018   2017   2016   2015

10   9   8   7   6   5   4   3   2   1

Contents

About the Editors

Andrea DeBruin-Parecki, Ph.D., Principal Research Project Manager, Educational Testing Service Early Childhood Research and Assessment Center, Princeton, New Jersey 08541

Dr. DeBruin-Parecki, a graduate of the Combined Program in Education and Psychology, University of Michigan, is recognized for her work in early and family literacy. She has written multiple books and articles and consistently presents at national conferences. As Senior Fulbright Specialist in Guatemala, she worked with teachers of young children. Her work has been in diverse communities, establishing effective literacy-related programs that positively affect families, teachers, and schools. She has worked directly with teachers through professional development, making positive, research-based changes resulting in more effective literacy instruction. She has authored two noted assessments: Early Literacy Skills Assessment (ELSA; High/Scope Press, 2004) and the Adult–Child Interactive Reading Inventory (ACIRI; available from Paul H. Brookes Publishing Co.). Her current research examines strategy instruction to promote young children's comprehension development and state and U.S. territory early literacy learning standards.

Anne van Kleeck, Ph.D., CCC-SLP, Professor and Callier Research Scholar, Callier Center for Communication Disorders, School of Behavioral and Brain Sciences, University of Texas at Dallas, Dallas, Texas 75235

Dr. van Kleeck's research focuses on language and emerging literacy skills in children with language impairments as well as the broader group of children who are at risk academically. Some specific areas of interests include parents' language socialization processes in the home that provide their young children with foundations for later literacy and academic success and issues related to language assessment in the preschool population. Her most recent work focuses on what she refers to as the academic talk register in preschoolers and its importance to later academic achievement. Dr. van Kleeck's previous publications include several edited books, nearly 50 peer-reviewed journal articles, and 25 book chapters. She has given several hundred invited and peer-reviewed presentations nationally and internationally.

Sabra Gear, Ph.D., Senior Lecturer, Department of Communication Disorders and Special Education, Darden College of Education, Old Dominion University, Norfolk, Virginia 23529

Dr. Gear teaches special education core courses: educational and diagnostic assessment, instructional methods, individual educational programming, directed field experience, collaboration, and transitions. Before teaching at Old Dominion University (ODU), she taught diverse learners in Grades pre-K–12, general and special education in public school, treatment programs, home-based instruction, and adult basic education. She has authored and coauthored book chapters and articles; has presented at international, national, and regional conferences; and is a member of the Council for Exceptional Children, including special interest divisions, and a member of the National Head Start Association. She is a reviewer for *National Head Start Association Dialog*. She is a contributing author and researcher for the Virginia Early Childhood Policy Center and the Teacher Immersion Residency Program at ODU. Her research goals include teacher and parent education to improve outcomes for children with disabilities.

About the Contributors

Sandra Barrueco, Ph.D., Associate Professor, Department of Psychology, O'Boyle Hall Room 314, Catholic University of America, Washington, DC 20064

Dr. Barrueco's expertise focuses on assessment and intervention approaches for young ethnically and linguistically diverse children and families, particularly of migrant and immigrant Latino communities. She has worked on research and clinical collaborations with communities, programs, and agencies throughout the United States and Puerto Rico. Dr. Barrueco is an Associate Professor of Psychology (Children, Families, and Cultures and Clinical Concentrations), Director of Latin American and Latino studies, and Policy Fellow at the Catholic University of America.

Kelly B. Cartwright, Ph.D., Professor, Psychology, Neuroscience, and Teacher Preparation, Christopher Newport University, 1 Avenue of the Arts, Newport News, Virginia 23693

Dr. Cartwright is a professor of psychology, neuroscience, and teacher preparation at Christopher Newport University, where she teaches courses on the development of thinking, learning, language and literacy, research, reading processes, and preschool and elementary reading. Her research focuses on the nature of skilled reading comprehension and the cognitive factors that underlie comprehension difficulties across the lifespan from preschool to adulthood.

Michael D. Coyne, Ph.D., Professor, Special Education, Neag School of Education, University of Connecticut, 249 Glenbrook Road, Unit 3064, Storrs, Connecticut 06269

Dr. Coyne is a professor of special education at the University of Connecticut. He is also a research scientist at the Center for Behavioral Education and Research. His research focuses on beginning reading and early vocabulary instruction and intervention, school-based experimental research, multitiered or response to intervention systems of support, and effective practices for students with learning disabilities.

Barbara E. Culatta, Ph.D., Associate Dean of Research, David O. McKay School of Education, Professor, Communication Disorders, 136 TLRB, Brigham Young University, Provo, Utah 84604

Dr. Culatta is a professor of communication disorders at Brigham Young University. She received her Ph.D. from the University of Pittsburgh and completed a postdoctoral fellowship at Johns Hopkins University. She has written books, articles, and chapters on language and literacy interventions and has received grants that resulted in the development of the Systematic and Engaging Early Literacy project (education.byu.edu/seel) and an app (Hideout: Early Reading).

Anne E. Cunningham, Ph.D., Professor, Graduate School of Education, 1501 Tolman Hall, University of California, Berkeley, Berkeley, California 94720

Dr. Cunningham is a professor in the Graduate School of Education at University of California, Berkeley. She examines the cognitive and motivational processes underlying reading ability and the interplay of context, development, and literacy instruction. Dr. Cunningham was a member of the National Early Literacy Panel and is coauthor of *Book Smart: How to Develop and Support Successful, Motivated Readers* (Oxford University Press, 2014).

David K. Dickinson, Ed.D., Professor, Department of Teaching and Learning, Peabody College, 230 Appleton Place, Vanderbilt University, Nashville, Tennessee 37203

Dr. Dickinson has long been interested in the relationship between language and early literacy development. Building on insights gained as part of a longitudinal study, he has developed tools to describe classrooms, has coauthored a curriculum, and currently is working on an intervention designed to teach vocabulary by combining book reading and supported play.

Caitlin McMunn Dooley, Ph.D., Associate Professor, Graduate Programs Coordinator, Early Childhood and Elementary Education, 30 Pryor Street, Georgia State University, Atlanta, Georgia 30303

Dr. Dooley's research investigates digital literacies, emergent comprehension, literacy instruction and testing in elementary grades, and teacher development. She is coeditor of *Language Arts,* the National Council of Teachers of English premier journal (2011–2016), and has led and evaluated funded research totaling more than $16.2 million. Follow Dr. Dooley via Twitter @Educateyourkido.

Nell K. Duke, Ed.D., Professor, School of Education, 610 East University Avenue, University of Michigan, Ann Arbor, Michigan 48109

Dr. Duke is a professor of literacy, language, and culture and faculty affiliate in the combined program in education and psychology at the University of Michigan and a member of the International Reading Association Literacy Research Panel. Dr. Duke's work focuses on early literacy development, particularly among children living in poverty. Her publications include *Literacy and the Youngest Learner: Best Practices for Educators of Children from Birth to Five* (Scholastic, 2005); *Beyond Bedtime Stories: A Parent's Guide to Promoting Reading, Writing, and Other Literacy Skills from Birth to 5* (Scholastic, 2014); and *The ABCs of Emergent Literacy* (Scholastic, 2012).

Billie J. Enz, Ph.D., Emeritus Professor, Mary Lou Fulton Teacher's College, 1050 South Forest Mall, Arizona State University, Tempe, Arizona 85281

Dr. Enz is an emeritus professor in Mary Lou Fulton Teacher's College at Arizona State University. During her 40 year career, she was a classroom teacher, university administrator, and faculty member in the early childhood department at Arizona State University, Mary Lou Fulton Teacher's College. Her research interests include teacher development, parent education, and family literacy.

Geraldine M. Fernández, B.S., Doctoral Candidate, Clinical Psychology, Department of Psychology, O'Boyle Hall Room 314, Catholic University of America, Washington, DC 20064

Ms. Fernández is a doctoral student in clinical psychology with a specialization in children, families, and cultures at the Catholic University of America. Her research and clinical interest focus on the relationship between acculturation-related risk factors and the development and maintenance of developmental psychopathology, particularly anxiety disorders and depression. Throughout her training, she has been dedicated to treating a range of emotional disorders in children and adolescents, including anxiety, depression, and trauma.

Roberta Michnick Golinkoff, Ph.D., Unidel H. Rodney Sharp Professor, School of Education, Willard Hall, University of Delaware, Newark, Delaware 19716

Dr. Golinkoff has won numerous awards for her work, including the Urie Bronfenbrenner lifetime achievement award from the American Psychological Association; the James McKeen Cattell Fellow Award for lifetime achievement in applied psychological research from the Association for Psychological Science; and the Francis Alison Award, the highest honor at her university. Her research, supported by federal grants, has resulted in more than 150 articles and 12 books. She is an expert on language development, playful learning, and children's early spatial knowledge and is passionate about the dissemination of psychological science. She cofounded the Ultimate Block Party movement to celebrate the science behind play and speaks all over the world.

Nicole Ruther Guajardo, Ph.D., Professor, Department of Psychology, Christopher Newport University, 1 Avenue of the Arts, Newport News, Virginia 23693

Dr. Guajardo is a professor of psychology at Christopher Newport University, where she teaches courses on human development across the lifespan, including physical, social, and cognitive development. Her research focuses on social-cognitive development during childhood with a focus on theory of mind and counterfactual reasoning. Her work has examined the roles of social and cognitive factors in how children come to reason about their own and others' mental states and behaviors.

Kendra M. Hall-Kenyon, Ph.D., Associate Professor, Department of Teacher Education, David O. McKay School of Education, 301 MCKB, Brigham Young University, Provo, Utah 84604

Dr. Hall-Kenyon is an associate professor in the Department of Teacher Education at Brigham Young University. She received her Ph.D. from Teachers College, Columbia University. Dr. Hall-Kenyon has multiple publications and presentations in the areas of early literacy instruction and assessment and early childhood teacher education.

Kathy Hirsh-Pasek, Ph.D., Debra and Stanley Lefkowitz Faculty Fellow, Department of Psychology, Temple University, Weiss Hall, 1701 North 13th Street, Philadelphia, Pennsylvania 19122

Dr. Hirsh-Pasek is the Debra and Stanley Lefkowitz Faculty Fellow at Temple University. A national expert in language and cognitive psychology, her research has been funded by the National Science Foundation, the National Institutes of Health and Human Development, and the Institute of Education Sciences, resulting in 11 books and more than 200 publications. She is the recipient of the American Psychological Association's Urie Bronfenbrenner Award for Lifetime Contribution to Developmental Psychology in the Service of Science and Society, and she is the president-elect of the International Society on Infant Studies. In addition, she is a fellow of the American Psychological Association and the American Psychological Society and has served as the associate editor of *Child Development.*

Janne Lepola, Ph.D., Researcher, University of Turku, Seminaarikatu 1, 26100 Rauma, Finland

Dr. Lepola has been conducting longitudinal studies on motivation and learning to read and focusing on those children who struggle in the acquisition of reading and math skills. Dr. Lepola recently carried out a longitudinal study on the development of children's narrative comprehension skills from preschool age to Grade 3.

Julie S. Lynch, Ph.D., Associate Professor, Department of Psychology, 7400 Bay Road, Saginaw Valley State University, University Center, Michigan 48710

Dr. Lynch earned a Ph.D. in educational psychology from the University of Minnesota. Her research explores the complex mental processes involved in producing and comprehending language. In addition to her ongoing work examining the development of children's narrative comprehension, she is also interested in the development of college students' writing skills.

John P. Madura, M.A., Program in Measurement, Evaluation and Research, Department of Educational Psychology, Neag School of Education, University of Connecticut, 249 Glenbrook Road, Unit 3064, Storrs, Connecticut 06269

Mr. Madura's substantive interests center on aspects of interpersonal perceptions and dyadic relationships that occur in school settings and affect both student achievement and teacher evaluation. His methodological research focuses broadly on structural equation modeling and multilevel modeling, as well as extensions that combine the strengths of the two approaches in the emerging area of multilevel structural equation modeling. He also maintains an interest in philosophical theories of psychological measurement.

D. Betsy McCoach, Ph.D., Coprincipal Investigator, Professor, Measurement, Evaluation, and Assessment, Department of Educational Psychology, Neag School of Education, University of Connecticut, 249 Glenbrook Road, Unit 3064, Storrs, Connecticut 06269

Dr. McCoach has extensive experience in hierarchical linear modeling, instrument design, factor analysis, and structural equation modeling. She is Director of the Data Analysis Training Institute of Connecticut at University of Connecticut (UConn) and teaches weeklong training courses in structural equation modeling and hierarchical linear modeling every summer. Dr. McCoach is also the founder and program chair of the Modern Modeling Methods conference, held annually at UConn. She has coauthored nearly 100 peer-reviewed journal articles, book chapters, and books, including *Instrument Design in the Affective Domain* (Springer, 2013) and *Multilevel Modeling of Educational Data* (Information Age Publishing, 2008). She is the current coeditor of the *Gifted Child Quarterly* and associate editor of *Frontiers in Quantitative Psychology and Measurement.*

Sabina Rak Neugebauer, Ed.D., Assistant Professor, Department of Education, Water Tower Campus, 820 North Michigan Avenue, Loyola University Chicago, Chicago, Illinois 60611

Dr. Neugebauer's research focuses on the language and literacy development of linguistically diverse students from childhood through adolescence. Her research aims to identify linguistic and affective factors that influence students' reading comprehension for improving the literacy outcomes of students in traditionally underserved schools. She received her doctorate from the Harvard Graduate School of Education. She has published in journals including *The Reading Teacher, Reading Psychology, Learning and Individual Difference,* and *Journal of School Psychology,* among others. Dr. Neugebauer has also taught and collaborated with teachers across multiple settings, including elementary and middle school classrooms in the United States and abroad.

Katherine M. Newman, M.S., Doctoral Student, Department of Teaching and Learning, Peabody College, 230 Appleton Place, Vanderbilt University, Nashville, Tennessee 37203

Ms. Newman is a doctoral student in the Department of Teaching and Learning at Vanderbilt University's Peabody College of Education and Human Development. Her research interests include early childhood language and literacy development and the role of adult-guided play in promoting literacy. She is particularly focused on improving educational opportunities for preschool children from low-income backgrounds.

Shana Pribesh, Ph.D., Associate Professor, Educational Research and Statistics, Old Dominion University, Hampton Boulevard, Norfolk, Virginia 23508

Dr. Pribesh is an Associate Professor of Educational Research and Statistics at Old Dominion University. She earned a Ph.D. in sociology from Ohio State University. She has more than 2 decades of educational research experience, having worked with organizations such as the American Institutes for Research, RAND, and the University of Michigan. She is interested in the intersection of poverty and educational inequality.

Jill Stamm, Ph.D., Associate Clinical Professor, Mary Lou Fulton Teacher's College, 1050 South Forest Mall, Arizona State University, Tempe, Arizona 85281

Dr. Stamm is a clinical associate professor in Mary Lou Fulton Teachers College at Arizona State University, where she teaches both graduate and undergraduate classes in educational psychology and in learning and instruction. Her research interests include the understanding of the development of brain systems that support early learning, specifically attention, bonding, and communication.

Sharon M. Ware, Ph.D., Research Associate, Neag School of Education, University of Connecticut, 249 Glenbrook Road, Unit 3064, Storrs, Connecticut 06269

Dr. Ware is an educational researcher at the University of Connecticut. She is also a research associate at the Center for Behavioral Education and Research. Her research interests focus on early vocabulary instruction and intervention and on the language and literacy development of struggling readers and English language learners.

Meghan M. Welch, M.S., Doctoral Fellow, Early Childhood Education, 30 Pryor Street, Georgia State University, Atlanta, Georgia 30303

Ms. Welch is a Ph.D. candidate in the Department of Early Childhood Education at Georgia State University. Previously a prekindergarten teacher and early education media specialist at WTTW in Chicago, Illinois, and Georgia Public Broadcasting in Atlanta, Georgia, she now works with the university to provide professional development for Georgia's pre-K teachers.

Jamie Zibulsky, Ph.D., Assistant Professor and Director, School Psychology MA/Certification Program, Fairleigh Dickinson University, 1000 River Road, Teaneck, New Jersey 07666

Dr. Zibulsky is the coauthor of *Book Smart: How to Develop and Support Successful, Motivated Readers* (Oxford University Press, 2014), a how-to guide for parents aimed at addressing the broad range of skills that foster reading success.

Foreword

Developing comprehension skills in early childhood has been a neglected topic in the field of early literacy. This book begins to build an important foundation for a better understanding of this important topic. It is a welcome addition to the corpus of research on the critical skills children will need to become successful readers and writers.

Understanding of early literacy in many ways has been informed by the notion of the "simple view." This is a formula posited by Gough and Tunmer (1986) to provide a parsimonious understanding of reading. It suggests the following: Reading Achievement (RA) = Decoding (D) × Language Comprehension (LC). Basically, it argues that to be able to read, children will need both strategies to decode words and the background knowledge and skills to understand them. It also recognizes that you can't have one without the other. Decoding, without comprehension, is not reading; comprehending words without strategies to decode new words is also not reading. Although there are critics who might say the "simple view" is far too simple, it still is an important equation to consider in early literacy learning.

Nevertheless, the bulk of the research in early literacy has often focused on the former part of the equation and not the latter. There are literally thousands of research studies on phonological awareness, phonemic awareness, and phonics, and the important roles they play in early literacy. The intent is not to diminish this important research, but, at the same time, there is a paucity of research on comprehension and its development in the early years.

Here's what is known about the other side of the equation: language comprehension. Oral language development, vocabulary learning, and children's beginning understandings of what they know (or their metacognition) are highly related to developing comprehension. And this volume has brought together some of the major scholars who have been at the forefront of this work together. Children's oral language, both receptive and expressive, highly predicts their listening comprehension. Activities such as play, informational text, digital texts, and other firsthand experiences support language development and comprehension.

Furthermore, children are highly capable of learning new words, both sophisticated and content-rich words, through various interventions. In other words, vocabulary is a highly alterable factor that can be influenced and accelerated through high-quality instruction. It does, however, often require a more intensive and longer-dosage approach to teaching than the constrained skills of alphabet knowledge—or phonics, for that matter. For example, meta-analyses (Marulis & Neuman, 2010; Marulis & Neuman, 2013) and research (Beck & McKeown, 2007) show that children will need explicit definitions, embedded practice using the words in meaningful contexts, practice, distributed review, and ongoing progress monitoring.

But language development and specific vocabulary learning doesn't help explain the whole construct of comprehension and what enables a child to become a good versus a poor comprehender. In other words, one cannot rely on vocabulary studies alone to improve comprehension. Yet to some extent, this is where many researchers and practitioners have come to a bit of a dead end. In terms of instructional practice, what other components might influence and, therefore, potentially be subject to more targeted intervention than vocabulary and overall general language skills?

In this volume, you'll read about some interesting new developments. For example, there is evidence that executive functioning plays an important role in early comprehension development. And there's evidence that multilingualism in early childhood helps develop cognitive skills that are related to greater comprehension development early on as well as later in students' achievement. Therefore, in this volume, you will read about some exciting new research that can inform instructional practices—areas that have not been considered to be at the center of early literacy learning.

Researchers are also coming to understand the enormous role that background knowledge plays in comprehension. In fact, experiments have begun to question whether comprehension, particularly in the early years, is a generic skill or one so closely tied to one's background knowledge that it may be hard to distinguish the two. For example, a child who knows a good deal about baseball is far more likely to comprehend a text about baseball than someone who has never watched the sport. Furthermore, if a child is very low in vocabulary knowledge but high in background knowledge on a topic, the background knowledge will often mitigate the vocabulary disadvantage. In addition, it has also been shown that interest and engagement in a subject or topic can play a tremendous role in reading comprehension for young children, supporting their learning despite some limitations in vocabulary or background knowledge.

The caregiver is so central to children's development that it would be difficult to talk about comprehension without reference to the parent and other supportive adults. Unlike later on, children are dependent on these adults to provide nurturance and care, education, cognitive experiences, values, and attitudes toward reading and writing that are surely to carry on throughout the child's development. As these chapters show, it is the parents and caregivers who support imaginative play, shared reading, and negotiating text and who help the young child begin to think like a reader and a writer. These early literacy lessons are crucial for the child's development, sense of security, and interest in learning.

All this is to say that this is an exciting field of research, with many new areas to explore. What the authors in this volume do especially well is that they understand early childhood development and the processes of early reading. They recognize that early reading development might look different from later reading and writing with print. They describe in beautifully articulated chapters the state of the field in developing comprehension. They also point to where the research must continue to explore in order to ensure that all children successfully become knowledgeable readers and writers.

Susan B. Neuman, Ed.D.
Professor of Early Childhood and Literacy
New York University

REFERENCES

Beck, I., & McKeown, M. (2007). Increasing young low-income children's oral vocabulary repertoires through rich and focused instruction. *Elementary School Journal, 107*(3), 251–271.

Gough, P., & Tunmer, W. (1986). Decoding, reading, and reading disabilities. *Remedial and Special Education, 7,* 6–10.

Marulis, L.M., & Neuman, S.B. (2010). The effects of vocabulary training on word learning: A meta-analysis. *Review of Educational Research, 80*(3), 300–335.

Marulis, L., & Neuman, S.B. (2013). How vocabulary interventions affect young children at-risk: A meta-analytic review. *Journal of Research on Educational Effectiveness, 6,* 223–262.

Preface

As decoding and comprehension have become more widely viewed as two separable aspects of reading, following the model of reading posited by Gough and Tunmer (1986), researchers have been able to discern the different preliterate foundations for each. In the past decades, a plethora of work on the code-related skills of phonological awareness, alphabet knowledge, and combinations of the two have greatly advanced our basic understanding of the role these skills play in the reading process (e.g., Melby-Lervàg, Lyster, & Hulme, 2012). This has resulted in many highly successful interventions for prereaders and early readers that have been discussed in a number of meta-analyses (Bus & van IJzendoorn, 1999; Ehri et al., 2001; Lonigan, Schatschneider, Westberg, & the National Early Literacy Panel, 2008; Wagner, 1988).

To date, interventions fostering foundations for later reading comprehension have primarily been focused on one particular activity—reading storybooks aloud to prereaders—and have typically considered child outcomes primarily in the areas of vocabulary, broader receptive and expressive language skills, participation level, and, in some cases, later decoding and reading comprehension abilities. Several reviews (e.g., Dickinson, Griffith, Golinkoff, & Hirsh-Pasek, 2012; Scarborough & Dobrich, 1994) and meta-analyses of this work have occurred over time (e.g., Blok, 1999; Bus, van IJzendoorn, & Pellegrini, 1995; Dunst, Simkus, & Hamby, 2012; Lonigan, Shanahan, Cunningham, & the National Early Literacy Panel, 2008; Mol & Bus, 2011; Mol, Bus, & de Jong, 2009; Mol, Bus, de Jong, & Smeets, 2008). The purpose of this volume is to include these important efforts focused on the storybook-sharing activity but also extend considerably beyond them in order to consider a number of additional issues and areas of development important to providing foundations for later reading comprehension during the preschool years. Our goal for the book is to communicate the importance of this wider array of concerns related to prereader comprehension to policy makers, researchers, and professional educators.

The authors whose writings appear within the 12 chapters and the foreword have concentrated on topics related to their own major contributions to early comprehension research, scholarship, and evidence-based practices. Some chapters translate existing knowledge for the benefit of parents and practitioners. Other chapters aim to fill gaps in current thinking and practices, thereby pointing the way for future work in this critically important area of school readiness. Finally, some chapters accomplish multiple goals.

The variety of important topics aligned with prereader comprehension easily supported the 12 chapters written for this book. DeBruin-Parecki and Pribesh, in Chapter 1, address a critical issue in education—narrowing the achievement gap in comprehension for school-age readers through early, effective, targeted strategy instruction. A preschool comprehension strategy curriculum developed by DeBruin-Parecki is presented along with evidence regarding the efficacy of educating early childhood teachers to implement this type of instruction in their classrooms.

In Chapter 2, Coyne, Neugebauer, Ware, McCoach, and Madura discuss the strong role that vocabulary plays in developing early comprehension. Coyne and his colleagues present four prominent hypotheses and a theoretical framework that links vocabulary and comprehension, followed by an overview of research trends since the mid-1980s on this topic. Finally, they present evidence from a vocabulary intervention they conducted that had a positive impact on children's listening comprehension.

In Chapter 3, Newman, Dickinson, Hirsh-Pasek, and Golinkoff build upon the role of oral language and vocabulary, providing insight into the comprehension process and demonstrating the importance and uses of teacher-guided social pretend play for children. These authors further describe how to implement appropriate practices that promote the successful understanding of narratives.

In Chapter 4, van Kleeck makes the case for reconceptualizing preschoolers' oral language to include two broad registers: casual talk and academic talk, with the latter being critically important to school success when used at school and at home during the preschool years. By reexamining existing research on mother–children interaction, she demonstrates that some preschoolers are consistently exposed to the academic talk register at home, whereas other preschoolers experience far less exposure to this type of talk. This author synthesizes and conceptually organizes research and scholarship from a wide array of disciplines to flesh out the many distinctions between these two registers.

Fusing comprehension with technology, in Chapter 5, Dooley and Welch describe a child's view of making meaning from the plethora of information-rich sources that exist in the digital world. These authors explain how symbol systems can be used to enhance children's language and literacy experiences, contributing to the development of emergent comprehension. Dooley and Welch also offer pragmatic ideas and recommendations for parents and teachers to take advantage of the latest digital applications that have been shown to benefit children's comprehension.

In Chapter 6, Hall-Kenyon, Culatta, and Duke provide a rationale for using informational texts in the preschool classroom to build knowledge and comprehension, thereby elaborating on a key requirement in the Common Core State Standards. Hall-Kenyon and colleagues describe the abundant possibilities and benefits to children as more attention is focused on including information in preschool curricula. These efforts will build important awareness of the different structure of informational texts and also help build children's world knowledge, both of which will be critical to their later reading comprehension.

The next two chapters address the needs of specific populations of children: those with disabilities and those who are dual- or multilingual learners. In Chapter 7, Gear delivers a guide for preschool teachers and family members who work with children with disabilities. Data on the increasing prevalence and diversity of disability characteristics given in this chapter provide a compelling rationale for early identification and intervention to improve prereader comprehension and help to prevent later school failure. Gear offers specific recommendations for effective, evidence-based interventions that can be implemented by parents and teachers in everyday adult–child interactions. In Chapter 8, Barrueco and Fernández address the continual growth of multilingualism in the United States and relate this information specifically to the educational needs of children who speak languages other than (or in addition to) English in the home. These authors illuminate the many complexities that are often encountered in considering the early comprehension development of bilingual and multilingual children. Barrueco and Fernández also describe evidence-based assessments and interventions that are most appropriate for this population of young children.

In Chapter 9, Cartwright and Guajardo discuss the neuroscience behind complex processes involved in prereader comprehension, focusing specifically on various aspects of executive function. These authors review research supporting the critical role of different dimensions of executive function in prereader comprehension. They organize their treatment of this topic by examining cool functions (cognitive functions such as planning, working memory, and inhibition) and hot functions (which hone in on social, emotional, and motivational components of self-regulation). The practical implications for preschool teachers include how to enhance different aspects of executive function during such activities as story reading, story mapping, and guided discussions.

Because the cycle of teaching and learning necessitates gathering relevant information, Lynch and Lepola's Chapter 10 focuses on issues related to the assessment of comprehension. These authors provide a comprehensive overview of assessment methods for teachers and professionals who develop, administer, and interpret measures of comprehension. They also identify a number of challenges unique to assessing complex comprehension processes in young children and respond to those challenges with suggested practical applications of current, commercially available assessments.

In Chapter 11, Enz and Stamm focus on the child's first teachers—their parents—and consider the critically important parent–child interactions from birth through early childhood that potentially influence a child's understanding of his or her world. Enz and Stamm also review the research that supports the effectiveness of parent–child interactive, shared reading in promoting prereader comprehension.

Finally, in Chapter 12, Zibulsky and Cunningham present a developmental continuum related to comprehension growth. They discuss both listening and reading comprehension and the similarities and differences between them. The authors emphasize the shared, interactive nature of comprehension development, how it relates to children's cognitive and oral language development, and what teachers and parents can do to help their children in classrooms and at home.

Taken together, these chapters provide ample evidence that the realm of reading comprehension is indeed a very complex one and that researchers are just beginning to understand some of the foundations for reading comprehension that potentially emerge during the preschool years. Naigles (2002) published an article titled "Form Is Easy, Meaning Is Hard: Resolving a Paradox in Early Child Language." She provided ample evidence that in oral language acquisition, learning form is easy, as even infants have remarkable abilities in this respect. However, linking knowledge of language form to meaning is a far more difficult and prolonged process.

The same can be said for the later acquisition of written language. Written word identification, which includes decoding ability and sight word recognition, is a relatively simple and straightforward process. Researchers have done much to understand this process and to develop effective interventions for teaching it. Attaching meaning to what is read, however, is anything but simple and straightforward. All of us interested in preparing preschoolers for the later demands of reading comprehension have a great deal of work to do in further fleshing out our basic understanding of the development of comprehension and its accompanying elements. By learning more in this area, it will become increasingly apparent how to foster those skills in children in feasible and effective ways. It is our hope that the varied contributions in this volume will help to move those efforts forward.

REFERENCES

Blok, H. (1999). Reading two young children in educational settings: A meta-analysis of recent research. *Language Learning, 49*(2), 343–371.

Bus, A.G., & van IJzendoorn, M.H. (1999). Phonological awareness and early reading: A meta-analysis of experimental training studies. *Journal of Educational Psychology, 91,* 403–414.

Bus, A.G., van IJzendoorn, M.H., & Pellegrini, A. (1995). Joint book reading makes for success in learning to read: A meta-analysis on intergenerational transmission of literacy. *Review of Educational Research, 65,* 1–21.

Dickinson, D.K., Griffith, J.A., Golinkoff, R.M., & Hirsh-Pasek, K. (2012). How reading books fosters language development around the world. *Child Development Research.* Article ID 602807. Retrieved from http://dx.doi.org/602810.601155/602012/602807

Dunst, C.J., Simkus, A., & Hamby, D.W. (2012). Effects of reading to infants antivirus on their early language development. *Center for Early Literacy Learning Reviews, 5*(4), 1–7.

Ehri, L.C., Nunes, S.R., Willows, D.M., Schuster, B.V., Yaghoub-Zadeh, Z., & Shanahan, T. (2001). Phonemic awareness instruction helps children learn to read: Evidence from the National Reading Panel's meta-analysis. *Reading Research Quarterly, 36*(3), 250–287.

Gough, P.B., & Tunmer, W.E. (1986). Decoding, reading, and reading disability. *Remedial and Special Education, 7,* 6–10.

Lonigan, C.J., Schatschneider, C., Westberg, L., & the National Early Literacy Panel. (2008). Impact of code-focused interventions on young children's early literacy skills. In National Early Literacy Panel (Ed.), *Developing early literacy: Report of the National Early Literacy Panel* (pp. 107–151). Washington, DC: National Institute for Literacy.

Lonigan, C.J., Shanahan, T., Cunningham, A., & the National Early Literacy Panel. (2008). Impact of shared-reading interventions on young children's early literacy skills. In National Early Literacy Panel (Ed.), *Developing early literacy: Report of the National Early Literacy Panel* (pp. 153–171). Washington, DC: National Institute for Literacy.

Melby-Lervàg, M., Lyster, S.H., & Hulme, C. (2012). Phonological skills and their role in learning to read: A meta-analytic review. *Psychological Bulletin, 138*(2), 322–352.

Mol, S.E., & Bus, A.G. (2011). To read or not to read: A meta-analysis of print exposure from infancy to early adulthood. *Psychological Bulletin.*

Mol, S.E., Bus, A.G., & de Jong, M.T. (2009). Interactive book reading in early education: A tool to stimulate print knowledge as well as oral language. *Review of Educational Research, 79*(2), 979–1007.

Mol, S.E., Bus, A.G., de Jong, M.T., & Smeets, D.J.H. (2008). Added value of dialogic parent-child book readings: A meta-analysis. *Early Education and Development, 19*(1), 7–26.

Naigles, L.R. (2002). Form is easy, meaning is hard: Resolving a paradox in early child language. *Cognition, 86,* 157–199. doi: 10.1016/S0010-0277(02)00177-4

Scarborough, H.S., & Dobrich, W. (1994). On the efficacy of reading to preschoolers. *Developmental Review, 14,* 245–302.

Wagner, R.K. (1988). Causal relations between the development of phonological processing abilities and the acquisition of reading skills: A meta-analysis. *Merrill-Palmer Quarterly, 34*(3), 261–279.

1

Evening the Playing Field

The Importance of Teaching All Young Children Comprehension Strategies

ANDREA DEBRUIN-PARECKI AND SHANA PRIBESH

When two specific words—*achievement* and *gap*—are put together, they result in a multitude of various people expressing passionate concern and promising to work hard to facilitate positive change. The *achievement gap* is defined as occurring "when one group of students outperforms another group and the difference in average scores for the two groups is statistically significant (that is larger than the margin of error)" (National Center for Education Statistics, 2014). The achievement gap has existed for a very long time and has most affected children in poverty, particularly those who are African American and Hispanic (Hemphill & Vanneman, 2010; Vanneman, Hamilton, Baldwin Anderson, & Rahman, 2009). Although the achievement gap can be the result of multiple factors in children's lives that occur within many contexts, this chapter focuses only on school. One specific means of attempting to narrow this gap—comprehension strategy instruction in preschool—is proposed with the aim of getting children ready to enter school better prepared to succeed.

EVIDENCE OF THE NEED FOR EARLY COMPREHENSION STRATEGY INSTRUCTION

The National Assessment of Educational Progress (NAEP) Reading Assessment measures reading and comprehension skills by having students read age-appropriate passages and answer related questions. The cognitive targets being assessed are the understanding of written text; the development and interpretation of meaning; and the appropriate use of meaning concerning the type of text, purpose, and situation—all skills directly related to reading comprehension. The 2013 NAEP report results reported no improvement in reading for fourth-grade students. Up to 65% of all fourth-grade children in the United States are reading either at or below the basic level. There are still large differences among racial groups in terms of those reading below reading proficiency levels. Blacks have the highest percentage of fourth-grade students who are reading below proficiency (83%), and Latinos (81%) and American Indians (78%) are not far behind. This is in comparison to the lower percentages of their white (55%) and Asian fourth-grade counterparts (49%). In addition, 93% of students whose first language is not English are below proficient in reading, and their proficiency rates have not improved in the last 10 years (Annie E. Casey Foundation, 2014).

The Reading First Impact Study (Gamse, Bloom, Kemple, & Jacob, 2008) adds to the reading achievement gap information by revealing that on average, across participating sites, Reading First did not increase the percentages of students whose reading comprehension scores were at or above grade level in the first, second, or third grade, as fewer than half of the students in these grades were reading at or above grade level. Those children reading below grade level who cannot understand short paragraphs such as those appearing in age-appropriate books will only continue to have problems understanding text across all subject areas.

All this evidence leads to the conclusion that children who struggle with reading comprehension continue to lag behind those who do not and need earlier intervention to assist them in developing their comprehension abilities before they get frustrated, lose motivation to learn, and continue to fail. If students are fluent in reading by decoding but do not understand what they are reading, they are not learning and therefore fall behind. Teaching comprehension strategies to promote understanding at a younger age is an effective method of promoting future reading success and leads to increased learning and accomplishment. Comprehension strategy instruction cannot wait until children learn to read. They can learn listening comprehension strategies that studies have shown transfer to reading comprehension (Garner & Bochna, 2004; Kendeou, van den Broek, White, & Lynch, 2007). These strategies must be taught earlier to provide children with the tools they need to become successful readers (DeBruin-Parecki & Squibb, 2011; DeBruin-Parecki & Vaughn, 2014; Hansen, 2004; Morrow, 1985; Paris & Paris, 2007).

WHAT IS PRESCHOOL COMPREHENSION STRATEGY INSTRUCTION?

What does comprehension mean for preschool children? It typically refers to listening comprehension that occurs when children link ideas and concepts to create meaning through listening and personal interaction (Dickinson & Tabors, 2001; Morrow, 1988; Teale, 1985). The more familiar term "reading comprehension" is aimed at older children who are able to directly read written text to make meaning (Hoover & Gough, 1990; Snow, 2002). The development of comprehension begins with listening and oral interaction and the strategies learned to effectively advance listening comprehension. Children also learn strategies that enable them to use pictures to create understanding. These early comprehension strategies help to build the bridge to learning to read and comprehend text (Kendeou, van den Broek, White, & Lynch, 2007; Perfetti, Landi, & Oakhill, 2005). For an excellent discussion of the links between listening and reading comprehension, see Chapter 12 by Zibulsky and Cunningham.

Developing preschool children's comprehension abilities can be accomplished by teaching them specific strategies. Here a strategy is defined as a method of assisting a child to reach a goal—in this case, learning to comprehend. Dymock noted, "Research indicates that comprehension strategies should be explicitly taught and modeled long term at all grade levels" (2007, p. 161; see also Pressley, 2002). Students should practice strategies with guidance in a variety of contexts with multiple texts until they understand the strategy and when and how to apply it (Pressley, 2002). For a discussion of the cognitive aspects of children's learning strategies, see Chapter 9 by Cartwright and Guajardo and Chapter 12 by Zibulsky and Cunningham.

Over the years, there has been some debate about which strategies are best to teach young children. Many studies exist that have an emphasis on teaching children comprehension strategies, but typically they have focused on one type of skill such as inferencing, often called predicting (Kendeou, Bonn-Gettler, White, & van den Broek, 2008; Morrow, 2005; Reed & Vaughn, 2012; van Kleeck, 2008). For more detailed information about inferencing and retelling (recalling), please see Chapter 3 by Newman, Dickinson, Hirsh-Pasek, and Golinkoff; Chapter 10 by Lynch and Lepola; and Chapter 12 by Zibulsky and Cunningham.

In a longitudinal research study by Bianco et al. (2010) that focused on children in preschool and kindergarten, multiple comprehension strategies including inferencing, knowledge activation (background knowledge), and monitoring (thinking aloud and inconsistency checking and resolving) were taught. Children participated in one of three conditions: component skills of comprehension, storybook reading with no explicit comprehension instruction, or phonological awareness. Results showed that those in the comprehension component skills group improved their oral comprehension beyond that of the other two groups. The training was long term (two semesters), and effects still existed 9 months after the program ended. The storybook group showed no improvement in comprehension. Phonological awareness training improved phonological awareness but not comprehension, and comprehension training improved comprehension but not phonological awareness, demonstrating that these skills develop separately, as many have claimed (Kendeou, van den Broek, White, & Lynch, 2009; Paris & Paris, 2003). As a result of this study, researchers concluded that instruction in oral language skills and multiple comprehension strategies must begin at a young age because this knowledge transfers to later reading comprehension (Bianco et al., 2010). Others also agree that a focus on specific areas of early literacy instruction such as prereader comprehension development can have a positive effect on later reading comprehension (Oakhill & Cain, 2012; Snow, Burns, & Griffin, 1998).

In a more recent study examining the impact of oral comprehension strategy training on reading achievement in the first grade, Bianco et al. (2012) found that listening and reading comprehension skills are highly correlated in children. This provides even further evidence of the importance of teaching young children how to comprehend (Bianco et al., 2012). Learning useful strategies that assist in developing listening comprehension abilities brings children to the core of text comprehension. "this is the only way to accompany children on the pathway toward reading mastery and towards acquiring the ability to understand and learn from what they read" (Bianco et al., 2012, p. 446).

WHY HAS COMPREHENSION STRATEGY INSTRUCTION NOT BEEN A FOCUS OF PRESCHOOL CURRICULA?

Although many preschool curricula include comprehension in the form of vocabulary instruction or scripted read-alouds, there is little time spent on the strategies that would help children learn to comprehend. Teachers often spend a cursory amount of time on comprehension and focus a great deal more on easily measured skills such as alphabet and phonological awareness, the skills children most typically will be tested on and for which teachers will be held accountable. These constrained skills—skills mastered quickly—can provide more accurate measures, allowing for easily presented results and clearer, sounder empirical study (Paris, 2005; Paris & Luo, 2010; Paris & Paris, 2006). Comprehension is complex and composed of a multitude of unconstrained skills—skills learned throughout a lifetime. "Comprehension in its different forms cannot be quantified and assessed easily along a single dimension—unlike phenomena such as height, weight, and perhaps even basic reading skills such as vocabulary and phonological awareness" (Kendeou et al., 2005, p. 92). Until early comprehension measurement catches up to the multitude of constrained skills measures on the market, it is unlikely that it will easily become a major focus of preschool classroom instruction. (See Chapter 10 by Lynch and Lepola for a comprehensive review of early comprehension assessment.)

COMPREHENSION STRATEGY CURRICULUM: ENHANCING PRESCHOOLERS IN COMPREHENSION

As mentioned previously, Bianco et al. (2012) found that early comprehension strategy training is indeed possible and helps young children improve their ability to comprehend. In addition, they discovered that for the training to be successful, it needs to contain well-defined comprehension-focused activities and must be consistent and occur over a long time period—in their case, the equivalent of two school semesters. Finally, teachers need to receive effective training to not only teach strategies but also understand the theory and purpose behind them.

How can these results be transferred into a comprehension strategy curriculum that spans the school year yet does not displace the required curriculum many preschool teachers are asked to follow? This question led to the creation of a research-based, teacher-friendly, child-engaging supplementary comprehension curriculum—Enhancing Preschoolers in Comprehension (EPIC)—that is designed to take place 2 days a week for a maximum of 3 hours total (DeBruin-Parecki, 2010, 2013; DeBruin-Parecki & Squibb, 2011). The focus is on narrative listening comprehension.

EPIC was designed to target the development and integration of four research-based comprehension strategies most commonly discussed in the literature about young children's comprehension: connection to life (activating background knowledge), prediction (inference), retelling (recall), and increasing vocabulary. This choice of strategies was based on extensive theoretical and empirical support (see Table 1.1 and multiple chapters in this book for further evidence) and ease of strategy instruction within meaningful and engaging contexts. What follows is a brief summary of the importance of these strategies, beginning with connection to life.

Connection to life, or bridging ideas to prior knowledge, is how children first learn to comprehend. It requires children to make sense of ideas and encourages them to reflect on the content of stories and find ways to make information relevant by "building links between the text and their prior knowledge to fill in information that is left implicit" (Brandao & Oakhill, 2005, p. 698). Children who are skilled in comprehending also integrate

Table 1.1.   Research supporting chosen comprehension strategies

Strategy	Supporting research
Connection to life (background knowledge)	Brandao & Oakhill (2005); Bransford & Johnson (1972); Chiesi, Spilich, & Voss (1979); Hirsch (2003); Roberts (2013); Snow, Burns, & Griffin (1998)
Vocabulary	Beck & McKeown (2001); Dickinson & Smith (1994); Neuman & Dwyer (2009); Neuman, Newman, & Dwyer (2011); Nielsen & Friesen (2012); Sénéchal, Ouellette, & Rodney (2006)
Prediction (inference)	Cain & Oakhill (1999); Florit, Roch, & Levorato (2011); Hansen (2004); Kendeou et al. (2008); Kendeou et al. (2012); Tompkins, Guo, & Justice (2013); van Kleeck (2008)
Retelling (recall)	Cairney (1990); Hansen (2004); Morrow (1985); Reed & Vaughn (2012); Roberts, Good, & Corcoran (2005); Zampini, Suttora, D'Odorico, & Zanchi (2013)

information from the story with relevant background knowledge to build understanding (Brandao & Oakhill, 2005).

Increasing vocabulary allows children to go beyond understanding a limited number of words, which can hinder comprehension (Biemiller, 2003). Children can learn new and rare words in the context of story reading (Dickinson & Tabors, 2001) when teachers define them, provide examples of other circumstances where the word might be used, allow children to own words through their self-generated examples, or add the vocabulary to everyday classroom conversations. As children's vocabularies grow, they will be able to better understand concepts and words in stories, leading to deeper comprehension of ideas and storylines (Beck & McKeown, 2007).

Retelling a story requires the listener to think about what was heard or seen in pictures and construct a coherent representation of it (Cairney, 1990). When children retell a story, either in part or entirely, they are being asked to recall key elements from the beginning, middle, and/or end of a story, including characters and plot; solve problems and address solutions (Hansen, 2004). Very young children often recall a stream of information about a story when asked, without regard for the sequence of ideas in the story. As this skill develops, children start to provide more cohesive and sequential retellings that demonstrate their clear understanding of organization and story content, leading them to deeper comprehension (Pellegrini & Galda, 1982).

Prediction is activated in young children listening to or having heard stories and allows them to go beyond the information provided in the book to fill in ideas needed to understand and elaborate on the story. They are taught to use evidence from the book or classroom discussions about the book to make relevant predictions. Preschoolers are clearly able to engage in this strategy to demonstrate their capability to comprehend (van Kleeck, 2008).

EPIC instruction was presented 2 days a week over four thematic units, with each unit lasting 8 weeks. The units focused on friendship, imagination, other people/other places, and change over time. Each week's instruction was centered on one of eight selected storybooks per thematic unit. Books were chosen based on their complexity, inclusion of rare vocabulary words, and interest to children of varied cultures.

Comprehension strategy instruction typically takes place for 75–90 minutes per day, 2 days per week. The teacher presents approximately 30 minutes of whole-group instruction in the context of circle time and storybook reading focused on the specific book used that week in the EPIC lesson, followed by about 45 minutes of small-group, activity-based instruction directly related to the target strategy being taught that day. Whole-group lessons include vocabulary introduction, shared book reading, and interactive discussion with children to promote oral language skills as well as comprehension. (See Chapter 4 by van Kleeck for a discussion of the importance of interacting with children using academic talk.) Selected vocabulary is introduced to children during whole-group lessons using cards with pictures of the terms being taught. Target words are selected from curriculum storybooks and are considered rare words unlikely to be known to children yet integral to understanding the text (e.g., *luminous, disappear, adventure*). An average of 7 words per book is taught for a total of 56 vocabulary words per thematic unit. Teachers introduce the word and provide a child-friendly, age-appropriate definition that provides a simplified version of the meaning. Children also see a picture related to the meaning of the word on the card the teacher holds up while introducing the word to them. Children are asked to give a "thumbs up" when they hear the word during read-alouds, and when children do this, they are asked to contribute what they remember and know about the word. In addition, target words are often posted on word walls or other designated areas in the classroom and are integrated into multiple classroom contexts and used by teachers and children throughout the day. Teachers integrate the words into daily conversations that go beyond discussion of the book. This may occur during playtime, meals, center time, and walks down the hall. A target word used during the first unit is *navigate.* One day, as the children were walking to lunch, they put their hands to their foreheads as if looking farther down the hall, and they talked about navigating to the cafeteria. This target word was not a word used that week but a word they had learned and remembered and could now use in different contexts.

Shared reading takes place 2 days per week; books are read in two parts between these two sessions. On day 2, teachers help children remember where they left off in the story by either doing a picture-walk (i.e., using illustrations to describe the narrative of the story) to the place they stopped reading or asking children multiple questions about the story up to that point. Interactive discussion includes specific strategy development and practice with weekly target strategies or integration of strategies. Strategies were selected due to repeated emphasis in the literature and connections to reading comprehension skills. The order was determined by the strategy that was developed earliest in life (i.e., connection to life, or background knowledge, comes first, followed by developing more extensive vocabulary). Retelling and prediction are more advanced cognitive skills and are learned later. Specific emphasis is placed on developing target strategies through multiple examples and applications within and between selected books. See Table 1.2 for the order in which the strategies are taught in each unit.

Immediately following the whole-group instructional session are the 45-minute small-group activity-based sessions designed to link specifically to the week's target strategy or strategy integration. Children work closely with teachers or teacher assistants on

Table 1.2. Comprehension strategy instruction

Week	Strategy	Practice
1	Connection to life	Books with relevant themes and plots chosen; whole group/activity-based small groups Student-generated oral, pictorial, and print experiences connecting text to their lives and linking new knowledge to what they already know
2	Vocabulary	Books and target words chosen to enhance comprehension of story; whole group/activity-based small groups Focus on both teacher-generated and child-generated definitions, including non-text-based contexts of target words Instruction delivered using word cards, word walls, and activity-based review
3	Integration of connection and vocabulary	Books chosen to facilitate integration of strategies; whole-group/activity-based small groups; child as author and illustrator; art activities; songs and drama; scavenger hunts; activities designed to increase vocabulary and background knowledge
4	Prediction	Use of predictive stories; whole group/activity-based small groups Priority given to using evidence to support predictions and evaluation of predictions based on evidence
5	Retelling	Use of stories that provide multiple opportunities for retelling; whole group/activity-based small groups Use of story-based sequencing cards, dramatic interpretation, manipulatives, and props
6	Integration of retelling and prediction	Books chosen to facilitate integration of strategies; whole-group/activity-based small groups; child as author and illustrator; art activities; songs and drama; scavenger hunts; activities designed to increase vocabulary and background knowledge
7, 8	Integration of all strategies	

From DeBruin-Parecki, A., & Squibb, K. (2011). Promoting at-risk preschool children's comprehension through research-based strategy instruction. *Reading Horizons, 51*(1), 41–62; adapted by permission.

these activities, which include school-based scavenger hunts where children make predictions based on evidence and dramatic retellings of a story. See Table 1.3 for an example of a complete 1-day lesson.

This lesson is based on the book *Edwina, the Dinosaur Who Didn't Know She Was Extinct,* by Mo Willems (2006). The story is about Edwina, a dinosaur who plays with children, helps old ladies cross the street, and bakes yummy chocolate chip cookies. Everyone loves Edwina except for Reginald Von Hobbie-Doobie, who doesn't believe she is real because he knows all dinosaurs are extinct. Reginald goes to great lengths to convince everyone that Edwina is extinct. In the end, no one cares, and Reginald finds himself sitting and eating delicious chocolate chip cookies baked by Edwina, who may not really be extinct.

Before using EPIC, teachers receive intensive professional development that includes children's comprehension development, the use and purpose of the curriculum, detailed explanations of the strategies, the reasons they are important to future reading comprehension, and observational monitoring of children's comprehension development. It is important that teachers continue to receive knowledge and support through coaches, knowledgeable others, or their own study groups. If possible, the use of EPIC in the

Table 1.3.   Example of a complete 1-day lesson

Unit 2: Imagination
Week 5, day 2
Book: *Edwina, the Dinosaur Who Didn't Know She Was Extinct* by Mo Willems
Target strategy: Prediction

Lesson objectives

1. Children will connect the concept of imagination to the new book.
2. Children will predict events that might occur in the story during whole-group reading and small-group activities.
3. Teacher will remind children that prediction is being able to guess what will happen next in the story or after the story ends. Children can use clues from the story to help them decide what will happen.
4. Children will demonstrate an understanding of prediction through a variety of activities related to the book and to their own life experiences.
5. Children will be able to predict events in a book other than the one read in class.

Large group: 30–45 minutes

Before reading, the teacher will use the vocabulary cards to review the words learned the day prior, use the vocabulary words in a sentence, and introduce the new words for the day. He or she will remind the children to give a "thumbs up" when they hear a vocabulary word in the story:

Protest: When you don't agree with something and you might make signs or pass out papers to tell everyone
Persuade/convince: When you try to get other people to believe the same things that you believe
Shock: When you're so surprised that you don't even know what to say

- Picture-walk the first half of the book and then read the second half of *Edwina, the Dinosaur Who Didn't Know She Was Extinct.*
- Why do you think the children and others didn't believe that Edwina was extinct?
- After Reginald sat and cried, a voice from behind him said, "I'll listen to you." Whom do you think that voice belonged to? Why?
- After Reginald told Edwina all the reasons she was extinct, Edwina was shocked. What do you think she will do next?
- Talk to the children about all the ways that Reginald tried to convince everyone that Edwina was imaginary. Did they work? At the beginning of the story, Reginald seemed somewhat mad at Edwina—what about now? What happened? (They're friends now.) Why do you think they're friends now? Do you think Edwina is real or imaginary now that we've read the whole book? Why or why not?

Small group: 30–45 minutes

Materials:
Edwina story templates
Pencils/crayons/markers

- Each child will have a story template paper with space to draw and empty lines on which to write his or her story.
- Ask children about whether there are any other dinosaurs living in the town in the book. Ask the children, "Do you think Edwina is lonely?" She has some people friends, but she doesn't have any dinosaur friends.
- Tell the children to draw a picture of some dinosaur friends Edwina might like to have (suggest that children use markers or crayons for the illustration).
- On the lines, they will tell a story predicting what Edwina might do with her dinosaur friends (suggest that children use pencils for their story).
- Write dictated stories on the back of children's stories.

classroom should be monitored to ascertain whether it is being implemented correctly and strategies learned are transferred to multiple contexts throughout the day (DeBruin-Parecki & Vaughn, 2014). It is clear from the research that consistent support in terms of pedagogical methods and regular provision of information on the purpose and content of materials can have a positive impact on helping preschool teachers maintain more effective instruction (Powell, Diamond, Burchinal, & Koehler, 2010).

DOES ENHANCING PRESCHOOLERS IN COMPREHENSION WORK?

To illustrate the efficacy of using a supplementary comprehension strategy curriculum for preschoolers, two studies are presented in the following sections: one that was done in a Head Start center and the other that took place in a university preschool program. These studies differed in sample demographics, design, and duration. The Head Start study used the EPIC Comprehension Strategy Curriculum comprehension program with 85 Head Start students and compared them to 84 Head Start students who did not receive EPIC but had the same teachers. The second university study examined EPIC at various dosage levels, meaning that not all classes received all parts of the EPIC curriculum. One group of children did not receive EPIC and served as the control group. Another group of children were taught by a teacher who was given early childhood comprehension training but was not provided EPIC materials. A third group of children were given instruction by a teacher who was provided with the full complement of EPIC materials and was given early childhood comprehension training. In addition, teachers in the university study were interviewed concerning their perceptions of early childhood comprehension, and the teachers using EPIC was asked how it might have influenced children's development of comprehension. The combination of studies indicates students—regardless of race and socioeconomic status and setting—whose teachers used EPIC to teach comprehension strategies are likely to see improvement in early comprehension.

Head Start Center Study

The EPIC curriculum was implemented in five Head Start classrooms in the southeastern United States in 2011. These students, 3–5 years old, were then compared to another group of children in the same Head Start classrooms in 2012 who were not exposed to the EPIC curriculum, thus holding teacher effects constant. EPIC is a materials-based curriculum with coaching support. Thus in 2012, EPIC materials were physically removed from the Head Start building along with the questioning guides, wall materials, and weekly coaching. Concerns about diffusion of treatment (the fear that the trained teachers would continue to try to mimic EPIC in 2012) were addressed through fidelity observations. The teachers were observed in 2011 to determine that they were implementing the EPIC program correctly. With formative corrections from the coaches, the research team determined that EPIC was fully implemented. Conversely, in 2012, the same teachers were observed to determine if they were still attempting to implement EPIC even though the materials and coaches had been removed. The research team determined that they were not using EPIC in 2012. Children who may have received EPIC in 2011 and were still present in 2012 were excluded from the analysis.

The two groups—treatment, who were exposed to EPIC in 2011, and control, with no EPIC in 2012—each contained approximately 80 students who lived in low-income households and were primarily African American (96%). Importantly, the two groups performed the same on the Peabody Picture Vocabulary Test (PPVT; Dunn & Dunn, 2007) ($F(1,164) = 3.165, p = .077$) and the Early Literacy Skills Assessment (ELSA) comprehension scores (DeBruin-Parecki, 2004) ($F(1,167) = 1.561, p = .213$) at the beginning of the respective years.

The ELSA is a comprehensive assessment that measures comprehension, phonological awareness, alphabetic principle, and concepts about print (DeBruin-Parecki, 2004). The ELSA is constructed to resemble a children's storybook with items embedded within the storyline and has been found to be a reliable and valid measurement instrument (Cheadle, 2007). For this study, only the comprehension data were used and included three strategies: connection to life, prediction, and retelling.

Results of the study found that children exposed to EPIC were likely to score significantly higher on the ELSA comprehension measure ($Madj$ = 8.396, SE = .429) than their counterparts who had no EPIC exposure ($Madj$ = 6.679, SE = .386) ($F(1, 120)$ = 8.819, p = .004, partial eta-squared = .068) even after controlling for the ELSA pretest (Adj R^2 = .222) (see Table 1.4 and Figure 1.1). The differences were broken down by comprehension strategy. Children exposed to EPIC were likely to score higher on questions concerned with connections to life ($F(1,120)$ = 13.953, p < .001, partial eta-squared = .104) and prediction ($F(1,120)$ = 7.423, p = .007, partial eta-squared = .058), whereas the two groups were not different in terms of retelling (p = .745) (DeBruin-Parecki & Vaughn, 2014; DeBruin-Parecki, Vaughn, & Squibb, 2012; see Figure 1.2).

The effect sizes, partial eta-square, represent the variance in ELSA scores that is explained by the EPIC treatment versus no treatment after excluding the variance of the ELSA pretest. When using analysis of covariance (ANCOVA), effect sizes that range from .02 to .13 are considered to be small effects (Field, 2013). Thus the effects of EPIC on early childhood comprehension in this study are considered to be small yet statistically significant.

Table 1.4.   ANCOVA of Head Start ELSA posttest comprehension scores on EPIC and control groups when controlling for ELSA pretest

Source	Type III sum of squares	df	Mean square	F	Sig.	Partial eta-squared
Corrected model	370.980[a]	2	185.490	18.374	.000	.234
Intercept	1958.878	1	1958.878	194.040	.000	.618
ELSA comp Pretest	254.915	1	254.915	25.251	.000	.174
EPIC or not	89.025	1	89.025	8.819	.004	.068
Error	1211.427	120	10.095			
Total	8404.000	123				
Corrected total	1582.407	122				

Key: ANCOVA, analysis of covariance; ELSA, Early Literacy Skills Assessment; EPIC, Enhancing Preschoolers in Comprehension; df, degrees of freedom; F, F-test; Sig., significance.

[a] R^2 = .234 (adjusted R^2 = .222).

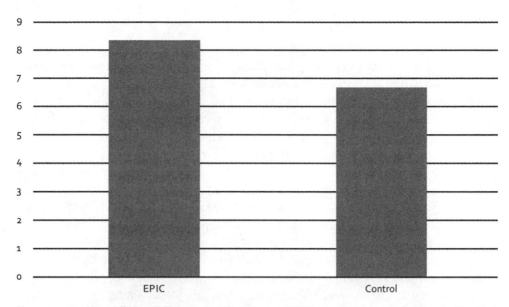

Figure 1.1.   Head Start differences in Early Literacy Skills Assessment (ELSA) comprehension scores for Enhancing Preschoolers in Comprehension (EPIC) and control groups after controlling for ELSA pretest.

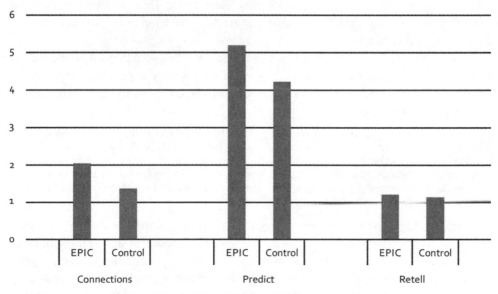

Figure 1.2.   Head Start differences in Early Literacy Skills Assessment (ELSA) comprehension component scores for Enhancing Preschoolers in Comprehension (EPIC) and control groups after controlling for ELSA pretest.

University Preschool Study

Three classrooms at a university preschool program were used as intact groups to compare student comprehension gains at different levels of comprehension strategy implementation (Cartwright & DeBruin-Parecki, 2014). Classes of approximately 15 students were randomly assigned to receive one of three treatment levels: 1) EPIC fully implemented, 2) EPIC not used but teacher received instruction on literal comprehension, and 3) no EPIC or comprehension supports. Both EPIC and literal comprehension groups used the same books. The control class proceeded with business as usual. The study was run over the course of 16 weeks. The students ranged in age from 3 to 5 years old but, unlike the Head Start study, hailed from predominantly affluent households and most were Caucasian (66%) or Asian/American Indian (22%). The three groups were equivalent in terms of ELSA comprehension scores ($F(2, 40) = .937$, $p = .400$) and PPVT-4 ($F(2, 41) = .347$, $p = .709$) prior to the start of the study.

Results showed that the preschool children exposed to EPIC were likely to score significantly higher on the ELSA comprehension measure ($Madj = 12.517$, $SE = 1.138$) than students whose teacher was given literacy supports ($Madj = 8.722$, $SE = 1.292$) or those who had no comprehension or literacy support ($Madj = 8.705$, $SE = 1.147$) ($F(2, 38) = 3.590$, $p = .037$, partial eta-squared = .159), even after controlling for the ELSA pretest (adjusted $R^2 = .367$; see Table 1.5 and Figure 1.3). The differences were broken down by comprehension strategy. Children exposed to EPIC were likely to score higher on all three strategies—connections to life ($F(2,38) = 3.394$, $p = .044$, partial eta-squared = .152), prediction ($F(2,38) = 5.887$, $p = .006$, partial eta-squared = .237), and retelling ($F(2,38) = 3.426$, $p = .043$, partial eta-squared = .153)—even after controlling for ELSA levels from the fall (see Figure 1.4). When using ANCOVA, effect sizes that range from .13 to .26 are considered to be medium effects (Field, 2013). Thus the effects of EPIC on early childhood comprehension in this study are all considered to be medium size and statistically significant.

When the study was completed, the teachers were asked what they knew about early childhood comprehension. The answers reflected the teachers' exposure to comprehension curricula. The teacher of the control group (with no comprehension training) struggled to define comprehension:

> Primarily . . . it means to be sometimes repetitious . . . a lot of times what they need is the same thing kind of over and over again to really absorb the information. It needs to be in a concrete form a lot of times or at least concrete representation so that they have a visual or something even sensory oriented to help them to comprehend what is going on. Abstract concepts are really often times lost on them. Then there also needs to be in a language level that they understand. You have to be careful of the vocabulary. I guess that's really about it.

The teacher who received some support in terms of literal comprehension and books to use but no training in early comprehension strategies guessed at the meaning of comprehension: "I guess I would assume it's just the knowledge of building on their understanding and teaching them how to understand certain vocabulary or sequencing or graphing or anything like that." However, the teacher who received training in comprehension strategies and EPIC curricular supports had a very concrete view of the different components of comprehension including retelling, prediction, and vocabulary.

Table 1.5. ANCOVA of university ELSA posttest comprehension scores on EPIC and control groups when controlling for ELSA pretest

Source	Type III sum of squares	df	Mean square	F	Sig.	Partial eta-squared
Corrected model	519.318[a]	3	173.106	8.920	.000	.413
Intercept	276.396	1	276.396	14.242	.001	.273
ELSA comp pretest	345.449	1	345.449	17.800	.000	.319
EPIC or not	139.353	2	69.676	3.590	.037	.159
Error	737.468	38	19.407			
Total	5517.000	42				
Corrected total	1256.786	41				

Key: ANCOVA, analysis of covariance; ELSA, Early Literacy Skills Assessment; EPIC, Enhancing Preschoolers in Comprehension; df, degrees of freedom; F, F-test; Sig., significance.

[a] R^2 = .413 (adjusted R^2 = .367).

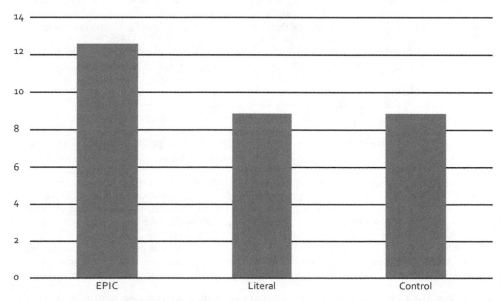

Figure 1.3. University preschool differences in Early Literacy Skills Assessment (ELSA) comprehension scores for Enhancing Preschoolers in Comprehension (EPIC) and control groups after controlling for ELSA pretest.

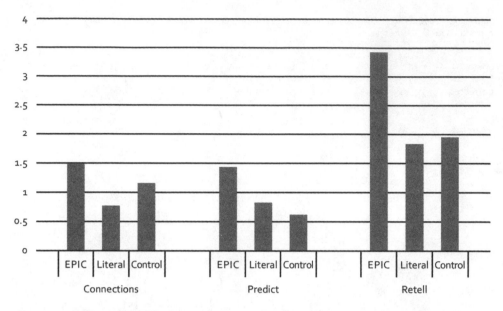

Figure 1.4. University preschool differences in Early Literacy Skills Assessment (ELSA) comprehension component scores for Enhancing Preschoolers in Comprehension (EPIC) and control groups after controlling for ELSA pretest.

Vocabulary came up repeatedly as something the students particularly liked. The EPIC teacher had a lot to say about it:

> I think that the words stuck a little bit more by going through and finding specific words that were in the book that you were reading . . . but they got really excited when they would actually hear one of the words that they were supposed to be listening for and I think it really stuck with them and even when we read books now they still will point out those words like . . . "I heard faint" or "I heard backwash."

The vocabulary words from stories carried over into real-life situations. For example, the EPIC teacher talked about when the students learned about a particular word:

> The children learned about the word squint. I can't remember what book it was in, but they really liked that word, and then when we would go to the playground, they were squinting their eyes because the sun was out.

When vocabulary was broached by the teacher who was provided some literal comprehension supports, it reflected a much more haphazard approach:

> Vocabulary words . . . usually I don't do [those] in the circle times. . . . I do them in morning meetings which is earlier in the day. I'll incorporate them sometimes through circle time and through centers but . . . usually . . . you know . . . I give them a word and have them sound it out and see if they can figure it out . . . let the kids define the word . . . I define the word. We put it on the word wall and then we'll play games like "I spy . . . like . . . I spy a word that means" . . . whatever it might mean. . . . Bonjour . . . or hello in French and you know . . . the kids would find Bonjour . . . but that's not . . . well. . . . while I'm reading a story and I come across a word that I find interesting or that they find interesting we stop and talk about it. But, typically, I don't pull out words specifically for the readings while I'm reading.

When the EPIC teacher was asked to comment on the EPIC curriculum specifically and how it related to early childhood comprehension, she quickly related to the number of questions that created opportunities for increasing background knowledge and under-standing: "With EPIC, there are a *lot* of questions. . . . I think that we thought we asked a lot of questions . . . but they had a lot more questions within their lesson plans." She also thought EPIC assisted with "figuring out a way to get children to ask more about what they don't understand" (EPIC teacher).

It is clear that EPIC does work in terms of increasing early childhood comprehension. In two different studies with vastly different student samples, the students who received EPIC scored higher on an early childhood comprehension test than students who did not. These results were consistent across racial groups—African American students benefited from EPIC in the same manner as white and Asian students. Students living in or around the poverty level benefited from EPIC in the same way as affluent children, and it did not matter about the preparation of the teacher. The teachers in the Head Start study had bachelor degrees but were not certified teachers. At the university preschool, the teachers had Master's degrees and were certified teachers. Yet students of teachers who used EPIC, regardless of educational preparation, were likely to show higher levels of early childhood comprehension than those who had teachers who did not use EPIC.

IMPLICATIONS

This chapter has provided a means of putting to practical use much of the research that will be discussed in the chapters to follow. A supplementary research-based comprehension strategy curriculum was presented that can easily be used by preschool teachers of all educational levels. Children's added comprehension growth has been documented when this curriculum was used in classrooms. This is just one example of how we can add to a teacher's instructional toolbox to create opportunities for all young children, regardless of race or socioeconomic status, to learn important prereader comprehension strategies. These strategies will later translate to reading comprehension and the ability to learn across all content areas. As early childhood scholars, it is important for us to be able to translate what we study and learn into teacher-friendly, theoretically sound materials that can positively affect the comprehension growth of young children of diverse racial and economic backgrounds and begin to narrow the achievement gap.

REFERENCES

Annie E. Casey Foundation. (2014, January). *Early reading proficiency in the United States.* Retrieved from http://www.aecf.org/~/media/Pubs/Initiatives/KIDS%20COUNT/E/EarlyReadingProficiency/Early ReadingProficiency2014.pdf

Beck, I., & McKeown, M. (2001). Text talk: Capturing the benefits of read-aloud experiences for young children. *The Reading Teacher, 55*(1), 10–20.

Beck, I., & McKeown, M. (2007). Increasing young low-income children's oral vocabulary repertoires through rich and focused instruction. *The Elementary School Journal, 107,* 251–271.

Bianco, M., Bressoux, P., Doyen, A., Lambert, E., Lima, L., Pellenq, C., & Zorman, M. (2010). Early training in oral comprehension and phonological skills: Results of a three-year longitudinal study. *Scientific Studies of Reading, 14*(3), 211–246.

Bianco, M., Pellenq, C., Lambert, E., Bressoux, P., Lima, L., & Doyen, A. (2012). Impact of early code-skill and oral comprehension training on reading achievement in the first grade. *Journal of Research in Reading, 34*(4), 427–455.

Biemiller. A. (2003). Vocabulary: Needed if more children are to read well. *Reading Psychology, 24,* 323–335.

Brandao, A.C.P., & Oakhill, J. (2005). "How do you know this answer?": Children's use of text data and general knowledge in story comprehension. *Reading and Writing, 18*(7–9), 687–713.

Bransford, J.D., & Johnson, M.K. (1972). Contextual prerequisites for understanding: Some investigations of comprehension and recall. *Journal of Verbal Learning and Verbal Behavior, 11,* 717–726.

Cain, K., & Oakhill, J.V. (1999). Inference making ability and its relation to comprehension failure in young children. *Reading and Writing, 11,* 489–503.

Cairney, T. (1990). *Teaching reading comprehension.* Bristol, PA: Open Court Press.

Cartwright, K., & DeBruin-Parecki, A. (2014, July). *The role of theory of mind and executive skills in preschoolers' expressive vocabulary, narrative comprehension, and response to comprehension intervention.* Paper presented at the National Head Start Research Conference, Washington, DC.

Cheadle, J. (2007). *The Early Literacy Skills Assessment (ELSA) Psychometric Report for both English and Spanish versions.* Retrieved from http://www.highscope.org/file/Assessment/ELSAJacobs.pdf

Chiesi, H.L., Spilich, G.J., & Voss, J.F. (1979). Acquisition of domain-related information in relation to high and low domain knowledge. *Journal of Verbal Learning & Verbal Behavior, 18*(3), 257–273.

DeBruin-Parecki, A. (2004). *The Early Literacy Skills Assessment (ELSA): Violet's adventure/La aventura de Violetta* (C. Magana, Trans.). Ypsilanti, MI: High/Scope Press.

DeBruin-Parecki, A. (2010, May). *Providing at-risk preschoolers strategies for developing deeper understandings.* Paper presented at the Annual Meeting of the International Reading Association, Chicago, IL.

DeBruin-Parecki, A. (2013, April). *The value of prereader comprehension strategy instruction: Giving young children tools to build understanding.* Paper presented at the International Reading Association Conference, San Antonio, TX.

DeBruin-Parecki, A., & Squibb, K. (2011). Promoting at-risk preschool children's comprehension through research-based strategy instruction. *Reading Horizons, 51*(1), 41–62.

DeBruin-Parecki, A., & Vaughn, E.S. (2014, April). *The value of comprehension strategy instruction for Head Start children.* Paper presented at the Annual Meeting of the American Educational Research Association, Philadelphia, PA.

DeBruin-Parecki, A., Vaughn, S., & Squibb, K. (2012, June). *Growing understanding through research-based instruction: Head Start children learn comprehension strategies.* Paper presented at the National Head Start Research Conference, Washington, DC.

Dickinson, D.K., & Smith, M.W. (1994). Long-term effects of preschool teachers' book readings on low-income children's vocabulary and story comprehension. *Reading Research Quarterly, 29*(2), 104–122.

Dickinson, D.K., & Tabors, P.O. (Eds.). (2001). *Beginning literacy with language: Young children learning at home and school.* Baltimore, MD: Paul H. Brookes Publishing Co.

Dunn, L.M., & Dunn, D.M. (2007). *Peabody Picture Vocabulary Test, Fourth Edition (PPVT-4).* Minneapolis, MN: Pearson.

Dymock, S. (2007). Comprehension strategy instruction: Teaching narrative text structure awareness. *The Reading Teacher, 61*(2), 161–167.

Fields, A. (2013). *Discovering statistics using IBM SPSS Statistics* (4th ed.). Thousand Oaks, CA: Sage.

Florit, E., Roch, M., & Levorato, M.C. (2011). Listening text comprehension of explicit and implicit information in preschoolers: The role of verbal and inferential skills. *Discourse Processes, 48*(2), 119–138.

Gamse, B.C., Bloom, H.S., Kemple, J.J., & Jacob, R.T. (2008). *Reading first impact study: Interim report.* Washington, DC: Institute of Educational Sciences.

Garner, J.K., & Bochna, C.R. (2004). Transfer of listening comprehension strategy to independent reading in first-grade students. *Early Childhood Education Journal, 32,* 69–74.

Hansen, J. (2004). *"Tell me a story": Developmentally appropriate retelling strategies.* Newark, DE: International Reading Association.

Hemphill, F.C., & Vanneman, A. (2010). *Achievement gaps: How Hispanic and white students in public schools perform in mathematics and reading on the National Assessment of Educational Progress* (NCES 2011-459). Washington, DC: National Center for Education Statistics, Institute of Education Sciences, U.S. Department of Education.

Hirsch, E.D., Jr. (2003). Reading comprehension requires knowledge—of words and the world. *American Educator, 27,* 1316–1322, 1328–1329, 1348.

Hoover, W.A., & Gough, P.B. (1990). The simple view of reading. *Reading and Writing: An Interdisciplinary Journal, 2,* 127–160.

Kendeou, P., Bohn-Gettler, C., White, M.J., & van den Broek, P. (2008). Children's inference generation across different media. *Journal of Research in Reading, 31*(3), 259–272.

Kendeou, P., Lynch, J.S., van den Broek, P., Espin, C.A., White, M.J., & Kremer, K.E. (2005). Developing successful readers: Building early comprehension skills through television viewing and listening. *Early Childhood Education Journal, 33*(2), 91–98.

Kendeou, P., van den Broek, P., White, M.J., & Lynch, J. (2007). Comprehension in preschool and early elementary children: Skill development and strategy interventions. In D.S. McNamara (Ed.), *Reading comprehension strategies: Theories, interventions, and technologies* (pp. 27–45). Mahwah, NJ: Erlbaum.

Kendeou, P., van den Broek, P., White, M.J., & Lynch, J.S. (2009). Predicting reading comprehension in early elementary school: The independent contributions of oral language and decoding skills. *Journal of Educational Psychology, 101*(4), 765–778.

Kendeou, P., Papadopoulos, T.C., & Spanoudis, G. (2012). Processing demands of reading comprehension tests in young readers. *Learning and Instruction*, 22(5), 354–367.

Lepola, J., Lynch, J., Laakkonen, E., Silvén, M., & Niemi, P. (2012). The role of inference making and other language skills in the development of narrative listening comprehension in 4–6-year-old children. *Reading Research Quarterly, 47*, 259–282.

Morrow, L.M. (1985). Retelling stories: A strategy for improving young children's comprehension, concept of story structure, and oral language complexity. *Elementary School Journal, 85*, 647–651.

Morrow, L.M. (1988). Young children's responses to one-to-one story readings in school settings. *Reading Research Quarterly, 23*(1), 89–107.

Morrow, L.M. (2005). *Literacy development in the early years: Helping children read and write* (5th ed.). Boston, MA: Allyn–Bacon.

National Center for Education Statistics. (2013). *The nation's report card: A first look: 2013 mathematics and reading* (NCES 2014-451). Washington, DC: Institute of Education Sciences, U.S. Department of Education.

National Center for Education Statistics. (2014, January 30). *National Assessment of Educational Progress*. Retrieved from http://nces.ed.gov/nationsreportcard/studies/gaps

Neuman, S.B., & Dwyer, J. (2009). Missing in action: Vocabulary instruction in pre-K. *The Reading Teacher, 62*(5), 384–392.

Neuman, S.B., Newman, E.H., & Dwyer, J. (2011). Educational effects of a vocabulary intervention on preschoolers' word knowledge and conceptual development: A cluster-randomized trial. *Reading Research Quarterly, 46*, 249–272.

Nielsen, D.C., & Friesen, L.D. (2012). A study of the effectiveness of a small-group intervention on the vocabulary and narrative development of at-risk kindergarten children. *Reading Psychology, 33*(3), 269–299.

Oakhill, J.V., & Cain, K. (2012). The precursors of reading ability in young readers: Evidence from a four-year longitudinal study. *Scientific Studies of Reading, 16*(2), 91–121.

Paris, A., & Paris, S. (2003). Assessing narrative comprehension in young children. *Reading Research Quarterly, 38*(1), 36–76.

Paris, A.H., & Paris, S.G. (2007). Teaching narrative comprehension strategies to first graders. *Cognition and Instruction, 25*(1), 1–44.

Paris, S.G. (2005). Reinterpreting the development of reading skills. *Reading Research Quarterly, 40*(2), 184–202.

Paris, S.G., & Luo, S.W. (2010). Confounded statistical analyses hinder interpretation of the NELP report. *Educational Researcher, 39*(4), 316–322.

Paris, S.G., & Paris, A.H. (2006). Assessments of early reading. In W. Damon, R.M. Lerner, K.A. Renninger, & I.E. Sigel (Eds.), *Handbook of child psychology* (Vol. 4, pp. 211–246). Hoboken, NJ: John Wiley & Sons.

Pellegrini, A.D., & Galda, L. (1982). The effects of thematic-fantasy play training on the development of children's comprehension. *American Educational Research Journal, 19*, 443–452.

Perfetti, C.A., Landi, N., & Oakhill, J. (2005). The acquisition of reading comprehension skill. In M.J. Snowling & C. Hulme (Eds.), *The science of reading: A handbook* (pp. 227–247). Oxford, UK: Blackwell.

Powell, D.R., Diamond, K.E., Burchinal, M.R., & Koehler, M.J. (2010). Effects of an early literacy professional development intervention on Head Start teachers and children. *Journal of Educational Psychology, 102*, 299–312.

Pressley, M. (2002). Comprehension strategies instruction: A turn of the century status report. In C.C. Block & M. Pressley (Eds.), *Comprehension instruction: Research-based recommended practices* (pp. 11–27). New York, NY: Guilford Press.

Reed, K., & Vaughn, S. (2012). Retell as an indicator of reading comprehension. *Scientific Studies of Reading, 16*(3), 187–217.

Roberts, G., Good, R., & Corcoran, S. (2005). Story retell: A fluency-based indicator of reading comprehension. *School Psychology Quarterly, 20*(3), 304–317.

Roberts, K.L. (2013). Comprehension strategy instruction during parent-child shared reading: An intervention study. *Literacy Research and Instruction, 52*(2), 106–129.

Sénéchal, M., Ouellette, G., & Rodney, D. (2006). The misunderstood giant: On the predictive role of early vocabulary to future reading. In D.K. Dickinson & S.B. Neuman (Eds.), *Handbook of early literacy research* (Vol. 2, pp. 173–182). New York, NY: Guilford Press.

Snow, C. (2002). *Reading for understanding: Toward an R&D program in reading comprehension*. Santa Monica, CA: RAND Corporation.

Snow, C.E., Burns, M.S., & Griffin, P. (1998). *Preventing reading difficulties in young children*. Washington, DC: National Academy Press.

Teale, W.H. (1985). Parents reading to their children: What we know and what we need to know. *Language Arts, 58*(8), 902–912.

Tompkins, V., Guo, Y., & Justice, L.M. (2013). Inference generation, story comprehension, and language skills in the preschool years. *Reading and Writing, 26*(3), 403–429.

van Kleeck, A. (2008). Providing preschool foundations for later reading comprehension: The importance of and ideas for targeting inferencing in storybook-sharing interventions. *Psychology in the Schools, 45*(7), 627–643.

Vanneman, A., Hamilton, L., Baldwin Anderson, J., & Rahman, T. (2009). *Achievement gaps: How black and white students in public schools perform in mathematics and reading on the National Assessment of Educational Progress* (NCES 2009-455). Washington, DC: National Center for Education Statistics, Institute of Education Sciences, U.S. Department of Education.

Willems, M. (2006). *Edwina, the dinosaur who didn't know she was extinct*. White Plains, NY: Disney-Hyperion.

Zampini, L., Suttora, C., D'Odorico, L., & Zanchi, P. (2013). Sequential reasoning and listening text comprehension in preschool children. *European Journal of Developmental Psychology, 10*, 563–579.

2

Vocabulary and Its Role in Early Comprehension Development

MICHAEL D. COYNE, SABINA RAK NEUGEBAUER,

SHARON M. WARE, D. BETSY MCCOACH, AND JOHN P. MADURA

A large body of research evidence supports the strong and sustained positive relationship between vocabulary knowledge and comprehension (e.g., Elleman, Lindo, Morphy, & Compton, 2009; Ouellette, 2006). This evidence comes from correlational research documenting the association between vocabulary knowledge and comprehension (e.g., students with larger vocabularies are better comprehenders) as well as experimental research documenting the causal effects of vocabulary instruction and intervention on comprehension outcomes (e.g., vocabulary instruction improves comprehension). Most of this research has focused on the *reading* comprehension of students in third grade and beyond with established or at least fundamental reading skills. There is much less research, however, on the role of vocabulary in the development of students' *listening* comprehension (McKeown & Beck, 2011). This is particularly true for research with young students who are at the beginning stages of learning to read. Listening comprehension, or linguistic comprehension, refers to students' ability to comprehend language, particularly language in an academic setting (e.g., listening to text read aloud).

Although there is less research on the connections between vocabulary and listening comprehension, there is strong theoretical support for the central role of listening comprehension in the development of reading comprehension (Perfetti, 2007; Scarborough, 2001). The simple view of reading (Gough & Tunmer, 1986), a widely accepted conceptual model of reading comprehension, suggests that two components are necessary for successful reading comprehension: decoding and listening comprehension. In essence, the simple view suggests that students apply the same meaning-making processes when understanding oral language as they do with written language once it is decoded. In other words, in reading comprehension, when students decode text, they are translating written language into oral language. At that point, students essentially use their listening comprehension skills to construct meaning from what they have read.

According to the simple view, listening comprehension is a primary contributor to reading comprehension, and young students' listening comprehension should directly influence later reading comprehension. Therefore, supporting the development of listening comprehension should be a primary focus for teachers and schools in the early grades because these skills serve as a necessary precondition for successful reading comprehension. Listening comprehension instruction is particularly important for students with less developed oral language skills or those who are not yet proficient readers.

The purpose of this chapter is to explore the role of vocabulary in the listening comprehension of young students. First, we describe a theoretical framework for understanding the relationship between vocabulary knowledge and listening comprehension. We then provide an overview of research that has examined the associations between vocabulary and listening comprehension as well as research that has investigated the effects of teaching vocabulary on listening comprehension outcomes. In particular, we share results from a program of research that developed vocabulary instruction and intervention and evaluated its effects on the vocabulary development and listening comprehension of kindergarten students.

THEORETICAL FRAMEWORK FOR THE RELATIONSHIP BETWEEN VOCABULARY KNOWLEDGE AND LISTENING COMPREHENSION

In this section, we present four prominent hypotheses for explaining the relationship between vocabulary knowledge and reading comprehension. We also describe how these hypotheses are equally relevant for examining the relationship between vocabulary and listening comprehension.

The first three hypotheses we review were originally proposed in a seminal paper by Anderson and Freebody (1981). The first of these, the instrumentalist hypothesis, suggests a straightforward and direct relationship between vocabulary knowledge and comprehension: The greater the number of words you know in a text, the more likely you are to comprehend that text (Stahl, 1991; Stahl & Nagy, 2006).

Moreover, the deeper one understands a word—for example, its multiple meanings (e.g., a *bug* can refer to an insect, but to *bug* can refer to the act of bothering another person), different syntactic uses (e.g., you have a *bug* on you, I am *bugging* you), or knowledge of synonyms related to the word (e.g., *bother, annoy, pick on*)—the more one can construct a rich and versatile understanding of how that word contributes to the overall meaning of the text. In other words, the more you know about a word's meaning, the more agile you are in using this knowledge flexibly to comprehend text (Ouellette, 2006). In addition, these more defined representations of a word increase the rate with which it can be retrieved from memory. This increased ability to access a word from memory can also accelerate comprehension processes (Mezynski, 1983; Perfetti, 2007).

Although the majority of studies exploring the instrumentalist hypothesis have focused on reading comprehension, the same mechanism explaining the link between vocabulary knowledge and reading comprehension can also theoretically explain the relationship between vocabulary and listening comprehension. For example, a student who understands the meaning of the word *murky* is more likely to comprehend the meaning of the sentence "The watch fell to the bottom of the murky water, but Marco could still see something glimmer from deep below." Students who know the word *murky* will better understand this sentence whether reading it or listening to it spoken aloud (e.g., they will understand that Marco's watch is in dark, muddy water). In addition, by an instrumental-ist account, another benefit of students knowing the meaning of *murky* is they may also be better able to infer the meaning of the word *glimmer* (e.g., to see something through "murky" water, it must be bright and shiny).

Using this rationale, learning the meanings of words creates a generative snowball effect, where students are better able to not only comprehend language that includes known words but also leverage their understanding of new vocabulary to infer the mean-ings of additional words that are heard in conjunction with other words they know. The instrumentalist hypothesis supports the idea that knowledge of individual words is the vehicle for learning new words heard in the context of known words. Therefore, a more distal effect of this cumulative learning is that students will expand their general vocabu-lary beyond just words taught, and this accumulated word knowledge will influence gen-eral vocabulary and comprehension outcomes.

Two additional hypotheses proposed to explain the connection between vocabulary knowledge and reading comprehension include Anderson and Freebody's (1981) knowl-edge and aptitude hypotheses. We describe these two hypotheses together because both theorize that vocabulary and reading comprehension are linked by a third underlying factor that influences each. The knowledge hypothesis states that vocabulary and read-ing comprehension are both influenced by conceptual or content knowledge. According to this hypothesis, when conceptual knowledge increases, there are concurrent increases in vocabulary and comprehension as a result. For example, a child who learns about the concept of mummification in ancient Egypt on a visit to a museum is more likely to know the words *cadaver* and *papyrus*. With his or her new knowledge of mummification, the child is also more likely to be able to comprehend the written or spoken sentence "They covered the cadavers with linen and papyrus from head to toe." In this explanation, it is the knowledge of the concept of mummification that facilitates the child's understanding of the words and the meaning of the sentence rather than decontextualized knowledge of the individual words *cadaver* and *papyrus*. Without this conceptual knowledge, the child might understand this sentence to mean covering a body with some type of blan-ket rather that understanding the wrapping process associated with mummification. In Chapter 6, Hall-Kenyon, Culatta, and Duke describe the benefits of using informational texts to build comprehension.

The aptitude hypothesis suggests that the underlying factor that influences vocabu-lary and comprehension is general intelligence (Anderson & Freebody, 1981; Nagy, 2007; Pearson, Hiebert, & Kamil, 2007). By this logic, it is a students' general verbal ability that explains the link between vocabulary and comprehension skills. Thus a student with strong language skills will perform well across language tasks. This explanation is trou-bling for educators and researchers alike, as general intelligence is usually conceptualized as a characteristic that is fixed and not influenced by instruction.

Additional work beyond that of Anderson and Freebody (1981) has focused on another potential underlying third factor, one that is theoretically and in practice respon-sive to experience and instruction: metalinguistic awareness (Nagy, 2007). Metalinguistic awareness "is the ability to reflect on and manipulate the structural features of language" (Nagy & Anderson, 1995, p. 2), written and spoken, in a thoughtful and flexible manner.

The metalinguistic hypothesis suggests that awareness of, and sensitivity to, the linguistic elements that convey a message—not just the content of the message—influences vocabulary and comprehension alike. Metalinguistic awareness can describe knowledge of a variety of language skills (i.e., knowledge of different phonemes or knowledge of word parts such as prefixes or suffixes). However, we focus here on how metalinguistic awareness might be particularly relevant for understanding the relationship between vocabulary learning and listening comprehension. Vocabulary learning is multifaceted with knowledge of a word requiring an understanding of meaning across contexts, syntax, relationships between words, and word parts (i.e., prefixes, suffixes). All of these aspects of a word are thought to reflect metalinguistic ability.

Vocabulary instruction that includes opportunities for students to manipulate language, actively engage with words across different contexts, and explore word usage in a supportive and reflective manner can increase students' word consciousness and metalinguistic awareness (Beck, McKeown, & Kucan, 2013). Students who develop strong metalinguistic awareness skills have more complex lexical representations for words. For example, if we return to the preceding sentence regarding Marco's watch that disappeared in the "murky water," students with strong metalinguistic skills will understand that the word *murky* in this sentence describes the dark quality of the water, but they also know that the word *murky* can refer to other contexts (e.g., a murky night) or even to a more abstract idea (e.g., a murky statement, which is vague or unclear). A proximal consequence of increases in metalinguistic awareness is that students will be better able to consolidate, synthesize, and access lexical knowledge about a specific word as well as be more active word learners, where they are better equipped to take advantage of naturalistic word-learning opportunities. A more distal implication of increases in metalinguistic awareness may be that students who are more attuned to words and language will be more likely to infer new words and comprehend language naturally occurring in their environment and could experience growth on standardized measures of comprehension and general vocabulary knowledge. Although we have reviewed these various hypotheses separately, it is also possible, and in fact likely, that multiple mechanisms may be occurring simultaneously and may be reciprocal in nature. See Chapter 9 by Cartwright and Guajardo for a comprehensive discussion on developing children's executive functioning and theory of mind as they relate to pre-reader comprehension.

INVESTIGATING THE RELATIONSHIP BETWEEN VOCABULARY KNOWLEDGE AND LISTENING COMPREHENSION

In the preceding section, we discussed multiple hypotheses explaining the connection between vocabulary knowledge and comprehension, including listening comprehension. In this section, we provide a brief summary of research documenting the strong relationship between vocabulary knowledge and reading and listening comprehension. We then present an overview of a study that investigated empirically the relationships among vocabulary learning, listening comprehension, and general vocabulary knowledge in kindergarten students and discuss which hypotheses could potentially explain the mechanisms underlying these relationships.

A large body of research has consistently found a strong positive relationship between vocabulary knowledge and reading comprehension. In fact, vocabulary emerges consistently as one of the strongest predictors of reading comprehension across studies (Sénéchal, Ouellette, & Rodney, 2006; Snow, Burns, & Griffin, 1998). For example, vocabulary knowledge in the elementary grades is strongly related to students' current reading comprehension and continues to predict reading comprehension in high school and beyond (Cunningham & Stanovich, 1997).

Although not as numerous as studies examining the relationship between vocabulary and reading comprehension, evidence also supports the strong relationship between vocabulary knowledge and listening comprehension. For example, Potocki, Ecalle, and Magnan (2013) investigated whether the cognitive and linguistic predictors of reading comprehension in elementary students were the same for listening comprehension in 5-year-old prereaders. Vocabulary knowledge, as well as syntactic and morphological knowledge, was related to young children's listening comprehension scores.

Study Examining Mechanisms Among Vocabulary Knowledge, Response to Vocabulary Instruction, and Listening Comprehension

Although correlational research supports the relationship between vocabulary and listening comprehension, few studies have empirically investigated different hypotheses explaining the association among vocabulary knowledge, response to vocabulary instruction, and literacy-related skills, including listening comprehension (Coyne et al., 2010). In 2012, we conducted a study that explored these relationships through the lens of both an instrumentalist and/or metalinguistic hypothesis for kindergartners receiving high-quality classroom and small-group vocabulary instruction (Coyne et al., 2012; Neugebauer et al., 2012). We also explored how these relationships might operate for students who received different degrees of instructional intensity, comparing students who received only classroom vocabulary instruction to students who received both classroom instruction and a supplemental Tier 2 vocabulary intervention.

Nineteen kindergarten classrooms from seven elementary schools participated in this study of multitiered vocabulary instruction called Project Intensive Vocabulary Intervention (Project IVI). At the beginning of the school year, we screened all students on receptive vocabulary knowledge, using the Peabody Picture Vocabulary Test, Fourth Edition (PPVT-4). Students who scored above the 30th percentile ($n = 177$) were considered not at risk for language and literacy difficulties and were assigned to receive only Tier 1 classroom vocabulary instruction. Students performing at or below the 30th percentile ($n = 78$) were considered at risk for language and literacy difficulties and at risk for not responding to classroom vocabulary instruction. These students were assigned to receive small-group Tier 2 vocabulary intervention in addition to the classroom vocabulary instruction. A subset of students from two schools ($n = 15$) qualified to receive the supplemental small group intervention based on their PPVT-4 score but did not receive the vocabulary intervention because the school did not have the personnel to provide Tier 2 support. In our analysis, these students are included with the group of students who scored above the 30th percentile and who received only Tier 1 classroom vocabulary instruction.

Classroom Instruction

In a multitiered study of vocabulary instruction, an important goal is to support the vocabulary learning of all students through consistent, high-quality, evidenced-based Tier 1 classroom vocabulary instruction. In this study we used a commercially available classroom-based vocabulary program, *Elements of Reading Vocabulary (EOR-V),* developed by Beck and McKeown (2004). We chose EOR-V because it includes all the components of effective vocabulary instruction, and there is evidence supporting its effectiveness (Apthorp et al., 2012; Beck & McKeown, 2004).

Classroom instruction took place 5 days a week for about 20 minutes each day. On the first day of instruction, teachers read a story to the class and introduced five new vocabulary words. According to Beck and McKeown (2004), the target words chosen for instruction in this curriculum are common in children's literature but are not typically used by children in conversation; they are sophisticated words for concepts that children understand, such as using the word *collide* to describe bumping into something. The target words were defined by the teacher using simple full-sentence explanations that were easy for students to understand. For example, the target word *glance* was defined by the teacher saying, "If you *glance* at something or someone, you look at them very quickly and then look away." Teachers also showed picture cards that provided students with visual representations of the words. On subsequent days, teachers used the picture cards to review definitions of new words and engaged students in a variety of activities that gave them practice using the new words in different contexts. Students acted out words and had opportunities to relate new words to their own experiences. On the final day of the 5-day lesson, teachers reviewed the vocabulary words for the week, assessed vocabulary learning, and briefly reviewed the words taught the prior week.

Supplemental Intervention

The supplemental Project IVI vocabulary intervention was designed by our research team to align closely with the classroom vocabulary EOR-V program and included instructional strategies shown to be effective in previous vocabulary intervention research (e.g., Beck & McKeown, 2007; Biemiller & Boote, 2006; Coyne et al., 2010; Coyne, McCoach, Loftus, Zipoli, & Kapp, 2009; Justice, Meier, & Walpole, 2005; Silverman, 2007). The intervention was delivered by school-based personnel who were trained by the research team. Some of the interventionists were speech-language pathologists or retired teachers, whereas others were paraprofessionals, but we found that they all delivered the intervention with high fidelity of implementation.

Each intervention group met four times per week for 15–20 minutes. Interventionists reviewed three of the five words taught in the classroom lesson. The supplemental intervention was designed to be direct and explicit and included a significant amount of interventionist modeling, scaffolding, and corrective feedback. Students had many opportunities to practice using new words by talking about pictures and using the words to describe their own experiences. The interventionists supported students' use of expanded language.

At the beginning of each lesson, interventionists reintroduced and reviewed three of the five words that had been taught in the classroom. Interventionists modeled the pronunciation and definition of each word: "Our first magic word is *drenched*. Everyone say *drenched*." Then they would follow by saying, "*Drenched* means really wet. Everyone say, '*Drenched* means really wet.' This picture can help us remember what *drenched* means. In the picture, you can see that the boys are getting very wet. Now I'm going to talk about the picture using our magic word *drenched*. 'The boys are *drenched!*' Everyone say, 'The boys are *drenched!*' In the picture you can see that the boys are really wet, or *drenched*."

The small-group, Tier 2 setting provided students with many opportunities to refine their understanding of the words and numerous occasions to practice using the words in varied and expanded contexts. For example, in one activity, the interventionist reviewed the words and then presented students with several pairs of pictures showing examples and nonexamples of each target word. Students were instructed to put their thumbs up and say, "That's drenched," or thumbs down and say, "That's not drenched." In another activity, students practiced using target words to describe pictures and were supported in generating sentences, using the target word, to relate a personal experience. Interventionists were taught to use explicit scaffolding and feedback procedures to support each student at their individual level and to encourage elaboration: "Great job! Can you tell even more about it?" "Can you say it like this?" or "Can you say that again and use our magic word *drenched?*" The small-group setting allowed for increased instructional intensity by providing more direct feedback, modeling, and scaffolding and giving students more opportunities to respond. These instructional strategies have been shown to support word learning with struggling learners (Loftus, Coyne, McCoach, Zipoli, & Pullen, 2010). For additional discussion on the importance of academic talk and prereader comprehension, see Chapter 4 by van Kleeck.

Analytic Techniques

During our study, we were interested in the relationship between vocabulary knowledge and listening comprehension. In particular, we wanted to know whether students who learned more target vocabulary as the result of instruction and intervention would also demonstrate greater listening comprehension of passages that contained target vocabulary, controlling for their overall level of vocabulary knowledge assessed before the start of instruction. We used structural equation modeling to examine the mechanisms that might potentially explain the relationships among students' initial vocabulary knowledge, response to vocabulary instruction and intervention, and listening comprehension outcomes (Torppa et al., 2007).

We created a latent variable to represent students' initial vocabulary knowledge measured in the fall of kindergarten before the start of instruction. This variable included a standardized measure of both receptive vocabulary (PPVT-4; Dunn & Dunn, 2007) and expressive vocabulary (Expressive Vocabulary Test, Second Edition [EVT-2]; Williams, 2007). The listening comprehension outcome was assessed at posttest using a series of researcher-developed passages that contained target vocabulary words. We created a latent variable that included three different indicators: 1) answers to comprehension questions about the passages, 2) number of target words used in a retell of the passages, and 3) lexical diversity in the retells (e.g., number of different words in students' retells).

Students' responsiveness to the intervention was measured using a researcher-developed expressive measure of students' knowledge of target word definitions.

We estimated structural models, first conducting bootstrap analyses to evaluate the stability of the model parameter estimates in a multigroup hybrid model. A hybrid model, which modeled the effects of students' initial general vocabulary scores on target vocabulary and listening comprehension for both the intervention and classroom-only groups, displayed an adequate fit for the assumption of equal measurement weights of the factors for each latent variable (i.e., general vocabulary knowledge and listening comprehension). A systematic exploration of the paths provided evidence that the best-fit model permitted the path between pregeneral vocabulary knowledge and listening comprehension to vary between the intervention- and classroom-only group but constrained the other paths to be equal across groups. A conceptual figure of these structural paths is presented in Figure 2.1.

Results and Discussion

Results revealed that the target word learning of students receiving classroom-only instruction predicted their listening comprehension of passages that contained those target words. However, students' general vocabulary knowledge assessed at the

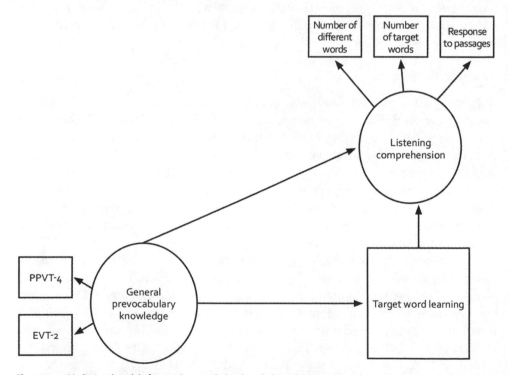

Figure 2.1.   Mediational model of general prevocabulary knowledge to listening comprehenson and general postvocabulary knowledge. (*Key*: PPVT-4, Peabody Picture Vocabulary Test, Fourth Edition [Dunn &Dunn, 2007]; EVT-2, Expressive Vocabulary Test, Second Edition [Williams, 2007].)

beginning of the year before the start of instruction also predicted their listening comprehension scores. For the students receiving classroom vocabulary only, listening comprehension was explained by both entry-level vocabulary knowledge and also their response to vocabulary instruction. It is likely that these students were not only using their knowledge of the target words taught during instruction but also leveraging their general vocabulary knowledge to comprehend the passages presented in the listening comprehension task.

In contrast, for students receiving intensive vocabulary intervention as well as classroom instruction, general vocabulary knowledge assessed at the beginning of the year did not directly predict students' performance on the listening comprehension measure when students' target vocabulary learning was included in the model. Instead, students' responsiveness to the intervention (i.e., learning target words) fully mediated the relationship between general vocabulary knowledge and listening comprehension scores. These findings suggest that students who received intensive intervention were able to use their newly acquired deep knowledge of words taught during instruction to comprehend passages that included those words.

These results are consistent with an instrumentalist explanation for the relationship between target word learning and listening comprehension and add to the relatively limited literature examining these mechanisms with younger learners. It makes sense that a deeper understanding of the meanings of words included in a passage would be associated with greater comprehension of that passage, and our findings support that explanation.

Moreover, finding that response to intervention fully mediated the predictive relationship between general vocabulary assessed at pretest and listening comprehension for those students who received the intensive intervention highlights the promise of supplemental intervention for preventing students who are at risk from falling further behind their peers. The Matthew effect (i.e., the rich get richer and the poor get poorer) describes the process where students with stronger general vocabulary ability are better able to comprehend text than their peers with weaker vocabulary ability because they have richer language resources available to do so (Stanovich, 1986). This differential learning widens the gap, with students with less-developed vocabulary knowledge falling further and further behind. In this case, however, intensive vocabulary intervention may have helped to mitigate the Matthew effect for these students. Students who received intensive intervention were able to use their deep and rich understandings of words taught during instruction to comprehend passages presented orally and did not have to rely on their general vocabulary knowledge.

We also considered whether a metalinguistic hypothesis might help to explain the findings from our study, particularly for students who received the intensive vocabulary intervention. The extended vocabulary instruction in the intensive intervention was characterized by highly interactive activities that purposely drew students' attention to words and their meanings. The small-group intervention also allowed students to discuss words in different contexts, see connections and relationships between words, and connect them to their own experiences. It is possible that this type of intensive and extended instruction helped students develop their word consciousness and metalinguistic awareness (e.g., flexible understanding of word meanings across contexts, syntax, and relationships between words). When students develop metalinguistic awareness, they attend to words more carefully and may become more independent and active word learners and comprehenders. According to this hypothesis, students who develop metalinguistic awareness may demonstrate literacy learning on transfer tasks beyond those that include words taught during vocabulary instruction.

We conducted additional analyses that may provide at least tangential support for the metalinguistic hypothesis. Our findings demonstrated that students' response to intensive vocabulary instruction and intervention was related to not only their listening comprehension of passages that included target words but also their overall general vocabulary learning. Although students' general vocabulary knowledge assessed at the start of the study was still the strongest predictor of general vocabulary at the end of the study, response to vocabulary instruction and intervention predicted additional variance in general vocabulary outcomes. Because none of the words we taught were included on the measure of overall vocabulary knowledge, it seems unlikely that knowledge of the target words by itself could logically explain general vocabulary outcomes. Instead, it may be that response to the intervention could also be acting as an indicator of metalinguistic awareness that could be helping to predict general vocabulary outcomes and could also theoretically support general comprehension outcomes. These findings provide initial evidence for a different and perhaps more powerful mechanism between vocabulary learning instruction and listening comprehension.

Although our analyses were exploratory and do not provide any conclusive or causal evidence about what mechanisms explain the relationship between response to vocabulary instruction and listening comprehension, our findings suggest that that both the instrumentalist and metalinguistic hypotheses offer reasonable explanations and are likely working together to explain outcomes. Finally, our analyses did not include a direct measure of metalinguistic awareness, and future research should more fully and explicitly model the role of metalinguistic awareness in vocabulary and listening comprehension outcomes.

INVESTIGATING THE CAUSAL IMPACTS OF VOCABULARY INSTRUCTION AND INTERVENTION ON LISTENING COMPREHENSION OUTCOMES

Correlational research can help us understand the relationship between vocabulary knowledge and listening comprehension and can help explore theoretical hypotheses about the nature of this relationship. Experimental intervention research, on the other hand, can provide information about the causal effects of vocabulary instruction on language and comprehension outcomes.

A number of meta-analyses have reviewed research on the effects of vocabulary interventions on reading comprehension outcomes. In a seminal review, Stahl and Fairbanks (1986) reported an average effect size of .97 for researcher-developed comprehension measures and .30 for global measures of comprehension. (Effect sizes in this chapter refer to Cohen's d [Cohen, 1988], which indicates the magnitude of effects of an intervention, with effect sizes of .20 and below generally considered small, effect sizes of .50 considered moderate, and effect sizes of .8 and above considered large.) In a 2009 meta-analysis, however, Elleman et al. used a more conservative methodology and found a mean effect of .50 for researcher-developed comprehension measures and a nonstatistically significant effect of only .10 for standardized measures of comprehension.

Very little intervention research has evaluated the effects of vocabulary instruction and intervention on the listening comprehension of younger students. However, in a 2013 study, Baker et al. reported on the effects of a read-aloud intervention for first-grade students in classrooms that were assigned either to teach the read-aloud strategies implemented over 19 weeks or to serve as comparison classrooms following typical practice. Their read-aloud intervention was developed to provide explicit instruction in listening comprehension strategies and vocabulary instruction within the context of read-aloud storybook lessons. They found that the intervention had significant effects on students' performance on word learning and on retelling a narrative passage. The effect size for vocabulary gains on an experimenter measure of depth of knowledge was .93. The effect size on a standardized measure of narrative retell was moderate at .42. Baker et al. did not find any statistically significant effects of the intervention on expository retell or on the subtest of listening comprehension of the Gates-MacGinitie Reading Tests (Gates & MacGinitie, 1964).

Another study by McKeown and Beck (2011) examined the effects of two different approaches to vocabulary instruction on students' language processing. In the interactive instructional condition, students were provided with rich instruction in which they were asked to think about target word meanings and to discuss the use of the target word in multiple potential contexts. In the repetition condition, students learned and practiced the meanings of target words in game-like activities such as concentration and matching that paired the word with its definition. Outcomes for the instructional conditions were compared with a control group.

Students in both instructional conditions outperformed the control group on an experimenter measure of word learning, with an effect size of .35 for the repetition condition and .44 for the interactive condition. Students' listening comprehension processing was assessed using two researcher-developed measures: passage retell and context integration. There were no statistically significant effects for passage retell in either instructional condition. The context integration measure required students to use their knowledge of a target word to make sense of a sentence. For example, students were asked, "Jim had to *insist* that Freddy go on the merry-go-round. What did Freddy think about the merry-go-round?" Students in the interactive instruction condition demonstrated more complete sentence-level understanding with answers such as "Maybe he got sick to his stomach" and "It was scary—it went too fast," whereas students in the repetition instruction group and the control group were more likely to answer with "It was fun" or another answer that indicated they did not understand the meaning of *insist*.

Study Examining the Effects of Vocabulary Instruction on Listening Comprehension

In a different study, we evaluated a kindergarten vocabulary intervention in schools that served large percentages of students at risk for experiencing literacy and language difficulties and measured its impact on listening comprehension outcomes (Coyne et al., 2010). In this quasi-experimental study, five classrooms were assigned to treatment or control conditions at two schools. There were 52 students in the three treatment classes and 22 students in the two control classes. In a third school, individual students were assigned to instructional groups with 23 students receiving small-group vocabulary instruction and 21 students in the control group. Students received a 20-minute vocabulary intervention 2 days per week over 18 weeks in either the whole-class or small-group settings.

The vocabulary instruction was similar to the instruction described earlier and is also included in Coyne et al. (2010). We developed the intervention around 18 storybooks (such as *Tar Beach* by Faith Ringgold and *The Three Little Pigs* by James Marshall) that were read aloud to students followed by interactive postreading activities. We selected storybooks that would be of high interest to kindergarten students; they included engaging narratives, rich language, and illustrative pictures. Priority was given to storybooks that depicted multicultural characters and themes. We chose three target vocabulary words from each storybook to teach directly (54 total). At the beginning of each storybook reading session, interventionists introduced the three target words and had students pronounce them. Students were then encouraged to listen for each of the "magic words" during the story reading and to raise their hands whenever they heard one. Interventionists acknowledged students when they recognized target words and then reread the sentence containing the word (e.g., "Oh, good. Some of you raised your hands! What word did you hear? Yes, *peculiar*. 'When Anansi said the word *seven*, a *peculiar* thing happened'"). Interventionists then provided students with a simple definition of the word (e.g., "*Peculiar* means strange or different"). Next, interventionists reread the sentence and replaced the target word with its definition (e.g., "Now I'll say the sentence again with the words that mean peculiar. 'When Anansi said the word *seven*, a *strange* thing happened'"). Interventionists then reinforced the story context by referring to the illustration: "In the picture, you can see that something strange or peculiar happened to Anansi that sent him flying through the air." Finally, students again pronounced the target word to strengthen phonological representations (e.g., "Everyone say *peculiar*"). The purpose of these procedures was to offer students both a simple definition of each target word and contextual support for the word's use in the story (Stahl & Fairbanks, 1986).

After each story reading, interventionists engaged students in activities that provided them with opportunities to interact with target words in rich and varied contexts beyond those offered in the story (Beck et al., 2013). First, students were reintroduced to each target word by reviewing how it was used in the story (e.g., "One of the magic words we learned in the story was *peculiar*. *Peculiar* means strange or different. 'When Anansi said the word *seven*, a peculiar thing happened.' In the picture, you can see that something strange or peculiar happened to Anansi that sent him flying through the air"). Next, interventionists provided students with examples of the target word used in other contexts (e.g., "Other things could be peculiar too. If a person were wearing a bathing suit outside on a snowy day, he or she would look peculiar. If you saw a cat driving a car, that would be a peculiar thing. If a boy always walked backward, that would look peculiar or strange and different"). Students then engaged in different interactive activities that focused on recognizing examples and nonexamples of target words used in different contexts and asked open-ended questions to encourage students to extend and elaborate on their initial responses. Interventionists provided additional individual turns to students who may have been having difficulty. Review activities reinforced definitions and encouraged deep processing of word meanings through opportunities to interact with words in novel contexts and explore the relationships between target words and previously known words and concepts.

We evaluated the effects of the vocabulary instruction on measures of target word learning (i.e., words taught directly during instruction) as well as a measure of listening comprehension. We developed a story that contained 18 of our target words. Students listened to the story read aloud while following along with pictures in a wordless storybook. After the reading, students were asked 10 literal and inferential questions about the story. Answers to questions were scored as either correct or incorrect.

To determine the impact of the vocabulary intervention, we estimated the effect of the treatment after controlling for initial receptive vocabulary knowledge (PPVT-4). Originally, we had intended to use an analysis of covariance to analyze our data. However, we failed to meet the assumption of homogeneity of regression slopes across treatment and control groups. Instead, we consistently found an interaction between the covariate (initial PPVT-4) and treatment. Therefore, we used a multiple regression test to analyze our data. For each dependent variable, we estimated a model that included the treatment condition, the centered initial PPVT-4 score, and the Treatment × PPVT-4 interaction.

As expected, students who received the vocabulary instruction learned the words that were targeted for instruction, with large effect sizes favoring the treatment students. We also found a moderate effect of the vocabulary instruction on our measure of listening comprehension, with an overall effect size of .42. This finding suggested that extended vocabulary instruction increased students' ability to comprehend stories read aloud that included words taught during instruction.

These results are consistent with findings in the meta-analysis conducted by Elleman and her colleagues (2009). They reported an average effect size of .50 for the impact of vocabulary instruction on researcher-developed measures of reading comprehension. Findings of our study suggested that the impact of vocabulary instruction on the listening comprehension of younger students may be similar to the impact of instruction on the reading comprehension of older students.

CONCLUSION

In this chapter, we reviewed theory and research suggesting that there is a strong positive relationship between vocabulary knowledge and listening comprehension, similar to the well-researched relationship between vocabulary knowledge and reading comprehension. We presented hypotheses that may explain this association between vocabulary and listening comprehension. Prominent among these are the instrumentalist hypothesis, which suggests that learning vocabulary directly increases listening comprehension because the more words students understand in a sentence or passage that is read aloud, the better they will be able to comprehend the overall meaning of that sentence or passage. Another complimentary hypothesis is the metalinguistic hypothesis, which suggests that students who are able to reflect on and manipulate language on a number of levels and who are actively engaged in word learning will develop word consciousness and metalinguistic awareness, which in turn supports both additional vocabulary learning and listening comprehension.

We presented the findings of a study that suggests that both the instrumentalist and metalinguistic hypotheses may be working together to support kindergarten students' listening comprehension. Students who received explicit and robust vocabulary instruction in kindergarten were able to leverage their knowledge of words taught during instruction to better understand an oral passage that included those words—in support of the instrumentalist hypothesis. In addition, we found that students' response to rich vocabulary instruction and intervention was also associated with overall vocabulary outcomes—which provides at least initial and intriguing evidence that vocabulary instruction may strengthen metalinguistic awareness, another mechanism that could support listening comprehension. Finally, we presented results of a study in which directly teaching vocabulary to kindergarten students increased their listening comprehension of passages that included words targeted during instruction.

In sum, we believe the results of these studies as well as others support the important connections between early vocabulary development and students' listening comprehension. Moreover, findings highlight the central role of vocabulary instruction and intervention in the early grades. This instruction can accelerate the development of students' vocabulary knowledge and metalinguistic awareness, which in turn supports listening comprehension.

REFERENCES

Anderson, R.C., & Freebody, P. (1981). Vocabulary knowledge. In J.T. Guthrie (Ed.), *Comprehension and teaching: Research reviews* (pp. 77–117). Newark, DE: International Reading Association.

Apthorp, H., Randel, B., Cherasaro, T., Clark, T., McKeown, M., & Beck, I. (2012). Effects of a supplemental vocabulary program on word knowledge and passage comprehension. *Journal of Research on Educational Effectiveness, 5*(2), 160–188.

Baker, S.K., Santoro, L.E., Chard, D.J., Fien, H., Park, Y., & Otterstedt, J. (2013). An evaluation of an explicit read aloud intervention taught in whole-classroom formats in first grade. *Elementary School Journal, 113,* 331–358. doi:10.1086/668503

Baumann, J.F., Kame'enui, E.J., & Ash, G. (2003). Research on vocabulary instruction: Voltaire redux. In J. Flood, D. Lapp, J.R. Squire, & J. Jensen (Eds.), *Handbook of research on teaching the English language arts* (2nd ed., pp. 752–785). Mahwah, NJ: Erlbaum.

Beck, I.L., & McKeown, M.G. (2004). *Elements of reading: Vocabulary, teacher's guide—level K.* Austin, TX: Steck-Vaughn.

Beck, I.L., & McKeown, M.G. (2007). Increasing young low-income children's oral vocabulary repertoires through rich and focused instruction. *Elementary School Journal, 107,* 251–271. doi:10.1086/511706

Beck, I.L., McKeown, M.G., & Kucan, L. (2013). *Bringing words to life: Robust vocabulary instruction* (2nd ed.). New York, NY: Guilford Press.

Biemiller, A., & Boote, C. (2006). An effective method for building meaning vocabulary in primary grades. *Journal of Educational Psychology, 98,* 44–62. doi:10.1037/0022-0663.98.1.44

Cohen, J. (1988). *Statistical power analysis for the behavioral sciences* (2nd ed.). Hillsdale, NJ: Erlbaum.

Coyne, M., McCoach, D., & Kapp, S. (2007). Vocabulary intervention for kindergarten students: Comparing extended instruction to embedded instruction and incidental exposure. *Learning Disability Quarterly, 30,* 74–88. doi:10.2307/30035543

Coyne, M., McCoach, D., Loftus, S., Zipoli, R., & Kapp, S. (2009). Direct vocabulary instruction in kindergarten: Teaching for breadth vs. depth. *Elementary School Journal, 110,* 1–18. doi:10.1086/598840

Coyne, M.D., McCoach, D., Loftus, S., Zipoli, R., Ruby, M., Crevecoeur, Y.C., & Kapp, S. (2010). Direct and extended vocabulary instruction in kindergarten: Investigating transfer effects. *Journal of Research on Educational Effectiveness, 3,* 93–120. doi:10.1080/19345741003592410

Coyne, M.D., Neugebauer, S., Ware, S., Madura, J., McCoach, D., & Capozzoli-Oldham, A. (2012, February). *Exploring relationships between vocabulary intervention and literacy outcomes.* Paper presented at the Pacific Coast Research Conference, San Diego, CA.

Cunningham, A.E., & Stanovich, K.E. (1997). Early reading acquisition and its relation to reading experience and ability 10 years later. *Developmental Psychology, 33,* 934–945. doi:10.1037/0012-1649.33.6.934

Dunn, L.M., & Dunn, D.M. (2007). *Peabody Picture Vocabulary Test, Fourth Edition (PPVT-4).* Minneapolis, MN: Pearson.

Elleman, A.M., Lindo, E.J., Morphy, P., & Compton, D. (2009). The impact of vocabulary instruction on passage-level comprehension of school-age children: A meta-analysis. *Journal of Research on Educational Effectiveness, 2,* 1–44. doi:10.1080/19345740802539200

Gates, A., & MacGinitie, W.H. (1964). *Reading tests.* New York, NY: Teachers College Press.

Gough, P., & Tunmer, W. (1986). Decoding, reading, and reading disability. *Remedial and Special Education, 7,* 6–10. doi:10.1177/074193258600700104

Justice, L., Meier, J., & Walpole, S. (2005). Learning new words from storybooks: An efficacy study with at-risk kindergartners. *Language, Speech, and Hearing Services in Schools, 36,* 17–32. doi:10.1044/0161-1461(2005/003)

Loftus, S.M., Coyne, M., McCoach, D., Zipoli, R., & Pullen, P. (2010). Effects of a supplemental vocabulary intervention on the word knowledge of kindergarten students at-risk for language and literacy difficulties. *Learning Disabilities Research & Practice, 25,* 124–136. doi:10.1111/j.1540-5826.2010.00310.x

McKeown, M.G., & Beck, I.L. (2011). *Two approaches to vocabulary instruction for kindergarteners: Comparing effects on comprehension.* Paper presented at the American Educational Research Association Conference, New Orleans, LA.

Mezynski, K. (1983). Issues concerning the acquisition of knowledge: Effects of vocabulary training on reading comprehension. *Review of Educational Research, 53,* 253–279. doi:10.3102/00346543053002253

Nagy, W.E. (2007). Metalinguistic awareness and the vocabulary-comprehension connection. In R.K. Wagner, A.E. Muse, & K.R. Tannenbaum (Eds.), *Vocabulary acquisition: Implications for reading comprehension* (pp. 52–77). New York, NY: Guilford Press.

Nagy, W.E., & Anderson, R.C. (1995). *Metalinguistic awareness and literacy acquisition in different languages* (Center for the Study of Reading Technical Report No. 618). Retrieved from http://hdl.handle.net/2142/17594

National Institute of Child Health and Human Development. (2000). *Report of the national reading panel. Teaching children to read: An evidence-based assessment of the scientific research literature on reading and its implications for reading instruction* (NIH Publication No. 00-4769). Washington, DC: U.S. Government Printing Office. Retrieved from http://www.nichd.nih.gov/publications/pubs/nrp/Pages/smallbook.aspx

Neugebauer, S.R., Madura, J., Coyne, M., McCoach, B., Ware, S., & Capazolli, A. (2012, July). *Examining instrumentalist and metalinguistic hypotheses: What mechanisms explain the relationships among general vocabulary knowledge, response to an intensive vocabulary intervention, and literacy-related outcomes?* Poster session presented at the annual meeting of the Society for the Scientific Study of Reading, Montreal, Canada.

Ouellette, G.P. (2006). What's meaning got to do with it: The role of vocabulary in word reading and reading comprehension. *Journal of Educational Psychology, 98,* 554–566. doi:10.1037/0022-0663.98.3.554

Pearson, P.D., Hiebert, E.H., & Kamil, M.L. (2007). Theory and research into practice: Vocabulary assessment: What we know and what we need to know. *Reading Research Quarterly, 42*(2), 282–296. Retrieved from http://www.jstor.org/stable/4151794

Perfetti, C.A. (2007). Reading ability: Lexical quality to comprehension. *Scientific Studies of Reading, 11,* 357–383. doi:10.1080/10888430701530730

Potocki, A., Ecalle, J., & Magnan, A. (2013). Narrative comprehension skills in 5-year-old children: Correlational analysis and comprehender profiles. *Journal of Educational Research, 106,* 14–26. doi:10.1080/00220671.2012.667013

Scarborough, H.S. (2001). Connecting early language and literacy to later reading (dis)abilities: Evidence, theory, and practice. In S. Neuman & D. Dickinson (Eds.), *Handbook of early literacy research* (Vol. 1, pp. 97–110). New York, NY: Guilford Press.

Sénéchal, M., Ouellette, G., & Rodney, D. (2006). The misunderstood giant: On the predictive role of early vocabulary to future reading. In D.K. Dickinson & S.B. Neuman (Eds.), *Handbook of early literacy research* (Vol. 2, pp. 173–182). New York, NY: Guilford Press.

Silverman, R. (2007). Vocabulary development of English-language and English-only learners in kindergarten. *Elementary School Journal, 107*(4), 365–383. doi:10.1086/516669

Snow, C., Burns, M., & Griffin, P. (1998). *Preventing reading difficulties in young children.* Washington, DC: National Academy Press.

Stahl, S.A. (1986). Three principles of effective vocabulary instruction. *Journal of Reading, 29*(7), 662–668. Retrieved from http://www.jstor.org/stable/40029695

Stahl, S.A. (1991). Beyond the instrumentalist hypothesis: Some relationships between word meanings and comprehension. In P. Schwanenflugel (Ed.), *The psychology of word meanings* (pp. 157–178). Hillsdale, NJ: Erlbaum.

Stahl, S., & Fairbanks, M. (1986). The effects of vocabulary instruction: A model-based meta-analysis. *Review of Educational Research, 56,* 72–110. Retrieved from http://www.jstor.org/stable/1170287

Stahl, S.A., & Nagy, W. (2006). *Teaching word meanings.* Mahwah, NJ: Erlbaum.

Stanovich, K.E. (1986). Matthew effects in reading: Some consequences of the individual differences in the acquisition of literacy. *Reading Research Quarterly, 21,* 360–407. Retrieved from http://www.jstor.org/stable/747612

Torppa, M., Poikkeus, A.-M., Laakso, M.-L., Tolvanen, A., Leppänen, P., Puolakanaho, A., & Lyytinen, H. (2007). Modeling the early paths of phonological awareness and factors supporting its development in children with and without familial risk for dyslexia. *Scientific Studies of Reading, 11,* 73–103. doi:10.1080/10888430709336554

Vaughn, S., Gersten, R., & Chard, D. (2000). The underlying message in LD intervention research: Findings from research synthesis. *Exceptional Children, 67,* 99–114. Retrieved from http://search.ebscohost.com.ezproxy.lib.uconn.edu/login.aspx?direct=true&db=psyh&AN=2003–08625–001&site=ehost-live&scope=site

Williams, K.T. (2007). *Expressive Vocabulary Test, Second Edition (EVT-2).* Minneapolis, MN: Pearson.

3

Using Play to Promote Language Comprehension in Preschoolers

KATHERINE M. NEWMAN, DAVID K. DICKINSON,
KATHRYN HIRSH-PASEK, AND ROBERTA MICHNICK GOLINKOFF

A perspective shared by other chapters is that it is important to begin cultivating oral language–based higher-order comprehension processes in preschool-age children to ensure reading success when children move from listening to stories to reading stories. In this chapter, we introduce the relationship among comprehension of narratives, vocabulary, and reading and argue that adult-supported play provides a promising means to engage children in language-rich activity that can foster growth of critical abilities essential for later comprehension.

Comprehension processes are supported by three language-based skills that relate to reading success: skill in comprehending narratives, ability to make inferences, and deep knowledge of vocabulary. (See Chapter 6 by Hall-Kenyon, Culatta, and Duke for an extensive discussion on the topic of comprehension and informational texts.) Models of the reading process view language comprehension as central to reading comprehension (Kendeou, White, van den Broek, & Lynch, 2009; Tunmer & Chapman, 2012; Vellutino, Tunmer, Jaccard, & Chen, 2007). The ability to comprehend narratives draws on vocabulary and discourse-level language abilities that are interrelated in the preschool years (National Institute of Child Health and Human Development [NICHD] Early Child Care Research Network, 2005; Sénéchal, Ouellette, & Rodney, 2006; Tilstra, McMaster, van den Broek, Kendeou, & Rapp, 2009; Tunmer & Hoover, 1992), and early language competencies predict comprehension in the primary grades (Kendeou et al., 2009; Storch & Whitehurst, 2002), which is predictive of later reading comprehension (Nation & Snowling, 2004).

This chapter presents an argument that social pretend play may cultivate this complex array of skills in developmentally appropriate ways for preschool-age children who find this type of play enjoyable. The first part of the chapter reviews the development of these prereader comprehension skills. The rest discusses how play may help foster the

This chapter reports research conducted as part of award #R305A110128 from the Institute for Educational Science, U.S. Department of Education to Vanderbilt University, Temple University, the University of Delaware, and Lehigh University. The views expressed are those of the authors.

acquisition of these competencies using results from a play-based intervention being developed to support preschoolers' word learning and narrative comprehension.

THE COMPREHENSION PROCESS

The groundwork for written text comprehension is laid as children listen to and use extended language to communicate experiences and ideas. As teachers and children read stories, they may discuss questions such as the motivations for a character's actions or the likely outcome of an event. Such analytical talk about stories encourages children to listen to the text, using their emerging linguistic skills to comprehend the words and sentences as they draw on personal experiences, knowledge of the world, and information provided by the pictures to build a mental model of the story world. As they weave together their multiple sources of information, they are learning to engage in the kind of intellectual activity that later is needed to comprehend what one is reading. Evidence that such conversations in preschool classrooms may foster later comprehension comes from a longitudinal study in which language use across the day was observed and children's language and reading were assessed in kindergarten and fourth grade (Dickinson & Porche, 2011). Children whose teachers more often engaged them in analytical discussions of books had stronger language and print skills at the end of kindergarten, and these abilities were associated with stronger reading comprehension at the end of Grade 4.

An influential approach to describing how support for language and comprehension in preschool may foster later comprehension is provided by the landscape model of reading comprehension (van den Broek, Young, Tzeng, & Linderholm, 1999). It proposes that successful reading comprehension involves "interpretation of the information in the text, the use of prior knowledge to do so, and, ultimately, the construction of a coherent representation or picture of what the text is about in the reader's mind" (van den Broek et al., 2005, p. 109). Central to understanding text is the process of drawing on background knowledge and information from the text to create a mental representation. A mental representation is like a network made up of nodes that correspond to individual facts and events from the text and connections between the nodes that stand for the meaningful relations among them (van den Broek, Young, Tzeng, & Linderholm, 1999; Rapp, van den Broek, McMaster, Kendeou, & Espin, 2007). According to this theory, the reader generates inferences to identify the meaningful relations between parts of the text with the support of vocabulary knowledge and knowledge of the causal structure of narratives. In Chapter 9, Cartwright and Guajardo explain the roles executive function and theory of mind play in comprehension.

Prereaders engage in the same comprehension processes as do older children and adults (van den Broek et al., 2005). Preschool children draw on cognitive processes to understand events they experience with the support of three language-based abilities: skill in comprehending narratives, ability to generate inferences, and deep knowledge of vocabulary (Florit, Roch, Altoè, & Levorato, 2009; Lynch et al., 2008).

Narrative Comprehension

The ability to make causal connections within and between narrative events is particularly important for narrative comprehension. Causal connections are made when readers recognize that one event motivates, facilitates, psychologically induces, or physically brings about another event described in the narrative (Trabasso, van den Broek, & Suh, 1989). For example, the king is angry with the dragon for setting things on fire, causing the dragon to hide. Studies of adult comprehension suggest that mature readers encode the causal connections in a coherent mental representation of the narrative (Rapp & Taylor, 2004). After reading, adults and elementary students remember events from narratives that have more causal connections better than they remember events with fewer connections (Goldman & Varnhagen, 1986; van den Broek, 1988). In other words, readers are sensitive to the causal structure of narratives: They recognize an important event occurring early in the text that begins a chain of connected events throughout the text.

Prereaders are also sensitive to causal structure in narratives. Children as young as 2 years old recall causally related events more easily than arbitrarily sequenced events (Wenner & Bauer, 1999). By 5 years of age, children begin producing narratives that contain simple yet causally coherent events (Baumer, Ferholt, & Lecusay, 2005; Trabasso & Nickels, 1992), and forming causal connections is also important for establishing coherence when prereaders attend to nontext materials. For example, van den Broek and colleagues (1996) found that 4-year-olds were more likely to recall events from a short, audiovisual narrative that had more causal connections than events with fewer connections. For example, an event such as "The money Jimmy counted was not enough to buy a bike" contains more causal connections than "Jimmy walked to school one morning." Young children appear to create emergent network representations of narratives with an emphasis on the causal connections between events. These representations likely benefit memory for story events and the capacity to comprehend them when they are referenced in conversations or reading because preschoolers use these causally connected network representations to recall narratives and answer comprehension questions (Lynch et al., 2008). Finally, causal connections are often implicit; therefore, children listening to narratives must make inferences as they identify connections and integrate them into a developing mental representation. This activity is not simply an automatic memory-based process; rather, it may well require active constructive effort by the child.

Inference Ability

Competence in drawing inferences is essential to listening and reading comprehension, as authors and speakers leave many thoughts and actions in a narrative implicit (Bowyer-Crane & Snowling, 2005; Oakhill & Cain, 2012). When children make inferences, they draw conclusions about the points of view or motives of characters and make predictions about causes or outcomes of events that are not explicitly stated in texts (van Kleeck, Vander Woude, & Hammett, 2006). For example, a child might infer that the bear in a story feels upset because his friend the little bird is leaving the forest even though the book text does not state that the bear feels upset. Cain, Oakhill, and Bryant (2004) studied comprehension among children from ages 8 to 11 and found that, after taking into account working memory, inference-making skill predicted unique variance in comprehension. Inference generation supports prereaders' understanding of narratives through similar processes (van den Broek et al., 2005). Studies of preschoolers' comprehension across media types (e.g., audiotaped stories, television narratives) demonstrate that children make knowledge-based and text-based inferences about characters' internal states and emotions and the causal connections between events. Furthermore, these inferences contribute significantly to prereaders' comprehension (Florit, Roch, & Levorato, 2011; Kendeou, Bohn-Gettler, White, & van den Broek, 2008).

One of the ways in which young children may develop the ability to generate inferences well before they are able to read text is through high-level conversations with adults during book reading (van Kleeck et al., 2006). However, it is still unclear how these conversations promote children's inferential language development and comprehension. Zucker and colleagues (2010) have proposed that adults' use of inferential talk gives rise to children's use of higher-level talk in the moment, which, over time, benefits associated language skills. Indeed, early experience with inferential language has been associated with children's later ability to make predictions and explain concepts (van Kleeck, Gillam, Hamilton, & McGrath, 1997) and vocabulary knowledge (Dickinson & Porche, 2011), all of which support reading comprehension. Listening to and participating in high-level conversations about books in preschool could also support the internalization of inferential thinking about narratives. In other words, high-level conversations with prereaders could lead to the habitual practice of generating inferences that, if used when children begin reading narratives, strengthen the coherence of their mental representations and thus enhance comprehension. When children make inferences, they are connecting ideas and filling in details that are not explicitly mentioned and thus accessing the deeper meaning of narratives as opposed to attending to literal facts and details that provide only a surface-level understanding. See Chapter 4 by van Kleeck for a comprehensive discussion of children's academic talk as it relates to language and comprehension.

Depth of Vocabulary Knowledge

Vocabulary knowledge can be described in terms of two dimensions: breadth and depth. *Breadth of knowledge* refers to the number of words stored in a child's lexicon, whereas *depth of knowledge* includes elements of form, meaning, and use. Knowledge of form includes the word's pronunciation, spelling, and morphological features (Read, 2004). It also includes the elaborated and specific knowledge of a word's meaning, such as awareness of polysemous meanings and the ability to discern between commonplace and more technical word meanings. The concept of depth can be understood as a robust network of knowledge that supports the ability to distinguish between, categorize, and connect semantically related words (e.g., the ability to distinguish terms such as *cheerful, contented, ecstatic,* and *delighted;* Henriksen, 1999; Read, 2004). Finally, depth of vocabulary knowledge includes the ability to fluently access the correct meaning and syntactic form.

The influence of depth of vocabulary knowledge on reading comprehension can be understood when reading is considered using the lens of the lexical quality hypothesis (LQH; Perfetti, 2007). The LQH claims that comprehension depends on a reader's ability to retrieve word identities that fit the context of a particular narrative and associated concepts by drawing on background knowledge associated with the word. The greater the lexical quality of words, the more efficiently and accurately a reader can derive adequate explanations for story events that occurred previously in the text. Evidence supporting this position is that depth of vocabulary knowledge is a unique predictor of comprehension

(Ouellette, 2006; Roth, Speece, & Cooper, 2002), and early ability to define words, an indicator of deep vocabulary knowledge, is associated with later reading performance (Snow, Tabors, Nicholson, & Kurland, 1995).

A greater depth of vocabulary knowledge, also conceptualized by the LQH as robust lexical representations, may facilitate the retrieval of concepts from prior reading cycles (i.e., a previous sentence) or from relevant background knowledge and thus, according to the landscape model of comprehension, enrich the reader's mental representation and understanding of the text (van den Broek et al., 2005). In addition, studies on the role of language skills in reading demonstrate that word-level semantic knowledge also supports inferential processes, which bolster comprehension (Nation, Clarke, Marshall, & Durand, 2004). Prereaders likewise rely on vocabulary knowledge as they identify meaningful connections between events in stories that are read to them and between these events and their background knowledge (Florit et al., 2009; van den Broek et al., 2005). See Chapter 2 by Coyne, Neugebauer, Ware, McCoach, and Madura for additional theoretical perspectives and research on the role of vocabulary instruction and comprehension.

PRETEND PLAY

Children everywhere engage in play, and many have speculated that it plays an important role in fostering literacy development (Hirsh-Pasek, Golinkoff, Berk, & Singer, 2009; Roskos & Christie, 2013). Play is an activity that engages children in interactions with others and ways of using their language and minds that helps build children's ability to comprehend narratives, generate inferences, and acquire deep knowledge of vocabulary. Play may foster growth of competencies associated with comprehension because, as children engage in social pretend play, they adopt character roles and jointly construct narratives. By creating and living through stories, children have opportunities to engage in the kind of intentional interweaving of jointly produced language and personal experiences that also is required for reading comprehension.

Research examining the association between play and literacy includes a diverse array of studies on the relationship between play and emergent literacy skills that support comprehension development, including narrative recall and vocabulary (for a review, see Lillard et al., 2012). In discussing the literature, we use the term *pretend play* to describe the type of playful activity that has been characterized by play scholars as pleasurable, spontaneous, nonliteral, all-engrossing, and having no extrinsic goals (Fein, 1981; Weisberg, Zosh, Hirsh-Paske, & Golinkoff, 2013). This type of play, during which children experiment with different roles, has been referred to as make-believe, fantasy, symbolic, sociodramatic, and dramatic play (Bodrova & Leong, 2007; Roskos & Christie, 2013). Examples of pretend play include pretending to run an ice cream stand or pretending to go on a picnic. Here we discuss results from a project in which we are helping teachers to engage children in pretend play, and we use this term to encompass what other play researchers refer to as make-believe, fantasy, and symbolic play. Although we describe our approach as one that fosters playful learning, due to the fact that play is used to achieve educational outcomes and there is some degree of adult direction, some features typically associated with definitions of play must be relaxed.

One strand of research on play has maintained that children from middle-income families reap many benefits from engaging in pretend play with peers without adult involvement, with these benefits including opportunities to practice more syntactically and semantically complex language (reviewed by Lillard et al., 2012; Vedeler, 1997). Another research tradition surmises that some children do not reap the benefits of pretend play without adult support. Intervention studies have demonstrated the narrative- and language-based benefits of adult guidance during pretend play, with the benefits being especially noteworthy for children from families with less education and families where the dominant language of the country is not spoken (Christakis, Zimmerman, & Garrison, 2007; Han, Moore, Vukelich, & Buell, 2010; Smilansky, 1968). See Chapter 8 by Barrueco and Fernández for a discussion highlighting the linkages between multilingualism and comprehension in early childhood.

Play Develops Children's Narrative Comprehension

Enacting narrative episodes is a central feature of children's pretend play (Nicolopoulou & Ilgaz, 2013; Pellegrini & Galda, 1990). Researchers have observed structural parallels between preschoolers' pretend play and narratives. These parallel structures include setting, a central problem that develops over a number of episodes, and a resolution (Eckler & Weininger, 1989). Based on the correspondence between narrative structure and pretend play, researchers have engaged children in pretend play story reenactments in an effort to improve narrative comprehension.

In an effort to determine the strength of evidence that play has beneficial effects for narrative and language development, Lillard and her colleagues (2012) conducted a wide-ranging review of research on play and found the evidence to be sparse and inconclusive. They recommended more rigorous experiments, pointing out that the majority of studies linking play to narrative development have methodological shortcomings. Limitations include small sample sizes and the use of activities that could be viewed as outside the realm of children's everyday pretend play, such as reenacting researcher-selected stories. Despite methodological flaws, they concluded that correlational and experimental studies have produced "qualified results for the hypothesis that pretend play causes narrative development" (Lillard et al., 2012, p. 21).

In a study of low-income preschoolers, Dansky (1980) randomly assigned children to three conditions in which they participated for 30-minute sessions per week for 3 weeks. In the sociodramatic condition, children were encouraged to engage in pretend play on everyday themes such as "shopping for groceries." An experimenter participated in the children's play by modeling pretense or suggesting further actions. During free play, children had access to the same toys from the sociodramatic condition; however, the experimenter only answered children's questions and refrained from guiding, modeling, or providing themes. During exploration training, children were encouraged to interact with each other and the experimenter to equalize adult contact. There was a focus on investigating, explaining, and discussing the physical properties and functions of objects, and there was no pretense. Children in the sociodramatic condition scored higher on 9 of 10 measures of story memory and quality of narrative production.

In a correlational study, Williamson and Silvern (1992) investigated whether kindergartners' comprehension of fairy tales that were heard and then reenacted was related to the act of engaging in pretense, metaplay, or general productive language competence.

Metaplay was defined as verbal and nonverbal behaviors when children were "out of role" and were used to set the stage for the next pretend episode (i.e., talk used to negotiate actions and resolve situations relating to the play). Only one component of metaplay—directing, or telling another child to perform a specific act—contributed significantly to comprehension. This result may indicate that, when engaging in metaplay, children are gaining a generalized awareness of roles and actions as they actively construct stories and that having opportunities to engage in pretend play may provide more opportunities for such interaction, thereby fostering story comprehension.

A related line of research explores the benefits of a play- and narrative-based activity that is broadly based on Paley's work (1990). In this practice, preschool children are invited to dictate a story to a teacher at a particular time each day, such as during center time activities. Later in the day, the teacher reads each story aloud while the author of the story and a few classmates of the author's choosing act it out. The remaining classmates serve as the audience. In an exploratory study of these methods, Nicolopoulou (2002) found that participating in these activities fosters children's narrative production abilities. Data from a large-scale study directed by Nicolopoulou and colleagues (2010, 2013) that suggest these methods also promote narrative comprehension are forthcoming. Investigating the efficacy of the storytelling and story-acting activities, which build on children's skills and motivation as they compose and then enact their own stories, provides a much-needed complement to the studies of children enacting researcher-selected narratives.

Research from other domains describes complementary mechanisms through which play may support narrative comprehension. Pretend play may enhance memory for narratives because the story events are experienced through movement and in relation to props, resulting in improvement in what is called an *embodied representation,* whereby words and phrases are indexed to objects and actions with positive effects on memory retrieval (Glenberg, 1997; Glenberg, Gutierrez, Levin, Japuntich, & Kaschak, 2004). Also, enacting action sequences may enhance memory for story events (Biazak, Marley, & Levin, 2010), possibly by improving the ability to recognize and construct causal links between events. For example, using toys to act out events described in a story, such as getting eggs from a chicken in the barn, can help a child remember and comprehend the text. Evidence suggestive of long-term benefits of play comes from a longitudinal study that examined features of teacher–child interactions during free play in preschool and found that the percentage of teacher utterances meant to encourage the child to remain on the same topic was positively related to narrative production in kindergarten (Dickinson & Tabors, 2001). Given than nearly half of children's talk was coded as "pretend," many of these teacher–child conversations could have occurred as teachers encouraged children to elaborate pretend-based narratives. Other interactions that may have scaffolded narrative skills were when children, with teacher support, shared stories about past experiences. In sum, whether engaging in metaplay, physically enacting narratives, or conversing with responsive adults, producing narratives through play may help children develop mental representations that are thought to support comprehension (Graesser, Golding, & Long, 1991). Because children often develop and act out narratives during pretend play, it is not surprising that evidence suggests a positive relationship between play and narrative comprehension (Lillard et al., 2012). As Nicolopoulou and Ilgaz note, "It seems plausible that these two types of activity would draw on, and promote, some of the same skills and capacities" (2013, p. 60). One of the skills that prereaders draw on in comprehending narratives is the ability to generate inferences.

Play and Making Inferences

There are important parallels between constructing shared meaning during collaborative pretend play and the oral language abilities required for inference making. As children work to construct shared meaning with play partners (i.e., using language to create imaginary worlds; Bruner, 1983), they practice the type of cognitive problem solving that is required to comprehend narratives by making explicit information that may be implicit in a story. They verbally exchange ideas, negotiate intentions, and share symbolic concepts (e.g., a child communicates that the stick he holds is "a trumpet for the marching band"). In doing so, they must recognize and accommodate their play partner's point of view regarding the unfolding play episode in relation to their own ideas—skills that foster their ability to represent and coordinate multiple points of view. A parallel process occurs as children make inferences to comprehend narratives they hear and read. For example, when a child concludes that his or her play partner is planning a birthday party based on the fact that she announces, "I'm going to the store to buy candles," she is engaging in the type of inferential thinking that support children's comprehension of narratives, which often leave important connections between story events implicit. Coordinating perspectives and making inferences based on partners' play actions are reflected in children's language use during play. Evidence to support this hypothesis comes from observational studies that seek to understand how young children use communication strategies to establish, structure, and sustain pretend play.

Children engage in talk as they attempt to establish shared meaning. Although the frequency and type of talk varies by age, children between 3 and 5 years old rely on verbal strategies during pretend play to confer meaning on their actions and convey their ideas (Cohen & Uhry, 2007; Osório, Meins, Martins, Martins, & Soares, 2012). Although both simple and sophisticated verbal strategies are important for initiating and sustaining play, the more complex language uses—called *semantic ties* (Corsaro, 1983; Howe, Petrakos, Rinaldi, & LeFebvre, 2005)—are of particular interest in relation to inferential processes. Semantic ties include several strategies that children use to add new semantic elements to the developing play episode: 1) extending a partner's idea, which implies that the child understands and agrees with his or her partner's idea; 2) building on one's own idea to contribute to shared play; and 3) providing an explanation or justification that develops shared understanding between players (e.g., "That's a horse because it has a nice long tail. Dogs have short tails"). In doing so, they must accommodate at least some of their partners' suggestions and therefore take into account different perspectives.

Evidence suggests that this type of higher-level talk occurs more frequently in interactive and pretense-heavy types of play. Sibling dyads between 3 and 5 years old who engaged in more pretend enactments used more semantic ties (Howe et al., 2005). When they were engaged in cooperative pretend play and relatively long stretches of play, same-sex 3- and 4-year-old dyads used significantly more high-level semantic ties than they did less cognitively demanding strategies (Farver, 1992). Similarly, cooperative play among a sample of mixed-income 4-year-olds was related to more verbalizations on a higher cognitive distancing level than when initiating play or playing alone (Leseman, Rollenberg, & Rispens, 2001). *Distancing acts* were defined as "all verbal and nonverbal actions that required children (and teachers) to distance themselves from the immediate situation, both in producing these actions and in reacting to or extending the actions of others" (Leseman et al., 2001, p. 366). Examples of distancing acts were object substitutions (such as using a block for a phone) and instances in which a child indicated that she accepted another child's object substitution by acting in accordance with it. Leseman and colleagues (2001) therefore concluded that preschoolers who played cooperatively, as opposed to playing alone, exhibited a higher level of talk as they inferred cause and effect or a partner's reasoning. (See Chapter 4 by van Kleeck for additional analysis on children using academic talk.)

Despite differences in age, groupings, and background characteristics of children in these studies, they all use language to construct shared meaning during pretend play. They may negotiate the setting and shifts in time and place, discuss characters' actions and motivations for acts, and describe objects they are playing with and their uses. The language they use reflects the type of inferences children must generate when constructing meaning from narratives.

Play Fosters Depth of Vocabulary

Pretend play can build the third precursor for strong comprehension—deep knowledge of vocabulary—by enabling children to hear and use words across varied contexts as they elicit, respond to, and perform activities during imaginary episodes (Weisberg et al., 2013). Evidence indicates that a link exists between play and language skills such as vocabulary development and depth of word knowledge. However, reviews of research on the play–language connection (Lillard et al., 2012; Roskos & Christie, 2013; Weisberg et al., 2013) raise important issues about the correlational nature of the work and uncertainty about the direction of causation between the two domains. It could be that children with superior language skills tend to play more or that playing more results in improved language skills. Similarly, it remains unclear which mechanism of adult-supported play interventions contributes to positive language effects. Increased adult interaction and conversation may lead to improvements in language outcomes, not the increase in pretend play (e.g., Christakis et al., 2007; Lovinger, 1974). Nonetheless, it may be that pretend play provides motivation for increased language use and a setting for meaningful language input from play partners, both of which may contribute to development of language skills such as deep knowledge of vocabulary.

In very young children, play behaviors have been positively linked to receptive and expressive language (Ungerer & Sigman, 1984) and with the semantic diversity (e.g., categories of speech represented) of spontaneous utterances (Tamis-LeMonda & Bornstein, 1994), reflecting grasp of interconnections among words, which is an aspect of deep knowledge of word meanings. Although few preschool studies have measured depth of vocabulary in relation to play, a convergence of observational and experimental evidence suggests that play encourages the type of linguistic experiences theorized to improve the lexical representations of words and the ability to come up with the appropriate word with ease in varied situations.

When children engage in pretend play with others, they use words in appropriate syntactic frames for varied purposes as they talk about events and roles. For example, they use "toothbrush" when pretending to be a dentist, or they may say "boil" when pretending to be a chef. There are multiple ways in which this activity may improve lexical representations. It is likely that pronouncing target vocabulary during verbally engaging activities such as play enhances word learning through the encoding of phonological representations (e.g., saying "toothbrush" and "boil" helps the child remember the words). Moreover, increasing the precision and stability of a word's phonological representation is likely occurring as the meaning component is enriched over multiple exposures and opportunities to use the word while interacting with play partners. Observations of preschool-age children playing at home reveal that children indeed use language to create pretend worlds, which requires comprehending and then adding new information to a partner's previous contribution (Farver, 1992; Howe et al., 2005).

Using a target word in conversation may also expand knowledge of the word's grammatical classes, an additional marker of high-quality lexical representations (Perfetti, 2007; Read, 2004). Pretend play appears to provide an engaging environment for this increased language use with benefits for lexical representations. Observational evidence indicates that during pretend play, middle-class children use complex syntax, including auxiliaries, verb expansions, and temporal clauses (Ervin-Tripp, 1991); more complete syntactic utterances (Vedeler, 1997); and linguistic verbs (e.g., *say, tell, explain*; Pellegrini & Galda, 1990). For example, a child establishing pretend roles may say to a peer, "She was the little brother who could make-believe he was the lion." In a 2013 investigation of teacher–child conversations during playdough sessions in classrooms serving low-income preschoolers, Justice, McGinty, Zucker, Cabell, and Piasta found that children mirrored teachers' use of syntactically complex utterances, such as "They won't go if it's raining." Children's word learning during play could be enriched due to play's support for increased conversation with a more advanced partner and related complex syntax use. Hearing and producing target words in more complex utterances may contribute to knowledge of the grammatical forms and morphosyntactic inflections applicable to target words. Support for this finding comes from data we collected in 2012 related to books about knights and dragons. Consider uses of *charge,* one of the words we sought to teach. It was used in the future tense by a teacher: "The dragon's going to go *charging* at the knight." Later during the same play session, the teacher and a child were acting out the role of the dragon and the knight and negotiating whether or not they should fight. The child provided the following explanation as to why they should remain friends, and in doing so, she used the infinitive form of the target word, which serves as a direct object in this utterance: "When you're enemies, you're not friends, and then you have *to charge* at each other." Engaging in pretend play provided an opportunity for the child to hear and use different grammatical forms of the word *charge,* which may have deepened the child's knowledge of the word. Finally, producing target words across varied play scenarios reflects the ability to efficiently retrieve appropriate lexical items, another important aspect of depth of knowledge. Such linguistic experiences may help secure connections among the word's knowledge components so that all components are retrieved in synchronicity, a process that may aid comprehension once preschoolers begin to read text (Perfetti, 2007).

Building on the strength of correlational data relating play to increases in language, a small number of experimental studies—or "play training"—have fostered preschoolers' pretend play and thus their language development, with a few focusing specifically on vocabulary. During play training, adults first observe children as they explore sociodramatic play centers. Then depending on the level of spontaneous play exhibited by the children, adults employ one of two strategies: They 1) join children as coplayers in order to model pretend behaviors and related language use or 2) act as play directors and offer suggestions to further develop children's play (e.g., Smilansky, 1968). Effects of play training have been found on children's expressive vocabulary and grammatical development (Christakis et al., 2007; Lovinger, 1974). An intervention study by Han, Moore, Vukelich, and Buell (2010) addressed whether adult-supported play benefited low-income preschoolers' word learning. Children in one condition received explicit instruction on word meanings through book reading. Children in the explicit instruction *plus* play condition were taught new words during book reading and then engaged in pretend play episodes that featured the words and related props (e.g., for the word *bake*, the adult encouraged the children to act out baking a cake) with support from adult tutors. The time spent on instruction in both conditions was limited to 30 minutes per session. Children in the explicit instruction plus play condition showed more growth on curriculum-specific measures of receptive and expressive vocabulary than did children in the explicit instruction condition. Finally, several play training researchers have shown that adult support increases children's language and target vocabulary use *during* play (Dansky, 1980; Levy, Wolfgang, & Koorland, 1992).

In sum, evidence indicates that play can contribute to the component skills necessary for reading comprehension, particularly through the strengthening and enriching of lexical representations and enhanced capacity to represent narrative events and the relationships between them. However, research exploring the play–language connection has been hampered by the correlational nature of much of the work and the disparate types of play and outcomes that have been explored (Roskos & Christie, 2013). There is a need for greater methodological rigor in studies of the potential of play to bolster children's prereader skills (Lillard et al., 2012). We seek to bring such rigor to the study of play and reading. The next section describes results from a study supporting the hypothesis that play benefits prereader comprehension development by improving vocabulary knowledge and narrative skills.

READ, PLAY, LEARN PROJECT

The Read, Play, Learn project is a collaboration among Vanderbilt University, Temple University, Lehigh University, and the University of Delaware, led by David Dickinson, Kathy Hirsh-Pasek, Ageliki Nicolopoulou, and Roberta Golinkoff. It is striving to develop and test methods that can be used by preschool teachers to draw children into language-rich play by linking repeated reading of books to teacher-guided play that occurs with small groups. The goal is to provide teachers with materials that will enable them to read books, teach vocabulary, and engage children in play. The broader goal is to illustrate the power of playful learning to teachers who may improve their ability to scaffold children's learning.

Two themes were developed around the intervention: dragons and farms. Two books per theme were chosen for shared book readings based on the presence of an entertaining plot and characters that provided narrative scaffolding and appealing roles for children's pretend play.

Replica play kits were created for each book with props chosen to represent concrete nouns that would be taught (e.g., a *throne*) or to encourage the enactment of target verbs (e.g., a horse for the verb *gallop*). One larger prop established a setting for each theme: a castle for the dragon theme and a farmhouse for the farm theme.

In small-group settings that combined book reading and 10-minute play sessions, the children were taught Tier 2 words, or sophisticated words found in a variety of texts that children are not likely to learn through everyday conversation (Beck, McKeown, & Kucan, 2002). The children came from programs in two different communities that serve low-income children. After book reading, children experienced one of three types of play: 1) free play, 2) directed play, or 3) guided play. In *free play,* the researcher distributed props after the book was read, let children play, and intervened only to maintain order, such as when children needed help sharing props. In two different play conditions, teachers were active participants and used target words and encouraged children to use them. In *directed play,* the researcher assigned each child a role and led the group through a reenactment of the book narrative by prompting children to act out events and encouraging the use of dialogue from the book. In *guided play,* the researcher encouraged children to engage in play based on their own interests. Children were free to act out the story or invent their own pretend scenarios. The researcher observed the children's play for opportunities to build on and respond to children's initiatives by taking on a pretend role and asking questions meant to emphasize target words. These strategies are illustrated in Box 3.1.

A preliminary finding of particular relevance to the issue of story comprehension came from our assessment of children's abilities to retell the stories. Children retold the story while reviewing a booklet with 11 pictures from the story. They were awarded credit for recalling informational elements (e.g., describing the settings, actions, events and outcomes; describing character intentions; Rivera & Dickinson, 2013). Initial findings suggest that children who participated in the adult-supported play sessions performed better on this retelling measure than children who engaged in free play after the reading (Rivera & Dickinson, 2013). For additional exploration of parent-supported children's language and comprehension, see Chapter 11 by Enz and Stamm.

Preliminary results also suggest that adult-supported play coupled with book reading improved children's receptive and expressive vocabulary knowledge. However, play coupled with book reading appears to be more effective than book reading alone in improving children's expressive vocabulary scores. This finding has importance for reading comprehension because depth of vocabulary knowledge is associated with stronger reading comprehension (Ouellette, 2006; Vellutino et al., 2007). Taken together, these initial results indicate that when children engage in play supported by adults in ways that highlight word meanings and draw children to recall the story, children acquire deeper knowledge of words and gain a better understanding of the story.

Box 3.1. Transcript of play session from the dragon theme. The teacher is enacting the cook role and the student, Rob, is enacting the knight role.

Teacher/cook: [crying] I'm so sad that the king kicked me out of the castle. *Enacts character and prompts child use of target word through play role*

Rob/knight: Here's a **handkerchief**. [hands teacher/cook the handkerchief prop]

Teacher/cook: Oh, thank you so much for the **handkerchief**.

Rob/knight: [giggles]

Teacher/cook: I use it to blow. You can use it to blow your nose. It's tissue made of cloth. *Explains word meaning*

Teacher: Do you throw out a **handkerchief** or do you keep it? *Closed-ended question*

Rob/knight: You keep it.

Teacher: Why is the cook using a **handkerchief**? *Open-ended question*

Rob/knight: 'Cause he's crying.

Note: Target words are shown in boldface; teacher strategies are shown in italics; and player's actions are shown in brackets.

CONCLUSION

Since the mid-1990s, the focus on academic skills in preschool classrooms has led to more didactic instruction and fewer opportunities for play, yet curricula based on children's need for playful engagement in learning have been found to result in higher achievement (Hirsh-Pasek et al., 2009). Our findings are consistent with prior research in demonstrating the positive impact of adult-supported pretend reenactment of stories on prereaders' narrative retelling and comprehension (Baumer et al., 2005; Pellegrini & Galda, 1982). Furthermore, prereader ability to comprehend narratives is a skill that predicts reading comprehension in elementary school (van den Broek et al., 2005). Fostering prereader comprehension development has both short- and long-term benefits.

Successful comprehension relies on a family of skills and activities. These include working memory capacity and skills such as the ability to make inferences and the deep knowledge of vocabulary that result in a coherent mental representation of the narrative. Our findings demonstrate the positive effect of play on several of these component skills, including vocabulary knowledge. Although book reading supports receptive and expressive word learning, play appears to be particularly valuable for fostering children's ability to provide definitional information about words, a skill that has been associated with later reading comprehension (Snow, Cancino, DeTemple, & Schley, 1991).

Play is an appealing medium to use for building prereader comprehension because it is an activity that is motivating for many young children and appears to foster three language-based skills central to understanding stories: 1) the comprehension of narratives, 2) the ability to generate inferences, and 3) the deep knowledge of words. As children play, they are reenacting and, in some cases, creating novel narratives that include consideration of character motivations and feelings, important sources of information for drawing inferences. They may also be using language in interaction with play partners in ways that support depth of vocabulary knowledge. Thus as children engage in pretend play, they are acquiring capacities that nourish both prereader comprehension and the ability to understand written texts.

Additional methodologically strong research that includes fine-grained study of teacher–child interactions during play will help us learn more about how adult-supported play enhances children's comprehension development. Even if play can be shown convincingly to result in improved academic outcomes, research must be done in classrooms to determine the most effective and efficient ways to help teachers implement those methods. Teachers currently are not encouraged or trained to engage children in play or learning to interact playfully. Although pursuing an instructional agenda is complex, effective and efficient coaching methods are needed to help teachers. For empirical research involving teachers using comprehension strategy instruction to support prereader comprehension in the classroom, see Chapter 1 by DeBruin-Parecki and Pribesh. Despite the challenges, we are hopeful because the field is starting to recognize that the groundwork for reading comprehension is laid in the preschool years, and language-rich interactions are a critical element. Teacher-guided play provides one promising method for building these critical skills.

REFERENCES

Baumer, S., Ferholt, B., & Lecusay, R. (2005). Promoting narrative competence through adult-child joint pretense: Lessons from the Scandinavian educational practice of playworld. *Cognitive Development, 20*(4), 576–590. doi:10.1016/j.cogdev.2005.08.003

Beck, I.L., McKeown, M.G., & Kucan, L. (2002). *Bringing words to life: Robust vocabulary instruction.* New York, NY: Guilford Press.

Biazak, J.E., Marley, S.C., & Levin, J.R. (2010). Does an activity-based learning strategy improve preschool children's memory for narrative passages? *Early Childhood Research Quarterly, 25*(4), 515–526. doi:10.1016/j.ecresq.2010.03.006

Bodrova, E., & Leong, D.J. (2007). Play and early literacy: A Vygotskian approach. In K.A. Roskos & J.F. Christie (Eds.), *Play and literacy in early childhood: Research from multiple perspectives* (2nd ed., pp. 185–200). New York, NY: Erlbaum.

Bowyer-Crane, C., & Snowling, M.J. (2005). Assessing children's inference generation: What do tests of reading comprehension measure? *British Journal of Educational Psychology, 75*(2), 189–201. doi:10.1348/000709904x22674

Bruner, J. (1983). Play, thought, and language. *Peabody Journal of Education, 60*(3), 60–69.

Cain, K., & Oakhill, J. (1999). Inference making ability and its relation to comprehension failure in young children. *Reading and Writing, 11*, 489–503.

Cain, K., Oakhill, J., & Bryant, P. (2004). Children's reading comprehension ability: Concurrent prediction by working memory, verbal ability, and component skills. *Journal of Educational Psychology, 96*(1), 31–42. doi:10.1037/0022-0663.96.1.31

Christakis, D.A., Zimmerman, F.J., & Garrison, M.M. (2007). Effect of block play on language acquisition and attention in toddlers: A pilot randomized controlled trial. *Archives of Pediatrics & Adolescent Medicine, 161*(10), 967–971.

Cohen, L., & Uhry, J. (2007). Young children's discourse strategies during block play: A Bakhtinian approach. *Journal of Research in Childhood Education, 21*(3), 302–315.

Corsaro, W. (1983). Script recognition, articulation, and expansion in children's role play. *Discourse Processes, 6,* 1–19.

Dansky, J.L. (1980). Cognitive consequences of sociodramatic play and exploration training for economically disadvantaged preschoolers. *Journal of Child Psychology and Psychiatry, 20,* 47–58.

Dickinson, D.K., & Porche, M.V. (2011). Relation between language experiences in preschool classrooms and children's kindergarten and fourth-grade language and reading abilities. *Child Development, 82*(3), 870–886. doi:10.1111/j.1467-8624.2011.01576.x

Dickinson, D.K., & Tabors, P.O. (Eds.). (2001). *Beginning literacy with language: Young children learning at home and school.* Baltimore, MD: Paul H. Brookes Publishing Co.

Eckler, J.A., & Weininger, O. (1989). Structural parallels between pretend play and narratives. *Developmental Psychology, 25*(5), 736–743.

Ervin-Tripp, S. (1991). Play and language development. In B. Scales, M. Almy, A. Nicolopoulou, & S. Ervin-Tripp (Eds.), *Play and the social context of development in early care and education* (pp. 84–97). New York, NY: Teachers College Press.

Farver, J.A.M. (1992). Communicating shared meaning in social pretend play. *Early Childhood Research Quarterly, 7*(4), 501–516. doi:10.1016/0885-2006(92)90047-3

Fein, G.G. (1981). Pretend play in childhood: An integrative review. *Child Development, 52*(4), 1095–1118.

Florit, E., Roch, M., Altoè, G., & Levorato, M.C. (2009). Listening comprehension in preschoolers: The role of memory. *British Journal of Developmental Psychology, 27*(4), 935–951.

Florit, E., Roch, M., & Levorato, M.C. (2011). Listening text comprehension of explicit and implicit information in preschoolers: The role of verbal and inferential skills. *Discourse Processes, 48*(2), 119–138. doi:10.1080/0163853X.2010.494244

Glenberg, A.M. (1997). What memory is for. *Behavioral and Brain Sciences, 20*(1), 1–55.

Glenberg, A.M., Gutierrez, T., Levin, J.R., Japuntich, S., & Kaschak, M.P. (2004). Activity and imagined activity can enhance young children's reading comprehension. *Journal of Educational Psychology, 96*(3), 424–436.

Goldman, S.R., & Varnhagen, C.K. (1986). Memory for embedded and sequential story structures. *Journal of Memory and Language, 25*(4), 401–418.

Graesser, A., Golding, J.M., & Long, D.L. (1991). Narrative representation and comprehension. In R. Barr, M.L. Kamil, P.B. Mosenthal, & D.P. Pearson (Eds.), *Handbook of reading research* (Vol. 2, pp. 171–205). New York: Longman.

Han, M., Moore, N., Vukelich, C., & Buell, M. (2010). Does play make a difference? How play intervention affects the vocabulary learning of at-risk preschoolers. *American Journal of Play, 3*(1), 82–105.

Henriksen, B. (1999). Three dimensions of vocabulary development. *Studies in Second Language Acquisition, 21*(2), 303–317.

Hirsh-Pasek, K., Golinkoff, R.M., Berk, L.E., & Singer, D.G. (2009). *A mandate for playful learning in preschool.* New York, NY: Oxford University Press.

Howe, N., Petrakos, H., Rinaldi, C.M., & LeFebvre, R. (2005). "This is a bad dog, you know…": Constructing shared meanings during sibling pretend play. *Child Development, 76*(4), 783–794.

Justice, L.M., McGinty, A.S., Zucker, T.A., Cabell, S.Q., & Piasta, S.B. (2013). Bidirectional dynamics underlie the complexity of talk in teacher–child play-based conversations in classrooms serving at-risk pupils. *Early Childhood Research Quarterly, 28*(3), 496–508. doi:10.1016/j.ecresq.2013.02.005

Kendeou, P., Bohn-Gettler, C., White, M.J., & van den Broek, P. (2008). Children's inference generation across different media. *Journal of Research in Reading, 31,* 259–272.

Kendeou, P., White, M.J., van den Broek, P., & Lynch, J.S. (2009). Predicting reading comprehension in early elementary school: The independent contributions of oral language and decoding skills. *Journal of Educational Psychology, 101*(4), 765–778. doi:10.1037/a0015956

Leseman, P.P.M., Rollenberg, L., & Rispens, J. (2001). Playing and working in kindergarten: Cognitive coconstruction in two educational situations. *Early Childhood Research Quarterly, 16*(3), 363–384. doi:10.1016/S0885-2006(01)00103

Levy, A.K., Wolfgang, C.H., & Koorland, M.A. (1992). Sociodramatic play as a method for enhancing the language performance of kindergarten age students. *Early Childhood Research Quarterly, 7*(2), 245–262. doi:10.1016/0885-2006(92)90007-L

Lillard, A.S., Lerner, M.D., Hopkins, E.J., Dore, R.A., Smith, E.D., & Palmquist, C.M. (2012). The impact of pretend play on children's development: A review of the evidence. *Psychological Bulletin, 139*(1), 1–34. doi:10.1037/a0029321

Lovinger, S.L. (1974). Sociodramatic play and language development in preschool disadvantaged children. *Psychology in the Schools, 11*(3), 313–320. doi:10.1002/1520-6807(197407)

Lynch, J.S., van den Broek, P., Kremer, K.E., Kendeou, P., White, M.J., & Lorch, E.P. (2008). The development of narrative comprehension and its relation to other early reading skills. *Reading Psychology, 29*(4), 327–365.

Nation, K., Clarke, P., Marshall, C.M., & Durand, M. (2004). Hidden language impairments in children: Parallels between poor reading comprehension and specific language impairment? *Journal of Speech Language and Hearing Research, 47,* 199–211.

Nation, K., & Snowling, M.J. (2004). Beyond phonological skills: Broader language skills contribute to the development of reading. *Journal of Research in Reading, 27*(4), 342–356. doi:10.1111/j.1467-9817.2004.00238.x

National Institute of Child Health and Human Development Early Child Care Research Network. (2005). Pathways to reading: The role of oral language in the transition to reading. *Developmental Psychology, 41*(2), 428–442.

Neuman, S.B., & Roskos, K. (1992). Literacy objects as cultural tools: Effects on children's literacy behaviors in play. *Reading Research Quarterly, 27*(3), 202–225.

Nicolopoulou, A. (2002). Peer-group culture and narrative development. In S. Blim-Kulka & C.E. Snow (Eds.), *Talking to adults: The contribution of multiparty discourse to language acquisition* (pp. 117–152). Mahwah, NJ: Erlbaum.

Nicolopoulou, A., Cortina, K.S., Brockmeyer, C., de Sá, A., & Ilgaz, H. (2013). *Using a narrative- and play-based activity to promote low-income preschoolers' oral language, emergent literacy, and social competence.* Manuscript submitted for publication.

Nicolopoulou, A., de Sá, A.B., Ilgaz, H., & Brockmeyer, C. (2010). Using the transformative power of play to educate hearts and minds: From Vygotsky to Vivian Paley and beyond. *Mind, Culture, and Activity, 5,* 61–71.

Nicolopoulou, A., & Ilgaz, H. (2013). What do we know about pretend play and narrative development? A response to Lillard, Lerner, Hopkins, Dore, Smith, and Palmquist on "The impact of pretend play on children's development: A review of the evidence." *American Journal of Play, 6*(1), 55–81.

Oakhill, J.V., & Cain, K. (2012). The precursors of reading ability in young readers: Evidence from a four-year longitudinal study. *Scientific Studies of Reading, 16*(2), 91–121. doi:10.1080/10888438.2010.529219

Osório, A., Meins, E., Martins, C., Martins, E.C., & Soares, I. (2012). Child and mother mental-state talk in shared pretense as predictors of children's social symbolic play abilities at age 3. *Infant Behavior and Development, 35*(4), 719–726.

Ouellette, G.P. (2006). What's meaning got to do with it: The role of vocabulary in word reading and reading comprehension. *Journal of Educational Psychology, 98*(3), 554–566. doi:10.1037/0022-0663.98.3.554

Paley, V.G. (1990). *The boy who would be a helicopter: The uses of storytelling in the classroom.* Cambridge, MA: Harvard University Press.

Pellegrini, A.D., & Galda, L. (1982). The effects of thematic-fantasy play training on the development of children's story comprehension. *American Educational Research Journal, 19*(3), 443–452.

Pellegrini, A.D., & Galda, L. (1990). Children's play, language, and early literacy. *Topics in Language Disorders, 10*(3), 76–88.

Perfetti, C. (2007). Reading ability: Lexical quality to comprehension. *Scientific Studies of Reading, 11*(4), 357–383.

Rapp, D.N., & Taylor, H.A. (2004). Interactive dimensions in the construction of mental representations for text. *Journal of Experimental Psychology: Learning, Memory and Cognition, 30*(5), 988–1001. doi:10.1037/0278-7393.30.5.988

Rapp, D.N., van den Broek, P., McMaster, K.L., Kendeou, P., & Espin, C.A. (2007). Higher order comprehension processes in struggling readers: A perspective for research and intervention. *Scientific Studies of Reading, 11*(4), 289–312.

Read, J. (2004). Plumbing the depths: How should the construct of vocabulary knowledge be defined? In P. Bogaards & B. Laufer (Eds.), *Vocabulary in a second language: Selection, acquisition, and testing* (pp. 209–227). Amsterdam, Netherlands: John Benjamins.

Rivera, B., & Dickinson, D.K. (2013, April). Book reading and supported play fosters story recall by improving vocabulary. In D.K. Dickinson (Chair), *The mechanisms and impact of adult support for language learning in early childhood.* Symposium conducted at the biennial meeting of the Society for Research in Child Development, Seattle, WA.

Roskos, K.A., & Christie, J.F. (2013). Gaining ground in understanding the play literacy relationship. *American Journal of Play, 6*(1), 82–97.

Roth, P., Speece, D.L., & Cooper, D.H. (2002). A longitudinal analysis of the connection between oral language and early reading. *Journal of Educational Research, 95*(5), 259–272.

Sénéchal, M., Ouellette, G., & Rodney, D. (2006). The misunderstood giant: On the predictive role of early vocabulary to future reading. In D.K. Dickinson & S.B. Neuman (Eds.), *Handbook of early literacy research* (Vol. 2, pp. 173–182). New York, NY: Guilford Press.

Smilansky, S. (1968). *The effects of sociodramatic play on disadvantaged preschool children.* New York, NY: Wiley.

Snow, C.E., Cancino, H., DeTemple, J., & Schley, S. (1991). Giving formal definitions: A linguistic or metalinguistic skill? In E. Bialystock (Ed.), *Language processing and language awareness in bilingual children* (pp. 90–112). New York, NY: Cambridge University Press.

Snow, C.E., Tabors, P.O., Nicholson, P.A., & Kurland, B.F. (1995). SHELL: Oral language and early literacy skills in kindergarten and first-grade children. *Journal of Research in Childhood Education, 10*(1), 37–48.

Storch, S.A., & Whitehurst, G.J. (2002). Oral language and code-related precursors to reading: Evidence from a longitudinal structural model. *Developmental Psychology, 38,* 934–947.

Tamis-LeMonda, C.S., & Bornstein, M.H. (1994). Specificity in mother toddler language play relations across the second year. *Developmental Psychology, 30*(2), 283–292. doi:10.1037//0012-1649.30.2.283

Tilstra, J., McMaster, K., van den Broek, P., Kendeou, P., & Rapp, D. (2009). Simple but complex: Components of the simple view of reading across grade levels. *Journal of Research in Reading, 32*(4), 383–401. doi:10.1111/j.1467-9817.2009.01401

Trabasso, T., & Nickels, M. (1992). The development of goal plans of action in the narration of a picture story. *Discourse Processes, 15,* 249–275.

Trabasso, T., van den Broek, P., & Suh, S.Y. (1989). Logical necessity and transitivity of causal relations in stories. *Discourse Processes, 12*(1), 1–25.

Tunmer, W.E., & Chapman, J.W. (2012). The simple view of reading redux: Vocabulary knowledge and the independent components hypothesis. *Journal of Learning Disabilities, 45*(5), 453–466. doi:10.1177/0022219411432685

Tunmer, W.E., & Hoover, W.A. (1992). Cognitive and linguistic factors in learning to read. In P.B. Gough, L.C. Ehri, & R. Treiman (Eds.), *Reading acquisition* (pp. 175–214). Hillsdale, NJ: Erlbaum.

Ungerer, J.A., & Sigman, M. (1984). The relation of play and sensorimotor behavior to language in the second year. *Child Development, 55*(4), 1448–1455. doi:10.2307/1130014

van den Broek, P. (1988). The effects of causal relations and hierarchical position on the importance of story statements. *Journal of Memory and Language, 27*(1), 1–22.

van den Broek, P., Kendeou, P., Kremer, K.E., Lynch, J., Butler, J., White, M.J., & Lorch, E.P. (2005). Assessment of comprehension abilities in young children. In S. Stahl & S. Paris (Eds.), *Children's reading comprehension and assessment* (pp. 107–130). Mahwah, NJ: Erlbaum.

van den Broek, P., Lorch, E.P., & Thurlow, R. (1996). Children's and adults' memory for television stories: The role of causal factors, story-grammar categories, and hierarchical level. *Child Development, 67*(6), 3010–3028.

van den Broek, P., Rapp, D., & Kendeou, P. (2005). Integrating memory-based and constructionist processes in accounts of reading comprehension. *Discourse Processes, 39*(2–3), 299–316.

van den Broek, P., Young, M.D., Tzeng, Y., & Linderholm, T. (1999). The landscape model of reading: Inferences and the online construction of a memory representation. In H. van Oostendorp & S. Goldman (Eds.), *The construction of mental representations during reading* (pp. 62–87). Mahwah, NJ: Erlbaum.

van Kleeck, A., Gillam, R.B., Hamilton, L., & McGrath, C. (1997). The relationship between middle-class parents' book sharing discussion and their preschoolers' abstract language development. *Journal of Speech Language and Hearing Research, 40*(6), 1261–1271.

van Kleeck, A., Vander Woude, J., & Hammett, L. (2006). Fostering literal and inferential language skills in Head Start preschoolers with language impairment using scripted book-sharing discussions. *American Journal of Speech-Language Pathology, 15,* 85–95.

Vedeler, L. (1997). Dramatic play: A format for "literate" language. *British Journal of Educational Psychology, 67,* 153–167.

Vellutino, F.R., Tunmer, W.E., Jaccard, J.J., & Chen, R.S. (2007). Components of reading ability: Multivariate evidence for a convergent skills model of reading development. *Scientific Studies of Reading, 11*(1), 3–32.

Weisberg, D.S., Zosh, J.M., Hirsh-Pasek, K., & Golinkoff, R. (2013). Talking it up: Play, language development, and the role of adult support. *American Journal of Play, 6*(1), 39–54.

Wenner, J.A., & Bauer, P.J. (1999). Bringing order to the arbitrary: One- to two-year-olds' recall of event sequences. *Infant Behavior and Development, 22*(4), 585–590. doi:10.1016/S0163-6383(00)00013-8

Williamson, P.A., & Silvern, S.B. (1992). "You can't be grandma; You're a boy": Events within the thematic fantasy play context that contribute to story comprehension. *Early Childhood Research Quarterly, 7*(1), 75–93. doi:10.1016/0885-2006(92)90020-Y

Zucker, T.A., Justice, L.M., Piasta, S.B., & Kaderavek, J.N. (2010). Preschool teachers' literal and inferential questions and children's responses during whole-class shared reading. *Early Childhood Research Quarterly, 25*(1), 65–83. doi:10.1016/j.ecresq.2009.07.001

4

The Academic Talk Register
A Critical Preschool Oral Language
Foundation for Later Reading Comprehension

ANNE VAN KLEECK

More children fail in school, in the long run, because they cannot cope with "academic language" than because they cannot decode print.

—GEE (2005, P. 20)

What is it that differentiates students who make it from those who do not? This list is long, but very prominent among the factors is mastery of academic language.

—FILLMORE (2004)

The accepted view of preschoolers' oral language is that it consists of a number of subdomains related to language form, content, and use and that these subdomains combine into a single skill. In this chapter, I propose that, for preschoolers at risk for later difficulties with reading comprehension, we replace this idea of oral language as a unitary construct and reconceive of preschoolers' oral language skills as reflecting two distinguishable patterns of language use or *registers:* everyday *casual talk (CT)* and *academic talk (AT)*. In scholarship published to date, an overall weakness in preschoolers' oral language ability is viewed as predicting difficulties with later reading comprehension. I propose instead that it is a preschooler's command of the AT register more specifically that provides the strongest foundation for later reading comprehension and that familiarity with this register is often weak in many preschoolers at risk for later academic difficulties. Although other areas of preschool oral language, such as narrative development (i.e., the ability to cohesively link two or more sentences together; Kendeou, van den Broek, White, & Lynch, 2009) and using language to engage in inferencing (van Kleeck, 2008), are also important to later reading comprehension, in this chapter, I propose that we need to add academic talk to the list (see Chapter 10 by Lynch and Lepola for further discussion of narrative and

Acknowledgments: My sincere thanks to a number of people for listening to and commenting on earlier versions of these ideas, including the regular participants in the Callier Center for Communication Disorders FLASH research talk series, and also to the following individuals: Lisa Ahn, Suzanne Bonifert, Karen Clark, Julia Evans, John Locke, Jan Lougeay, Kathryn McCartney, Jennifer McGlothlin, Raúl Rojas, Amy Louise Schwarz, and Beth Steerman. Partial support for this work was provided by the Callier Research Scholar fund, provided to the author by the University of Texas at Dallas.

inferencing development and assessment; see Chapter 9 by Cartwright and Guajardo for discussion of executive functions related to prereaders' narratives skills).

My goals in this chapter are to 1) discuss the relationship of AT to reading comprehension; 2) establish the critical need to reconceptualize at-risk preschoolers' oral language skills from the perspective of the CT and AT registers; 3) distinguish between the CT and AT registers along conceptual, linguistic, and interactive levels; and 4) reinterpret several areas of extant research to demonstrate that there are different degrees of maternal use of AT in the home during the preschool years based on the mother's education level, which in turn influence a child's level of familiarity with AT upon school entry. To accomplish these goals, I pull together ideas and research that span many disciplines and focus on a broad age range of participants to provide a new perspective for thinking about and researching interventions focused on the oral language skills of preschoolers that are important to later reading comprehension.

I conceive of AT as a culturally determined pattern of language use—a register—that is employed when engaged primarily in teaching and learning; in contrast, CT is the pattern of language use employed "to get things done" and maintain relationships in everyday life. For AT, the cultural context is Western formal schooling. However, many features of the AT register are also widely used starting with the earliest parent–children interactions by parents who have spent relatively more years in this educational system. I elaborate on this point later in this chapter.

I have chosen to use the term *register,* following scholars such as Biber (1995), to indicate the different systematic co-occurring patterns of language features that reflect the different functions of oral language for everyday living purposes (CT) and for teaching and learning purposes (AT). With school-age children, others have used the term *discourse genres* to refer to a similar distinction between everyday casual talk and classroom talk (e.g., Lefstein & Snell, 2011). The two registers proposed here of course overlap. They share the same dimensions of language (e.g., the amount of support from the nonlinguistic context and the degree of explicitness) but are empirically distinguishable (at least among adults; Biber, 2003) by the prevalence of characteristics (e.g., having more or less support from the nonlinguistic context and being less or more explicit) of those dimensions in one register as compared with the other. In other words, although the registers are distinguishable, they are not discontinuous.

Although adults and older children may use many language registers, preschoolers have far less language at their command to be able to subtly adjust their language for different purposes. As such, I contend that young children initially have one major "native" register—the one that they typically learn from caregivers in their homes. I will also make the case that for some children (those with higher maternal education levels), this native register naturally incorporates many dimensions of AT into the everyday CT register. For others (those with lower maternal education levels), CT either does not incorporate characteristics of AT or does so to a lesser extent.

RELATIONSHIP OF ACADEMIC TALK TO READING COMPREHENSION

Many scholars focused on school-age children have directly addressed the ties between children's use of the oral language of instruction and their comprehension of the written language of textbooks (see Chapter 6 by Hall-Kenyon, Culatta, and Duke for discussion of expository or information texts, such as textbooks); that is, most view academic language as being one general style of language that can occur in either spoken or written form, described by terms such as *academic language* (Gee, 2005), *literate language* (Nelson, 1989), and *talking to learn* (Westby, 1985, 1995). In this chapter, the focus is on the oral language foundations for later reading comprehension in young children who cannot yet read—only 2% of children can read simple sight words upon kindergarten entry (Zill & West, 2001). As such, the term *talk* is used to emphasize the oral nature of the register at this developmental level (see Chapter 12 by Zibulsky and Cunningham for further discussion of the importance of oral language foundations for reading comprehension).

Among adults, work by Biber (2003) provides yet another source of evidence for the role of AT in supporting reading comprehension. In multivariate research conducted on naturally occurring corpora of adult language, Biber (2003) empirically demonstrated that the co-occurring linguistic features characteristic of the oral end of an oral-literate continuum are more prevalent in CT, whereas those at the other end are more prevalent in written academic language, such as textbooks. AT falls in between. As such, Biber's study empirically supports the claim that AT supports reading comprehension better than CT does because AT is more like academic written language.

These scholars focused on school-age children and adults align with a number of others who propose that there are certain dimensions of oral language used by and directed toward preschoolers that are associated with later literacy (e.g., Heath, 1983; Mehan, 1979; Scollon & Scollon, 1981; Watson, 2001; Wells, 1981). As Watson notes, "Literacy influences the forms of oral language," and "the forms of oral language associated with literacy can be orally transmitted and, once acquired, facilitate the acquisition of literacy-related skills and success in formal education" (2001, p. 43). In discussing preschoolers, the most frequently mentioned dimension is using oral language in a decontextualized fashion, meaning that the child has less support (than he or she would in everyday casual conversation) from either shared background knowledge with participants or the nonlinguistic context to help with understanding the language that is being used (e.g., Curenton & Justice, 2004; DeTemple & Beals, 1991; McKeown & Beck, 2003; Snow, 1983; Snow & Dickinson, 1991; Watson, 2001). Others have considered talk about linguistic and mental states as an important aspect of preschool oral language predictive of later literacy (e.g., Degotardi & Torr, 2007; Pelligrini, Galda, Bartini, & Charak, 1998). In this chapter, I extend substantially beyond decontextualized language and talk about linguistic and mental states when considering the features that compose the AT register.

RECONCEPTUALIZING PRESCHOOLERS' ORAL LANGUAGE SKILLS

The rationale for reconceptualizing at-risk preschoolers' oral language skills as consisting of two language registers—CT and AT—stems from several sources. First of all, an academic style of discourse that is distinguishable from everyday social discourse clearly exists, based on research with school-age children that began "well over a century ago" (Nystrand, 2006, p. 393), resulting in "tens of thousands of studies describing school environments" (Heath, 2012, p. 19). However, nearly all the work to date has focused on kindergarten and higher grade classrooms, with only a handful of studies considering interactions in preschool classrooms (e.g., Kantor, Green, Bradley, & Lin, 1992; Kleifgen, 1990; Kondyli & Lykou, 2008; Yifat & Zadunaisky-Ehrlich, 2008).

Although AT has very rarely been a focus of research with preschoolers (see Chapter 6 by Hall-Kenyon, Culatta, and Duke), it was suggested decades ago that some children arrive at school unfamiliar with the patterns of language used in classroom lessons (Heath, 1983; Michaels, 1981). Furthermore, once in school, children are not explicitly taught this vital pattern of language use, as it typically remains instead a part of the "hidden curriculum," which are aspects of the school experience that are critical to school success but are not explicitly taught (e.g., Giroux & Penna, 1979; Jackson, 1968). If some children arrive at school knowing the discourse patterns of the classroom, they have clearly learned this as preschoolers or even younger. Later in this chapter, I reinterpret various bodies of research focused on language used with preschoolers by mothers with different education levels to illuminate the source of differences in children's familiarity with AT upon arrival in school. This constellation of facts—that AT is important for school-age children, that children arrive at school with more or less familiarity with this register, and that those with less familiarity are not directly taught this register once they are in school—points to the need to seriously consider the AT register with preschool-age children.

Other reasons for focusing on AT at the preschool level stem from research directly focused on preschoolers. When tested rigorously in classroom contexts, there can be no doubt that our current efforts at fostering the oral language skills in of preschoolers at risk for later academic difficulties are not working. In the Preschool Curriculum Evaluation Research (PCER) initiative, randomized control trials were conducted in classrooms to test 13 different currently available preschool curricula focused on language and literacy skills. Only one curriculum resulted in significant but moderate ($d = .40$) improvements over "business as usual" on the two standardized language tests (one focused on vocabulary and one on grammar) that were used across all the studies (results are reported in Preschool Curriculum Evaluation Research Consortium, 2008).

And even the successful curriculum improved preschoolers' scores on the two norm-referenced language tests by less than one half of a standard deviation, closing only about half of the typical test score gap found in previous research between at-risk preschoolers' performance on norm-referenced language tests and the mean score of the norming sample (e.g., Qi, Kaiser, Milan, & Hancock, 2006; Qi, Kaiser, Milan, Yzquierdo, & Hancock, 2003). Children who score low on such norm-referenced language tests as preschoolers continue to score low on tests of both aspects of reading achievement (both decoding and comprehension) as they progress through the school years; that is, preschoolers' performance on norm-referenced language tests predicts their later reading comprehension (National Institute of Child Health and Human Development [NICHD] Early Child Care Research Network, 2005; Storch & Whitehurst, 2002).

Another line of research with preschoolers relates to the importance of teacher–child interactions in preschool classrooms. Wells notes that "at no stage is [the interactional relationship between the teacher and student] more important than in the child's first few months at school" (2006, p. 77). With growing numbers of children enrolled in preschool in the United States (74% of 4-year-olds in 2008–2009; Barnett, Epstein, Friedman, Sansanelli, & Hustedt, 2009) and with increasing numbers of them from nonmainstream backgrounds (e.g., Magnuson & Waldfogel, 2005), it is most often the preschool teacher who will need to be responsible for making sure children are adept in using the AT register. See Chapter 8 by Barrueco and Fernández for a conceptual model of comprehension for children who are multilingual.

A very large study conducted in 671 classrooms by Mashburn and colleagues (2008) empirically supports the need to focus on the teacher–child instructional interaction in preschool classrooms serving at-risk preschoolers for two reasons: first, because of its significant relationship to all the child language and academic skills of preschoolers that were measured, and second, because the quality of such interactions was empirically demonstrated to be quite poor in classrooms. The critical importance of teacher–child instructional interaction was further highlighted in this study by the lack of relationship between any of the other measures of classroom quality and children's posttest performance on several measures of language and academic skills.

There are many parallels between the way in which instructional interaction was defined and the characteristics of AT presented later in this chapter. Instructional interaction (or support) comprises concept development and quality of feedback (La Paro, Pianta, & Stulman, 2004).

> Concept development considers the strategies teachers employ to promote children's higher order thinking skills and creativity through problem solving, integration, and instructional discussions, [whereas] quality of feedback concerns the quality of verbal evaluation provided to children about their work, comments, and ideas. (Mashburn et al., 2008, p. 738)

Furthermore, specific aspects of feedback include such things as scaffolding students who are having trouble understanding a concept or answering a question, prompting students to explain their thinking, and providing additional information to expand student understanding (Pianta, La Paro, & Hamre, 2008). The findings of Mashburn et al. are also important because they found that instructional interactions are typically at a low level of quality in classrooms serving at-risk preschoolers, a finding supported by other large-scale research (Howes et al., 2008; LoCasale-Crouch et al., 2007; Pianta et al., 2005).

DISTINGUISHING THE CASUAL TALK AND ACADEMIC TALK REGISTERS

The discussion in this section combines ideas and evidence from disciplines such as linguistics (Biber, 2003; Chafe & Danielewicz, 1987; Scollon & Scollon, 1981), psychology (Bruner, 1966), applied linguistics in education (Gee, 2005; Wells, 1999), educational psychology (Watson, 1996, 2001; Watson & Shapiro, 1988), and communication sciences and disorders (Westby, 1985, 1995). In one way or another, all of these scholars attempted to consider the different ways language is used for different purposes, with the academic (or more literate or scientific) context being one of them. I have taken the liberty of applying their concepts to illuminate my idea of the CT and AT registers, even though none of these scholars were directly advocating for the existence of two distinct oral language registers in preschoolers as I propose here.

First I synthesize and organize how the CT and AT registers can be distinguished conceptually, and I follow that with a discussion of how the conceptual features are manifested in a variety of linguistic features that occur with greater or lesser frequency in the CT and AT registers. Finally, the differences between the two registers regarding the rules and opportunities for participation in the talk are presented, and many of these are also potentially quantifiable. It is important to note that there are no clearly fixed boundaries between these registers regarding how language is used in each. Rather, it is a matter of the relative frequency of use of various co-occurring characteristics along a number of dimensions that appears to separate the registers. So once again, the reader is reminded that it is important to view these dimensions as existing along continua, with one end having characteristics that tend to be more prevalent in CT, the other end having characteristics more prevalent in written academic language, and AT falling in between these two.

Conceptual Nature of the Talk in Each Register

Uses of Talk   In CT, the broadest goal of language is to serve daily living, and hence this register serves the functions of getting things done and having relationships with people (e.g., Gee, 2005; Westby, 1985). In AT, by contrast, the broadest goal of language is to serve formal learning, with the related functions of achieving cognitive clarity, precision, and accuracy in order to advance intellectual and scientific understanding (e.g., Bruner, 1966). In preschool classrooms, both of these goals of language use are present, and as such, both CT and AT are used, since preschoolers are learning to interact socially with their peers in the classroom as well as learning to use language in the context of various academic lessons. This is why I have referred to this register as academic talk rather than school talk, although I have used the latter term in previous publications (e.g., van Kleeck, 2006).

Topics of Talk   Very related to the functions and goals of the CT and AT registers is the nature of the topics that tend to occur in each register. Here I organize these dimensions into the descriptive categories of generality, familiarity, personal relevance, practicality, and redundancy. In CT, especially with preschoolers, we generally talk about specific people, objects, and events that are personally important to us. CT is about everyday life, so the topics are generally about familiar things (Westby, 1985) that are directly personally relevant to our daily lives (Bruner, 1966) and relationships. We engage in talk for the purposes of learning to do practical things related to daily living, getting those things done, and building and maintaining personal relationships with others. The topics in everyday casual talk often contain repetition, and information will be more redundant (Westby, 1985).

The knowledge being transmitted in Western culture schools is theoretical, scientific knowledge. Hence even in preschool, the topics of AT often focus on general characteristics and qualities of categories of people, animals, objects, places, and events (e.g., behaviors of bears in general, transportation, rainforests, forces that shape weather patterns; Wells, 1999). For younger children, specific things (e.g., a story about a particular bear who falls asleep for a long time) may provide a springboard for generating more general descriptions, explanations, and definitions (e.g., defining the word *hibernation* and how it is a behavior of bears in general and explaining the specifics of why, when, and where it typically takes place; Watson, 2001). As children mature cognitively and linguistically, topics in school will often move to "abstract things and relations among them; traits and quantification and categorization of traits" (Gee, 2005, p. 23). So later on, children might learn of many animals that hibernate and compare and contrast the specifics of how they do so.

Via the AT register, children are also often learning about unfamiliar people, objects, places, and events (e.g., George Washington, microscopes, Antarctica, the landing of the Pilgrims at Plymouth Rock) that may not be personally relevant to their daily lives and relationships (Bruner, 1966). The knowledge being transmitted in Western culture schools is not the practical, everyday kind of knowledge associated with being able to competently do concrete things in the material world that are related to daily living. It is theoretical, scientific knowledge—knowledge for knowledge's sake—and involves learning about things (and how to talk about things) rather than how to do things. For example, in discussing show-and-tell, Watson notes, "The discourse is organized around the signification and interpretation rather than the enactment of experience. What the child can do with the object is less important than the verbal reports she can produce" (2001, p. 50). Information presented in AT is also often more concise than that presented in CT (Westby, 1995).

Previous research has provided analyses of sharing time (also known as circle time, news time, and show-and-tell) in classrooms, during which children talk about something personally important to them in front of the class (see van Kleeck & Schwarz, 2011, for a discussion). This research illuminates how teachers, via the questions and comments they intersperse in children's sharing time narratives, indirectly *recontextualize* (Cazden, 2001) children's talk. This allows the teacher to use the child's specific and personal discussion as a catalyst for generating more general, depersonalized, scientific knowledge. However, as will be discussed in the final section of this chapter, teachers are often not successful in helping children who do not already know the AT register make this shift, which highlights the need for teachers to become consciously aware of the AT register and of the fact that not all children are equally familiar with it when they arrive in school.

Level of Cognitive Demand   In his work on bilingual children, Cummins (1979, 1984) discussed how the level of cognitive demand or challenge is typically greater in talk used in classrooms than it is in everyday casual communication. He distinguished the level of cognitive demand from the degree of contextual support provided as clues to the meaning of language. I have done the same in distinguishing CT and AT, as these two dimensions can certainly be orthogonal—one can engage in discussions of concrete things for which no contextual support is provided, and, conversely, one can engage in higher-level thinking about perceptually present objects and events.

Regarding the level of thinking required, I define it as being at the basic level when language is used to label, describe, and report on specific people, animals, objects, places, and actions/events (see van Kleeck, Gillam, Hamilton, & McGrath, 1997). It is often about concrete things and the changes they undergo (Gee, 2005). The higher-level thinking more prevalent in AT, and increasingly prevalent as children progress to higher grades, is discussed from a number of interrelated perspectives, often involving distinguishing between concrete and more abstract discussions. Inferencing, for example, requires that the child engage in higher-level reasoning when not all the information needed to understand and/or respond to language is directly provided in order to fill in the gaps (see van Kleeck, 2008, for a discussion of the importance of inferencing with preschoolers to their later reading comprehension). This is done by going "elsewhere"—perhaps earlier in the discussion, but more often by supplying information from one's background knowledge.

Hence the child combines what he or she already knows (or has just been told) with new information provided in order to explain, solve a problem, categorize, reorganize, generalize, define, predict, synthesize, summarize, conclude, critique, compare and contrast, analyze, evaluate, examine assumptions, and so forth (again, see van Kleeck et al., 1997). Bruner (1986) refers to analytic–reflective thought that is hierarchical (things and ideas are put in hierarchical relationships to each other) and paradigmatic (things and ideas are put into categories). As such, when using AT, we can discuss abstract things and the relations among them (Gee, 2005).

Gee (2005) discussed how the manner in which one goes about making sense varies in everyday versus academic contexts. In everyday contexts, sense is often made by juxtaposing images and themes to create patterns and associations that favor general and vague relationships. This process can create misleading symmetry and obscure systematic relationships. When making sense in academic contexts, it is crucial to consider both differences and the details of underlying mechanisms, such as causal relationships.

Although there are certainly other dimensions that can serve to increase the cognitive demand of language (such as language that is figurative instead of literal in meaning and communicative intents that are expressed implicitly rather than explicitly), I suggest that as these develop over time, they become increasingly important to both CT and AT (figurative language) or primarily to CT (implicit communicative intents), rather than distinguishing between these two registers.

Degree of Contextual Support   The level of challenge in producing or comprehending language can also be lessened or increased by the relationship of the talk to the ongoing social and physical (both present and nonpresent) context. In general, interpretation and production of talk in CT can rely more heavily on the social and physical context because it is most often conducted with familiar individuals with whom we are more likely to share a social history, a physical environment, or both (see also Chapter 6 by Hall-Kenyon, Culatta, and Duke). However, there can be cultural differences in the CT register depending on whether a culture is considered more collectivist (i.e., there is typically more shared information among speakers) or more individualistic (i.e., there is typically less shared information among speakers; see van Kleeck, 2013, for a discussion of individualist and collectivist communication styles).

Formal Linguistic Manifestations of the Conceptual Nature of the Two Registers

In considering the formal linguistic manifestations of the conceptual properties of the CT and AT registers, I focus in this section on easily measurable aspects of language form, including specific vocabulary and syntactic structures, as well as measures of word and sentence length. I refer to these as being formal in the sense that they relate to the language forms used. In the next section of this chapter, I discuss work by a linguist (Williams, 1995, 1999, 2001) who took a more functional approach to looking at the language of mothers, children, and teachers that was based on Halliday's (1970) systemic functional linguistics. Williams's results are not considered here, however, because he did not attempt to directly distinguish casual talk from more academic talk but instead considered how mothers from different social groups spoke differently to their preschoolers and how that language compared with the language of teachers.

Regarding the formal linguistic features that distinguish CT and AT, I found only one study that focused on children that quantified the frequency of specific co-occurring language characteristics that accompany these two general patterns of language use (Danielewicz, 1984). However, this study compared only two 8-year-olds and two 12-year-olds, which is not enough data for drawing even preliminary conclusions. The only quantitative investigations of this nature that I am aware of were conducted at the university level, and discourse related to CT and AT was analyzed for a wide variety of linguistic features (Biber, 2003; Chafe & Danielewicz, 1987).

Although conducted in very different ways, these two studies with adults each provide corroborative support for the other in making the claim that AT falls between CT and written academic prose along a number of linguistic dimensions. These two studies provide at least a starting point in demonstrating quantitatively that oral academic language is more similar to written academic language on a number of dimensions than is casual oral conversation. Although these distinctions are derived from naturalistic linguistic data provided by adults and, furthermore, from adults with high levels of formal education (college students and professors), they nonetheless provide at least a starting

Table 4.1. Data from Chafe and Danielewicz (1987) and Biber (2003) regarding language dimensions differing in casual conversation, classroom discussions, and academic written prose

| | Data source | Features of language | Data from Chafe & Danielewicz (1987)[a] | | |
			Casual conversation	Classroom informal lectures	Academic written prose
More oral	Data from Chafe & Danielewicz (1987) but supported by Biber (2003)	Contractions	High (37)	Medium (29)	None (0)
		First-person pronouns	High (48)	Medium (21)	Low (4)
		Temporal adverbials	High (16)	Medium (10)	Low (8)
		Conjoined clauses	High (34)	Medium (21)	Low (4)
		Location adverbials	High (14)	Medium (11)	Low (6)
	Data from Chafe & Danielewicz (1987) only	"You know"	High (11)	Low (2)	None (0)
		Colloquial vocabulary	High (27)	Medium (18)	Low (1)
			Data from Biber (2003)[b]		
	Data from Biber (2003) only (selected items)	Demonstrative pronouns	.91 loading		
		Indefinite pronouns	.79 loading		
		Present tense	.81 loading		
		Present progressives	.65 loading		
		Activity verbs	.58 loading		
		Pro-verb "do"	.56 loading		
		Adverbials: hedges	.55 loading		

(continued)

Table 4.1. *(continued)*

	Data source	Features of language	Casual conversation	Classroom informal lectures	Academic written prose
More literate	Data from Chafe & Danielewicz (1987) but supported by Biber (2003) findings	Nominalizations	Low (27)	Medium (56)	High (92)
		Prepositional phrase	Low (53)	Medium (88)	High (117)
		Attributive adjectives and nouns	Low (23)	Medium (56)	High (77)
		Conjoined phrases	Low (8)	Medium (12)	High (24)
		Passives	Low (3)	Medium (9)	High (22)
	Data from Chafe & Danielewicz (1987) only	Literary vocabulary	Low (8)	Medium (19)	High (46)
		Words per sentence	Low (6.2)	Medium (7.3)	High (9.3)
		Prepositional phrase sequences	Low (6)	Medium (14)	High (22)
		Abstract subjects	Low (21)	Medium (38)	High (48)
		Indications of probability	Low (4)	Medium (7)	High (10)
		Data from Biber, 2003[b]			
	Data from Biber (2003) only (selected items)	Word length	−.93 loading		
		Abstract nouns	−.82 loading		
		Relative clauses	−.55 loading		

Sources: Chafe and Danielewicz (1987); Biber (2003).
[a] Data represent mean number of occurrences per 1,000 words in each sample, except for mean number of words per sentence.
[b] Data represent loadings on the oral (vs. literate) dimension of the oral (vs. literate) factorial structure.

point for thinking about the ways in which various formal linguistic features of CT and AT may differ in the language used by and directed at preschoolers.

Chafe and Danielewicz's study (1987) compared the language of 20 professors and graduate students produced in three contexts that are of interest here: casual conversations, informal academic lectures, and academic papers. As shown in Table 4.1, these data were presented as the mean number of occurrences per 1,000 words in each sample, except for the mean number of words per sentence.

The Biber study (2003) looked at linguistic features of a 2.7 million-word corpus of language that occurred across many contexts encountered by students in a university setting. The contexts of interest here were the more casual conversations that occurred in service

encounters (e.g., book store, coffee shop, front desk of the dormitory), the language used during class sessions (classroom teaching), and the language used in textbooks (from six major
disciplines). Using a statistical method known as multidimensional analyses that allows a
large set of linguistic features to be simultaneously analyzed, Biber (2003) identified four
factors, with one showing contrasts between spoken and written contexts that was named
the oral-literate discourse dimension (oral having positive factor loadings and literate having negative factor loadings). On this dimension, mean dimension scores were 10.5 for service encounters, 4 for classroom teaching, and –9 for textbooks. So the oral language in the
classroom was in between more casual conversation and the language of textbooks. The
linguistic features defining the oral and the literate ends of this dimension and their factor
loadings are also noted in Table 4.1. For the formal linguistic features looked at in the Chafe
and Danielewicz (1987) and Biber (2003) studies, the findings are mutually supportive.

The linguistic features distinguishing CT from AT in both of these studies can be
tied in a general way to the conceptual features of CT and AT provided in the previous
section. For example, due to a lack of shared social and contextual support, AT needs to
be more explicit than CT. From the findings in Table 4.1, we can see that CT is less explicit
due to relatively more indefinite and demonstrative pronoun usage than is found in AT.
Also, AT has more relative clauses and more prepositional phrase sequences than CT.
Both of these linguistic features provide specification and hence more explicitness. It is
likely that being more explicit generally requires more talk per proposition, so it might
also be related to the longer sentence length found in AT than in CT.

Because of the generally greater shared social context in using CT, it tends to be less
formal than AT. Less formality is manifested in the language features of more colloquial
vocabulary, contractions, personal pronouns, active sentences, and appreciative markers
in CT, as compared with AT. Conversely, in AT as compared with CT, the findings of more
literary vocabulary and passives and fewer contractions and personal pronouns serve to
make it more formal.

The generally lower cognitive complexity of CT might account for the greater usage
of temporal and spatial adverbials and activity verbs than is found in AT. Conversely, AT
has fewer temporal and spatial adverbials but more mental verbs, nominalization, and
abstract subjects and nouns than CT. Higher cognitive complexity might also account for
the greater frequency of expressions of probability in AT than in CT.

Rules and Opportunities for Participation in the Talk

This section considers the rules and opportunities for participation in talk that are related
to the topic, the balance of contributions, the kinds of questions asked by parents and
teachers and the expected child responses to questions, and the degree of topic elaboration.

Topic   Regarding the topic, CT and AT tend to differ in who controls the topic. In
CT, participants tend to share control of the topic, assuming they are of equal status, and
in mainstream culture, young children are often treated as equal partners in conversation (see van Kleeck, 1994, for a discussion of cultural variation in children's conversational participation). In AT, the teacher tends to control the topic (e.g., Westby, 1995). The
preferred topic structure also tends to differ, with a more topic-associated or nonlinear

structure (where one topic can naturally lead to another) being very acceptable in CT, whereas a more topic-centered or linear structure (staying with a single topic) predominates in AT (e.g., Michaels, 1981). Topic structure is interrelated with topic spontaneity. In CT, participants are allowed to make spontaneous contributions to the topic, whereas in AT, the teacher often elicits and focuses the topic. Finally, CT will have more repetitive ideas and syntax, whereas AT will generally be more concise (Westby, 1985, 1995).

Balance of Contributions   CT will tend to have more balanced dialogues in which participants get more or less equal opportunity to talk, whereas AT will generally be less balanced, consisting of relatively more teacher monologues (e.g., Westby, 1995). As I will note shortly, this typical teacher domination of talk may not be the ideal situation.

Questions Asked/Expected Responses to Questions   Questions will often tend to function differently in CT and AT. In CT, questions are more likely to be eliciting genuine requests for information that the speaker does not already have, whereas in AT, many requests function to elicit verbal displays of knowledge from the child (e.g., Scollon & Scollon, 1981; Watson, 1996; Westby, 1995). This distinction relates directly to the expected responses to questions in CT and AT. In CT, one is expected to supply unknown information in response to questions. In contrast, in AT, the student responder is often expected to verbally display what he or she already knows and what the teacher knows as well (e.g., Scollon & Scollon, 1981).

Degree of Elaboration of Topic   It is difficult to discuss the issue of who talks and how they contribute to talk during classroom lessons without venturing into the realm of typical versus more ideal characteristics of the AT register in terms of the impact on learning more generally and reading comprehension more specifically. Van Kleeck and Schwarz (2011) suggest that verbal display in AT, in addition to displaying already acquired information, also sometimes involves requesting that children tell what they are thinking, often being elicited by more open-ended questions. This new usage to include the verbal display of thinking aligns with previous research on dialogic or discursive classroom interaction in school-age children (e.g., Rex & Schiller, 2009; Wells, 1999). When these more open-ended, authentic questions are part of small-group discussions in classrooms, students have opportunities for greater elaboration of ideas, which in turn generates higher-level thinking. When these discussions are based around a text, they generate high-level text comprehension (e.g., Soter et al., 2008). Hence I consider the degree of elaboration of a particular topic as a potential feature of AT. Children can also ask questions in classrooms, and although they do so rarely, there is evidence that student questions enhance student learning (e.g., Nystrand, Wu, Gamoran, Zeiser, & Long, 2003).

GENESIS OF CHILDREN'S REGISTER
FAMILIARITY AND USE IN MATERNAL TALK

In this section, I consider research supporting the idea that the "native register" of children whose mothers have lower education levels consists primarily of casual talk, or CT. In contrast, I contend that children whose mothers have higher education levels are more likely to have a native register in which CT and AT are woven together. Note that I am not suggesting that children whose mothers have higher education levels do not continue to considerably evolve their skill with the AT register and likely develop many variants of the AT registers as they progress through the school years—I am claiming only that they arrive at school with little separation between how they have learned to use language socially at home and how it is now used in the preschool classroom. Although some of the work consulted in this section has focused on social groups determined by socioeconomic status (SES) or race rather than by maternal education levels, the findings can nonetheless be used as preliminary support for the role of maternal education levels in children's development of the AT register because family income, parental education, race, and ethnicity covary significantly in the United States (Huston, McLoyd, & García Coll, 1994). The specific focus on education level in this chapter is supported overall by a line of research demonstrating that parents' education level is the most important dimension of socioeconomic influence on children's school performance (e.g., Myrberg & Rosén, 2009). In the research consulted in this chapter that specifies education level, it is only reported for mothers.

The pioneering work that most directly ties to the idea of there being a mismatch for some children between the language used at home and that used in early elementary school classrooms comes from Michaels (1981), although she framed the differences she observed as different styles of narrative. This work, conducted more than 30 years ago, looked at language use during sharing time in a first-grade classroom and showed that children arrive at school with language skills that tend to either match or mismatch the use of oral language in school.

Those children who matched their teacher's expectations for narrative production were receiving practice, via the teacher's collaboration, with what Michaels called a literate discourse style that provided the children with "oral preparation for literacy" (1981, p. 423). In contrast, for children who did not match the expected narrative style, the teacher's collaborative efforts were mostly unsuccessful. A 2008 synthesis of sharing time research conducted with low-SES African American children from kindergarten through the seventh grade supports Michaels's early findings that teachers often fail in their attempts to collaborate with children who do not produce the topic-centered kinds of narratives expected in school (Barletta, 2008). See Chapter 1 by DeBruin-Parecki and Pribesh for additional empirical research involving teachers using strategy instruction to improve comprehension in children, most of whom were from low-income, minority backgrounds.

Other research can be mined to illuminate how differences in experience with language in the home during the preschool years for children in families from different social groups might lead to the kinds of differences in children's subsequent familiarity with uses of language in the classroom found by Michaels. However, in contrast to Michaels's focus on narratives produced during sharing time, much of the research looking at social group differences in language used by parents and preschool children in the home has focused on the book-sharing activity. I will discuss this research first and then introduce work that has extended beyond the book-sharing activity.

Book Sharing with Preschoolers Across Social Groups

Both Heath (1982, 1983) and Wells and his colleagues (e.g., Moon & Wells, 1979) conducted seminal research that illuminated the different ways that parents from different social groups socialize their young children to use language. These researchers looked at how language is used by parents of preschoolers in the home in a variety of circumstances, but particularly during book sharing. Both Heath and Wells discussed how the ways in which parents use language with their young prereading children during book-sharing discussions with them provide different degrees of support for later academic success and literacy development. These researchers provided general evidence that differences in parents' talk in the home predicted children's later academic success and were related to their social group. Their work in this area spawned a great deal of additional research on social group differences in how parents conduct book sharing in the home that improved on their nascent work by providing detailed utterance-by-utterance analyses of intact book-sharing interactions.

Such studies have been conducted with Mexican American, African American, Argentinean, Israeli, and Dutch (including Surinamese and Turkish immigrants) mothers from different socioeconomic groups (Eisenberg, 2002; Hammer, 2001; Korat & Haglili, 2007; Korat, Klein, & Segal-Drori, 2007; Leseman & de Jong, 1998; Ninio, 1980; Peralta de Mendoza, 1995; Rodriguez, Hines, & Montiel, 2009). These studies used a wide variety of coding schemes and have observed young prereading children of a variety of different ages. Summarizing findings from across these studies, compared with lower-SES mothers, higher-SES mothers' extratextual talk provided significantly more utterances, elaborated language, distancing language, complex concepts, feedback, yes/no questions, discussion of the written system, and connections beyond the text. The higher-SES mothers' extratextual talk also contained significantly fewer directives and less paraphrasing of text. Relating these findings to characteristics of AT, the idea of distancing language relates to the degree of contextual support of CT and AT discussed earlier, with AT typically having less support from the social and physical contexts. The idea of complex concepts in this body of research appears to be aligned with the higher level of cognitive demand and more elaboration that is characteristic of AT. For a comprehensive discussion on the topic of executive function in prereader comprehension, see Chapter 9 by Cartwright and Guajardo.

A study by Williams (reported in his dissertation, 1995, and two book chapters, 1999, 2001) provides the only direct evidence to date that preschoolers from different social groups experience language at home during book sharing with their mothers that matches the language used by teachers during book sharing in school to a greater or lesser extent (note that although Williams did not directly define his groups based on maternal education level, he provided data that allowed me to do so). I review this study in more detail, as it provides a model for future research aimed at studying the CT and AT registers used with and by preschoolers. Williams's study included language produced by 1) mothers with higher education levels, which I refer to as the higher maternal education (HME) group (they all had 12 years of schooling, except for one who had 10 years); 2) mothers with lower education levels, which I refer to as the lower maternal education (LME) group (they had 8 to 12 years of schooling); 3) the preschoolers of both of these groups of mothers (a major improvement over the research on variation in book sharing across social groups just reviewed, since only adult language behavior during book sharing was observed in those studies; when child language was observed, it was done so using outcome measures and not during the book-sharing interactions); and 4) the language of kindergarten teachers in the two different catchment areas that would be serving the children the following year.

The details of Williams's very complex coding scheme are not available. Indeed, in his 931-page dissertation, Williams claimed that "within the available space, it is not possible to provide a comprehensive discussion of all aspects" (1995, p. 172). Although this lack of detail leads to methodological concerns—interjudge reliability of the coding scheme was not conducted and replication would be impossible to carry out—the coding scheme nonetheless allowed for a much more refined look at language use than is typical of book-sharing research because it went from superordinate categories of language function to various levels of subcategories. As such, it provides direction for future research on more functional aspects of adult–child interaction.

A general finding of Williams's study was that the mothers in the LME and HME groups did not differ in the number of text messages they read to their preschoolers (ages 3–6), indicating that the books they read did not appear to be significantly different in their overall length. In order to look at the discussions about the textual or extratextual messages, Williams conservatively chose four sessions with the largest number of extratextual messages for each dyad chosen for the LME group and the four sessions closest to the mean number of total extratextual messages per session for each dyad chosen for the HME group. Even with this constraint, the mothers in the HME group had 250% more extratextual messages in total (median = 563.0) than the mothers in the LME group (median = 224.5) and 275% more progressive messages, which were defined as messages with a major clause (HME median = 483.0; LME median = 175.0). So the HME mothers did not read more text, but they clearly engaged in far more discussion about the texts with their preschoolers than did the LME mothers.

Williams reported data combined for all classrooms because there were no significant differences between the sets of data from the classrooms in the two social locations (those serving children primarily from LME versus HME families). However, he did not directly statistically compare data from homes and classrooms because of the differences between an adult interacting with a single child versus an adult interacting with many children. Nevertheless, the medians in these different contexts can be informally compared.

Williams looked at demands for information (questions) and messages that were prefaced. At the broadest levels, the frequency of use of questions did not differ between the mothers in the HME and LME groups—they asked similar numbers of yes/no questions and questions requesting that the child provide specific information. As can be seen in Table 4.2, however, at the sublevels, there were a number of significant differences between these two groups. Furthermore, an informal comparison shows that the teachers' medians fell in between the HME group and the LME group on all the measures except for one in which they matched the median for the HME group.

And indeed, many of the characteristics differentiating the language used by the HME and LME groups can be related to dimensions of AT discussed earlier. Referring to the findings shown in Table 4.2, asking questions that require a child to explain something relates to the AT characteristic of higher-level thinking; asking the child to provide specific circumstances (about the location of a character or feature of the setting in an image in relation to other figures in the image) relates to the AT characteristic of being more explicit; and asking a child and go beyond specific information in her or his answer to a question relates to the characteristic of AT of going beyond the specific to consider the general.

Table 4.2. Williams's statistically significant findings regarding questions and prefaced messages presented as medians for each group

Semantic feature	HME mothers	Teachers	LME mothers
Yes-no questions			
• Check	5.5	4.0	2.0
Specific information questions			
• Explain	4.5	4.5	0.0
• Provide circumstance	5.0	2.0	0.0
• Go beyond specific information	16.0	9.0	6.0
Requests for extension beyond first specific response	58.5	24.5	7.0
Prefaced messages (overall)	51.0	35.0	7.0
• Child's state of consciousness; probability	14.5	9.5	2.5
• Adult state of consciousness	18.0	7.0	0.5
• Demands for information	7.0	4.5	0.0
• Ask child to inform with some specific information	4.5	1.5	0.0

Key: HME, higher maternal education; LME, lower maternal education.

AT also involves elaboration of topics. Williams captured an aspect of elaboration by looking at adult follow-up questions that requested that the children extend beyond their first specific response to a question. As shown in Table 4.2, mothers in the HME group provided substantially more utterances of this nature than did mothers in the LME group, and teachers fell in between. Similar to the mental state talk that has been put forth as a dimension of AT, Williams also looked at what he called projecting clauses that are not separate messages but instead signal a point of view via such devices as attitudinal, perceptual, cognitive, or mental verbs (*Did she say . . . , I hope . . . , I'm sure . . . , I'm glad . . .*). And here again, on a general level, but also at the more specific levels listed in Table 4.2, mothers in the HME group prefaced their messages significantly more frequently than mothers in the LME group, with the teachers' median falling in between.

Williams's results demonstrated that the mothers in the HME group provided even larger doses of various dimensions of AT to their children individually than did the teachers with their entire class. These results were obtained even though Williams selected samples with the greatest amount of extratextual utterances per session for the LME dyads but used samples closest to mean for the HME group and had social groups that were not very far separated in terms of maternal education.

Ultimately, the interest in maternal language practices (and how well they match or do not match the language of kindergarten teachers) is because of the impact mothers' language has on the language used by their children. As such, a critical piece of the picture is children's language use. Williams also analyzed aspects of the children's messages during book sharing at home and in classrooms (for those categories in which the children provided enough data for statistical comparisons). For the overall number of questions asked during book sharing at home, he found significant differences between the children in the HME group (median = 18.0) and the LME group (median = 5.0). At more refined levels, there were also significant differences for yes/no questions (HME median = 10.5; LME median = 1.5) and for questions that required specific information (HME median = 8.5; LME median = 3.0). In the classroom, at least during the beginning few weeks of the kindergarten year that were observed, the overall number of questions children asked was negligible, with the median for yes/no questions being 1.0 and the median for questions requiring specific information being 2.0.

Beyond the Book-Sharing Context

I have suggested that CT and AT are tightly woven together for many children whose mothers have relatively higher education levels. This would likely not be the case if AT was used only in the book-sharing context. Indeed, Watson suggested that "oral language developed in literate cultural traditions is passed on to children in daily interaction" (2001, p. 49). Evidence is beginning to accrue that can be reinterpreted to support this position on a general level, although, once again, the socialization of CT and AT as separate oral language registers was not a guiding construct in the research.

For example, in a sample of 72 low-income African American mother–child dyads, Roberts, Jurgens, and Burchinal (2005) found that a global measure of the home environment (e.g., primary caregivers' verbal and emotional responsivity, acceptance of a child's behavior, academic and language stimulation, organization of the environment) more consistently predicted language and literacy outcomes than did maternal use of book-sharing strategies (e.g., using simple and elaborate descriptions, linking the book to the world, predicting/inferencing, providing book concepts, referencing print, providing letter–sound relationships). To the extent that some of these book-sharing strategies and some of the measures of the home environment contained aspects of AT, this study suggests that looking beyond the book-sharing activity will likely be critical to making claims regarding how often AT is or is not used in the homes of children from different social groups.

Hasan carried out a series of studies on the same data set in the 1980s and 1990s that were updated and reprinted in 2009 (Hasan, 2009). Her research design was the basis Williams's study of book sharing discussed earlier. However, unlike Williams's focus on book sharing, Hasan looked at functional aspects of mothers' and children's language in a wide variety of daily activities in the home and compared the mothers' language to teachers' language during classroom lessons. Unfortunately, Hasan misapplied the statistical procedure she used—principal component analysis (PCA)—to a coding scheme consisting of categories that were subordinate and superordinate categories of each other. This can create spurious correlations among the variables entered into a PCA. As such, the findings of her potentially highly informative data set were rendered meaningless and will not be reported here (note that Williams did not use PCA). Had appropriate statistical methods been employed, these data would have potentially provided the most compelling evidence to date regarding the socialization of the CT and AT registers in the homes of preschoolers. General features of the design are nonetheless very worth considering in designing future research, and her work is mentioned for that reason.

Other research has documented differences based on maternal education level on various formal rather than functional aspects of language input to children and language produced by children. So, for example, the language used with toddlers and/or preschoolers by mothers with higher educational levels, compared with those with lower education levels, is associated with 1) more overall talk to the children in most (Hart & Risley, 1995; Hoff, 2003; Hoff-Ginsberg, 1991; Schacter, 1979; Vasilyeva, Waterfall, & Huttenlocher, 2008; Wells, 1985) but not all (Hammer & Weiss, 1999) studies (but note that this latter study focused on talk to 12- to 18-month-olds and compared African American mothers with lower and higher education levels that differed on average by only approximately 3 years); 2) greater sentence complexity and a longer mean length of utterance (MLU) in some (Hoff, 2003; Vasilyeva et al., 2008) but not all (Hammer & Weiss, 1999) studies; and 3) more word types and tokens (Hammer & Weiss, 1999; Hoff, 2003).

Regarding the spontaneously produced language of children, higher maternal education has been associated with a longer MLU and a greater number of different words in the spontaneous language samples of 3-year-olds (Dollaghan et al., 1999; this was still true when the group of mothers with less than a high school education, which consisted of 42% African Americans, was eliminated and only the mothers who were high school graduates versus those who were college graduates, and who were 84% and 96% European American respectively, were compared). These differences found by Dollaghan and her colleagues may have been due to differences in the use of complex syntax, since Vasilyeva and her colleagues (2008) did not find differences based on maternal education level in the simple syntax produced by children between 22 and 42 months of age. However, they did find that children whose mothers had higher education levels had earlier emergence of complex syntax, a higher total number of complex sentences, and a higher proportion of complex sentences. These findings fit with the idea that AT contains more complex syntax than CT.

Hoff (2003) presents one of the few studies that attempts to directly relate SES differences in maternal language to SES differences in the mothers' children's language, a connection that is often assumed but rarely empirically tested. Specifically, she tested the idea that SES-related differences in children's vocabulary development were the result of SES-related differences in their mothers' talk to them. As such, she was able to show that maternal input was the mediating variable for SES influences on this one aspect of children's language development. Her findings provide some additional support for the idea presented here that the register the mother uses with her preschooler at home determines the first register her child will learn to use with adults.

The findings that mothers with higher education levels, as compared with those with lower education levels, provide more language input to their young children and that their input contains sentences that are longer and more complex and vocabulary that is more varied fit in general ways with the idea that their language input combines AT and CT registers. Including more features of AT when using language for everyday social purposes requires that the language be more explicit. Being more explicit requires more talk, as well as longer and more complex sentences. The idea of being more explicit also fits with using more vocabulary in general, since one is generally relying less on the nonlinguistic physical and social context and more on language to convey meaning.

Data regarding differences even in the amount of talk that transpires between mothers and their children in different social groups suggests that perhaps even the act of talking with an adult may be more or less familiar for children from different backgrounds, and this could result in differences in their comfort levels for participating in classroom interactions with teachers in school. Indeed, in synthesizing literature on different cultural values and beliefs underlying how different cultural groups socialize their children to participate in conversations with adults, van Kleeck (1994) discusses a number of ways in which children from some social groups are encouraged to be more talkative with adults, whereas children from other social groups might be learning that being a quiet child is more valued. This could lead to a double risk for some children's classroom participation—they have not become as familiar with the AT register, and they have not been strongly encouraged to engage in any form of interaction with adults. It seems then that research on the AT register would need to go a bit deeper than looking at dimensions of the register and also include looking at general strategies (outlined by van Kleeck, 1994) for encouraging children to participate in interactions with adults.

CONCLUSION

The National Assessment of Educational Progress (NAEP) indicated that 33% of fourth graders in the United States were below a basic level of reading achievement in 2007, 2009, and 2011, and the incidence was strikingly higher for children from nonmainstream cultural backgrounds (e.g., 51% for African American and 49% for Hispanic children; National Center for Education Statistics, 2011). Evidence further shows that such gaps found in school achievement are presaged in preschool and upon school entry on assessments of language and code-related literacy skills (e.g., Aratani, Wright, & Cooper, 2011; Lee & Burkman, 2002; NICHD Early Child Care Research Network, 2005; Storch & Whitehurst, 2002). These gaps occurring all through school and those occurring before formal schooling are connected—children who start behind often stay behind. For additional suggestions about working with preschoolers with disabilities to improve comprehension, see Chapter 7 by Gear.

In this chapter I have suggested that viewing the oral language of preschoolers at risk for later reading comprehension difficulties from the perspective of two different registers—everyday casual talk (CT) and academic talk (AT)—might enable us to better match the oral language features we attempt to measure and teach in preschoolers with the patterns of language use found in academic texts and therefore needed for reading comprehension in school. Because discussions of the ways in which language is used to foster learning in Western culture formal educational settings stand at the nexus of the disciplines of linguistics, sociology, and education, my efforts to convince readers of the importance of AT during the preschool years have spanned these disciplines. Furthermore, given that I have marshaled support for my ideas from research focused on other age groups and designed for other purposes, the ideas are offered not as definitive conclusions but as springboards for further thought and inquiry.

Gee notes that

> Children from nonmainstream homes often do not get the opportunities to acquire the dominant secondary discourses—including those concerned with school—in their homes, due to their parents lack of access to these discourses. At school they cannot practice what they haven't yet got and they are exposed mostly to a process of learning and not acquisition. Therefore, little acquisition goes on. (1987, p. 9)

This chapter is a call to make the dominant discourse of classrooms explicit when it can potentially have the greatest impact—during the preschool years. AT needs to be made explicit first to researchers so they can endeavor to determine, from suggestions provided here, the co-occurring patterns of language use among preschoolers and adults who interact with them that define AT and distinguish it from CT. This will necessitate the use of multivariate statistical techniques such as the one used by Biber (2003). AT will then need to be made explicit to preschool teachers so they can begin to recognize which children are and are not proficient at using it. Finally, AT could be modeled explicitly for preschoolers who arrive at school less familiar and less comfortable with it so that this particular barrier to realizing their academic potential is removed.

REFERENCES

Aratani, Y., Wright, V.R., & Cooper, J.L. (2011). *Racial gaps in early childhood: Socio-emotional health, developmental, and educational outcomes among African-American boys.* New York, NY: New York Mailman School of Public Health, Columbia University.

Barletta, L.M. (2008). Teacher's differential of culturally and linguistically diverse students during sharing time. *Colorado Research in Linguistics, 21,* 1–21.

Barnett, W.S., Epstein, D.J., Friedman, A.H., Sansanelli, R.A., & Hustedt, J.T. (2009). *The state of preschool 2009: State preschool yearbook.* New Brunswick, NJ: The National Institute for Early Education Research, Rutgers University.

Biber, D. (1995). *Dimensions of register variation: A cross-linguistic comparison.* New York, NY: Cambridge University Press.

Biber, D. (2003). Variation among university spoken and written registers: A new multi-dimensional analysis. In P. Leistyna & C.F. Meyer (Eds.), *Language and computers, corpus analysis: Language structure and language use* (pp. 47–70). Amsterdam, Netherlands: Rodopi.

Bruner, J.S. (1966). *Toward a theory of instruction.* Cambridge, MA: Harvard University Press.

Bruner, J.S. (1986). *Actual minds, possible worlds.* Cambridge, MA: Harvard University Press.

Cazden, C.B. (2001). *Classroom discourse: The language of teaching and learning* (2nd ed.). Portsmouth, NH: Heinemann.

Chafe, W., & Danielewicz, J. (1987). Properties of spoken and written language. In R. Horowitz & S.J. Samuels (Eds.), *Comprehending oral and written language* (pp. 83–112). New York, NY: Academic Press.

Cummins, J. (1979). Cognitive/academic language proficiency, linguistic interdependence, the optimum age question and some other matters. *Working Papers on Bilingualism, 19,* 121–129.

Cummins, J. (1984). *Bilingualism and special education: Issues in assessment and pedagogy.* San Francisco, CA: College-Hill Press.

Curenton, S.M., & Justice, L.M. (2004). African American and Caucasian preschoolers' use of decontextualized language: Literate language features in oral narratives. *Language, Speech, and Hearing Services in Schools, 35,* 240–253.

Danielewicz, J. (1984). The interaction between text and context: A study of how adults and children use spoken and written language in four contexts. In A.D. Pelligrini & T.D. Yawkey (Eds.), *The development of oral and written language in social contexts* (pp. 243–260). Norwood, NJ: Ablex.

Degotardi, S., & Torr, J. (2007). A longitudinal investigation of mothers' mind-related talk to their 12- to 24-month-old infants. *Early Child Development and Care, 177*(6–7), 767–780.

DeTemple, J.M., & Beals, D.E. (1991). Family talk: Sources of support for the development of decontextualized language skills. *Journal of Research in Childhood Education, 6*(1), 11–19.

Dollaghan, C.A., Campbell, T.F., Paradise, J.L., Feldman, H.M., Janosky, J.E., Pitcairn, D.N., & Kurs-Lasky, M. (1999). Maternal education and measures of early speech and language. *Journal of Speech, Language, and Hearing Research, 42,* 1432–1443.

Eisenberg, A.R. (2002). Maternal teaching talk within families of Mexican descent: Influences of task and socioeconomic status. *Hispanic Journal of Behavioral Sciences, 24,* 206–224.

Fillmore, L.W. (2004). *The role of language in academic development.* Paper presented at the 13th Annual Administrator Conference, Sonoma County Office of Education, Sonoma, CA.

Gee, J.P. (1987). *Families and literacy.* Paper presented at the Marlman Foundation Conference on Families and Literacy, Harvard Graduate School of Education, Cambridge, MA.

Gee, J.P. (2005). Language in the science classroom: Academic social language as the heart of school-based literacy. In R.K. Yerrick & W.-M. Roth (Eds.), *Establishing scientific classroom discourse communities: Multiple voices of teaching and learning research* (pp. 19–37). Mahwah, NJ: Erlbaum.

Giroux, H.A., & Penna, A.P. (1979). Social education in the classroom: Dynamics of the hidden curriculum. *Theory and Research in Social Education, 7*(1), 21–42.

Halliday, M.A.K. (1970). Language structure and language function. In J. Lyons (Ed.), *New horizons in linguistics* (pp. 140–165). Harmondsworth, UK: Penguin.

Hammer, C.A. (2001). "Come sit down and let mama read": Book reading interactions between African American mothers and their infants. In J. Harris, A. Kamhi, & K. Pollock (Eds.), *Literacy in African American communities* (pp. 21–43). Mahwah, NJ: Erlbaum.

Hammer, C.A., & Weiss, A.L. (1999). Guiding language development: How African-American mothers and their infants structure play. *Journal of Speech, Language, and Hearing Research, 42,* 1219–1233.

Hart, B., & Risley, T.R. (1995). *Meaningful differences in the everyday experience of young American children.* Baltimore, MD: Paul H. Brookes Publishing Co.

Hasan, R. (2009). *Semantic variation: Meaning in society and sociolinguistics* (Vol. 2). London, UK: Equinox.

Heath, S.B. (1982). What no bedtime story means: Narrative skills at home and school. *Language in Society, 11,* 49–76.

Heath, S.B. (1983). *Ways with words: Language, life, and work in communities and classrooms.* New York, NY: Cambridge University Press.

Heath, S.B. (2012). *Words at work and play: Three decades in family and community life.* New York, NY: Cambridge University Press.

Hoff, E. (2003). The specificity of environmental influence: Socioeconomic status affects early vocabulary development via maternal speech. *Child Development, 74*(5), 1368–1378.

Hoff-Ginsberg, E. (1991). Mother-child conversation in different social classes and communicative settings. *Child Development, 62,* 782–796.

Howes, C., Burchinal, M., Pianta, R.C., Bryant, D., Early, D., Clifford, R., & Barbarin, O. (2008). Ready to learn? Children's preacademic achievement in prekindergarten programs. *Early Childhood Research Quarterly, 23,* 27–50.

Huston, A.C., McLoyd, V.C., & García Coll, C.T. (1994). Children and poverty: Issues in contemporary research. *Child Development, 65,* 275–282.

Jackson, P.N. (1968). *Life in classrooms.* New York, NY: Holt, Rinehart, and Winston, Inc.

Kantor, R., Green, J., Bradley, M., & Lin, L. (1992). The construction of schooled discourse repertoires: An interactional sociolinguistic perspective on learning to talk in preschool. *Linguistics and Education, 4,* 131–172.

Kendeou, P., van den Broek, P., White, M.J., & Lynch, J.S. (2009). Predicting reading comprehension in early elementary school: The independent contributions of oral language and decoding skills. *Journal of Educational Psychology, 101*(4), 765–778.

Kleifgen, J.A. (1990). Prekindergarten children's second discourse learning. *Discourse Processes, 13,* 225–242.

Kondyli, M., & Lykou, C. (2008). Defining and classifying in classroom discourse: Some evidence from Greek pre-school education. *Language and Education, 22*(6), 331–344.

Korat, O., & Haglili, S. (2007). Maternal evaluations of children's emergent literacy level, maternal mediation in book reading, and children's emergent literacy level: A comparison between SES groups. *Journal
of Literacy Research, 39*(2), 249–276.

Korat, O., Klein, P., & Segal-Drori, O. (2007). Maternal mediation in book reading, home literacy environment, and children s emergent literacy: A comparison between two social groups. *Reading and Writing,
20,* 361–398.

La Paro, K.M., Pianta, R.C., & Stulman, M. (2004). The Classroom Assessment Scoring System: Findings
from the prekindergarten year. *Elementary School Journal, 104*(5), 409–426.

Lee, V.E., & Burkman, D.T. (2002). *Inequality at the starting gate: Social background differences in achievement as children begin school.* Washington, DC: Economic Policy Institute.

Lefstein, A., & Snell, J. (2011). Promises and problems of teaching with popular culture: A linguistic ethno-
graphic analysis of discourse genre mixing in a literacy lesson. *Reading Research Quarterly, 46*(1), 40–69.

Leseman, P.P.M., & de Jong, P.F. (1998). Home literacy: Opportunity, instruction, cooperation and social-
emotional quality predicting early reading achievement. *Reading Research Quarterly, 33,* 294–318.

LoCasale-Crouch, J., Konold, T., Pianta, R.C., Howes, C., Burchinal, M., Bryant, D., . . . Barbarin, O.A.
(2007). Observed classroom quality profiles in state-funded prekindergarten programs and associations
with teacher, program, and classroom characteristics. *Early Childhood Research Quarterly, 22,* 3–17.

Magnuson, K.A., & Waldfogel, J. (2005). Early childhood care and education: Effects of ethnic and racial
gaps in school readiness. *Future of Children, 15*(1), 169–196.

Mashburn, A.J., Pianta, R.C., Hamre, B.K., Downer, J.T., Barbarin, O.A., Bryant, D., . . . Howes, C. (2008).
Measures of classroom quality in prekindergarten and children's development of academic, language, and
social skills. *Child Development, 79*(3), 732–749.

McKeown, M., & Beck, I. (2003). Taking advantage of read-alouds to help children make sense of decontextualized language. In A. van Kleeck, S.A. Stahl, & E. Bauer (Eds.), *On reading to children: Parents and
teachers* (pp. 159–176). Mahwah, NJ: Erlbaum.

Mehan, H. (1979). *Learning lessons.* Cambridge, MA: Harvard University Press.

Michaels, S. (1981). "Sharing time": Children's narrative styles and differential access to literacy. *Language
in Society, 10,* 423–442.

Moon, C., & Wells, G. (1979). The influence of home on learning to read. *Journal of Research in Reading, 2,*
53–62.

Myrberg, E., & Rosén, M. (2009). Direct and indirect effects of parents' education on reading achievement
among third graders in Sweden. *British Journal of Educational Psychology, 79,* 695–711.

National Center for Education Statistics. (2011). *The nation's report card: Reading 2011* (NCES 2012-457).
Washington, DC: National Center for Education Statistics.

National Institute of Child Health and Human Development (NICHD) Early Child Care Research Network.
(2005). Pathways to reading: The role of oral language in the transition to reading. *Developmental Psychology, 41*(2), 428–442.

Nelson, N.W. (1989). Curriculum-based language assessment and intervention. *Language, Speech, and Hearing Services in Schools, 20,* 170–184.

Ninio, A. (1980). Picture-book reading in mother-infant dyads belonging to two subgroups in Israel. *Child
Development, 51,* 587–590.

Nystrand, M. (2006). Research on the role of classroom discourse as it affects reading comprehension.
Research in the Teaching of English, 40, 392–412.

Nystrand, M., Wu, L.L., Gamoran, A., Zeiser, S., & Long, D.A. (2003). Questions in time: Investigating the
structure and dynamics of unfolding classroom discourse. *Discourse Processes, 35*(2), 135–198.

Pelligrini, A.D., Galda, L., Bartini, M., & Charak, D. (1998). Oral language and literacy learning in context:
The role of social relationships. *Merrill-Palmer Quarterly, 44.*

Peralta de Mendoza, O.A. (1995). Developmental changes and socioeconomic differences in mother–infant
picturebook reading. *European Journal of Psychology of Education, 10*(3), 261–272.

Pianta, R.C., Howes, C., Burchinal, M., Bryant, D., Clifford, R., Early, D.M., & Barbarin, O.A. (2005). Features of prekindergarten programs, classrooms, and teachers: Do they predict observed classroom quality
and child–teacher interactions? *Applied Developmental Science, 9*(3), 144–159.

Pianta, R.C., La Paro, K.M., & Hamre, B.K. (2008). *Classroom Assessment Scoring System® (CLASS™) manual,
Pre-K.* Baltimore, MD: Paul H. Brookes Publishing Co.

Preschool Curriculum Evaluation Research Consortium. (2008). Effects of preschool curriculum programs
on school readiness (NCER 2008–2009). Washington, DC: National Center for Education Research, Institute of Education Sciences, U.S. Department of Education.

Qi, C.H., Kaiser, A.P., Milan, S., & Hancock, T. (2006). Language performance of low-income African American and European American preschool children on the PPVT-III. *Language, Speech, and Hearing Services in Schools, 37*(1), 5–16.

Qi, C.H., Kaiser, A.P., Milan, S., Yzquierdo, Z., & Hancock, T.B. (2003). The performance of low-income, African American children on the Preschool Language Scale-3. *Journal of Speech, Language, and Hearing Research, 46*(3), 576–590.

Rex, L.A., & Schiller, L. (2009). *Using discourse analysis to improve classroom interaction.* New York, NY: Routledge.

Roberts, J., Jurgens, J., & Burchinal, M. (2005). The role of home literacy practices in preschool children's language and emergent literacy skills. *Journal of Speech, Language, and Hearing Research, 48,* 345–359.

Rodriguez, B.L., Hines, R., & Montiel, M. (2009). Mexican American mothers of low and middle socioeconomic status: Communication behaviors and interactive strategies during shared book reading. *Language, Speech, and Hearing Services in Schools, 40,* 271–282.

Schacter, F. (1979). *Everyday mother talk to toddlers: Early intervention.* New York, NY: Academic Press.

Scollon, R., & Scollon, S. (1981). *Narrative, literacy, and face in interethnic communication.* Norwood, NJ: Ablex.

Snow, C.E. (1983). Literacy and language: Relationships during the preschool years. *Harvard Educational Review, 53,* 165–189.

Snow, C.E., & Dickinson, D.K. (1991). Some skills that aren't basic in a new conception of literacy. In A. Purves & T. Jennings (Eds.), *Literate systems and individual lives: Perspectives on literacy and schooling* (pp. 175–213). Albany, NY: SUNY Press.

Soter, A.O., Wilkinson, I.A., Murphy, K., Rudge, L., Reninger, K., & Edwards, M. (2008). What the discourse tells us: Talk and indicators of high-level comprehension. *International Journal of Educational Research, 47*(6), 372–391.

Storch, S.A., & Whitehurst, G.J. (2002). Oral language and code-related precursors to reading: Evidence from a longitudinal structural model. *Developmental Psychology, 38*(6), 934–947.

van Kleeck, A. (1994). Potential cultural bias in training parents as conversational partners with their language-delayed children. *American Journal of Speech Language Pathology, 3,* 67–78.

van Kleeck, A. (2006). Cultural issues in promoting interactive book sharing in the families of preschoolers. In A. van Kleeck (Ed.), *Sharing books and stories to promote language and literacy* (pp. 179–230). San Diego, CA: Plural Publishing.

van Kleeck, A. (2008). Providing preschool foundations for later reading comprehension: The importance of and ideas for targeting inferencing in book-sharing interventions. *Psychology in the Schools, 45*(6), 627–643.

van Kleeck, A. (2013). Guiding parents from diverse cultural backgrounds to promote language skills in preschoolers with language disorders: Two challenges and proposed solutions for them. *Perspectives on Language Learning and Education, 20*(3), 78–85.

van Kleeck, A., Gillam, R., Hamilton, L., & McGrath, C. (1997). The relationship between middle-class parents' book-sharing discussion and their preschoolers' abstract language development. *Journal of Speech-Language-Hearing Research, 40,* 1261–1271.

Vasilyeva, M., Waterfall, H., & Huttenlocher, J. (2008). Emergence of syntax: Commonalities and differences across children. *Developmental Science, 11*(1), 84–97.

Watson, R. (1996). Talk about text: Literate discourse and metaliterate knowledge. In K. Reeder, J. Shapiro, R. Watson, & H. Goelman (Eds.), *Literate apprenticeships: The emergence of language and literacy in the preschool years* (pp. 89–100). Norwood, NJ: Ablex.

Watson, R. (2001). Literacy and oral language: Implications for early language acquisition. In S.B. Neuman & D.K. Dickinson (Eds.), *Handbook of early literacy development* (pp. 43–53). New York, NY: Guilford Press.

Watson, R., & Shapiro, J. (1988). Discourse from home to school. *Applied Psychology: An International Review, 37*(4), 395–409.

Wells, G. (1981). *Learning through interaction.* Cambridge, UK: Cambridge University Press.

Wells, G. (1985). *Language development in the preschool years* (Vol. 2). New York, NY: Cambridge University Press.

Wells, G. (1999). *Dialogic inquiry: Toward a sociocultural practice and theory of education.* Cambridge, UK: Cambridge University Press.

Wells, G. (2006). The language experience of children at home and at school. In J. Cook-Gumperz (Ed.), *The social construction of literacy* (pp. 76–109). Cambridge, UK: Cambridge University Press.

Westby, C.E. (1985). Learning to talk—talking to learn: Oral-literate language differences. In C. Simon (Ed.), *Communication skills and classroom success: Therapy methodologies for language-learning disabled students* (pp. 69–85). San Diego, CA: College-Hill.

Westby, C.E. (1995). Culture and literacy: Frameworks for understanding. *Topics in Language Disorders, 16*(1), 50–66.

Williams, G. (1995). *Joint book-reading and literacy pedagogy: A socio-semantic interpretation* (Unpublished doctoral dissertation). Macquarie University, Sydney, Australia.

Williams, G. (1999). The pedagogic device and the production of pedagogic discourse: A case example in early literacy education. In F. Christie (Ed.), *Pedagogy and the shaping of consciousness: Linguistic and social processes* (pp. 88–122). London, UK: Cassell Academic.

Williams, G. (2001). Literacy pedagogy prior to schooling: Relations between social positioning and semantic variation. In A. Morais, I. Neves, B. Davies, & H. Baillie (Eds.), *Towards a sociology of pedagogy: The contribution of Basil Bernstein to research* (pp. 17–45). New York, NY: Peter Lang.

Yifat, R., & Zadunaisky-Ehrlich, S. (2008). Teachers' talk in preschools during circle time: The case of revoicing. *Journal of Research in Childhood Education, 23*(2), 211–226.

Zill, N., & West, J. (2001). *Entering kindergarten: A portrait of American children when they begin school: Findings from the Condition of Education 2000.* Washington, DC: U.S. Government Printing Office.

5

Emergent
Comprehension in a Digital World

CAITLIN MCMUNN DOOLEY AND MEGHAN M. WELCH

Digital media use among children has become controversial. Thought leaders and professional organizations do not have consensus about when, how, or what digital tools should be introduced to young children. For example, in 2011, the National Association for the Education of Young Children (NAEYC) changed from advocating that young children (from birth through age 8) *not* use digital tools (NAEYC, 2011) to inviting children to engage with all that digital tools have to offer. This was a major shift in policy for the NAEYC. In addition, the new position statement broadens the term *technology* to include interactive tools such as multimedia games, e-books, and computers. However, the new statement does not include noninteractive media, such as television, at all; this is perhaps indicative of what society perceives to be the most important aspect of today's digital media: interactivity.

Like the NAEYC, other professional organizations have issued powerful position statements about children's digital interactions, both pro and con. These various stances and positions are intriguing because they are conflicting and because we know so little about how to prepare children for a world that is quickly changing (Leu, Kinzer, Coiro, Castek, & Henry, 2013). The National Council of Teachers of English (NCTE) and the International Reading Association (IRA) have policy statements that reinforce the educational potential of digital technologies, suggesting that educators explore this potential with vigor and enthusiasm (IRA, 2009; NCTE, 2008). However, the American Academy of Pediatricians (AAP) has not similarly embraced digital tools. The AAP's 2010 policy statement called for families to reject all types of digital technologies for children prior to age 2 and then significantly limit screen time after age 2 (AAP, 2010; U.S. Task Force on Childhood Obesity, 2011). The AAP warns of risks such as sexual and violent content, commercial consumerist messages, stereotypical depictions of racial and/or ethnic groups, and continuously stimulating light and sound waves. Early research suggests that these warnings are valid. Attention-deficit/hyperactivity disorder, obesity, irregular sleep patterns, and negative impacts on development (among others) have been linked to early media exposure (Brooks-Gunn & Donahue, 2008).

Meanwhile, as policy makers, professional organizations, and educators decide what position to take on whether and how children should use digital media, children find themselves growing up in a world increasingly saturated with technology. Born in 2010, Remy, coauthor Meghan's son, does not conceive of the digital world as being something new or different from the analog world. He has always lived with e-books, smartphones, and tablet computers. He enjoys reading hardcopy picture books, exploring digital texts and games, and video chatting with grandparents. His understanding of the world is shaped by digital media and the tools available to him. We offer Remy as the child-centric focus of this chapter to demonstrate how children are engaging in emergent comprehension in today's world.

Remy's emergent comprehension of texts began early—long before he could decode print and long before he could explain his strategies for thinking. Take, for example, the time he was caught texting his aunt when he was just 3 years and 3 months old (hereafter indicated as 3.3 years of age). Meghan notes,

> *My sister Kate and I send text messages to each other pretty regularly. One day we had been texting back and forth and I sent her a picture of Remy chilling out on the couch. Then I set my phone down. A while later, I picked up my phone and saw this (see Figure 5.1).*
>
> *When I asked Remy if he had used my phone, he nodded and said that he wanted to send a message to Aunt Kate. Interestingly, he had been learning the letters in his name and somehow found those letters on the keyboard.*

Figure 5.1.   Remy texts Kate at age 3.3.

When I saw the texts later in the day, I asked Remy if he had texted Aunt Kate. He said yes.

Remy knew that texting on the smartphone communicates meaning. He knew that there was an audience to this meaning (Kate). He knew that he could participate in meaning making by constructing a message (his own name). He constructed meaning—albeit an emergent level of meaning—with the symbols he recognized. He was not yet sounding out words, using conventional spelling, or reading Kate's earlier messages. But he still knew he was communicating by constructing meaning using the symbols available to him. This is what we mean by *emergent comprehension*. This chapter describes how young children's early experiences with symbol systems (such as texting and other digital media) can contribute to their emergent comprehension.

This chapter is divided into three main sections. This first section presents emergent comprehension as a lens by which to focus on young children's meaning making with texts and shows how children's early experiences might contribute to later reading development. Throughout this section, we use examples of Remy from 2.5 to 3.10 years of age to apply this theory of emergent comprehension to children's experiences with digital tools, such as smartphones, tablet computers, and software applications. The second section highlights the need to recognize Remy's position as a contributing factor to the types of literacy, digital or otherwise, afforded to him and other children of privilege. This section also points to the need for curricular focus on digital literacy to ensure that all children are afforded these privileges. The third and final section provides suggestions for policy and practice. Throughout this chapter, we use the terms *comprehension, meaning making,* and *understanding* interchangeably to mean the ways in which children construct meaning with symbols, including printed text.

THEORY OF EMERGENT COMPREHENSION

A framework for considering emergent comprehension contributes to a lifelong theory of literacy development as proposed by Alexander (2006). Alexander's view implies a developmental progression that involves acclimating to a literate environment, building competence as a literate being, and eventually developing expertise and proficiency. Alexander's model suggests that reading comprehension grows and develops throughout a literate person's lifetime. Other literacy researchers agree. Paris (2005) presented a theory in which decoding and phonics are important foci early in literacy development that top out and are discrete, whereas, comprehension develops early and continues to develop across a lifetime. Considering this theory of comprehension as an emerging and continuing process, we propose that digital media are as much of the context for literacy learning as traditional texts. Although the models developed to date and presented here are based on analog literacies, we hope to extend these theories by introducing a digital turn.

The social meaning-making process involved in *conventional* comprehension was originally described by the RAND Reading Study Group (2002) through a heuristic that involved the reader, text, and activity (i.e., the purpose[s] for a reading event). Dooley and Matthews (2009) adapted the RAND heuristic to describe young children's emergent comprehension. By mapping emergent comprehension to conventional comprehension, we can begin to examine developmental patterns that contribute to life-long literacy.

Meaning making with printed text is inherently social; thus, a sociocultural perspective (Vygotsky, 1978; Wells, 1999; Wertsch, 1991) situates a theory of emergent comprehension. Texts (not just "texting" but all texts, such as books, newspapers, and web pages) are created by a person (or people) to express meanings. The person or people engaging with texts construct meanings. This social transaction among reader, text, and meaning (or, as Rosenblatt [1965] called it, the poem) is comprehension. The sociocultural nature of comprehension is represented by the outer circle in Figure 5.2.

The inner circle of Figure 5.2 represents the RAND heuristic for conventional comprehension, including the reader, text, and activity as important elements to

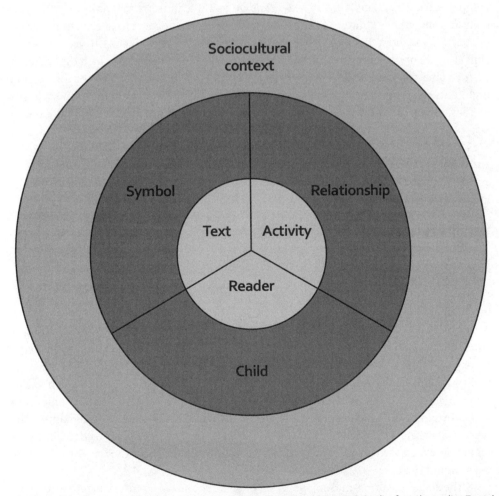

Figure 5.2. Visual representation of emergent comprehension. (From Snow, C.E. [2002]. *Reading for understanding: Toward an R&D program in reading comprehension.* Report prepared for the Office of Education Research and Improvement [OERI]. Santa Monica, CA: RAND Reading Study Group; adapted by permission. As adapted in Dooley, C.M., & Matthews, M.W. [2009]. Emergent comprehension: Understanding comprehension development among young literacy learners. *Journal of Early Childhood Literacy, 9*[3], 269–294.)

meaning making. The middle circle, consisting of the child, symbol, and relationship, represents emergent comprehension. We define *emergent comprehension* as meaning making that can contribute to the development of comprehension prior to conventional reading.

In light of Remy's experiences, we extend the principles of emergent comprehension to include digital media and to demonstrate how digital media contribute to comprehension development. Dooley and Matthews (2009) suggested that young children's emergent comprehension progresses according to three principles: 1) child: young children's meaning making construction proceeds in ways that are different from older children and adults; 2) symbol: young children's conceptions of an object, event, or action as a symbol develop across time and with socially interactive experiences; and 3) relationship: meaning making begins with interactions with primary caregivers and other important adults. In the next section, we describe each principle as distinctive only for the purpose of explanation. Indeed, in reality, any meaning-making transaction will involve permeable boundaries among the child, symbol, and relationships. How might Remy's experiences relate to emergent comprehension? Remy's world is inherently digital and analog, all at once. His literate comprehension will emerge from experiences that engage his interest and are supported by his relationships and semiotic (i.e., symbol-making) resources.

Principle 1: Child

Young children's meaning-making construction proceeds in ways that are different from those of older children and adults.

The first principle extends the RAND heuristic's *reader* to be considered a *child*. As adults, we must be attuned to (and respect) children's different characteristics, developmental phases, interests, and goals as we examine the "different paths to common [reading] outcomes" (Clay, 2001). Children experience the world in ways that are unique to their own cultural norms and habits, social relationships, interests, and developmental patterns (e.g., social and psychological development, including emotional and cognitive development). Clay (2001) warned that we adults cannot look at children's activities and assume adult-oriented goals; children pursue activities with their own goals and interests. For example, a child sitting on his or her mother's lap during bedtime book reading is not necessarily doing so in order to learn to read. Instead, the child may simply want to hear a story. Similarly, a child playing with toy trains may create a story narrative not to practice narrative story construction but as part of fantasy play. In other words, if an adult were to tell a child explicitly to create a story narrative, he or she may not understand what to do. Yet both children's activities (book reading and playful narratives) can contribute eventually to their comprehension development. See Chapter 3 by Newman, Dickinson, Hirsh-Pasek, and Golinkoff for an excellent discussion on using play to promote prereader comprehension.

Play is particularly essential to young children's developing minds, knowledge, and skills. In a review of 192 studies of play in early childhood, 67% indicated modest to large effects between play and the "early literacy comprehension" domain (Roskos,

Christie, Widman, & Holding, 2010). Play can support children's developing knowledge of narrative (Fivush, 2008); ability to infer (Dooley & Matthews, 2009); and ability to construct, respond to, and represent story worlds (Wohlwend, 2011). Playing supports children as they derive academic understandings and content knowledge that will assist their comprehension (Dooley, 2010; Siegel, Kontovourki, Schmier, & Enriquez, 2008; Wohlwend, 2011).

Dooley (2011) demonstrated how children between 2 and 5 years of age play with books in evolving and developmentally appropriate ways. At 2 years of age, the children used books as play props and toys: throwing them, cradling them, pushing them, and propping them up (called *book as prop*). Then they used books as invitations for social interactions (called *book as invitation*), perhaps mimicking the ways that books have been used to invite them into social rituals. Eventually, children attend to the content, images, and print as they echo story-like retellings and mimic read-alouds (called *book as script*). By the end of this 3-year longitudinal study, the young children (age 5) began to approximate readings and decode text within the books (called *book as text*). These evolving purposes demonstrate that children approach books—and other texts—through play and social interactions, eventually leading to the beginnings of conventional literate comprehension.

Remy's texting, writing, and talk about texts, books, and other stories demonstrate his playful interactions with text (see Figure 5.3). As Meghan explains, he approaches digital texts in ways that are similar to how children approach books (Dooley, 2010):

Figure 5.3.   Remy at the computer at age 2.5.

We live in an older home and, unfortunately, most doors don't completely close. When I write, I prop a heavy bag of books up against the door of my study and shut myself in. Within 15 minutes, tiny fingers creep through the crack and I hear a whisper, "Mommy, Mooooommmmmmmmy." From the time he could walk, Remy's ritual has been to visit me and spend 10 or so minutes "working" on the computer like me. Naturally, he is fascinated with the devices and screens capturing the attention of my husband and me.

During the first visits, I would open up a Word doc, make the document and font large, and let him type to his heart's content. When he started noticing and saying letters at about 2 years 5 months, "ABCs" he called them, I would point out and he would type the letters in his name. He also found great satisfaction in typing words like "TV" or "PJs"—words that he could spell by himself.

I think half the fun for him is feeling like he can operate the computer. He now talks himself through making the page and font bigger himself. For example, very matter-of-factly, he'll take control of the touchpad and say, "Okay, I need to make it bigger down here [referring to the page size], there we go, and I need to make this a 48 [referring to the font size], there we go, and press this [the caps lock]." He is then ready to work.

He now (age 3.10) asks how to spell names in our family or other words that are important to him. Yesterday, he asked how to spell "ketchup." Most of the time, he runs through the familiar favorites (Remy, Mac [his brother], and TV) and then moves on to a more challenging task like copying the print he sees around the house.

Remy's fantasy play will support the development of cognitive strategies, theories of mind, and narrative understandings such as character, sequence, and consequence (Seigel et al., 2008; Wohlwend, 2011), all of which will serve him well as a conventional reader. He creates playful fantasies that include writing and reading as essential activities. These playful interactions will contribute to his knowledge about texts and comprehension (Roskos et al., 2010).

Principle 2: Symbol

Young children's conceptions of an object, event, or action as a symbol develop across time and with socially interactive experiences.

The second principle extends the RAND heuristic's *text* to be considered as *symbols*. The field of semiotics has been helpful in explaining how symbols work within literacy (Berghoff & Harste, 2002; Kress, 2003; Street, 1995). Semiotics is the study of how symbols are developed through social interactions. Symbols do not have inherent meanings; they become meaningful because of human experience (DeLoache, 2005). Theorists who study the semiotic nature of literacy suggest that children pursue meanings by creating and acting on symbols (or signs) that they construe. Those symbols are multimodal; that is, children develop meanings through various modalities such as visual, verbal, gestural, and musical (among others; Kress, 2003; Mills, 2001). Prior to understanding printed texts as symbols, children learn to communicate with multiple symbol systems, such as gesture and physical movements, facial expressions, oral language, gaze, and then with drawings and writing (Rakoczy, Tomasello, & Striano, 2005). Hill and Nichols call this period of emergent literacy "symbols at work" (2006, p. 153).

Children do not come with expectations about what texts should look like; instead, they seek symbolic meanings as cues to understand their world (Rochat & Callaghan, 2005). Children's search for meanings is quite evident when we examine how young children approach books and other media. For example, in a study of children's (ages 4–6) meaning making with video and print stories, Paris and Paris (2003) found that children consistently constructed meaningful narratives of equal quality. In addition, several studies of children's readings of postmodern picture books (i.e., books that marry image and text to create nonlinear sequential plots often told from multiple perspectives) demonstrate that children seek to construct coherent narratives using multiple modes (e.g., Arizpe, 2001; Galda & Cullinan, 2002; Pantaleo, 2004). For example, Arizpe (2001) found that children sought meaning for any perceived symbol, whether conventionally considered symbolic or not. In other words, children constructed meaning from visual referents within the pictures, such as the colors and objects. Over time and with repeated readings, their constructed meanings gained depth and dimension.

Children's understandings of events, actions, and objects as symbols develop over time and with interaction with others (Namy & Waxman, 2005; Rochat & Callaghan, 2005). Namy and Waxman (2005) demonstrated that children, between the ages of 1 and 5 years, progress from no differentiation between the sign (e.g., object, event, activity) and its symbolic meaning to a more nuanced understanding of the distinctions between a sign and its symbolic meaning. In addition, Namy and Waxman (2005) demonstrated that children rely not necessarily on characteristics of an object (e.g., shapes, lines, points) but rather on the ways in which others (usually adults) have represented that object (e.g., referring to the object as a *frindle* or a *pen*).

Furthermore, routine exposure to symbolic meanings helps infants and young children appropriate their family's cultural values and concepts (Rakoczy et al., 2005). Whereas some families may have routines that are explicitly literacy related, such as book reading, other families may have routines that can also contribute to literacy (see Matthews, Dooley, & Czaplicki, 2011, for examples). These routines can provide opportunities for meaningful language and communication about topics that are important to the family or group (Dickinson, Golinkoff, & Hirsh-Pasek, 2010). They can also contribute to domain knowledge (Neuman, 2006) and strategic processing skills (Alexander, 2006) that will be helpful to comprehension development (Matthews et al., 2011). For further details on using activity-based intervention to embed language interactions in everyday routines, see Chapter 7 by Gear.

Remy has access to a broad range of experiences and text-related symbol systems. He makes meaning with environmental print (e.g., labels), books, Internet resources (e.g., YouTube), and other media. The symbolic meanings of these media are not necessarily conventional for Remy. Instead, he constructs meanings that are immediately meaningful to him and eventually tries to include others in that meaningful interaction. For example, Remy's texting episode mentioned at the start of this chapter could be conceived as evidencing the "invitation" phase of emergent comprehension (Dooley, 2010). He used smartphone texting in socially appropriate ways to invite attention and interaction with his aunt. He understood that print can carry meaning, and those meanings invite social interaction. This is an essential phase of development for emergent comprehension.

Children move from invention to convention through playful approximation. Children do not start like miniadults. Instead, they seek meaning and make meaning in inventive ways that are meaningful to themselves, not necessarily others. When Remy sat down to "work" at the computer, he approximated his mother's writing by sitting like her and typing like her. He did not copy her words. Nor did he worry that his meaning would be indecipherable to his mother. Similarly, when he texted Aunt Kate, he approximated the genre of texting by typing some letters and hitting send, then typing more letters and hitting send. He did not simply write shorter texts. His approximations of meaning were inventive and meaningful to him.

Too often early childhood curricula skip these playful inventions and approximations and skip to convention (Clay, 2001; Lonigan & Shanahan, 2010; McKeown & Beck, 2006; Wyse & Styles, 2007). Early childhood curricula require children to copy words, answer questions, or read nonsense words simply to mimic the act of writing and reading in ways that are not meaningful. These curricula miss that meaning making begins with inventive approximations that are meaningful to the meaning maker him- or herself. See Chapter 6 by Hall-Kenyon, Culatta, and Duke for additional, effective ways to use informational texts in building prereader comprehension.

Principle 3: Relationship

*M*eaning making begins with interactions with primary caregivers and other important adults.

The third principle extends the RAND heuristic's "activity" to be considered as "relationship." This principle is rooted in children's "basic affiliative need," or BAN (Rochat & Callaghan, 2005)—their desire to be with and like others who are important to them. Child developmental theorists consider the BAN to be a basic human survival strategy. In addition, children seek to be with others first and the environment next (Tomasello, Carpenter, Call, Behne, & Moll, 2005); therefore, they will seek connections with their caregivers and peers prior to seeking to understand their environment. The BAN demonstrates how children seek meanings that are consistent with their cultural group (Rogoff, 2003; Tomasello et al., 2005).

Whereas the RAND heuristic's "activity" explained how the purpose for reading contributes to comprehension, the "relationship" explains how a child's intentions develop and contribute to meaning making. This third principle emphasizes that children's early experiences are significant to them simply because of their need to be like, to be with, and to connect to others. Tomasello et al. (2005) describe how children learn to share intentions with caregivers. An infant comes to adults with a desire to share intentions—ultimately seeking to share beliefs, behaviors, and emotions. Dooley, Matthews, Matthews, and Champion (2009) demonstrated how young children engage with caregivers over time to share literacy-related intentions and make literate meaning. By playing with caring adults and peers, children develop understandings about when, how, and for what reasons literacy-related objects—such as books, pencils, crayons, and pens—might be useful for meaning making (Dooley, 2010; Rowe, 2008a, 2008b). Those early experiences and shared intentions can later contribute to comprehension of printed texts (Rowe, 2008a, 2008b).

Children's need to be near and like important others in their lives supplies their initial motivations to participate in literacy-related activities. Children do not explicitly seek to be literate or to comprehend text in conventional ways. Rather, they seek to make meaning because meaning making supports a social bond with important others in their lives. This is how their *interests, knowledge,* and *strategic processing*—important elements that contribute to lifelong literacy development (Alexander, 2006)—will emerge.

Meghan and Remy's mother and father provide a cultural model for what it is like to be literate in a digital world. Remy's early morning ventures into the study might have started because of his desire to be with his mother, evidence of his basic affiliate need to be with and like others who are important to him (Rochat & Callaghan, 2005). Furthermore, he sought to connect with his mother by doing something like her—writing on the computer (Rogoff, 2003; Tomasello et al., 2005). Eventually, he developed meanings that are similar to his mother's meanings—that texting is for communicating with Aunt Kate, computer writing is for writing words that are important to a person (e.g., "Mac" and "ketchup" for Remy, a dissertation for his mother), and YouTube is for finding great songs to listen to.

> One of Remy's particular online favorites is a video by the band Ok Go. Because we have helped him access the video before (on various screens—the television, my computer, my phone), he can now get to the YouTube search screen and type the band's name. Based on the pictures and word results (the band has many videos), he selects the song he wants to watch (see Figure 5.4).

Remy's interests guide his early playful engagements with text. His ability to search for his favorite band on YouTube was prompted by his interest in music. His willingness to write names and words stems from what interests him the most. Remy's interests will grow and develop as he grows up, but the knowledge that books, the Internet, YouTube, and other texts can feed those interests is an important concept that he has learned already. This knowledge will support his ability to seek information and answers through texts as he pursues meaning.

Taken together, these three principles relating to the child, symbol, and relationship provide a lens by which to investigate children's emergent comprehension. They provide theoretically grounded understandings about children's unique developmental qualities and the inherently social nature of symbolic meaning making.

PRIVILEGE AS INTERACTIVE PARTICIPATION

Not all children enjoy the same privileges as Remy of growing up in a literacy-rich environment. According to the Pew Research Center Internet Project Survey (2014), 47% of

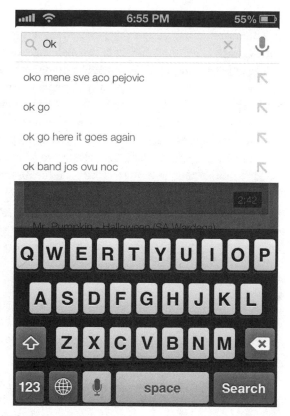

Figure 5.4. Remy searches for Ok Go video at age 3.9.

American adults making less than $30,000 per year own a smartphone and 81% of adults making $75,000 or more own smartphones. In addition, the U.S. Census from 2011 (published in 2013) reported that close to 35% of households with incomes below $25,000 do not have access to a computer or Internet. Thus there are vast socioeconomic differences that define privilege in the United States. Remy is indeed living in a privileged family with access to computers, smartphones, and the Internet. However, that is not his only privilege.

These statistical differences say nothing about how the smartphones are used and what skills and behaviors are encouraged in the young children observing and using digital tools. This gap between children who get to use digital media in their homes and communities and children who do not is called the *participation gap* (Palfrey & Gasser, 2008). Many parents demonstrate cultural models for how to use digital tools when they look up information on their computers, read on their smartphones, and text loved ones. Many children across socioeconomic statuses see their adult caregivers using these digital media (Rideout, 2014), and many themselves have been handed smartphones to play with, placed in front of computer games, and given e-books to read. Yet not all children's participation with these tools is equal. Although there is some evidence that children witness their parents and other adults as cultural models of how to use digital literacies and children demonstrate them through their play in early childhood classrooms (e.g., Wohlwend, 2013),

early childhood curricula have yet to embrace digital tools as legitimate texts for comprehension development (Davidson, 2011; Vasquez & Felderman, 2012). By leaving digital
media outside the scope of early childhood curricula, we also leave behind children who
have not had the privilege of witnessing adults at home use digital media.

The quality of participation with digital media is dependent on interactivity. The
three principles of emergent comprehension, described earlier, demonstrate that adult–
child interactions such as modeling, discussing, and providing feedback can create contexts in which comprehension emerges. Take, for example, Remy's texting his Aunt Kate.
The interactions that prompted his engagement were related to living in a home with a
smartphone, observing his mother text, and interacting with his mother's questions and
descriptions about texting (at that time as well as in prior experiences). Not all children
have this kind of interaction at home—the interaction is the privilege afforded here. If
educators do not offer guidance about how to create more interactive engagements, then
the "participation gap" with digital media will continue to widen (Palfrey & Gasser, 2008).

CONCLUSION

As texts change, what it means to be literate is changing (Brandt, 2001; Heath, 2013).
The digital disruptions to what used to be considered "text" cannot be underestimated;
the reality for young children today is ubiquitously digital. The digital turn raises some
important questions for emergent comprehension:

- How might digital technology such as touchscreen technologies, gesture-recognition
  tools, and virtual worlds support young children's playful and innovative literate
  interactions?

- What are the qualities of *good* child-friendly applications?

- Digital media have been proven to be highly engaging, perhaps more so than print media
  (Strasburger, Wilson, & Jordan, 2009). How might the highly engaging quality of digital
  media affect children's evolving interests? How might comprehension be affected?

- How might the ability to autocorrect/complete spellings help or hinder children's
  playful innovations as they approach more conventional meanings? When Remy
  searched for his favorite YouTube video, he approximated the search term by typing
  "Ok." Interestingly, the ability for the search tool to autocorrect made his approximation even more immediately conventional. We have yet to understand whether the
  ability for digital tools to more quickly adhere to conventional spellings and meanings
  will be helpful or hurtful to children's meaning making.

- How might the multiple modes that are available through digital media support (or
  not) the emergence of comprehension? What modes are helpful? Do the modes have
  to converge on a conventional meaning to assist young children's meaning making?
  (In some ways, Remy's ability to "write" at an earlier age [because of typing] is more
  conventional than if he did not have access to the assistive technology.)

These questions can help us understand more about how children are becoming literate in today's society; however, predicting what abilities and knowledge children will

need in 10 or 20 years is almost an impossible charge. Indeed, research has always been slow to catch up to the proliferation of digital media in children's lives (Leu et al., 2013; McPake, Stephen, & Plowman, 2013). Yet considering the reality of such ubiquitous digital technologies in children's worlds today, researchers can use the principles of emergent comprehension to provide a framework for considering how young children will learn. Researchers can only ask more questions and seek to understand children's emerging comprehension as they engage with the world around them.

Although there are no distinct answers yet to whether and how children should interact with digital media, we recommend several resources for learning more. Organizations such as Common Sense Media (http://www.commonsensemedia.org) and the Early Childhood Technology Network (http://www.ecetech.net) have emerged in the past few years to guide educators and families as they navigate this contested frontier. These organizations provide guidance and advice, such as how to choose developmentally appropriate digital tools, how to design a digitally enhanced curriculum in early childhood classrooms, and how to prepare children as "digital citizens" within a globally connected, digital society. Be cognizant of the policies and research accessible through organizations such as the NAEYC, the AAP and so forth. Their statements and popular media interpretations are often what teachers and parents turn to when thinking about digital tools and the emergent literacy of young children.

When preparing new teachers who will be interacting with young children and their families, here are a few guidelines to remember:

- *Encourage play.* You want teachers to encourage the play and exploration of the young children in their future classes. Therefore, teacher preparation should also include opportunities for play. Using their own or provided digital tools that might be in a child's environment will help a novice teacher approach and incorporate devices in ways that foster playful learning.

- *Challenge convention and highlight innovation.* Highlight examples and offer opportunities to use resources and digital tools in ways that are unconventional. Remind practitioners that young children will have unique understandings and uses for/of conventional literacy and digital tools. For example, creating nonlinear PowerPoint presentations in courses can be a way to create trivia games.

- *Emphasize relationships.* Young children thrive when relationships—with teachers, parents, and peers—are nurtured and emphasized as the foundation for any learning. Discussions of digital citizenship and online behaviors can also occur in preparation programs and with young children.

The digital revolution is perhaps the most amazing and disruptive change that our societies have experienced in a century. The authors contend that this revolution is changing what literacy is, how children become literate, and how educators and researchers think about literacy and literate comprehension. Like Remy, children are not aware of this changing landscape for literacy—it is all they have ever known. However, as researchers and educators, we are experiencing the disruptions caused by digital innovation like never before. Still, the principles of emergent comprehension are quite useful for understanding how children develop meanings as they engage with digital tools.

REFERENCES

Alexander, P.A. (2006). The path to competence: A lifespan developmental perspective on reading. *Journal of Literacy Research, 37,* 413–436.

American Academy of Pediatricians. (2010). Policy statement-media education. *Pediatrics, 126,* 1012–1017. Retrieved from http://www.pediatrics.org/cgi/doi/10.1542/peds.2010-1636

Arizpe, E. (2001). "Letting the story out": Visual encounters with Anthony Browne's *The Tunnel. Reading: Literacy and Language, 35*(3), 115–119.

Berghoff, B., & Harste, J. (2002). Semiotics. In B. Guzzetti (Ed.), *Literacy in America: An encyclopedia of history, theory, and practice* (pp. 580–581). Santa Barbara, CA: ABC-CLIO.

Blanchard, J., & Moore, T. (2010). *The digital world of young children: Impact on emergent literacy.* White paper presented by the Pearson Foundation. Retrieved from http://www.pearsonfoundation.org/downloads/EmergentLiteracy-ExecutiveSummary.pdf

Brandt, D. (2001). *Literacy in American lives.* Cambridge, UK: Cambridge University Press.

Brooks-Gunn, J., & Donahue, E.H. (2008). Introducing the issue. *The Future of Children, 18*(1), 3–10.

Clay, M.M. (2001). *Change over time in children's literacy development.* Portsmouth, NH: Heinemann.

Davidson, C. (2011). Young children's engagement with digital literacy in the home: Pressing matters for the teaching of English in the early years of schooling. *English Teaching: Practice and Critique, 8*(3), 36–54. Retrieved from http://files.eric.ed.gov/fulltext/EJ869393.pdf

DeLoache, J.S. (2005). The Pygmalion problem in early symbol use. In L. Namy (Ed.), *Symbol use and symbolic representation* (pp. 47–67). Mahwah, NJ: Erlbaum.

Dickinson, D.K., Golinkoff, R.M., & Hirsch-Pasek, K. (2010). Speaking out for language: Why language is central to reading development. *Educational Researcher, 39*(4), 305–310.

Dooley, C.M. (2010). Young children's approaches to books: The emergence of comprehension. *The Reading Teacher, 64*(2), 120–130.

Dooley, C.M. (2011). The emergence of comprehension: A decade of research 2000–2010. *International Electronic Journal of Elementary Education, 4*(1), 169–184. Retrieved from http://www.iejee.com/4_1_2011/10_IEJEE_4_1_Dooley.pdf

Dooley, C.M., & Matthews, M.W. (2009). Emergent comprehension: Understanding comprehension development among young literacy learners. *Journal of Early Childhood Literacy, 9*(3), 269–294.

Dooley, C.M., Matthews, M.W., Matthews, L., & Champion, R. (2009). Emergent comprehension: Preschool children's learning and intentions. *National Reading Conference Yearbook, 58,* 261–276.

Fivush, R. (2008). Sociocultural perspectives on autobiographical memory. In M. Courage & N. Cowan (Eds.), *The development of memory in children.* New York, NY: Psychology Press.

Galda, L., & Cullinan, B. (2002). *Literature and the child* (5th ed.). Belmont, CA: Wadsworth/Thomson Learning.

Healy, J.M. (2004). *Your child's growing mind.* New York, NY: Broadway Books.

Heath, S.B. (2013). *Words at work and play: Three decades in family and community life.* Cambridge, UK: Cambridge University Press.

Hill, S.E., & Nichols, S. (2006). Emergent literacy: Symbols at work. In B. Spodek & O. Saracho (Eds.), *Handbook of research on the education of young children* (2nd ed., pp. 153–165). Mahwah, NJ: Erlbaum.

International Reading Association. (2009). *New literacies and 21st-century technologies position statement.* Retrieved from http://www.reading.org/General/AboutIRA/PositionStatemetns/21stCenturyLiteracies.apspx

Kress, G. (2003). *Literacy in the new media age.* New York, NY: Routledge.

Leu, D.J., Kinzer, C.K., Coiro, J., Castek, J., & Henry, L.A. (2013). New literacies: A dual-level theory of the changing nature of literacy, instruction, and assessment. In R.B. Ruddell & D. Alverman (Eds.), *Theoretical models and processes of reading* (6th ed., pp. 1150–1613). Newark, DE: International Reading Association.

Lonigan, C.J., & Shanahan, T. (2010). Developing early literacy skills: Things we know and things we don't know. *Educational Researcher, 39,* 340–346. doi:10.31102/0013189X10369832

Lynch, J.S., van den Broek, P., Kremer, K.E., Kendeou, P., White, M.J., & Lorch, E.P. (2008). The development of narrative comprehension and its relation to other early reading skills. *Reading Psychology, 29,* 327–365.

Matthews, M.W., Dooley, C.M., & Czaplicki, K. (2011). Using parents' perceptions to gain insight into a young child's emergent literacy journey: A phenomenological study. *Literacy Research Association Yearbook, 59,* 224–238.

McKeown, M.C., & Beck, I.L. (2006). Encouraging young children's language interactions with stories. In D.K. Dickinson & S.B. Neuman (Eds.), *Handbook of early literacy research* (Vol. 2, pp. 281–294). New York, NY: Guilford Press.

McPake, J., Stephen, C., & Plowman, L. (2013). Pre-school children creating and communicating with digital technology at school and home. *British Journal of Educational Technology, 44*(3), 421–431.

Mills, K. (2001). "I'm making it different to the book": Transmediation in young children's multimodal and digital texts. *Australasian Journal of Early Childhood, 36*(3), 56–65.

Namy, L.L., & Waxman, S.R. (2005). Symbols redefined. In L.L. Namy (Ed.), *Symbol use and symbolic representation: Developmental and comparative perspectives* (pp. 269–277). Mahwah, NJ: Erlbaum.

National Association for the Education of Young Children. (2011). *Technology in early childhood programs serving children from birth through age 8.* Retrieved from http://www.naeyc.org/files/naeyc/file/positions/Draft%20Technology%20in%20Early%20Childhood%20Programs%24-29-2011.pdf

National Council of Teachers of English. (2008). *Reading and writing differently: An informational overview produced by the National Council of Teachers of English.* Retrieved from http://www.ncte.org/library/NCTEFiles/Resources/Journals/CC/0182-nov08/CC0182Reading.pdf

Neuman, S.B. (2001). The role of knowledge in early literacy. *Reading Research Quarterly, 36,* 468–475.

Neuman, S.B. (2006). The knowledge gap: Implications for early education. In D. Dickinson & S.B. Neuman (Eds.), *Handbook of early literacy research* (pp. 29–40). New York, NY: Guilford Press.

O'Neill, D.K., & Shultis, R.M. (2007). The emergence of the ability to track a character's mental perspective in narrative. *Developmental Psychology, 43*(4), 1032–1037. doi:10.1037/0012-1649.43.4.1032

Palfrey, J., & Gasser, U. (2008). *Born digital.* New York, NY: Basic Books.

Pantaleo, S. (2004). Young children interpret the metafictive in Anthony Browne's *Voices in the Park. Journal of Early Childhood Literacy, 4,* 211–233. doi:10.1177/1468798404044516

Paris, S. (2005). Reinterpreting the development of reading skills. *Reading Research Quarterly, 40,* 184–202.

Paris, S., & Paris, S.G. (2003). Assessing narrative comprehension in young children. *Reading Research Quarterly, 38,* 36–76.

Pew Research Internet Project. (2014). *Mobile technology fact sheet.* Retrieved from http://www.pewInternet.org/fact-sheets/mobile-technology-fact-sheet

Rakoczy, H., Tomasello, M., & Striano, T. (2005). How children turn objects into symbols: A cultural learning account. In L.L. Namy (Ed.), *Symbol use and symbolic representation: Developmental and comparative perspectives* (pp. 69–97). Mahwah, NJ: Erlbaum.

RAND Reading Study Group. (2002). *Reading for understanding: Towards an R&D program in reading comprehension.* Report prepared for the Office of Educational Research and Improvement, U.S. Department of Education. Retrieved from http://www.rand.org/content/dam/rand/pubs/monograph_reports/2005/MR1465.pdf

Rideout, V. (2014). *Learning at home: Families' educational media use in America.* The Joan Ganz Cooney Center: Families and Media Project. Retrieved from http://www.joanganzcooneycenter.org/publication/learning-at-home

Rochat, P., & Callaghan, T. (2005). What drives symbolic development? The case of pictorial comprehension and production. In L.L. Namy (Ed.), *Symbol use and symbolic representation: Developmental and comparative perspectives* (pp. 25–46). Mahwah, NJ: Erlbaum.

Rogoff, B. (2003). *The cultural nature of human development.* New York, NY: Oxford University Press.

Rosenblatt, L. (1965). *Literature as exploration.* New York, NY: D. Appleton-Century. (Original work published 1938)

Roskos, K.A., Christie, J.F., Widman, S., & Holding, A. (2010). Three decades in: Priming for meta-analysis in play-literacy research. *Journal of Early Childhood Literacy, 10,* 55–96. doi:10.11771468798409357580

Rowe, D.W. (2008a). Social contracts for writing: Negotiating shared understandings about text in the preschool years. *Reading Research Quarterly, 43,* 66–95.

Rowe, D. (2008b). The social construction of intentionality: Two-year-olds' and adults' participation at a preschool writing center. *Research in the Teaching of English, 42,* 387–434.

Siegel, M., Kontovourki, S., Schmier, S., & Enriquez, G. (2008). Literacy in motion: A case study of a shape-shifting kindergartener. *Language Arts, 86*(2), 89–98.

Strasburger, V.C., Wilson, B.J., & Jordan, A.B. (2009). *Children, adolescents, and the media* (2nd ed.). Los Angeles, CA: Sage.

Street, B. (1995). *Literacy in theory and practice.* Cambridge, UK: Cambridge University Press.

Tomasello, M., Carpenter, M., Call, J., Behne, T., & Moll, H. (2005). Understanding and sharing intentions: The origins of cultural cognition. *Behavioral and Brain Sciences, 28,* 675–735.

U.S. Department of Commerce. (2011). *Computer and Internet use in the United States.* Retrieved from http://www.census.gov/prod/2013pubs/p20-569.pdf

U.S. Task Force on Childhood Obesity. (2011). *White House Taskforce childhood obesity report to the president.* Retrieved from http://www.LetsMove.gov/white-house-task-force-childhood-obesity-report -president

van Kleeck, A., & Schwarz, A.L. (2011). Making "academic talk" explicit: Research directions for fostering classroom discourse skills in children from nonmainstream cultures. *Revue Suisse des Sciences de l'Éducation, 33*(1), 1–18.

Vasquez, V.M., & Felderman, C.B. (2012). *Technology and critical literacy in early childhood.* New York, NY: Routledge.

Vygotsky, L.S. (1978). *Mind in society: The development of higher psychological processes.* Cambridge, MA: Harvard University Press.

Wells, G. (1999). *Dialogic inquiry: Towards a socio-cultural practice and theory of education.* Cambridge, UK: Cambridge University Press.

Werstch, J.V. (1991). *Voices of the mind: Sociocultural approach to mediated action.* Cambridge, MA: Harvard University Press.

Wohlwend, K.E. (2011). *Playing their way to literacies: Reading, writing, and belonging in the early childhood classroom.* New York, NY: Teachers College Press.

Wohlwend, K.E. (2013). Playing Star Wars under the (teacher's) radar: Detecting kindergartners' action texts and embodied literacies. In V.M. Vasquez & J.W. Wood (Eds.), *Perspectives and provocations in early childhood education* [National Council of Teacher of English Early Childhood Assembly Yearbook] (pp. 105–115). Charlotte, NC: Information Age.

Wyse, D., & Styles, M. (2007). Synthetic phonics and the teaching of reading: The debate about England's "Rose Report." *Literacy, 41*(1), 35–42. doi:10.1111/j.1467-9345.2007.00455.x

6

Building Emergent
Comprehension Through Informational Texts

KENDRA M. HALL-KENYON, BARBARA E. CULATTA, AND NELL K. DUKE

Traditionally, narrative texts have been the focus of preschool literacy instruction; however, more recently, researchers have been calling for more access to and use of informational texts in all early childhood (pre-K–2) classrooms (e.g., Caswell & Duke, 1998; Duke, 2000; Hall & Sabey, 2007; Moss; 2008; Pappas, 1993; Pentimonti, Zucker, Justice, & Kaderavek, 2010; Yopp & Yopp, 2006; 2012). The Common Core State Standards (CCSS; National Governors Association Center for Best Practices & Council of Chief State School Officers, 2010) expect roughly equal attention to informational as to narrative reading and writing beginning in kindergarten, which may prompt pre-K teachers as well as K–2 educators to afford greater attention to informational texts. In addition, some states are creating or revising pre-K standards to include standards related to informational text skills (see Arizona, New Jersey, and Utah for examples). Access to and support for comprehending informational texts can prepare young children for acquiring information, developing critical thinking skills, and succeeding in school (Duke, 2010; Ogle & Blachowicz, 2002; Pappas, 2006; Venezky, 2000). The first section of this chapter describes the benefits of using informational texts and suggests ways of selecting and providing them for preschool use. The remainder of the chapter presents strategies for supporting preschool children's informational text comprehension.

USING INFORMATIONAL TEXTS IN PREKINDERGARTEN CLASSROOMS

Although many have argued for the importance of exposing young children to *informational text,* it still appears that these texts are not being used extensively in preschool or even primary grade classrooms (Duke, 2000; Jeong, Gaffney, & Choi, 2010; Pentimonti et al., 2010; Yopp & Yopp, 2006). The term "informational text," as used in the Common Core State Standards (CCSS, 2010) and other influential documents, is a broad term that refers to a number of different kinds of texts whose primary purpose is to convey information, such as to teach about the natural or social world (informative/explanatory text), to teach someone how to do something (procedural text), or to teach about a person's life (biographical text). As preschool teachers strive to increase the use of informational texts in their classrooms, they should understand the rationale behind exposing children to such texts, follow some basic criteria for selecting texts, and consider different ways to increase children's access to appropriate texts.

Rationale for Using Informational Texts with Young Children

The purposeful use of informational texts can provide both immediate and long-term benefits for young children. Informational texts can be used to help motivate young children's learning, build their knowledge, and support their language development.

Motivate Interest in Learning   Young children tend to be curious about their world, and informational texts can help them find answers to their questions, motivating them to explore topics more deeply through additional texts and experience (Conezio & French, 2002). Preschool teachers can build on children's natural interests by purposefully planning experiences that give them opportunities to ask/answer questions and explore their world (Chard, 1998; Helm & Katz, 2001). A teacher may introduce "studies" or "projects" that investigate interesting, meaningful topics. A study may begin with children brainstorming what they know and want to learn about a topic. The teacher provides support with questions or "wonderings" to stimulate the children's exploration and then guides the process of examining a variety of texts as one tool to address the questions (see Bellous, 2004).

Build Knowledge   One of the primary purposes of using informational text is to build children's content knowledge, which in turn becomes background for comprehending texts they will read in the future (Wilson & Anderson, 1986). Children often build knowledge by connecting information they encounter to their experiences, an important source for learning. However, when informational texts accompany firsthand experiences, children have access to content that extends what they can gain from a direct encounter alone. For example, using informational texts in conjunction with rock exploration activities can expand children's knowledge not only of the characteristics of rocks (e.g., layers, color, hardness) but of less apparent facts such as the way common rocks are formed (e.g., bits of soil, sand, and mud are pressed together and get hard over time).

Moreover, a good bit of developmentally appropriate knowledge cannot be gained firsthand (Tough, 1985), and informational texts can contribute significantly to filling in these areas (Duke, Halvorsen, & Knight, 2012). For example, certain insects might not be safe or even possible for children to handle physically. A teacher can build on children's knowledge of these as well as other insects through texts. When dealing with content that is removed from children's personal experience, the teacher should first connect to what children already know and can experience firsthand (e.g., familiar and safe local insects) and extend that knowledge through the use of varied informational texts (e.g., trade books, online content, videos, photographs, discussions).

Support Academic Language Development   Language is the chief medium by which informational texts convey knowledge about topics and events that are not always concrete, familiar, or accessible to children. Thus these texts must rely heavily on decontextualized academic language. Helping children to process oral or written texts that contain decontextualized language facilitates the development of early academic language skills that are essential for reading comprehension (McCabe, 2013; Nystrand, 2006; Stahl, 2013).

Now widely recognized as paramount in primary-grade classrooms, academic language development is also relevant to and should be fostered in pre-K classrooms (Blank, Marquis, & Kilmovitch, 1995; Dickinson & Tabors, 2001; see also Chapter 4 by van Kleeck). As children use language to gain information, they develop and refine their language skills—particularly the ability to represent ideas that are remote and abstract (Tough, 1985; Zwiers, 2008). Teachers should stimulate and guide practice in the use of language to gain information, think critically, and solve problems (Mashburn et al., 2008; Paul & Wang, 2012). See Chapter 4 by van Kleeck for a comprehensive discussion of the connections between young children's academic talk and comprehension.

Criteria for Selecting Appropriate Texts

As teachers make the decision to use informational texts in preschool classrooms, they must select the types of texts carefully, considering characteristics of these texts that make them appropriate for young children. This section focuses on text characteristics that are particularly important for preschool children: purpose, content, vocabulary, language, structure, and features.

Purpose   The purpose(s) of texts selected for classroom use should align with the purpose(s) for which the teacher is using them. For example, Eric Carle did not write *The Very Hungry Caterpillar* (1969) to teach children about metamorphosis, and as such, the book should not be used for that purpose. Informational texts are typically written to explain, describe, argue/persuade, instruct, or a combination of these purposes, and teachers should use informational texts for one or more of these purposes. Teachers should explicitly identify the purpose of using the text ("This book helps us learn about . . ." or "This book will tell how . . .") and should bear in mind that discussions, verbal explanations, videos, and other texts can be flexibly interwoven with hands-on experiences and printed text encounters to address their purposes.

Content   In selecting an informational text, a teacher should identify relevant and motivating content to address. The content can be a hook to entice children to engage with and process the text. Good texts must be accurate and contain interesting ideas presented at an appropriate level (Duke & Bennett-Armistead, 2003; Watanabe & Duke, 2013) and should represent a wide range of topics, not just animals, for example (Yopp & Yopp, 2012). To discern whether the text is appropriate, the teacher also needs to consider how much information will likely be unfamiliar to children. (See later in the chapter for a discussion of strategies to support children's experiences with unfamiliar content.)

Vocabulary   The vocabulary in informational texts often differs from the vocabulary children encounter in narratives or everyday conversations. Informational texts contain more technical words and fewer concrete nouns and verbs than fictional narratives or social exchanges (Zwiers, 2008). They include fewer high-frequency words, more generic or superordinate terms, and more words that signal relationships among ideas, such as *because, while, so, however,* and *but.* In addition, words like *problem, solution, compare, cause, alike,* and *different* tend to occur in informational texts because they relate to the purpose and organization of the text.

Teachers should carefully consider the vocabulary demands associated with the texts they select for use in their classrooms. If necessary, the vocabulary in informational texts can be simplified in oral interactions; however, teachers should be sure that the text does not contain too many obscure words. In selecting texts, teachers can use similar criteria that are recommended for teaching vocabulary—that is, focusing on texts that contain a few challenging words that are not too unusual (see Neuman & Wright, 2013) and have high utility (see Blachowicz, Fisher, Ogle, & Taffe, 2013).

Early Academic Language   Although young children cannot deal with complex academic texts, they do begin to develop academic language skills before entering kindergarten (Blank et al., 1995; see also Chapter 4 by van Kleeck). Thus, to support the development of this ability, texts selected for young children should convey some information in language that is not signaled redundantly in pictures. In addition, any content relating to events that are not pictured should be conveyed in explanations that the children are able to understand, along with references to familiar ideas or experiences. Some abstract or less familiar ideas can be made "realizable" through reference to language, pictures, and information that are concrete, familiar, and immediate (Blank, Marquis, & Kilmovitch, 1994, p. 30). Children develop higher-level language abilities by building from the language they already know to process new language and acquire new information.

Structure   Informational texts have a number of organizational structures that can be related to their varied functions. General structures include description, sequence, enumeration, compare/contrast, cause/effect, and problem/solution (Meyer & Freedle, 1984; Meyer & Poon, 2001). Although there is not a one-to-one correspondence between structure and purpose, informational texts are organized in ways that fit with or relate to their purpose:

- Texts that instruct or convey a set of procedures are likely to be organized as a set of steps listed in a sequence.

- Texts recounting past situations would likely be organized as a series of events placed in a time sequence.

- Informational texts that explain can follow several organizational patterns. For example, a text that deals with similarities and differences might compare and contrast two entities along several characteristics. Other explanatory texts might state problems and offer possible solutions.

- Texts that argue or persuade might enumerate reasons for believing or doing something.

Teachers should select texts with a clear structure that aligns well with the instructional purpose(s).

Features   Informational texts employ a variety of forms and features to present content. Navigational features (e.g., index, tables of content), headings, captions, and labels contribute to making texts accessible and appealing for young children (Duke & Bennett-Armistead, 2003). Text features often add to or elaborate on information in the running text, permitting the teacher to use the text in a topical, nonlinear fashion. Graphics (e.g., photos, diagrams) can contribute to making informational books visually appealing, and young children can acquire information from visual representations as well as from the text (Donovan & Smolkin, 2002). However, the children will need support in comprehending graphics and connecting them to the information in the running text (Barone & Morency, 2013; Duke et al., 2013; Norman, 2010).

Ways to Increase and Enhance Access to Informational Texts

After identifying appropriate informational texts, teachers should make them available for frequent and purposeful access. Informational text skills, like other literacy capabilities, develop with guided encounters with a variety of texts. Substantial experience with a genre is necessary if knowledge of that genre is to develop (Duke & Kays, 1998; Kamberelis, 1999; Pappas, 1993; Tower, 2003). This section describes ways that teachers can increase preschool children's access to informational texts and maximize that access for learning purposes.

Incorporate Informational Texts into Multiple Contexts   Informational texts are easily incorporated into multiple classroom contexts and connected to hands-on activities. For example, in the dramatic play area, children might utilize lists, menus, catalogs, invitations, announcements, and brochures as they relate to particular themes or contexts of play such as shopping, hosting a party, or traveling (Neuman, 2001). Simple "how-to" texts or manuals (e.g., cookbooks, directions for making paper airplanes, explanations of simple physical exercises) can be used authentically as small groups of children engage in cooking activities, crafts, or physical movement. Informational texts such as posters and children's dictations can be displayed on classroom walls for others to read and learn from.

Teachers can support children in understanding the print content through modeling and explanations. For example, a teacher may demonstrate how store workers use print as they stock shelves or wait on customers. Or during a cooking experience, the teacher could show the recipe written on chart paper and discuss with the children how the text tells them, in sequence, the steps they need to take to make the snack or food item (e.g., what to add, when to mix or pour ingredients, how long to cook).

Share Exemplary Informational Picture Books   Good informational picture books should be provided in the classroom library or book corner and be regularly included when the teacher reads aloud (Pentimonti et al., 2010). Many excellent picture books become classroom reference materials with information relevant to unit topics and to children's personal interests. Teachers do not need to read informational picture books in sequence or in their entirety. Just one page or small section of a book can be relevant to the topic of exploration. By choosing a particular segment, the teacher can model using the index to locate the information or show children how to build ideas by using content provided by graphics and written text from several picture books.

Help Children Compose Informational Texts   The teacher and children can compose informational texts using shared writing processes in which children contribute their ideas while the teacher serves as the scribe (Black, Hall-Kenyon, & Culatta, 2013). For example, teachers can guide children through the process of writing a "how-to" or procedural text as they discuss/describe the steps and processes they went through in conducting simple hands-on science observations or investigations. The discussion surrounding the creation of the text should support and elaborate on children's content knowledge and also contribute to children's understanding of the forms and functions of informational texts. Teachers can also provide additional support in the writing process through the use of high-quality informational texts. These exemplary or "mentor" texts (Dorfman & Cappelli, 2007, 2009) can help introduce and elaborate on content and also provide examples of some of the unique features of informational texts that the teacher can refer to as the class jointly creates a piece of informational writing—a strategy that has proved to be effective with primary-grade students (Bradley & Donovan, 2010). For example, in the book *Animal Babies* (Squire, 2001), there are two sections that explain the similarities and differences among baby animals that make them either dependent on or independent of their parents. The comparisons are made across several features (e.g., need of protection, capacity to get food, ability to get around). These sections contain several well-structured comparative statements that can serve as a source for a "mentor" compare/contrast text.

Incorporate Appropriate Digital Media Information does not only have to be conveyed through traditional informational books/text. Teachers can also utilize digital forms of text to convey information to young children. Digital media can expose children to information or experiences that would not otherwise be accessible in a classroom (e.g., large animals, oceans, space; Moses, 2013). Digital media also permit students to connect ideas and content from multiple sources. Video clips can be used effectively to make remote content immediate and concrete. The National Association for the Education of Young Children (NAEYC) supports the use of digital sources when they are combined with interactive instruction and the content fits with the classroom curriculum (NAEYC, 2012). For further discussion on the topic of supporting children's comprehension with digital media, see Chapter 5 by Dooley and Welch.

GUIDING EMERGENT COMPREHENSION OF INFORMATIONAL TEXTS

To be successful in comprehending informational texts and acquiring content knowledge, young children need the high levels of scaffolding provided by facilitative interactions within contexts of hands-on experiences. The following instructional strategies, many of which have been adapted for pre-K from the early primary grades, support functional knowledge and skills related to the aspects of informational texts earlier recommended as selection criteria: purpose, content, vocabulary, language, structure, and features. Although more research is needed on early informational text instruction, some work suggests that many of these strategies, when taught in developmentally appropriate ways, can be effective for young children in pre-K and kindergarten (Culatta, Hall-Kenyon, & Black, 2010; Dreher & Gray, 2009). For the purpose of this chapter, each of these aspects of informational text will be discussed separately; however, the strategies are all related and overlap to a significant degree. Thus teachers can draw upon multiple strategies across multiple texts to fortify instruction.

Purpose

Having a purpose for reading and writing, rather than reading or writing simply because the teacher asks or expects one to, appears to foster literacy development (e.g., Block, 2013; Purcell-Gates, Duke, & Martineau, 2007).

Provide Reasons to Access and Convey Information   Being aware of the circumstances in which young children require information (e.g., to solve a problem, address a question, figure out how to do something, decide between two options) can enable a teacher to find situations in which students need or want information from texts. For example, a teacher might make a paper airplane that does not fly and then engage children in following instructions to fix the problem. As another example, if a class is learning about living and nonliving things, the teacher might engage interest by showing the children two items: a plant and a rock. As he or she explains and invites discussion about differences between living and nonliving things, the teacher might record some of the children's ideas and help them to confirm or elaborate on their ideas by using a text such as *Living and Nonliving* by Lindeen (2008).

Teachers can also involve children in negotiating, persuading others, and making arguments, just as parents engage young children in such exchanges in their everyday lives (see Chapter 4 by van Kleeck). Young children and adults engage in conversations to make a point, assert a right, or demonstrate participation (Orsolini, 1993; Weiss & Sachs, 1991); such exchanges can be valued, encouraged, and highlighted in the classroom. For example, the teacher could read about hamsters and hermit crabs and then encourage children to make a case about which would make a better classroom pet.

Make Purpose Explicit   Teachers should explicitly state reasons for engaging with informational texts or engaging in information-based conversations. As they give reasons for gathering or conveying information, teachers can stimulate children's curiosity and provide an expectation for learning. For example, the teacher might say, "This book tells us about why so many animals live around ponds. I want to know about some of the animals that make their homes around ponds. What do you want to know?" Connecting the purpose of a text with its organization (or imposing an organization if the text is not well structured) can help children focus on main ideas and gain a deeper understanding of content because the structure is drawing their attention to the relationships among the ideas rather than isolated facts (Hall, Smith, & Losser, 2007). For example, the teacher might describe the purpose for reading a book about frogs and toads with a compare/contrast structure as follows: "This book can teach us how to tell the difference between a frog and a toad. Frogs and toads look alike in some ways, but we'll find out that they are actually pretty different."

Content

Teachers can support children's content learning with informational texts by using many strategies, including activating knowledge, providing hands-on experiences, relating content to personal experience, and connecting ideas across texts and contexts (Cervetti & Barber, 2008).

Activate and Elaborate Prior Knowledge   Prior knowledge in a targeted domain plays a significant role in children's ability to comprehend informational text (Best, Floyd, & McNamara, 2008). This appears to be a catch-22—children gain domain knowledge by accessing informational texts, but they need domain knowledge to access the text. Young children typically have limited world knowledge, so they need to recall what they already know about a particular topic as well as extend and expand that knowledge.

Teachers can use questioning in order to activate prior knowledge. Questions about what children already know can tap into their store of experiences and permit teachers to draw upon the funds of knowledge they have gained from their cultural backgrounds (Moll, Amanti, Neff, & Gonzales, 2005). Teachers must determine whether a particular text might be too far removed from children's experience. But often teachers can help children connect with texts by recognizing ways in which remote people and situations are similar to and different from their own experiences (Zarnowski, 2006), providing a meaningful and relevant emotional frame for or connection to the content (Sommers, 1981). For example, young children who have not lived on a farm may have relevant experience with and feelings about doing chores or taking care of pets (Westby, Culatta, & Hall-Kenyon, 2015).

Once activated, prior knowledge can be extended in a variety of ways. Teachers can plan multiple exposures to new content as part of thematic units (Ukrainetz, 2006). Conveying relevant real-life experiences of the teacher or of the children's friends and families can also give a personal perspective on informational content (Culatta et al., 2010). Providing hands-on experiences that relate to the ideas in the text is also an important strategy.

Provide Hands-On Experiences   Young children need real-world hands-on experience to help build knowledge. Simple construction projects, investigations, and exploration of materials can provide this sort of information. For example, children can learn about crabs by examining shells found on a beach and manipulating the claws; they can continue their exploration by using different tools (e.g., tongs) to grab items. With this experience to relate to, the teacher could expand into an informational book that shows pictures of a crab's claws and read and talk about how crabs use their claws to catch food and snap at other animals that get too close.

Give Accounts of Personal Experiences   Teachers can supplement children's own experiences by sharing accounts of others' experiences. Parents from various cultures can serve as experts, sharing personal accounts and bringing in artifacts from the children's homes and communities. Teachers can also share personal experiences, supported with pictures and props. A personal account can have emotional appeal if told with energy and excitement, even if the experience happened to someone other than the teller. In one pre-K project, the teacher brought in a harness used by a Seeing Eye dog and related a family's experiences training the dog before the animal was put into use. In another lesson, the teacher brought in a humane animal trap (e.g., have-a-heart trap) and told about using it to safely return a wild squirrel to the woods (Culatta et al., 2010).

Connect Content Across Multiple Texts and Contexts   Connecting content across texts and contexts is a useful strategy for extending knowledge (Culatta et al., 2010;

Dreher & Gray, 2009). Connecting ideas across texts and media (e.g., written text to written text or oral text to written text) also strengthens learning. For example, children might observe and discuss processes of growing plants from seeds and sprouts, recording their observations and comparing what they discover to pictures found online or in books. They can relate what they observed to a time-lapse YouTube video of a sprouting seed as they read about the stages of plant growth in a text. The teacher can read and reread informational books that elaborate on the growth of the plants the children are growing as well as less familiar plants. As they guide children in making varied connections, teachers may help them chart the information gained from multiple sources (Morris & Tchudi, 1996).

Vocabulary

Learning vocabulary increases children's knowledge of underlying content and concepts and supports developing comprehension (Elleman, Lindo, Morphy, & Compton, 2009; Stahl & Fairbanks, 1986). Teachers need to identify relevant words to teach, provide multiple examples, and deepen word knowledge.

Teach Relevant Words   Teachers should select words that are age appropriate and useful. Such words may come from those that apply to specific information domains and content (Neuman & Wright, 2013), those that can generalize to other contexts (Beck, McKeown, & Kucan, 2002), and those that deal with the nature of informational texts.

Many standards documents expect children in pre-K to develop content knowledge. Developing content-related vocabulary is a necessary part of that process. When selecting content-related words, teachers should focus on terms that are relevant to the discipline (Blachowicz et al., 2013; Neuman & Wright, 2013). However, experts suggest that selected words should not be overly numerous (no more than three to four in each text) or rare (overly technical and not useful in communicating about target content). For a unit on insects, for example, words that are relevant but not too obscure might include *insect* and *creep*.

In addition to discipline-specific terms, a teacher can identify words that are likely to be useful across content areas and contexts (Blachowicz et al., 2013). Some of these terms include words that describe process skills such as *predict* and *observe*, which are naturally used across content areas. Others might include words that are relevant to a particular unit but can also be applied to a number of other topics and/or situations. For example, in a unit on insects, words like *ability* (what a particular insect can do) or *cracks* (places where moths hide to lay eggs) can be taught and then revisited in other contexts. Additional words that tend to appear in informational texts and apply to varied situations include superordinate category terms that signal higher-order group membership: *insect* versus *ant* and *bee* or *vehicle* versus *truck* and *car*.

A third type of word teachers may select includes those related to the nature of informational texts (although they have relevance to some other types of text as well). For example, to express relationships among ideas or locate key information in informational texts, children might learn the following:

- For compare/contrast: *compare, same, different, alike*

- For problem/solution: *problem, solution, ways to fix the problem*

- For sequence: *steps, order, first/second/third*

- For causal relationships: *because, so, as a result*

- To locate information: *table of contents, index, headings*

To qualify a statement, they might learn *most, not always, some,* and so forth.

Provide Multiple Exposures and Examples   Multiple exposures to words help children understand their meaning and usage (Harris, Golinkoff, & Hirsh-Pasek, 2010; Nagy, Herman, & Anderson, 1985). Providing a number of examples is particularly important for teaching early academic vocabulary, including attributes and spatial, temporal, and quantity terms, as learning such words requires children to notice common feature(s) or characteristics in different instances. For example, learning the word *heavy* requires that the characteristic *weight* be abstracted from and applied to objects being manipulated.

One or two exposures to a word do not provide the opportunity for sufficient depth of word knowledge (Beck et al., 2002; Nagy, 1988). Children need to have reasons to notice the meaning of the word in arranged instructional contexts and to experience it repeatedly in naturally occurring settings. For example, a preschool teacher might introduce processes and terms involved with compare/contrast by matching and comparing footwear. Children can change in and out of shoes and boots that "got mixed up in a pile," chatting about which items were *the same, different, alike,* and *not alike.* A few hours later and on succeeding days, use of these words might also be incorporated into everyday contexts such as commenting on how carrot sticks and celery sticks are alike and different during snack time. With examples embedded into authentic contexts, contrived or real, children develop an increasingly automatic connection between the purpose for using a word and its meaning.

Deepen Word Knowledge   Children's comprehension of word meanings should go deeper than just recognizing the word in a narrow context (Pollard-Durodola et al., 2011). Teachers elaborate on the meaning of words encountered in book reading as they provide hands-on experiences (Justice, Meier, & Walpole, 2005; Riley-Ayers, 2013), give explanations, provide verbal examples, explain words in simple ways, make connections with other words (e.g., synonyms, antonyms, superordinate categories; Nagy, 1988; Neuman & Wright, 2013), make word maps or webs, and prompt children to act out words (Beck et al., 2002; Blachowicz & Fisher, 2004). They may associate the word with experiences familiar to the children, perhaps giving them a prompt to forge the link: "Have you ever accidentally *squashed* a bug?" "Did you ever have to *squash* or smash down garbage to make it take up less space?" See Chapter 2 by Coyne, Neugebauer, Ware, McCoach, and Madura for theoretical perspectives and further research involving vocabulary instruction and comprehension.

Early Academic Language

Strengthening early academic language is foundational to building text comprehension skills (McCabe, 2013; Riley-Ayers, 2013). As children engage with informational texts, they need support in dealing with the language demands. Preschool teachers can support children's acquisition of early academic language as they interweave contextualized with decontextualized language, expose children to higher-level functions, and adjust the complexity of the text. For a comprehensive discussion specific to academic talk and comprehension, see Chapter 4 by van Kleeck.

Interweave Contextualized with Decontextualized Language　For preschool children, decontextualized, academic language abilities develop through oral as well as written modes. The move from contextualized to decontextualized language entails a shift from talking about and understanding references to ostensible, perceptible objects and actions to talking about events that are more remote (or removed in time and space) and abstract. As previously noted, providing relevant, concrete hands-on activities gives teachers opportunities to talk about how concrete and familiar ideas relate to remote and abstract ones (Blank, Rose, & Berlin, 1978; see also Chapter 4 by van Kleeck).

To take early academic language beyond areas easily represented in hands-on activities, teachers can promote higher-level language through interactions around informational texts (Pappas, Varelas, Barry, & Rife, 2003). Preschool children can engage in conversations about decontextualized topics that are pictorially represented in texts, and their language gradually becomes more sophisticated with practice (Maduram, 2000; Paul & Wang, 2012). As they seek to understand facts by asking questions and engaging in conversations, language complexity increases for both children and adults. In one study, parents who shared informational texts with their children tended to use a higher number of feedback utterances, more differentiated language, longer extratextual utterances, and greater vocabulary diversity than they did when sharing narrative texts (Price, van Kleeck, & Huberty, 2009).

Engage Children in Higher-Level Exchanges　Engaging in higher-level language use (e.g., reasoning, explaining, arguing, problem solving) during conversations gives children valuable experience dealing with or processing the demands of informational texts (Feuerstein, Falik, Feuerstein, & Bohacs, 2012; Westby et al., 2015). In giving explanations or solving problems during classroom activities, teachers can clarify the function of certain objects (whiteboard and erasers), explain how simple machines work (a stapler or hole punch), or give a rationale for certain actions (posting classroom "job" assignments so students remember; Bova, 2011; Snow & Beals, 2006). Teachers can engage children in talking about procedures for doing things (e.g., steps in cleaning the hamster cage) or refer to causes and effects of actions (e.g., the role that hand washing can play in keeping children healthy). Teachers can model curiosity about a topic and ask interesting, thought-provoking questions. In such higher-level exchanges, teachers acknowledge and elaborate on children's contributions.

As teachers provide explanations and elaborations, they are helping children make inferences, a higher-level language skill (e.g., Anderson & Pearson, 1984). They supply the connection between what is stated and what is missing but assumed. In reading and/or talking about responsibility for taking care of pets, for example, the teacher can lead children to infer that if they are careless and let a dog or cat get lost, they may cause it to get hungry or be hurt. Addressing higher-level functions promotes the use of early academic language.

Adjust the Complexity of the Text   If the language of a text is too complex, the teacher can make adjustments while reading aloud (Blank et al., 1994; Feuerstein et al., 2012). In addition to explaining unfamiliar words before and during the reading, teachers can paraphrase important ideas to avoid overly complex terms and can add assumed or implied information.

Teachers can restate important ideas in simple ways to provide helpful redundancy. For example, the book *We Need Insects* (Prokos, 2005) has a section titled "The Earth Needs Insects," describing ways that insects are "an important part of nature": "Some insects help plants grow. Some eat other harmful insects. Some insects keep the soil healthy. Many insects are food for other living things" (p. 4). The teacher might restate and elaborate by explaining how insects help plants grow, keep the soil healthy, and so forth.

Structure

Awareness of text structure has long been understood as important in comprehending and learning from texts for upper elementary-age students (for a review of research in this area, see Ray & Meyer, 2011). However, there is also growing evidence that developing text structure awareness may also be an effective strategy for early primary-grade and even preschool-age children (Culatta et al., 2010; Dreher & Gray, 2009; Hall, Sabey, & McClellan, 2005; Reutzel, Smith, & Fawson, 2005; Williams et al., 2005). As such, preschool teachers need instructional strategies to help raise children's awareness of informational text structures.

Highlight Signal Words   An oral or written informational text with a clear, recognizable structure will likely indicate that structure with recognizable words (e.g., *similar, different, in contrast, but,* and *alike* to signal a comparison; Meyer & Rice, 1982). During a reading or oral retelling, words indicating text structure can be emphasized or added if not explicitly used (Price, van Kleeck, & Huberty, 2009). For example, a section titled "Starting at Home" in the book *Where Does Garbage Go?* (Asimov, 1992) begins, "You can help solve the garbage problem by throwing out less" (p. 20). Though the words *solve* and *problem* occur in the first sentence, no signal words appear in the rest of the passage, which lists some things that can be done to recycle, such as putting glass and plastic bottles in a recycling bin, using scrap paper for notes or gift wrap, and starting a compost pile with food scraps and grass clippings. If the children seem to be getting lost in the list, the teacher can add words and phrases to indicate that the suggested actions address the garbage issue: *so, things to try, solution, another way to fix the problem.* Highlighting and adding signal words to texts and oral discussions of informational content can call children's attention to text structure and expose them to organizational frameworks and important related ideas (Spyridakis & Standal, 1987). Pre-K teachers should not expect children to identify or use signal words, but they can help children notice how and when such words are used. Exposure to and supports for processing signal words help children make connections between ideas.

Focus on Well-Structured Texts   Researchers recommend teaching young children from informational texts that have a structure that is easy to discern (Dreher & Gray,

2009; Hall-Kenyon & Black, 2010; Williams et al., 2005). Working with one or two structures at a time and presenting the children with multiple examples can make them aware
of ways factual information can be organized.

Although many texts for children do not have an easy-to-discern structure, reasonable options are available. Teachers can choose to use just one well-structured section of
a book that has a more complicated overall organization. For example, *Bats!* (Iorio, 2005)
has a section titled "Bats Beware" that deals with possible dangers that bats face; this section can be presented alone as a problem/solution text. Given a particular instructional
purpose, teachers can also impose a structure on a text. For example, *Community Helpers*
(Kalman, 2011) provides descriptions of different jobs. But the teacher can also naturally
impose a compare/contrast structure by leading the children in a discussion about the
similarities and differences of some of the community helpers (e.g., whether they help
animals or people, whether they wear a uniform). When imposing a structure on a text,
it is important to explicitly highlight the structure by inserting keywords or representing
the ideas graphically in a chart or matrix.

In addition to finding well-structured informational texts, teachers can create their
own texts based on children's shared experiences that lend themselves to a particular
structure. Preschool children can understand the relationships involved with problem/
solution, compare/contrast, or time sequence, particularly when they encounter these
relationships in their lived experience: solving the problem of lacking all the ingredients for muffins during a cooking activity, examining two different kinds of rocks as a
comparison, or discussing steps in planting seeds as a sequence. After providing experiences with a clear structure, the teacher can involve children in a shared writing activity
designed to co-create a similarly structured text. This process may contribute to a foundation for comprehending more complex informational texts children will approach in the
future (Culatta et al., 2010).

Create Visual Representations   Teachers can support children's informational
text comprehension by guiding them through the process of creating simple visual representations for the relationships among ideas, particularly those that relate to higher-level
organization (Duke & Pearson, 2002). Connections between ideas are more easily understood as the organization of the text becomes visual and thus more explicit and concrete
(e.g., Carlisle, 1991; Chambliss & Calfee, 1989).

Visual forms such as a T-chart, matrix chart, or concept map are effective with
young children. In a study of the use of expository texts in early literacy, preschool teachers used a large, two-column T-chart to teach children to make comparisons by contrast-
ing information on the life of a gorilla in a zoo with the life of a gorilla in the wild (Culatta
et al., 2010). Children were given objects or pictures representing some of the things they
had learned about life situations of gorillas and took turns placing the pictures and objects
in the appropriate columns or on the center line if the item could apply to both conditions.

Co-constructing the charts gets the children actively involved in both the content
and the structural pattern of the text. The teacher involves children in a conversation while
constructing a graphic representation, calling attention to the important information and
the connections and relationships of the ideas. For example, as the children placed objects

on the gorilla chart, the teacher continually commented on how a gorilla's life in the wild is *different from* a gorilla's life in the zoo, repeating and emphasizing keywords such as *different, difference,* and *not the same.* Another encounter with a well-structured text can occur when the teacher and students retell the information from the graphic representation. The teacher does not expect the children to identify the organization of a text or map, but he or she labels or describes the organization for the children as the text is retold or rewritten from the visual.

Features

As explained earlier, informational texts can have a number of features—such as headings, captions, and graphics—that help to convey information. Devoting attention to these features introduces children to important comprehension aids.

Point Out Text Features   Research by Justice and colleagues indicates that explicitly referencing aspects of print during read-alouds supports literacy development (e.g., Justice & Ezell, 2004; Justice, McGinty, Piasta, Kaderavek, & Fan, 2010). Similarly, we believe that explicitly referencing informational text features during read-alouds and making use of those features with children can support informational reading and writing development.

Once children are familiar with some common features in informational books from read-alouds, the teacher can model these features during shared writing (see Duke & Bennett-Armistead, 2003), finding authentic reasons for using them to communicate information. If the children are writing about what they have learned about firefighters to share with another class, the teacher might encourage them to create headings using an approach similar to this one:

> You learned a lot about the different things that firefighters do, so our first heading could say "What Firefighters Do." [After discussing and writing content for that section, the teacher might say,] You also learned a lot about the equipment or tools that firefighters use to fight fires. What could our heading for that be? [And so forth.]

Demonstrate How to Locate Specific Information in a Text   Some studies have explored the impact of the awareness and use of text features on primary-grade informational text comprehension (Hall, 2007; Kelley & Clausen-Grace, 2010). However, in preschool the purpose would be limited to raising children's awareness of using informational text features to locate information and answer questions. For example, when reading aloud a text about diggers (e.g., *Diggers* by Askew, 2010), the teacher might say, "I want to find out what kinds of things diggers can do. Let's see where I could find information in this book that will help me answer my question." He or she could then model the process of using the table of contents to locate the sections "Digging and Moving," and/or "Breaking up Hard Ground," which are likely to have that information.

Treat Graphics as "Text"   In reading informational texts, teachers should focus on the meaning conveyed by both the written text and the graphics (Coleman, McTigue, & Smolkin, 2011; Roberts et al., 2013). Graphics such as drawings, photographs, diagrams, tables, and charts are visual representations of content (Norman, 2010). Teachers should help children understand how to "read" informational graphics and how to connect those graphics to the written text.

Graphics are common in young children's informational texts. To keep the written text simple, authors may depend on the graphics to add a great deal of information that children can "read" before they can decode words. For example, by examining pictures of spiders, children can learn how spiders' fangs allow them to suck their food or how their eyes allow them to see in multiple directions. From additional pictures in the same text or across texts, children might notice similarities and differences among spiders and other animals: "A spider and a daddy longlegs may look alike at first. But the pictures show that the spider has eight eyes and the daddy longlegs has only two."

Teachers can introduce children to other types of graphics (e.g., maps, charts) and demonstrate the use of each. In addition, they can help children become more familiar with the purposes of different graphics by constructing diagrams or charts from observations the children make (Duke & Bennett-Armistead, 2003)—possibly engaging the children in a discussion about the foods served at snack time and/or lunch and creating a pictograph to represent the food groups consumed across a few days. Once the graph is completed, the teacher could guide the children in "reading" it by summarizing or retelling the information from the graphic representation: "How many vegetables did we eat? Did we eat more fruits and vegetables than bread and other grains?" Graphs created by the children can help them express relationships among ideas they encounter during a lesson or across a unit of study (Culatta et al., 2010).

CONCLUSION

Historically, informational text comprehension has not been a focus of preschool instruction. However, the tide may be turning with the strong presence of informational text in the CCSS (NGACBP & CCSSO, 2010) and a growing body of research suggesting benefits of using informational texts with young children. Thoughtful use of informational texts has the potential to be engaging for preschool children while also supporting their knowledge, language, and overall comprehension development.

This chapter emphasizes the value of attending to informational texts in pre-K classrooms and suggests an assortment of instructional strategies and practices, including the following:

- Incorporating informational texts into multiple contexts

- Sharing exemplary informational picture books

- Helping children compose informational texts

- Incorporating appropriate digital media

- Providing reasons for children to access and convey information

- Making the purpose for reading and writing informational text explicit

- Activating background knowledge

- Providing hands-on experiences

- Relating content to personal experience

- Connecting ideas across texts and contexts

- Identifying relevant vocabulary to teach

- Providing multiple examples of words

- Elaborating on and explaining the meaning of words

- Interweaving contextualized with decontextualized language

- Exposing children to higher-level language functions

- Adjusting the complexity of the text

- Developing awareness of text structure (by highlighting signal words, focusing on well-structured texts, and creating visual representations)

- Pointing out informational text features

- Demonstrating how to locate specific information in a text

- Treating graphics as "text"

These practices can work together to support young children's comprehension of informational text. Whereas instructional strategies can individually address the various aspects of informational texts (purpose, content, vocabulary, academic language, text structure, and features), each component or strategy operates in conjunction with the others. The overlap among the various aspects of texts ensures that instruction is meaningful. Within a particular thematic or project-based unit, teachers can emphasize relevant content, teach new vocabulary, support the use academic language, draw attention to the relationships among ideas in a particular content area, and highlight important text features.

Careful attention to each of the instructional components is necessary because of the unique demands (e.g., decontextualized language, academic vocabulary, text structure and features) children face when encountering and comprehending informational texts. Interweaving contextualized and decontextualized language can help children to meet these demands. Vocabulary instruction with informational text is also essential: giving careful attention to selection of words, providing multiple exposures and examples, and using various strategies to deepen word knowledge. Text structure and text features are important foci of instruction with the emphasis on how structure and features help children learn more about the natural and social worlds and communicate what was learned to others. With the right kinds of support, even very young children can handle the demands associated with informational texts.

REFERENCES

Anderson, R.C., & Pearson, P.D. (1984). A schema-theoretic view of basic processes in reading comprehension. In P.D. Pearson, R. Barr, M.L. Kamil, P. Mosenthal, & R. Dykstra (Eds.), *Handbook of reading research* (pp. 255–292). New York, NY: Longman.

Asimov, I. (1992). *Where does garbage go?* New York, NY: Gareth Stevens.

Askew, A. (2010). *Diggers.* London, UK: QED.

Barone, D., & Morency, A. (2013). New perspectives on literature for young children. In D. Barone & M. Mallette (Eds.), *Best practices in early literacy instruction* (pp. 119–134). New York, NY: Guilford Press.

Beck, I.L., McKeown, M.G., & Kucan, L. (2002). *Bringing words to life: Robust vocabulary instruction.* New York, NY: Guilford Press.

Bellous, K. (2004). Looking at the trees around us. *Early Childhood Research and Practice, 6*(1). Retrieved from http://ecrp.illinois.edu/v6n1/Bellous.html

Best, R.M., Floyd, R.G., & McNamara, D.S. (2008). Differential competencies contributing to children's comprehension of narrative and expository texts. *Reading Psychology, 29,* 137–164.

Blachowicz, C., & Fisher, P. (2004). Vocabulary lessons. *Educational Leadership, 61*(6), 66–69.

Blachowicz, C., Fisher, P., Ogle, D., & Taffe, S.W. (2013). *Teaching academic vocabulary K–8: Effective practices across the curriculum.* New York, NY: Guilford Press.

Black, S., Hall-Kenyon, K., & Culatta, B. (2013). Learning about the world: Exploring and comprehending expository texts. In B. Culatta, K. Hall-Kenyon, & S. Black (Eds.), *Systematic and engaging early literacy: Instruction and intervention.* San Diego, CA: Plural Publishing.

Blank, M., Marquis, M.A., & Kilmovitch, M.O. (1994). *Directing school discourse.* Tucson, AZ: Communication Skill Builders.

Blank, M., Marquis, M.A., & Kilmovitch, M.O. (1995). *Directing early discourse.* Tucson, AZ: Communication Skill Builders.

Blank, M., Rose, S.A., & Berlin, L. (1978). *The language of learning: The preschool years.* New York, NY: Grune & Stratton.

Block, M.K. (2013). *The impact of identifying a specific purpose and external audience for writing on second graders' writing quality* (Unpublished doctoral dissertation). Michigan State University.

Bova, A. (2011). Functions of "why" questions asked by children in family conversations. *Procedia—Social and Behavioral Sciences, 30,* 776–782.

Bradley, L.G., & Donovan, C.A. (2010). Information book read-alouds as models for second-grade authors. *The Reading Teacher, 64*(4), 246–260.

Carlisle, J.F. (1991). Language comprehension and text structure. In J.F. Kavanagh (Ed.), *The language continuum from infancy to literacy* (pp. 115–145). Parkton, MD: York Press.

Caswell, L.J., & Duke, N.K. (1998). Non-narrative as a catalyst for literacy development. *Language Arts, 75,* 108–117.

Cervetti, G.N., & Barber, J. (2008). Text in hands-on science. In E.H. Hiebert & M. Sailors (Eds.), *Finding the right texts: What works for beginning and struggling readers* (pp. 89–108). New York, NY: Guilford Press.

Chambliss, M.J., & Calfee, R.C. (1989). Designing science textbooks to enhance student understanding. *Educational Psychologist, 24*(3), 307–322.

Chapman, M., Filipenko, M., McTavish, M., & Shapiro, J. (2007). First graders' preferences for narrative and/or information books and perceptions of other boys' and girls' book preferences. *Canadian Journal of Education, 30,* 531–553.

Chard, S.C. (1998). *The project approach: Making the curriculum come alive.* New York, NY: Scholastic.

Coleman, J.M., McTigue, E.M., & Smolkin, L.B. (2011). Elementary teachers' use of graphical representations in science teaching. *Journal of Science Teacher Education, 22,* 613–643.

Conezio, K., & French, L. (2002). Science in the preschool classroom: Capitalizing on children's fascination with the everyday world to foster language and literacy development. *Young Children, 57,* 12–18.

Culatta, B., Hall-Kenyon, K.M., & Black, S. (2010). Teaching expository comprehension skills in early childhood classrooms. *Topics in Language Disorders, 30*(4), 323–338.

Cummins, J. (2000). *Language, power and pedagogy: Bilingual children in the crossfire.* Buffalo, NY: Multilingual Matters.

Dickinson, D.K., & Tabors, P.O. (Eds.). (2001). *Beginning literacy with language: Young children learning at home and school.* Baltimore, MD: Paul H. Brookes Publishing Co.

Donovan, C.A., & Smolkin, L.B. (2002). Considering genre, content and visual features in the selection of trade books for science instruction. *The Reading Teacher, 55*(6), 502–520.

Dorfman, L., & Cappelli, R. (2007). *Mentor texts: Teaching writing through children's literature: K–6.* Portland, ME: Stenhouse.

Dorfman, L., & Cappelli, R. (2009). *Nonfiction mentor texts: Teaching informational writing through children's literature: K–8.* Portland, ME: Stenhouse.

Dreher, M.J., & Gray, J.L. (2009). Compare, contrast, comprehend: Using compare-contrast text structures with ELLs in K–3 classrooms. *The Reading Teacher, 63*(2), 132.

Duke, N.K. (2000). 3.6 minutes per day: The scarcity of informational texts in the first grade. *Reading Research Quarterly, 35,* 202–224.

Duke, N.K. (2010). The real world reading and writing U.S. children need. *Phi Delta Kappan, 91*(5), 68–71.

Duke, N., & Bennett-Armistead, S. (2003). *Reading & writing informational text in the primary grades.* New York, NY: Scholastic.

Duke, N.K., Halvorsen, A., & Knight, J.A. (2012). Building knowledge through informational text. In A.M. Pinkham, T. Kaefer, & S.B. Neuman (Eds.), *Knowledge development in early childhood: Sources of learning and classroom implications* (pp. 205–219). New York, NY: Guilford Press.

Duke, N., & Kays, J. (1998). "Can I say 'once upon a time'?": Kindergarten children developing knowledge of information book language. *Early Childhood Research Quarterly, 13,* 295–318.

Duke, N.K., Norman, R.R., Roberts, K.L., Martin, N.M., Knight, J.A., Morsink, P.M., & Calkins, S.L. (2013). Beyond concepts of print: Development of concepts of graphics in text, pre-K to Grade 3. *Research in the Teaching of English, 48,* 175–203.

Duke, N.K., & Pearson, P.D. (2002). Effective practices for developing reading comprehension. In A.E. Farstrup & S.J. Samuels (Eds.), *What research has to say about reading instruction* (3rd ed., pp. 205–242). Newark, DE: International Reading Association.

Elleman, A.M., Lindo, E.J., Morphy, P., & Compton, D.L. (2009). The impact of vocabulary instruction on passage-level comprehension of school-age children: A meta-analysis. *Journal of Research on Educational Effectiveness, 2*(1), 1–44.

Feuerstein, R., Falik, L.H., Feuerstein, F., & Bohacs, K. (2012). *A think-aloud and talk aloud approach to building language: Overcoming disability, delay and deficiency.* New York, NY: Teachers College Press.

Hall, K.M. (2007, December). *Dealing with informational text in the primary grades: Instructional strategies that improve young children's comprehension.* Paper presented at the National Reading Conference, Austin, TX.

Hall, K.M., & Sabey, B.L. (2007). Focus on the facts: How to use informational texts effectively in early elementary classrooms. *Early Childhood Education Journal, 35*(3), 261–268.

Hall, K.M., Sabey, B.L., & McClellan, M. (2005). Expository text comprehension: Helping primary grade teachers use expository texts to their full advantage. *Reading Psychology, 26*(3), 211–234.

Hall, K.M., Smith, L.K., & Losser, J.L. (2007, December). *Cooperative inquiry as professional development: Learning how to use literacy skills to enhance content learning.* Paper presented at the National Reading Conference, Austin, TX.

Hall-Kenyon, K.M., & Black, S. (2010). Learning from expository texts: Classroom-based strategies for promoting comprehension and content knowledge in the elementary grades. *Topics in Language Disorders, 30*(4), 339–349.

Harris, J., Golinkoff, R.M., & Hirsh-Pasek, K. (2010). Lessons from the crib for the classrooms: How children really learn vocabulary. In S.B. Neuman & D.K. Dickinson (Eds.), *Handbook of early literacy research* (pp. 49–66). New York, NY: Guilford Press.

Helm, J.H., & Katz, L.G. (2001). *Young investigators: The project approach in the early years.* New York, NY: Teachers College Press.

Iorio, N. (2005). *Bats.* New York, NY: HarperCollins.

Jeong, J.S., Gaffney, J.S., & Choi, J.O. (2010). Availability and use of informational text in second, third, and fourth grades. *Research in the Teaching of English, 44,* 435–456.

Justice, L.M., & Ezell, H.K. (2004). Print referencing: An emergent literacy enhancement strategy and its clinical applications. *Language, Speech, and Hearing Services in Schools, 35*(2), 185–193.

Justice, L.M., McGinty, A., Piasta, S.B., Kaderavek, J.N., & Fan, X. (2010). Print-focused read-alouds in preschool classrooms: Intervention effectiveness and moderators of child outcomes. *Language, Speech, and Hearing Services in Schools, 41*(4), 504–520.

Justice, L.M., Meier, J., & Walpole, S. (2005). Learning new words from storybooks: An efficacy study with at-risk kindergartners. *Language, Speech, and Hearing Services in Schools, 36,* 17–32.

Kalman, B. (2011). *Community helpers.* New York, NY: Crabtree Publishing.

Kamberelis, G. (1999). Genre development and learning: Children writing stories, science reports, and poems. *Research in the Teaching of English, 33,* 403–460.

Kelley, M.J., & Clausen-Grace, N. (2010). Guiding students through expository text with text feature walks. *The Reading Teacher, 64*(3), 191–195.

Lindeen, C.K. (2008). *Living and nonliving.* Mankato, MN: Capstone Press.

Maduram, I. (2000). "Playing possum": A young child's responses to information books. *Language Arts, 77*(5), 391–297.

Mantzicopoulos, P., & Patrick, H. (2011). Reading picture books and learning science: Engaging young children with informational text. *Theory into Practice, 50,* 269–276.

Mashburn, A.J., Pianta, R.C., Hamre, B.K., Downer, J.T., Barbarin, O.A., Bryant, D., . . . Howes, C. (2008). Measures of classroom quality in prekindergarten and children's development of academic, language, and social skills. *Child Development, 79*(3), 732–749.

McCabe, A. (2013). A comprehensive approach to building oral language in preschool: Prerequisites to literacy. In D. Barone & M. Mallette (Eds.), *Best practices in early literacy instruction* (pp. 26–41). New York, NY: Guilford Press.

Meyer, B.J.F. (1975). Identification of the structure of prose and its implications for the study of reading and memory. *Journal of Reading Behavior, 7,* 7–47.

Meyer, B.J.F., & Freedle, R.O. (1984). Effects of discourse type on recall. *American Educational Research Journal, 21,* 121–143.

Meyer, B.J.F., & Poon, L.W. (2001). Effects of structure training and signaling on recall of text. *Journal of Educational Psychology, 93*(1), 141–159.

Meyer, B.J.F., & Rice, G.E. (1982). The interaction of reader strategies and the organization of text. *Text: An Interdisciplinary Journal for the Study of Discourse, 2,* 155–192.

Mohr, K.A.J. (2006). Children's choices for recreational reading: A three-part investigation of selection preferences, rationales, and processes. *Journal of Literacy Research, 38*(1), 81–104.

Moll, L., Amanti, C., Neff, D., & Gonzales, N. (2005). Funds of knowledge for teaching: Using a qualitative approach to connect homes and classrooms. In N. Gonzalez, L.C. Moll, & C. Amanti (Eds.), *Funds of knowledge* (pp. 71–87). Mahwah, NJ: Erlbaum.

Morris, P.J., & Tchudi, S. (1996). *The new literacy: Moving beyond the 3Rs.* San Francisco, CA: Jossey-Bass.

Moses, A. (2013). What, when and how electronic media can be used in an early literacy classroom. In D. Barone & M. Mallette (Eds.), *Best practices in early literacy instruction* (pp. 96–118). New York, NY: Guilford Press.

Moss, B. (2008). The information text gap: The mismatch between non-narrative text times in basal readers and 2009 NAEP recommended guidelines. *Journal of Literacy Research, 40*(2), 201–219.

Nagy, W.E. (1988). *Teaching vocabulary to improve comprehension.* Newark, DE: International Reading Association.

Nagy, W.E., Herman, P., & Anderson, R.C. (1985). Learning words from context. *Reading Research Quarterly, 20*(2), 233–253.

National Association for the Education of Young Children. (2012). *Technology and interactive media as tools in early childhood programs serving children from birth through age 8: A position statement.* Washington, DC: Author.

National Governors Association Center for Best Practices & Council of Chief State School Officers. (2010). *Common Core State Standards for English language arts and literacy in history/social studies, science, and technical subjects.* Washington, DC: Authors. Retrieved from http://www.corestandards.org/assets/CCSSI_ELA%20Standards.pdf

Neuman, S.B. (2001). The role of knowledge in early literacy. *Reading Research Quarterly, 36*(4), 468–475.

Neuman, S.B., & Roskos, K. (2012). Helping children become more knowledgeable through text. *The Reading Teacher, 66*(3), 207–210.

Neuman, S.B., & Wright, T.S. (2013). *All about words.* New York, NY: Teachers College Press.

Norman, R.R. (2010). Picture this: Processes prompted by graphics in informational text. *Literacy Teaching and Learning, 14*(1–2), 1–39.

Nystrand, M. (2006). Research on the role of classroom discourse as it affects reading comprehension. *Research in the Teaching of English, 40*(4), 392–412.

Ogle, D., & Blachowicz, C.L.Z. (2002). Beyond literature circles: Helping children comprehend informational text. In C.C. Block & M. Pressley (Eds.), *Comprehension instruction: Research-based best practices* (pp. 259–274). New York, NY: Guilford Press.

Orsolini, M. (1993). "Because" in children's discourse. *Applied Psycholinguistics, 14,* 89–120.

Page, J., & Culatta, B. (1986). Incorporating relational vocabulary training into classroom procedures. *Journal of Childhood Communication Disorders, 9*(2), 157–168.

Pappas, C.C. (1993). Is narrative "primary"? Some insights from kindergarteners' pretend readings of stories and information books. *Journal of Reading Behavior, 25,* 97–129.

Pappas, C.C. (2006). The information book genre: Its role in integrating science literacy research and practice. *Reading Research Quarterly, 44*(2), 226–250.

Pappas, C.C., Varelas, M., Barry, A., & Rife, A. (2003). Dialogic inquiry around information texts: The role
of intertextuality in constructing scientific understandings in urban primary classrooms. *Linguistics and
Education, 13*(4), 435–482.

Paul, P., & Wang, Y. (2012). *Literate thought: Understanding comprehension and literacy.* Sudbury, MA: Jones
& Bartlett Learning.

Pentimonti, J., Zucker, T.A., Justice, L.M., & Kaderavek, J.N. (2010). Informational text use in preschool
classroom read-alouds. *The Reading Teacher, 63*(8), 656–665.

Pollard-Durodola, S.D., Gonzalez, J.E., Simmons, D.C., Davis, M.J., Simmons, L., & Nava-Walichowski,
M. (2011). Using knowledge networks to develop preschoolers' content vocabulary. *The Reading Teacher,
65*(4), 265–274.

Price, L.H., van Kleeck, A., & Huberty, C.J. (2009). Talk during book sharing between parents and preschool
children: A comparison between storybook and expository book conditions. *Reading Research Quarterly,
44*(2), 171–194.

Prokos, A. (2005). *We need insects.* Parsippany, NJ: Pearson.

Purcell-Gates, V., Duke, N.K., & Martineau, J.A. (2007). Learning to read and write genre-specific text: Roles
of authentic experience and explicit teaching. *Reading Research Quarterly, 42,* 8–45.

Ray, M.N., & Meyer, B.J. (2011). Individual differences in children's knowledge of expository text structures:
A review of literature. *International Electronic Journal of Elementary Education, 41*(1), 67–82.

Reese, E., Cox, A., Harte, S., & McAnally, H. (2003). Diversity in adult's styles of reading books to children. In A. van Kleeck, S.A. Stahl, & E.B. Bauer (Eds.), *On reading books to children: Parents and teachers*
(pp. 37–57). Mahwah, NJ: Erlbaum.

Reutzel, D.R., Smith, J.A., & Fawson, P.C. (2005). An evaluation of two approaches to teaching reading comprehension strategies in the primary years using science information texts. *Early Childhood Research
Quarterly, 36,* 468–475.

Riley-Ayers, S. (2013). Supporting language and literacy development in quality preschools. In D. Barone &
M. Mallette (Eds.), *Best practices in early literacy instruction* (pp. 58–78). New York, NY: Guilford Press.

Roberts, K.L., Norman, R.R., Duke, N.K., Morsink, P., Martin, N.M., & Knight, J.A. (2013). Diagrams, time-
lines, & tables, oh my! Concepts and comprehension of graphics. *The Reading Teacher, 61,* 12–24.

Snow, C., & Beals, D.E. (2006). Mealtime talk that supports literacy development. *New Directions for Child
and Adolescent Development, 111,* 52–66.

Sommers, S. (1981). Emotionality reconsidered: The role of cognition in emotional responsiveness. *Journal
of Personality and Social Psychology, 41*(3), 553–561.

Spyridakis, J.H., & Standal, T.C. (1987). Signals in expository prose: Effects on reading comprehension.
Reading Research Quarterly, 22, 285–298.

Squire, A.O. (2001). *Animal babies.* New York, NY: Children's Press.

Stahl, K. (2013). Reading to learn from the beginning: Comprehension instruction in the primary grades. In
D. Barone & M. Mallette (Eds.), *Best practices in early literacy instruction* (pp. 175–190). New York, NY:
Guilford Press.

Stahl, S.A., & Fairbanks, M.M. (1986). The effects of vocabulary instruction: A model-based meta-analysis.
Review of Educational Research, 56(1), 72–110.

Thomas, J., & Pagel, D. (2006). *The ultimate book of kid concoctions.* Nashville, TN: B & H Publishing.

Tough, J. (1985). *Listening to children talk: A guide to the appraisal of children's use of language.* London, UK:
Ward Lock Educational.

Tower, C. (2003). Genre development and elementary students' informational writing: A review of the literature. *Reading Research and Instruction, 42*(4), 14–39.

Ukrainetz, T. (2006). *Contextualized language intervention: Scaffolding pre K–12 literacy achievement.* Austin, TX: PRO-ED.

van Kleeck, A. (2006). Fostering inferential language during book sharing with preschoolers: A foundation
for later text comprehension strategies. In A. van Kleeck (Ed.), *Sharing books and stories to promote language and literacy* (pp. 269–318). San Diego, CA: Plural.

van Kleeck, A. (2008). Providing preschool foundations for later reading comprehension: The importance of
and ideas for targeting inferencing in storybook-sharing interventions. *Psychology in the Schools, 45*(7),
627–643.

Venezky, R.L. (2000). The origins of the present-day chasm between adult literacy needs and school literacy
instruction. *Scientific Studies of Reading, 4*(1), 19–39.

Watanabe, L., & Duke, N. (2013). Read all about I.T.! Informational text in the early childhood classroom. In D. Barone & M. Mallette (Eds.), *Best practices in early literacy instruction* (pp. 135–154). New York, NY: Guilford Press.

Weiss, D.M., & Sachs, J. (1991). Persuasive strategies used by preschool children. *Discourse Processes, 14,* 55–72.

Westby, C., Culatta, B., & Hall-Kenyon, K. (2015). Informational discourse: Teaching the main course of schooling. In T. Ukrainetz (Ed.), *School-age language intervention: Evidence-based practices.* Austin, TX: PRO-ED.

Williams, J.P., Hall, K.M., Lauer, K.D., Stafford, K.B., DeSisto, L.A., & deCani, J.S. (2005). Expository text comprehension in the primary grade classroom. *Journal of Educational Psychology, 97*(4), 538–550.

Wilson, K., Trainin, G., Laughridge, V., Brooks, D., & Wickless, M. (2011). Our zoo to you: The link between zoo animals in the classroom and science and literacy concepts in first-grade journal writing. *Journal of Early Childhood Literacy, 11*(3), 275–306.

Wilson, P.T., & Anderson, R.C. (1986). What they don't know will hurt them: The role of prior knowledge in comprehension. In J. Oransano (Ed.), *Reading comprehension from research to practice* (pp. 31–48). Hillsdale, NJ: Erlbaum.

Yopp, R.H., & Yopp, H.K. (2006). Informational text as read-alouds at school and home. *Journal of Literacy Research, 38*(1), 37–51.

Yopp, R.H., & Yopp, H.K. (2012). Young children's limited and narrow exposure to informational text. *The Reading Teacher, 64*(7), 480–490.

Zarnowski, M. (2006). *Making sense of history.* New York, NY: Scholastic.

Zwiers, J. (2008). *Building academic language: Essential practices for content classrooms.* Newark, DE: International Reading Association.

7

Special Education

A Guide to Working with
Preschool Children with Disabilities in
Inclusive Classrooms to Improve Comprehension

SABRA GEAR

Effective early interventions need to take into account child characteristics, family norms and expectations of the settings in which the child and family live, and the nature of interactions between the child and those with whom the child interacts.

—HESTER ET AL. (2004, P. 7)

Prereader comprehension and how it facilitates reading success must be priorities of teachers and families working with children with disabilities. Failure in learning to read and comprehend text is often related to early problems in cognitive and oral language processing (Hulme & Snowling, 2011; Justice, Mashburn, & Petscher, 2013). These early learning problems can be identified with appropriate assessments and considerably improved with effective instruction, early intervention, and progress monitoring (Buysse & Peisner-Feinberg, 2010; Fricke, Bowyer-Crane, Haley, Hulme, & Snowling, 2013). See Chapter 10 by Lynch and Lepola for a thorough discussion of comprehension skills assessment in preschool children.

The purpose of this chapter is to guide teachers and families working with preschool children with disabilities in inclusive environments to increase their opportunities for effective adult–child interactions. Effective interactions between children and those with whom they work are essential to improving comprehension. Literature on the use of inclusive practices, effective early intervention, and instruction for children with disabilities is included throughout the chapter because comprehension is necessary for long-term reading success (Fuchs et al., 2012; Kendeou, van den Broek, White, & Lynch, 2009). The chapter first discusses characteristics and prevalence of disabilities identified in young children and then provides a brief overview of challenges and practices related to inclusion. Finally, the chapter reviews research and recommendations for effective instruction and intervention to improve children's comprehension.

CHARACTERISTICS AND PREVALENCE OF DISABILITIES IN CHILDREN THAT CONTRIBUTE TO COMPREHENSION PROBLEMS

Snowling and Hulme (2012) proposed that reading comprehension problems should be classified under specific learning disabilities as a separate learning disorder from dyslexia. Children with reading comprehension problems may decode accurately and fluently, whereas children with dyslexia often lack fluency and misread words. Comprehension problems cause children to misunderstand the meaning of the words, sentences, or passages they read. Snowling and Hulme underscored that poor reading comprehension can be an outcome of a number of disabilities or disorders, such as speech or language impairment, autism, attention-deficit/hyperactivity disorder, and intellectual disabilities, among others.

Spencer, Quinn, and Wagner (2014) agree that poor reading comprehension unrelated to dyslexia presents a major problem, but their research hypothesis, which is based on the simple view of reading (Tunmer & Chapman, 2012), points to the influence of oral language comprehension of vocabulary as the general culprit. Spencer and colleagues found that less than 1% of first-, second-, and third-grade children with adequate decoding and vocabulary abilities scored poorly on measures of reading comprehension. Regardless of the specific classification or underlying causes, it is important to realize that most children with reading disabilities are neither identified nor provided with services until they are in the elementary grades (Fuchs et al., 2012). However, for preschool children with disabilities that presage later difficulties with reading comprehension, effective early intervention is the key to improving comprehension and preventing major reading problems later in school.

The prevalence of specific learning disabilities in the United States has stabilized over the past two decades relative to other disability categories, such as developmental delays or disabilities and other health impairments (Boyle et al., 2011; Hallahan, Keller, Martinez, Byrd, Gelman, & Fan, 2007). According to Boyle and her colleagues (2011), the prevalence of developmental delays or disabilities in U.S. children ages 3 through 17 *increased* by 17% over a 12-year period, based on annual data from the National Health Interview Surveys between 1997 and 2008. Three categories increased most: autism (289.5%); attention-deficit/hyperactivity disorder (33%; usually included in the category of "other health impairment"); and other developmental delays (24.7%). Two categories decreased: intellectual disability (1.5%) and moderate to profound hearing loss (31%). Boyle and colleagues (2011) proposed that more research, specialized services, and early intervention are needed to meet current challenges facing more young children with disabilities and their families.

Preschool children (from the ages of 3 through 5 years) with disabilities are usually found eligible for and may receive early childhood special education and related services under Part B of the Individuals with Disabilities Education Improvement Act (IDEA) of 2004 (PL 108-446). IDEA defines special education as "specially designed instruction, at no cost to parents, to meet the unique needs of a child with a disability" (§1401 [29]). Examples of related services that can be provided to help a child gain educational benefits include speech-language therapy, physical therapy, occupational therapy, audiology, hearing services, medical and nursing services, nutrition, counseling, psychological and transition services, and assistive technology and training.

There are 13 disability categories through which children may receive special education and related services: autism, deafblindness, developmental delay (physical, cognitive, communication, social, emotional, and/or adaptive), emotional disability, hearing impairment, intellectual disabilities, multiple disabilities, other health impairment, orthopedic impairment, specific learning disability, speech or language impairment, traumatic brain injury, and visual impairment. Most categories include eligibility criteria considered substantial risk factors for developing comprehension problems, including impairments in speech, language, and nonverbal communication; sensory, perceptual, physical, and motor functions; interpersonal relationships; psychosocial, emotional, and adaptive behavior; intellectual functioning; information processing; memory; reasoning; abstract thinking; judgment and problem solving; alertness and attention; hyperactivity; and acute and chronic health conditions (Data Accountability Center, 2013).

The numbers of preschool children identified for early childhood special education, along with their educational settings, are published through the U.S. Department of Education's (DOE) Office of Special Education Programs (OSEP) on the sponsored web site IDEA Data Center (http://www.ideadata.org). The state and national database is shared, in part, to inform providers so they might better plan for education services to meet the special needs of children with disabilities.

In 2012, throughout the 50 states and U.S. territories, 750,131 children from 3 to 5 years of age were served under IDEA. Speech or language impairment (SLI) was the largest disability category for which education services were provided to 335,128 children in the 3- to 5-year-old age group, representing over 24% of all children identified with SLI. The next largest disability category was developmental delay (DD), through which services were provided to 279,225 children, or 69% of the 3- to 5-year-olds. About 82% of children with disabilities, from ages 3 through 5, received services for either SLI or DD. The majority of children with disabilities, including 65% of 3- to 5-year-olds, were placed in general early childhood education programs with their peers without disabilities. About 26% of children, 3 through 5 years of age, were in a separate preschool class for children with disabilities. The remaining 9% of children in this age group were in residential facilities, outpatient clinics or hospitals, or at home.

Three main points can be made and supported by the data collected on more than 6.9 million individuals, birth through 21 years old, who received early intervention or special education in 2012. First, one of six children was under 5 years old and represented a large, highly vulnerable population of children with disabilities. Second, at least 75% of children with disabilities, birth through 5 years old, received services at home, in community-based settings, or in general education programs. In those inclusive settings, the primary caregiver or teacher is ideally situated to work with a special educator or related service provider (e.g., speech-language pathologist) on how to deliver effective early interventions. Third, over 87%, or at least 8 in 10 children (birth to 5 years old), are placed at risk of developing comprehension problems based on increasing prevalence of developmental delays or disabilities or speech-language impairment.

The information reviewed in this section shows increases in the prevalence and diverse characteristics of preschool children with disabilities requiring effective early intervention and special education for comprehension problems. The next step is to recognize a number of challenges to working with included children with disabilities and consider how inclusive practices can help teachers and families collaborate to improve child outcomes.

CHALLENGES TO WORKING WITH CHILDREN WITH DISABILITIES IN INCLUSIVE CLASSROOMS

With the beginning of early interventions in the 1970s, most children with disabilities from birth to age 3 have continued to learn and grow in their natural settings (Bricker, 2000; Kaiser & Hester, 1994). The majority of preschool children with disabilities from 3 to 5 years old are identified with speech-language impairment or developmental delays, both of which carry increased risk of poor comprehension-related outcomes. Because of strong individual differences among young children's background experiences, vocabulary knowledge, and language skills related to early comprehension development, early childhood educators face constant challenges in their efforts to design and deliver a high-quality early education to meet the needs of all children (Odom, Buysse, & Soukakou, 2011). As a subset of that changeable field, early childhood special education has responded with inclusive practices for children with disabilities from birth to age 8 (Raver, 2009). Although inclusive practices have become more family centered and community centered, teachers' roles have also broadened, encompassing increasingly dynamic, multifaceted functions related to these innovations (Raver, 2005). One of most far-reaching challenges is the full inclusion of young children with disabilities in early childhood programs that were designed primarily to serve children with typical development (Lieber, Horn, Palmer, & Fleming, 2008).

Definition of Inclusion

Whereas inclusion is not universally defined, four core features are expressed in the literature (e.g., Hunt, Soto, Maier, Liborion, & Bae, 2004; Idol, 2006). First, inclusion occurs when children with disabilities are members in the same settings as their peers who are typically developing. Second, included children receive the necessary services to accomplish the goals established by their education team, including parents and professionals. Third, the team assesses and makes educational decisions informed by monitoring progress toward expected outcomes (Hunt et al., 2004). Fourth, inclusion occurs along a continuum of the percentage of time spent in general education programs from no inclusion to full inclusion (Idol, 2006). Full inclusion is when children with disabilities spend 100% of their time in the general education program in which more than 50% of the children require no special education services (Guralnick, Neville, Hammond, & Conner, 2008). Partial inclusion is described as children spending most of the time in general education and part in a separate special education program (Guralnick et al., 2008; Idol, 2006). A reverse inclusion program includes some children without disabilities in a special education program that is designed primarily to serve children with disabilities (e.g., Rafferty & Griffin, 2005). However, both full inclusion and partial inclusion provide more opportunities for children with disabilities to be educated to the greatest extent possible with their peers without disabilities. Inclusion may be best described as a process of increasing opportunities for preschool children with disabilities to interact with others in their natural learning environments rather than a specific placement or classroom.

Inclusive Practices

Jackson attends Sunny View Child Development Center and receives individualized instruction using the *Carolina Curriculum for Preschoolers with Special Needs* (Johnson-Martin, Hacker, & Attermeier, 2004). Jackson is 4 years old and has a receptive language impairment that interferes with his understanding and ability to follow directions and engage in social conversations. Jackson also needs to learn to answer *wh*- questions (e.g., who, what, when, where, why, and how) to improve his ability to comprehend information within story narratives and expository texts. Jackson's individualized education program (IEP) includes a specific measurable goal to correctly answer three *wh*- questions when prompted by the teacher, with a minimum of five embedded learning opportunities throughout the day in the preschool setting. When discussing the habitats of frogs, Jackson's teacher asks him contextual questions, such as "Where do frogs live?," "What kinds of things do frogs like to eat?," and "How do frogs get from place to place?"

The development of inclusive practices that provide ample learning opportunities is one of the most salient determinants of a high-quality education for included children. Examples of inclusive practices involve authentic assessment and progress monitoring (Johnson-Martin et al., 2004; Raver, 2003, 2004), collaborative problem solving and planning for individualization (DeVore & Russell, 2007; Gable, Mostert, & Tonelson, 2004; Grisham-Brown, Pretti-Frontczak, Hawkins, & Winchell, 2009; Hunt et al., 2004), and teacher training for inclusion (Buysse & Hollingsworth, 2009; Campbell, Milbourne, Silverman, & Feller, 2005).

Accurate and consistent assessment, including comprehension measures, begins the teaching-learning cycle of providing effective, individualized instruction for children with disabilities. Johnson-Martin et al. (2004) developed a criterion-based authentic assessment and planning guide that can be embedded in daily routines for children with disabilities in inclusive programs. The assessment is used to track children's performance across measurable objectives, including comprehension (e.g., listening and following directions, answering questions about a story, memory of content and concepts, completing a story, imitating actions and words), using a predetermined indicator under given learning conditions and a specified number of opportunities to correctly respond to teacher-directed prompts. The *Carolina Curriculum for Preschoolers with Special Needs* was reorganized, aligning assessment items with inclusion class routines (Johnson-Martin et al., 2004). Systematic use of the tool and planning guide adds to its validity and reliability by assessing a child across a variety of inclusive settings (e.g., large group, small group, inside, outside, transitions).

Inclusion teachers need to monitor children's progress toward specific learning objectives on a frequent, regular basis during embedded classroom activities and routines. Raver (2003, 2004) developed a user-friendly group objective matrix, listing measurable skills or behaviors for each child in the group to learn across developmental domains (e.g., receptive and expressive language; cognitive, personal, social, and self-help; fine and gross motor). Using the matrix, teachers follow a three-step process: 1) identify the skills or behaviors that children need to be taught, 2) teach the skills or behaviors within and across the appropriate contexts in which the children will use them, and 3) decide when and how progress monitoring will occur and the acceptable criteria for mastering the skills or learned behaviors. A progress-monitoring portfolio (PMP; Stockall, Dennis, & Rueter, 2014) is one way to collect and share data with the team, providing evidence of achievement: indicators of language and learning growth over time with curriculum-based measurement (CBM; Deno, 1985, 2003), activity logs and anecdotal records of child observations (e.g., dramatic and sensory play, listening library, manipulative materials), and parental input about what the child knows and can do at home (e.g., interactive reading). Children with disabilities are best served when teachers use authentic assessments to collaboratively problem-solve and plan effective instruction for each included child.

A survey of 453 preschool classroom teachers from a number of U.S. states (Texas, Kentucky, and Ohio) by Grisham-Brown and Pretti-Frontczak (2003) found that most teachers reported a wide range of instructional planning times from a half-hour to 25 hours per week. Teachers reported using allotted instructional planning time for a number of other activities (e.g., talking with parents, attending meetings, completing paperwork). In the absence of intentional and collaborative planning for effective individualized instruction, learning opportunities for children with disabilities could be significantly lessened or thwarted.

On a 2-year mission to find long-range solutions to effectively plan, implement, and sustain the successful inclusion of preschool children with disabilities, DeVore and Russell (2007) began with a small collaborative team of three educators. Their team grew into a 20-member stakeholder group of educators, service providers, and family members working together to prepare children with disabilities for smoother transitions from an inclusive preschool program to the kindergarten classrooms. Although stakeholders remarked that collaborative problem solving facilitated successful inclusion, no specific child outcomes were reported in the study. Hunt and colleagues (2004) examined the effectiveness of collaborative teaming to support included children, reporting substantial gains in class participation and learning engagement for 3- to 4-year-olds with significant and severe disabilities. Their research assisted teachers to collaborate on a regular monthly basis with parents in creating Unified Plans of Support (UPS), which involved teaching language, communication, and social skills for included children. Gable and his colleagues (2004) also recognized the many challenges that professionals face in evaluating special education services on included children's learning outcomes. Thus they developed a model for assessing the collaborative problem-solving process and gathering information from stakeholders involved at all levels of inclusion.

Another way to improve learning for included children is through teacher training followed by classroom observations, measuring improved child learning environments and outcomes (Campbell et al., 2005). Campbell et al. used the Early Childhood Environment Rating Scale (ECERS; Harms, Clifford, & Cryer, 2005) as a pre- and postobservation tool, evaluating the Philadelphia Inclusion Network, a teacher-training program designed to help include infants and young children and to provide high-quality care for all children. Changes in environment quality ratings showed significant differences with medium effect sizes. Results suggested a relatively short (e.g., 3–4 month) training program can promote significant learning gains for children. Buysse and Hollingsworth (2009) proposed there is a need to create even stronger connections between the quality of inclusive early childhood programs and professional development. Their recommendations include the following: consider the characteristics of the adult learners and the professional development leaders; redefine the content consistent with current standards of program quality, practices, and measures; and employ evidence-based professional development practices infused with experiential learning opportunities to improve both program and inclusion quality.

In sum, inclusive practices such as authentic assessment to inform instruction, collaborative problem solving and planning, and efficacious teacher training offer workable solutions to including children with disabilities in ways that improve outcomes. The final section of this chapter offers effective intervention and instructional approaches for inclusion teachers and parents to use in addressing specific learning needs in pre-reader comprehension.

EFFECTIVE INSTRUCTION AND INTERVENTION FOR PRESCHOOL CHILDREN'S SPECIFIC LEARNING NEEDS IN COMPREHENSION

Effective instruction and early intervention for preschool children with disabilities is necessary to raise the trajectory of comprehension development and reading outcomes in a more positive direction. Despite persistent achievement gaps in language and literacy skills between children with disabilities and their typically developing peers, the onset of difficulties in language and prereading comprehension must be met with early identification, prompt intervention response, and high-quality instruction (Green, Terry, & Gallagher, 2014). Instruction and intervention need to be scientifically based at a minimum on moderate to strong evidence in the research literature that is appropriate to the developmental age of the child, considerate of the family's strengths and concerns, and sensitive to cultural and linguistic differences (Dunst & Trivette, 2009; Watson & Lee, 2014). Dunst and Trivette defined evidence-based practices as

> Informed by research findings demonstrating a (statistical or functional) relationship between the characteristics and consequences of a planned or naturally occurring experience or opportunity where the nature of the relationship directly informs what a practitioner or parent can do to produce a desired outcome. (2009, p. 41)

This final section is intended to inform teachers and parents about a selected segment of the research that includes statistical or functional relations between interventions and child outcomes that can lead to improvements in comprehension.

Language Interventions

In a randomized controlled trial, Fricke et al. (2013) investigated language intervention effectiveness for 4-year-old children ($N = 90$) with oral language impairments. The intervention improved children's development in language areas related to prereader comprehension and emergent reading with the following effect sizes and/or effect size ranges (Cohen's d): general language (0.80–0.83), vocabulary (0.83–1.18), narrative (0.30–0.39), listening comprehension (0.33–0.57), expressive naming (0.83–1.11), definitions (1.08–1.18), phonemic awareness (0.49), and letter knowledge (0.41).

Teaching assistants trained in fidelity of implementation procedures delivered the 30-week intervention through three teaching components: 1) multisensory techniques to teach children new vocabulary centered around common themes, such as growing, journeys, self-awareness, and time, and to teach parts of speech, such as nouns, verbs, adjectives, pronouns, prepositions, and question words; 2) group activities to teach children to create and act out narratives, identify and sequence narrative elements, teach story grammar, and use expressive language; and 3) a game to teach children to listen for sounds, such as phoneme blending and segmenting, and to match sounds to letters. Fricke and colleagues (2013) found the improvements on children's outcomes remained 6 months after the intervention ended. In fact, children's reading comprehension measures obtained 6 months postintervention were on par with their typically developing peers. This study reinforces that specifically targeted language intervention can have a positive impact on children's oral and reading comprehension.

Wilcox, Gray, Guimond, and Lafferty (2011) conducted a randomized controlled trial on the effectiveness of the preschool curriculum *Teaching Early Literacy and Language (TELL)* for children with developmental speech or language impairment. The TELL curriculum combines manipulative materials and structured activities infused throughout the inclusive preschool classroom daily schedule during circle, story, and snack times; teacher-led activities; and integrated writing. A modified sample from the curriculum's teaching practices is listed in Table 7.1. The sample represents some of the teaching practices that generally support and explicitly instruct children in their language learning in the preschool setting. Other teaching practices embedded within the curriculum address vocabulary, phonological awareness, concepts about print, and alphabet knowledge. The curriculum includes a supplement for teacher training to promote implementation and to maintain procedural fidelity.

Compared with their peers, children with speech and language impairments who were taught in the TELL curriculum classes made gains based on effect sizes (Cohen's *d*) of significantly higher mean length of utterances (0.82), indicating increases in sentence length and complexity and uses of new grammar and additional descriptors within their sentences. Furthermore, effect size gains were made in vocabulary, both expressive (1.32) and receptive (0.56). Children's language skills were incorporated into their daily conversations and narratives. Their ability to use and understand language improved significantly over and above the skills of children in classrooms where the traditional curriculum was taught. Wilcox and colleagues describe the TELL curriculum as a universally designed, collaborative project by researchers, regular and special education teachers, and speech-language pathologists whose mutual goals included meeting the unique needs of all preschoolers, including children with a broad range of developmental characteristics.

To summarize and emphasize the benefits of teacher- and parent-directed language interventions, recommendations by Sinatra, Zygouris-Coe, and Dasinger offer evidence-based activities (2012, pp. 347–348) shown to improve children's oral language and vocabulary development related to prereading comprehension.

- Provide opportunities for teachers and parents to read storybooks aloud, accompanied by richly worded explanations, questions, discussions, and presentations of new words before, during, and after reading. Use hands-on props that connect to the words in the story and children's real-world experiences. Provide parent training of vocabulary strategies to follow-up classroom lessons.

Table 7.1.   Teaching Early Literacy and Language (TELL) curriculum: Evidence-based practices in supporting and teaching language

Generally supportive practices of language	Explicit teaching of language
Use a slow rate of speech to support children's information processing and comprehension.	Use words to label immediately perceptible objects and events.
Use consistent gestures and signals that accompany speech to support comprehension.	Use words to demonstrate relations between and among objects (e.g., prepositional, directional, categorical concepts).
Simplify and rephrase questions and comments when they are not understood by the child.	Use embedded verbal definitions of words within phrases and sentences.
Engage the child's attention before providing directives.	Provide examples of attributes or adjectives of objects.
Interact with the child verbally and nonverbally at his or her eye level.	Demonstrate concepts with words, props, and manipulative materials.
Provide at least a 5-second wait time for the child to respond to questions and directives.	Preteach new vocabulary words.
Provide opportunities for the child to direct his or her peers or teachers in an activity.	Connect vocabulary words to the child's real-life experiences.
Provide wait time for the child to verbally request manipulative materials or turn taking.	Provide linguistic mapping to the child by noting the focus of his or her attention and using a sentence to label the object or define the meaning of the activity; the child's reply is not required.
Provide verbal options to the child when she or he is unable to answer a direct question.	Provide verbal recasts and expansions of children's language use.
Select and structure activities that require peer interactions.	Model the child's language use with explicit prompts—for example, "Say, 'Please help me.'"
Encourage peers to read to each other.	Provide the child with prompts and cues for more complex forms of language in conversations.
When it is appropriate, redirect the child to ask a peer for help when he or she requests adult assistance.	Provide the child with verbal and nonverbal story modeling.

Source: Wilcox, Gray, Guimond, and Lafferty (2011).

- Provide multiple opportunities for children's story retelling with verbal and nonverbal expressions of personal reactions, feelings, and understandings about how to use and repeat new words across multiple contexts.

- Provide nonverbal instruction, using pictures and real objects, body language and facial expressions, and gestures and pointing to storybook illustrations.

- Provide opportunities for embedding phonemic awareness, phonics, and word recognition strategies.

- Pronounce and demonstrate word spellings to highlight phonological and orthographic features of vocabulary words.

The literature demonstrates that early childhood special education models of prevention, early identification, and intervention may guide educators, parents, and other caregivers to develop children's prerequisite knowledge and skills needed to decipher the language clues and promote prereader comprehension. The subsection that follows includes activity-based intervention, representing another evidence-based teaching approach. This approach is intended to be implemented in collaboration with educators, parents, or other early childhood education providers across natural and inclusive settings, preschool classrooms, community child care centers, and the home.

Activity-Based Intervention

Rowan is a 4-year-old preschooler with a diagnosis of attention-deficit/hyperactivity disorder. He frequently gets distracted and talks about off-topic, extraneous, and unrelated details with assigned manipulatives (i.e., toys, dramatic and creative play materials) or picture prompts instead of answering teacher-directed questions related to those class activities. Consequently, Rowan also has difficulty learning to make inferences and predictions. He receives special education services for a developmental delay in his inclusion preschool classroom. His IEP includes a specific, measurable goal for Rowan to learn to make age-appropriate inferences and predictions, three times out of five given opportunities, that relate to daily classroom activities: dramatic play themes (e.g., going to the store), creative arts (e.g., finger painting), and storybook reading. For positive reinforcement, Rowan receives specific teacher praise plus a sticker to place on his chart, measuring progress toward the IEP goal, every time he makes an appropriate inference and/or prediction.

Activity-based intervention (ABI) is an effective teaching approach delivered in natural environments (Bricker, Pretti-Frontczak, & McComas, 1998; Macy, 2007; Pretti-Frontczak & Bricker, 2001). ABI can be used by teachers and family members to promote children's language, behavioral, and social-emotional functioning within adult–child interactions (Campbell & Sawyer, 2007; Campbell, Milbourne, Silverman, & Feller, 2005; Delaney & Kaiser, 2001; Hart, 2000; Raver, 2005; Sawyer & Campbell, 2012). Child language outcomes, including comprehension, can be improved through collaboratively planned activities centering on adult–child interactions that are tailored to individual needs. Authentic assessments linked to targeted child outcomes are gathered by direct observations within and across environments, providing data-driven decisions for multidisciplinary teams (Bagnato, McLean, Macy, & Neisworth, 2011; Macy, Bricker, & Squires, 2005; Raver, 2005). ABI empirical research has generally used single-subject methods to determine whether functional relations are established, suggesting effectiveness between the intervention and its intended outcomes (Barton & Fettig, 2013).

ABI involves social, behavioral, and cognitive principles that, when implemented effectively and with fidelity, increased children's engagement in meaningful daily activities that are planned to meet individual goals (Bricker et al., 1998; Macy, 2007). Four components are essential to success: 1) developing functional or educational goals for children that will generalize across time, settings, events, and people; 2) implementing planned, routine, and spontaneous child-initiated activities to achieve individual goals; 3) providing opportunities for children to receive immediate feedback (e.g., praise) and other positive reinforcements (e.g., rewards); and 4) providing a variety of opportunities for children to achieve their goals. Four studies are presented (Delaney & Kaiser, 2001; Gear, 2010; Hemmeter & Kaiser, 1994; Hester, Kaiser, Alpert, & Whiteman, 1996) that have demonstrated effective interventions particularly relevant to parent-supported child language learning and emergent reading skills. Teachers can also use this approach with their students with disabilities (or at risk for disabilities) and in their parent education programs.

Milieu teaching (Hemmeter & Kaiser, 1994) is a naturalistic approach, similar to ABI, used to improve children's language outcomes by incorporating environmental stimuli (e.g., toys and materials of interest to the child) as prompts for parent–child interactions and conversations. Children in the study by Hemmeter and Kaiser ranged in age from 2 to 5 years old and were identified with developmental delays (e.g., Down syndrome, pervasive developmental disorder, cerebral palsy, language and behavior delays) in receptive and expressive language. Parents in the study included three mothers and one father. Though effect sizes were not reported, parent-implemented intervention showed a functional relation to improvements in child language targets as noted through visual analysis of graphed single-subject data. Intervention consisted of the following strategic components: arranged environmental stimuli (e.g., using specific toys) to increase opportunities for children's learning and practicing of language, selected elements of responsive interactions (e.g., target words) to increase the frequency of parental language modeling, and increased semantic contingencies (e.g., specific feedback) to become more child centered. Hemmeter and Kaiser also recommended establishing mastery criteria upon child language measures rather than parent performance measures of strategy use. As parents learn to effectively use the intervention, they can generalize its use at home, in the car, on the playground, and in community settings (Hester, Baltodano, Gable, Tonelson, & Hendrickson, 2003).

In a follow-up study, Hester and her colleagues (1996) investigated training three research apprentices to teach six parents to use enhanced milieu language teaching strategies with their preschool-age children. All six parents reached criterion level and generalized their training to their home setting with their children. On the basis of established functional relations indicated by single-subject visual data analysis, each child showed modest improvements in using language and in his or her communications with parents at home.

In 2001, Delaney and Kaiser implemented a unique ABI approach focusing on four components to prevent children's learning and behavior problems: 1) balanced parent and child turn taking, 2) provision of meaningfully responsive parental feedback, 3) parent dialogue targeted to the child's language development level, and 4) parent expansion and modeling of new forms of language. Delaney and Kaiser found that parent–child communication and behavioral responsiveness improved. Children increased their utterances by about 30% from baseline through intervention (no effect sizes reported). Parents reported they felt secure in their abilities to better manage their children's behavior and language problems.

Building upon this foundation of ABI research, Gear (2010) conducted a study teaching six parents who lived in a culturally, linguistically, and ethnically diverse urban region to implement a dialogic reading, activity-based intervention with preschool children. Each of the six children (4–5 years old) was placed at risk for reading disabilities due to socioeconomic disadvantage or had a history of developmental delay (e.g., speech-language, social-emotional, attention-behavioral). With their preschool children, parents learned to implement two strategic researcher-developed interventions, titled PETER–PIPER, that were based on dialogic reading guidelines and prompts (Whitehurst et al., 1988; Ziolkowski & Goldstein, 2008). For a detailed explanation of the processes and outcomes of dialogic reading, please see Chapter 11 by Enz and Stamm. This particular ABI was designed to help children develop their phonological awareness and emergent reading skills. Embedded within each intervention strategy, using the mnemonic devices (e.g., PETER–PIPER), were opportunities for parents to reinforce children's oral language and comprehension skills. An overall description of the PETER–PIPER intervention strategies is presented in Table 7.2, and the strategy bookmarks used by parents are provided in Figure 7.1.

Single-subject research findings showed parents applied the strategies in dialogic reading with their children at the preschool center and at home with a relatively high degree of fidelity. The children showed gains (as determined by the percentage of all non-overlapping data converted to estimated Cohen's d effect sizes; see Parker & Hagan-Burke, 2007) in their responses to the following:

- Parental strategy prompting of picture labeling ($d = 1.20$)

- Predicting story events ($d = 1.00$)

- Ending (rhyming) sounds ($d = 1.60$)

- Talking about the tale (relating to experience; $d = 1.20$)

- Eliciting details ($d = 1.40$)

Table 7.2. PETER–PIPER phonodialogic reading strategies

	Intervention conditions	
Strategies	PETER (rhyming)	PIPER (alliteration)
Prompt picture labeling/story predicting.	P	P
Eavesdrop/evaluate; ask child to identify rhyming words; complete sentence with rhyming words.	E	
Identify initial sounds; ask the child to complete word or sentence with the initial sound of words.		I
Talk about the tale by relating story events to child's experiences.	T	
Pose purposeful *wh-* questions about the story events.		P
Expand/elaborate on child responses, eliciting the child for more story details.	E	E
Reinforce/praise correct responses.	R	R

From Gear, S.B. (2010). *Parent interventionists in phonodialogic emergent reading with preschool children: PIPER training manual* (Doctoral dissertation). Retrieved from Old Dominion University Libraries database. (odu.b3257812)

- Identifying initial (alliteration) sounds ($d = 1.70$)

- Posing *wh-* questions ($d = 0.90$)

Limitations in the study that must be mentioned are that phonological awareness was the primary dependent variable outcome measured, the study had a small sample size, and the intervention was only 8 weeks in duration. The following parent-implemented strategy prompts demonstrated an increase from the largest to the smallest mean percentage of change:

- Ending sounds (748%)

- Reinforcement and praise (393%)

- Initial sounds (269%)

- Predicting story events (267%)

- Picture labeling (110%)

- Relating story to experience (58%)

- *Wh-* questions (17%)

- Eliciting story details (14%)

However, the study adds to the evidence for including ABI as one way to improve children's emergent reading and expands the opportunities for teachers and parents to facilitate prereader comprehension.

ABI offers an effective intervention approach to building children's prereading abilities supported by a rigorous measurement system based on behavioral principles (Hancock, Kaiser, & Delaney, 2002; Macy, 2007). Losardo and Bricker (1994) found that ABI was instrumental in generalizing children's language abilities significantly over direct

PETER (rhyming)	PIPER (alliteration)
Prompt picture labeling and **predicting** events.	**Prompt picture labeling** and **predicting** events.
Eavesdrop and **evaluate** your child's responses. Point to the **rhyming words**. **Pause** for your child to **fill in the rhymes**.	**Identify initial letter sounds.** **Pause** for your child to complete the word or sound.
Talk about the **tale** and how story **relates** to life experiences.	**Pose purposeful questions** "who, what, when, where, why, and how" to **prompt** your child's responses.
Expand and **elaborate** on your child's responses. Elicit more **details** about the story.	**Expand** and **elaborate** on your child's responses Elicit more **details** about the story.
Reinforce your child's right responses with **positive remarks** and **praise**. Repeat the reading.	**Reinforce** your child's right responses with **positive remarks** and **praise**. Repeat the reading.

Figure 7.1.   PETER–PIPER intervention strategy bookmarks. (From Gear, S.B. [2010]. *Parent interventionists in phonodialogic emergent reading with preschool children: PIPER training manual* [Doctoral dissertation]. Retrieved from Old Dominion University Libraries database. [odu.b3257812])

instruction. ABI has enhanced the quality of parent–child interaction by teaching parents to be more responsive to children's initial learning efforts, leading to increases in participation in daily learning activities and routines (Dunst et al., 2001). Thus ABI combined with early prereading strategies may help teachers and parents improve children's comprehension, among other early reading competencies, through everyday opportunities to play and read together (see Chapter 3 by Newman, Dickinson, Hirsh-Pasek, and Golinkoff). Given the strong relation between children's language and cognition, the next section describes how cognitive strategy instruction complements language intervention in improving comprehension.

Cognitive Strategy Instruction

Lynlee is a 5-year-old preschooler who produces frequent speech articulation errors and is delayed in her oral vocabulary development and prereader comprehension. She is undergoing a comprehensive evaluation to determine eligibility for special education and related services (e.g., speech-language services). Lynlee's preschool teacher in the inclusion classroom is implementing cognitive strategy instruction to help Lynlee expand her oral vocabulary and develop her comprehension skills. For example, prior to telling or reading a story to Lynlee, her teacher identifies the new vocabulary words in the story and embeds definitions and context clues to the meanings of the new words within the story. As Lynlee's teacher tells or reads the story, the teacher systematically pauses to ask inferential or prediction questions and provides verbal prompts for story retelling and making connections to personal life experiences.

The comprehension process requires that children construct mental models to be able to understand the meaning of the content that is presented, sensed, and perceived and to which they have attended and recalled (van den Broek, Kendeou, Lousberg, & Visser, 2011). For a review of the comprehension process, see Chapter 3 by Newman, Dickinson, Hirsh-Pasek, and Golinkoff.

Children begin developing their cognitive skills to process meaning before they learn to read and decode text, and parents and teachers can use cognitive strategy instruction (CSI) to promote comprehension. CSI includes multiple-component solutions to the specific problems children might face in developing comprehension, such as working memory, executive function, attention, and inhibition among others involved in understanding meaning (Cartwright, 2012). For a more detailed analysis of executive function, see Chapter 9 by Cartwright and Guajardo. Although there are areas of overlap with language interventions, as in building vocabulary knowledge, the focus of CSI is on teaching children solutions that are aligned with specific cognitive areas of difficulty (Watson, Gable, Gear, & Hughes, 2012).

For example, research by van den Broek and colleagues (2011) found children's best answers to causally connected questions within narratives occurred when the questions were posed during listening to the narrative, not afterward. In a cross-age comparison study between the 2- to 3-year-old prereader group ($N = 40$) and the young reader group of 8- to 9-year-old children in third grade ($N = 42$), both groups of children gained higher comprehension scores for questions asked during listening rather than after listening to the narratives. This research suggests the value of using questioning during listening comprehension for prereaders and young readers. One practical implication for teachers and parents would be to provide strategy instruction, focusing on one skill or task at a time (van den Broek et al., 2011).

Comprehension strategy instruction has been shown to help young children at risk for reading disabilities due to low socioeconomic and cultural or linguistic differences make gains in listening comprehension (DeBruin-Parecki & Squibb, 2011). Thirty children across two public prekindergarten classes participated in an 8-week comprehension curriculum that incorporated four strategy categories: 1) connecting the narrative content to children's background knowledge; 2) elaborating on understood narrative content to make predictions and forecast events; 3) retelling the sequence of key elements in the narrative; and 4) preteaching new words from the narrative, especially rare and unknown words, linking new vocabulary to well-known concepts and personal experiences (DeBruin-Parecki & Squibb, 2011, pp. 45–47). Across categories and on total comprehension scores, children made statistically significant gains over the 8-week intervention program. Implications for educators include more training and coaching for preschool and elementary teachers to use comprehension strategy instruction for prereaders as part of the continuum of literacy, incorporating strategy instruction alongside traditional strategies to assist poor comprehenders, and observing and supporting teacher candidates in their field placements to implement comprehension strategy instruction. Chapter 1 by DeBruin-Parecki and Pribesh reviews the detailed descriptions and analyses on comprehension strategy instruction.

CONCLUSION

Teachers and family members are encouraged to use the information presented in this chapter as one resource on the path to identifying child strengths and special needs, establishing goals, and providing and monitoring early intervention and long-term instructional strategies for improving children's comprehension. Within this chapter, information about the current increasing prevalence and diverse characteristics of disabilities is provided as a rationale and impetus for action. Indeed, teachers and parents are well situated to work together on determining specific comprehension problem areas for individual children (e.g., oral language, cognitive processes) and planning to use the most efficacious and feasible evidence-based solutions. Teachers must be well trained in methods of instruction that will engage and increase participation of included children with disabilities and in the implementation and progress monitoring of effective strategies to increase prereader comprehension. Those reviewed in this chapter include language-based interventions, ABI, and cognitive and comprehension strategy instruction. It should be cautioned that too much emphasis on the interventions or strategies themselves can detract from the intended purpose, goals, and positive outcomes for children. First and foremost, the absolute priority of researchers and practitioners must be placed upon enhancing children's construction of meaningful interactions with family, teachers, peers, and the learning materials arranged in their natural environments.

REFERENCES

Alpert, C.L., & Kaiser, A.P. (1992). Training parents to do milieu language teaching with their language-impaired preschool children. *Journal of Early Intervention, 16,* 31–52.

Bagnato, S.J., McLean, M., Macy, M., & Neisworth, J.T. (2011). Identifying instructional targets for early childhood via authentic assessment: Alignment of professional standards and practice-based evidence. *Journal of Early Intervention, 33,* 243–253. doi:10.1177/1053815111427565

Barton, E.E., & Fettig, A. (2013). Parent-implemented interventions for young children with disabilities: A review of fidelity features. *Journal of Early Intervention, 35,* 194–219. doi:10.1177/1053815113504625

Boyle, C.A., Boulet, S., Schieve, L.A., Cohen, R.A., Blumberg, S.J., Yeargin-Allsopp, M. . . . Kogan, M.D. (2011). Trends in the prevalence of developmental disabilities in US children, 1997–2008. *Pediatrics, 127,* 1034–1104. doi:10.1542/peds.2010-2989

Bricker, D.D. (2000). Inclusion: How the scene has changed. *Topics in Early Childhood Special Education, 20,* 14–19.

Bricker, D.D., Pretti-Frontczak, K.L., & McComas, N.R. (1998). *An activity-based approach to early intervention* (2nd ed.). Baltimore, MD: Paul H. Brookes Publishing Co.

Buysse, V., & Hollingsworth, H.L. (2009). Program quality and early childhood inclusion: Recommendations for professional development. *Topics in Early Childhood Special Education, 29,* 119–128. doi:10.1177/0271121409332233

Buysse, V., & Peisner-Feinberg, E. (2010). Recognition and response: Response to intervention for PreK. *Young Exceptional Children, 13,* 2–13.

Campbell, P., Milbourne, S., Silverman, C., & Feller, N. (2005). Promoting inclusion by improving child care quality in inner-city programs. *Journal of Early Intervention, 28,* 65–79.

Campbell, P.H., & Sawyer, L.B. (2007). Supporting learning opportunities in natural settings through participation-based services. *Journal of Early Intervention, 29,* 287–305. doi:10.1177/105381510702900402

Cartwright, K.B. (2012). Insights from cognitive neuroscience: The importance of executive function for early reading development and education. *Early Education and Development, 23,* 24–36.

Data Accountability Center. (2013). *IDEA, Part B, data dictionary* (rev. ed.). Rockville, MD: Westat. Retrieved from https://tacc-epic.s3.amazonaws.com/uploads/product/3621/32527d78417311e38cbaae9ee814a6e3/bdatadictionary_final_1-23-13.pdf?AWSAccessKeyId=AKIAIMS3GHWZEDKKDRDQ&Expires=1390421463&Signature=HA3vMiOk%2B40nFvKFey8A8jZp%2B%2FI%3D

DeBruin-Parecki, A., & Squibb, K. (2011). Promoting at-risk preschool children's comprehension through research-based strategy instruction. *Reading Horizons, 51*(1), 41–62.

Delaney, E.M., & Kaiser, A.P. (2001). The effects of teaching parents blended communication and behavior support strategies. *Behavioral Disorders, 26*(2), 93–116.

Deno, S.L. (1985). Curriculum-based measurement: The emerging alternative. *Exceptional Children, 52,* 219–232.

Deno, S.L. (2003). Developments in curriculum-based measurement. *Journal of Special Education, 37,* 184–192.

DeVore, S., & Russell, K. (2007). Early childhood education and care for children with disabilities: Facilitating inclusive practice. *Early Childhood Education Journal, 35,* 189–198.

Dunst, C.J. (2012). Parapatric speciation in the evolution of early intervention for infants and toddlers with disabilities and their families. *Topics in Early Childhood Special Education, 21,* 208–215. doi:10.1177/0271121411426904

Dunst, C.J., Bruder, M.B., Trivette, C.M., Hamby, D., Raab, M., & McLean, M. (2001). Characteristics and consequences of everyday natural learning opportunities. *Topics in Early Childhood Special Education, 21,* 68–92.

Dunst, C.J., & Trivette, C.M. (2009). Using research evidence to inform and evaluate early childhood intervention practices. *Topics in Early Childhood Special Education, 29,* 40–52. doi:10.1177/0271121408329227

Fricke, S., Bowyer-Crane, C., Haley, A.J., Hulme, C., & Snowling, M. (2013). Efficacy of language intervention in the early years. *Journal of Child Psychology and Psychiatry, 54,* 280–290. doi:10.1111/jcpp.12010

Fuchs, D., Compton, D.L., Fuchs, L.S., Bryant, J., Hamlett, C.L., & Lambert, W. (2012). First-grade cognitive abilities as long-term predictors of reading comprehension and disability status. *Journal of Learning Disabilities, 45,* 217–231. doi:10.1177/0022219412442154

Gable, R.A., Mostert, M.P., & Tonelson, S.W. (2004). Assessing professional collaboration in schools: Knowing what works. *Preventing School Failure, 48*(3), 4–8.

Gear, S. (2010). *Parent interventionists in phonodialogic emergent reading with preschool children.* (Unpublished doctoral dissertation.). Old Dominion University, Publication No. AAT 3428820.

Green, K.B., Terry, N.P., & Gallagher, P.A. (2014). Progress in language and literacy skills among children with disabilities in inclusive Early Reading First classrooms. *Topics in Early Childhood Special Education, 33,* 249–259. doi:10.1177/0271121413477498

Grisham-Brown, J., & Pretti-Frontczak, K. (2003). Using planning time to individualize instruction for pre-schoolers with special needs. *Journal of Early Intervention, 26,* 31–46.

Grisham-Brown, J., Pretti-Frontczak, K., Hawkins, S.R., & Winchell, B.N. (2009). Addressing early learning standards for all children within blended preschool classrooms. *Topics in Early Childhood Special Education, 29,* 131–142. doi:10.1177/0271121409333796

Guralnick, M. (2011). Why early intervention works: A systems perspective. *Infants and Young Children, 24,* 6–28. doi:10.1097/IYC.0b013e3182002cfe

Guralnick, M.J., Neville, B., Hammond, M.A., & Connor, R. (2008). Continuity and change from full-inclusion early childhood programs through the early elementary period. *Journal of Early Intervention, 30,* 237–250.

Hallahan, D.P., Keller, C.E., Martinez, E.A., Byrd, E.S., Gelman, J.A., & Fan, X. (2007). How variable are interstate prevalence rates of learning disabilities and other special education categories? A longitudinal comparison. *Exceptional Children, 73,* 136–146.

Hancock, T.B., Kaiser, A.P., & Delaney, E.M. (2002). Teaching parents of preschoolers at high risk: Strategies to support language and positive behavior. *Topics in Early Childhood Special Education, 22,* 191–222.

Harms, T., Clifford, R.M., & Cryer, D. (2005). *Early Childhood Environment Rating Scale* (rev. ed.). New York, NY: Teachers College Press.

Hart, B. (2000). A natural history of early language experience. *Topics in Early Childhood Special Education, 20,* 28–32.

Hemmeter, M.L., & Kaiser, A.P. (1994). Enhanced milieu teaching: Effects of parent-implemented language intervention. *Journal of Early Intervention, 18,* 269–289.

Hester, P.P., Baltodano, H.M., Gable, R.A., Tonelson, S.W., & Hendrickson, J. (2003). Early intervention with children at risk of emotional/behavioral disorders: A critical examination of research methodology and practices. *Education and Treatment of Children, 26,* 362–381.

Hester, P.P., Baltodano, H.M., Hendrickson, J.M., Tonelson, S.W., Conroy, M., & Gable, R.A. (2004). Lessons learned from research on early intervention: What teachers can do to prevent children's behavior problems. *Preventing School Failure, 49,* 5–10.

Hester, P.P., Kaiser, A.P., Alpert, C.L., & Whiteman, B. (1996). The generalized effects of training trainers to teach parents to implement milieu teaching. *Journal of Early Intervention, 20,* 30–51. doi:10.1177/105381519602000105

Hulme, C., & Snowling, M. (2011). Children's reading comprehension difficulties: Nature, causes, and treatments. *Current Directions in Psychological Science, 20,* 139–142. doi:10.1177/0963721411408673

Hunt, P., Soto, G., Maier, J., Liboiron, N., & Bae, S. (2004). Collaborative teaming to support preschoolers with severe disabilities who are placed in general education early childhood programs. *Topics in Early Childhood Special Education, 24,* 123–142.

Idol, L. (2006). Toward inclusion of special education students in general education: A program evaluation of eight schools. *Remedial and Special Education, 27,* 77–94.

Individuals with Disabilities Education Improvement Act (IDEA) of 2004, PL 108-446, 20 U.S.C. §§ 1400 *et seq.* Retrieved from http://www.copyright.gov/legislation/pl108-446.pdf

Johnson-Martin, N.M., Attermeier, S.M., & Hacker, B.J. (2004). *The Carolina Curriculum for Infants and Toddlers with Special Needs* (3rd ed). Baltimore, MD: Paul H. Brookes Publishing Co.

Justice, L., Mashburn, A., & Petscher, Y. (2013). Very early language skills of fifth-grade poor comprehenders. *Journal of Research in Reading, 36,* 172–185. doi:10.111/j.1467-9817.2011.01498x

Kaiser, A., & Hester, P. (1994). Generalized effects of enhanced milieu teaching. *Journal of Speech & Hearing Research, 6,* 1320–1341.

Kendeou, P., van den Broek, P., White, M.J., & Lynch, J.S. (2009). Predicting reading comprehension in early elementary school: The independent contributions of oral language and decoding skills. *Journal of Educational Psychology, 101,* 765–778. doi:10.1037/a0015956

Lieber, J., Horn, E., Palmer, S., & Fleming, K. (2008). Access to the general education curriculum for preschoolers with disabilities: Children's school success. *Exceptionality, 16,* 18–32. doi:10.1080/09362830701796776

Losardo, A., & Bricker, D.D. (1994). Activity-based intervention and direct instruction: A comparison study. *American Journal on Intellectual disability, 98,* 744–765.

Lynch, J.S., van den Broek, P., Kremer, K.E., Kendeou, P., White, M.J., & Lorch, E.P. (2008). The development of narrative comprehension and its relation to other early reading skills. *Reading Psychology, 29,* 327–365. doi:10.1080/02702710802165416

Macy, M. (2007). Theory and theory-driven practices of activity based intervention. *Journal of Early and Intensive Behavior Intervention, 4*(3), 561–585.

Macy, M.G., Bricker, D.D., & Squires, J.K. (2005). Validity and reliability of a curriculum-based assessment approach to determine eligibility for Part C services. *Journal of Early Intervention, 28,* 1–16. doi:10.1177/105381510502800101

Odom, S.L., Buysse, V., & Soukakou, E. (2011). Inclusion for young children with disabilities: A quarter century of research perspectives. *Journal of Early Intervention, 33,* 344–356. doi:10.1177/1053815111430094

Parker, R.I., & Hagan-Burke, S. (2007). Useful effect size interpretation for single case research. *Behavior Therapy, 38,* 95–105.

Pretti-Frontczak, K.L., & Bricker, D.D. (2001). Use of the embedding strategy by early childhood education and early childhood special education teachers. *Infant and Toddler Intervention: The Transdisciplinary Journal, 11,* 111–128.

Rafferty, Y., & Griffin, K.W. (2005). Benefits and risks of reverse inclusion for preschoolers with and without disabilities: Perspectives of parents and providers. *Journal of Early Intervention, 27,* 173–192.

Raver, S.A. (2003). Keeping track: Routine-based instruction and monitoring. *Young Exceptional Children, 6,* 12–20.

Raver, S.A. (2004). Monitoring child progress in early childhood special education settings. *TEACHING Exceptional Children, 36,* 52–57.

Raver, S.A. (2005). Using family-based practices for young children with special needs in preschool programs. *Childhood Education, 82,* 9–13.

Raver, S.A. (2009). *Early childhood special education—0 to 8 years: Strategies for positive outcomes.* Upper Saddle River, NJ: Pearson.

Sawyer, B.E., & Campbell, P.H. (2012). Early interventionists' perspectives on teaching caregivers. *Journal of Early Intervention, 34,* 104–124. doi:10.1177/1053815112455363

Sinatra, R., Zygouris-Coe, V., & Dasinger, S.B. (2012). Preventing a vocabulary lag: What lessons are learned from research. *Reading and Writing Quarterly: Overcoming Learning Difficulties, 28,* 333–357. doi:10.1080/10573569.2012.702040

Snowling, M.J., & Hulme, C. (2012). Annual research review: The nature and classification of reading disorders—a commentary on proposals for DSM-5. *Journal of Child Psychology and Psychiatriy, 53,* 593–607. doi:10.1111/j.1469-7610.2011.02495.x

Spencer, M., Quinn, J.M., & Wagner, R.K. (2014). Specific reading comprehension disability: Major problem, myth, or misnomer? *Learning Disabilities Research & Practice, 29,* 3–9.

Stockall, N., Dennis, L.R., & Rueter, J.A. (2014). Developing a progress monitoring portfolio for children in early childhood special education programs. *TEACHING Exceptional Children, 46*(3), 32–40.

Tunmer, W.E., & Chapman, J.W. (2012). The simple view of reading redux: Vocabulary knowledge and the independent components hypothesis. *Journal of Learning Disabilities, 45,* 453–466. doi:10.1177/0022219411432685

van den Broek, P., Kendeou, P., Lousberg, S., & Visser, G. (2011). Preparing for reading comprehension: Fostering text comprehension skills in preschool and early elementary school children. *International Electronic Journal of Elementary Education, 4,* 259–268.

Watson, S.M.R., Gable, R.A., Gear, S.B., & Hughes, K.C. (2012). Evidence-based strategies for improving the reading comprehension of secondary students: Implications for students with learning disabilities. *Learning Disabilities Research and Practice, 27,* 79–89. doi:10.1111/j.1540-5826.2012.00353x

Watson, S.M.R., & Lee, T. (2014). *Virginia's guidelines for educating students with specific learning disabilities.* Richmond, VA: Virginia Department of Education. Retrieved from http://www.doe.virginia.gov/special_ed/disabilities/learning_disability/learning_disabilities_guidelines.pdf

Whitehurst, G.J., Falco, F.L., Lonigan, C.J., Fischel, J.E., DeBaryshe, B.D., Valdez-Menchaca, M.C., & Caulfield, M. (1988). Accelerating language development through picture book reading. *Developmental Psychology, 24,* 552–559.

Wilcox, M.J., Gray, S.I., Guimond, A.B., & Lafferty, A.E. (2011). Efficacy of the *TELL* language and literacy curriculum for preschoolers with developmental speech and/or language impairment. *Early Childhood Research Quarterly, 26,* 278–294. doi:10.1016/j.ecresq.2010.12.003

Ziolkowski, R.A., & Goldstein, H. (2008). Effects of embedded phonological awareness intervention during repeated book reading on preschool children with language delays. *Journal of Early Intervention, 31*(1), 67–90.

8

Multilingualism in Early Childhood

Comprehension Development, Assessment, and Intervention

SANDRA BARRUECO AND GERALDINE M. FERNÁNDEZ

Recent decades have witnessed a growth in multilingualism across the country. From an estimated 11% in 1980 to roughly 20% in 2010, the percentage of individuals over the age of 5 who begin to develop two or more languages from an early age is indisputably on the rise in the United States (Grosjean, 2010; Ryan, 2013). Among the youngest portion of the population (upon whom this book is centered), an even greater proportion are multilingual. Such impacts are particularly noted within low-income communities, which are disproportionally composed of immigrant and ethnocultural communities. Federally funded preventive intervention programs for young impoverished children, such as Early Head Start and Head Start, report that approximately 40% of participants' families speak a language other than English at home (Administration for Children and Families, 2006, 2009). Such statistics underscore the importance of building a thorough knowledge base about multilingualism among young children, both in the empirical field as well as in the care, education, and health fields.

A full review of the multilingual literature is beyond the scope of the present chapter (for thorough discussions, see Goldstein, 2012; Paradis, Genesee, & Crago, 2011). Yet highlights from the field are incorporated in order to provide readers with an integrated and contextualized understanding of the interrelationship of multilingualism and the development of comprehension among young children. Notably, few studies directly examine comprehension skills, particularly in emergent literacy; most investigations with multilingual children assess lexical and/or alphabetic abilities. As these studies contribute to a deeper understanding of comprehension, they are incorporated into the chapter. To the extent possible, studies examining multilingual comprehension in early childhood are also underscored.

The chapter begins by grounding the reader in the terminology of the field, particularly as it has shifted over time. A conceptual model of comprehension among young multilingual children is subsequently presented that unpacks the elements intrinsic to multilingual comprehension; the model also describes the multiplicity of factors contributing to development in this area. The remainder of the chapter incorporates key considerations related to assessment and intervention approaches, as well as recommendations for future research, practice, and policy endeavors.

MULTILINGUALISM

A myriad of terms have been used to refer to children learning more than one language, including *bilinguals, multilinguals, emergent bilinguals, heritage language speakers, simultaneous and sequential language learners, language minority, English as a second language (ESL) learners,* and *limited English proficient (LEP),* among others (Leos, 2014). In more recent years, the terms *dual language learners (DLLs)* and *English language learners (ELLs)* have gained in popularity in the early childhood and general educational fields, respectively (Nemeth, 2014). DLL can be considered an umbrella term to describe children who are in the process of learning two languages, regardless of their level of proficiency in each one (Castro, García, & Markos, 2013; Espinosa, 2013; Paradis et al., 2011). Thus this approach encompasses children with varying proficiencies in both languages as well as children who are in the process of developing English language abilities. In turn, ELL is a subclassification under DLL that identifies children at their earliest stages of English acquisition (Administration for Children and Families, 2008). Within the school-age population, ELLs may qualify for legally required educational support services (Iglesias & Rojas, 2012; Leos, 2014).

Variation in children's development of multiple languages has often been incorporated in theoretical conceptualizations throughout the years (Bloomfield, 1933; Butler & Hakuta, 2004; Grosjean, 1989, 2010; Haugen, 1953; MacLeod, Fabiano-Smith, Boegner-Page, & Salome Fontolliet, 2013). Bilingualism was initially conceptualized as the attainment of complete language fluency within *and* across both languages (Bloomfield, 1933). Later models incorporated the potential for uneven abilities across languages (Grosjean, 1989; Grosjean, 2010), as well as the existence of various types and degrees of multilingualism (Bialystok, 2001; Dopke, 1992). As is discussed throughout the course of this chapter, the degree to which an individual develops linguistic and literacy competencies in each language is dependent on a range of factors. Thus bilingualism is a dynamic and multidimensional phenomenon (Grosjean, 2010).

A critique that can be directed to many of the present models and terminologies (including *DLLs)* is the exclusion in consideration of children who are developing abilities in more than two languages. Immigrant families from the southern states of Mexico may speak indigenous languages along with Spanish; now living in the United States, these families have burgeoning English proficiency. The immigration of families speaking indigenous languages from Mexico is on the rise (U.S. Department of Labor, 2005). In turn, children of farm workers from Haiti, Africa, or other nations may attend Migrant and Seasonal Head Starts where English and Spanish are more likely to be spoken due to the high prevalence of Hispanics in the industry (U.S. Department of Labor, 2005). Given these considerations, the terms *multilingualism* and *multilingual children* are utilized in the present chapter. When applicable, greater specificity is provided and the terms *ELLs, DLLs, sequential bilingual,* and *simultaneous bilingual* are utilized.

CONCEPTUAL MODEL: THE DEVELOPMENT OF COMPREHENSION AMONG YOUNG MULTILINGUAL CHILDREN

As emphasized throughout this book, comprehension is a critical component of young children's development, both as a medium for subsequent growth as well as an important outcome in its own right. The act of comprehension is made up of multiple components, including the abilities of young children to identify words; assign meaning to words; understand grammatical rules and social norms; and, ultimately, gather meaning from combinations of words, format, and presentation. Thus lexical, semantic, syntactic, and contextual cues are key agents in the development of comprehension (see Chapter 2 by Coyne, Neugebauer, Ware, McCoach, and Madura; Chapter 4 by van Kleeck; and Chapter 10 by Lynch and Lepola).

Multilingual children undertake this process within each language as well as across languages (see Figure 8.1). To some degree, the task may be facilitated by cross-linguistic

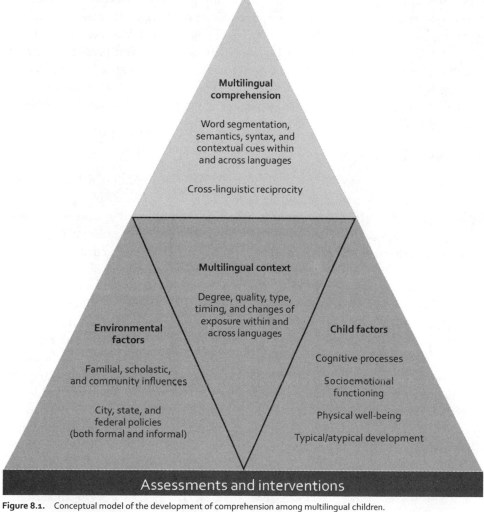

Figure 8.1. Conceptual model of the development of comprehension among multilingual children.

transfer, where knowledge and skills are shared or made accessible across languages (Cummins, 1979, 1981, 2008). The degree of which reciprocity due to cross-linguistic transfer may be present can relate to the degree to which the languages are similar in their lexicon, meanings, format (including alphabetic code), and usage (e.g., Kelley & Kohnert, 2012). Furthermore, cross-linguistic transfer may only occur for some domains and may be context dependent on the language of instruction, among other considerations (Cárdenas-Hagan, Carlson, & Pollard-Durodola, 2007; Goodrich, Lonigan, & Farver, 2013). In addition, higher-level cognitive processes may be implicated in the degree of reciprocity among language systems (e.g., Gottardo & Mueller, 2009).

Within the area of early childhood language and literacy, there are no known studies examining cross-linguistic transfer of comprehension abilities among multilingual children. Comparatively, the linguistic and emergent literacy building blocks to comprehension have been examined at a molar level for their degree of reciprocity. In a sample of Spanish–English bilingual preschoolers, Dickinson, McCabe, Clark-Chiarelli, and Wolf (2004) identified interdependence across a 7-month period in the areas of phonological awareness, letter and word knowledge, print concepts, and sentence memory. Not only is there evidence of the cross-linguistic transfer of phonological awareness skill (Lindsey, Manis, & Bailey, 2003), but phonological awareness in one language predicts word identification skills a year later and reading ability 2 years later in another language (Manis, Lindsey, & Bailey, 2004). Hammer, Lawrence, and Miccio (2007) also found that growth in English and Spanish receptive language abilities among bilingual children related to later reading abilities within and across the languages.

Environmental Factors

The development of comprehension abilities among young multilingual children is a multifaceted process, with contributing factors from a wider array of sources beyond cross-language transfer. As evidenced in Figure 8.1, multilingual comprehension does not develop in a vacuum. Rather, three principal sources can be considered as potential catalysts or deterrents to young multilingual child development: 1) environmental factors, 2) the multilingual context, and 3) children's personal characteristics.

First, the familial, scholastic, and community environments of multilingual children have been found to contribute to their linguistic and literacy development in a plethora of manners (for reviews, see Hammer & Rodríguez, 2012; Paradis et al., 2011). Key considerations in the environmental realm include parental educational levels, immigration status, household composition, the home and school settings, teacher qualifications and teaching style, and broader interactions in the community. For example, the type of dialogue Latina mothers engage in during storytelling predicts their young children's emergent literacy skills (Caspe, 2009). In addition, improvements in vocabulary and socioemotional functioning among low-income Latino children have been longitudinally linked to parental literacy activities as well as parental stress levels (Farver, Xu, Eppe, & Lonigan, 2006). Within early childhood settings, Spanish-speaking children improve most over the course of an academic year in classrooms with responsive and sensitive teachers who used the home language (Burchinal, Field, López, Howes, & Pianta, 2012).

A preponderance of additional evidence points to the positive contributions of early care and education for young multilingual children. At preschool entry, monolingual and Spanish–English bilingual children differ in emergent phonological awareness skills, oral language skills, letter knowledge, and spelling; comparatively, morphological skills are similar (Morgan, Restrepo, & Auza, 2013; Páez, Tabors, & López, 2007; Tabors, Páez, & López, 2003). Emergent literacy skills of predominantly Spanish-speaking bilingual, impoverished children can be well below average in vocabulary, early writing, and letter recognition upon entering Head Start (U.S. Department of Health and Human Services, 2003).

Montrul (2008) described and differentiated incomplete acquisition from protracted language development in bilinguals. Incomplete acquisition describes bilingual children who, unlike their monolingual peers, do not acquire full language and literacy abilities in one of the languages. Protracted language acquisition refers to bilingual children whose skills are delayed at a particular point in time but who continue to develop their skills in both languages (Montrul, 2008). Several studies measuring the language and literacy development of sequential learners in Head Start programs have found evidence of protracted language acquisition that results in substantial gains over time in the majority language (Hammer, Lawrence, & Miccio, 2006; Hammer, Lawrence, & Miccio, 2007; Miccio, Hammer, Davison, & Scarpino, 2006). Montrul (2006) argued that although protracted language acquisition can result in incomplete acquisition, it does not necessarily imply an end state; that is, under certain circumstances, the individual can at a later point potentially continue to develop his or her skills in the language.

Indeed, differences between monolingual and bilingual children appear to dissipate following formal schooling over a period of time, with studies finding evidence of bilingual children potentially outperforming their monolingual peers on word identification, reading tasks, spelling (Lesaux & Siegel, 2003), executive control, and metacognitive and metalinguistic skills (Bialystok, 2007a). Furthermore, Gathercole and Thomas (2009) found that when language development for both languages was supported through high-quality linguistic environments, the language abilities of bilingual children were comparable to those of monolingual children by middle school. Comprehension skills unfortunately were not directly assessed in the studies. Nevertheless, the findings are suggestive of the important role that early care and educational environments can play and suggest that, although the language and literacy skills of multilingual children may be initially weaker than those of monolingual peers, these can become comparable and potentially advanced over time.

Relatively few investigations have focused on the broader role of policies in multilingual children's development. Yet both positive and negative influences of policies among multilingual children have been demonstrated in areas such as early childhood education (e.g., Buysse, Peisner-Feinberg, Páez, Hammer, & Knowles, 2013) and even deportation (e.g., Chaudry et al., 2010). Rigorous attention is increasingly placed on utilizing research findings to inform policies affecting multilingual children, since policies developed are often devoid of an empirical basis and can even stand contrary to substantiated findings about multilingualism (Castro et al., 2013).

Multilingual Context

Considerable empirical attention has been paid to elucidating the key features of multilingual environments that relate to children's linguistic and literacy development within and across languages. Specifically, research has attempted to unpack how the degree, quality, type, and timing of language exposure and utilization influence the development of multilingual children (for reviews, see Paradis et al., 2011; Goldstein, 2012). The overwhelming majority of these investigations have focused on school-age children; the literature base within early childhood has only begun to flourish within the past decade. Similarly, the literature has primarily centered on basic receptive, expressive, and literacy skills, with little examined in the broader domain of comprehension. To the extent possible, studies about the multilingual context are highlighted in the following text as they relate to early childhood and the development of comprehension.

The acquisition of multiple languages during early childhood can occur in several manners. Romaine (1999) described six distinct linguistic input patterns through which children can develop multilingual abilities, each accounting for the native language of the parent(s), the dominant language of the community, and the method by which the child receives the language from the parent(s). This distinction highlighted two key principles of multilingual development. First, it underscored the heterogeneous conditions that facilitate multilingualism, implying that there is no one set course or circumstance for acquiring languages in childhood. Second, it elucidated the decisive role of the environment; specifically, varying degrees of linguistic exposure and input result in different levels of competency in both languages (Bialystok, 2001).

Bornstein (2013) emphasizes the moderating role of the setting condition, person, language, time, mechanism, and outcome in the acquisition and development of multiple languages. As noted by Bialystok (2001), bilingual competencies can vary significantly across individuals, with some individuals considered to be productive bilinguals and others receptive bilinguals (Dopke, 1992). Whereas the former refers to individuals who are able to speak two languages to some degree, the latter refers to individuals who can understand and/or read but not speak or write the second language. These distinctions have been fundamental to defining multilingualism and for recognizing the factors that account for different levels of proficiency. Languages are often uneven in development, and multilingual children tend to be more proficient in one language over the other, particularly when the child's linguistic experiences in the home environment differ from those in the academic and social environment (Paradis et al., 2011).

Research on the course of language development among young bilingual children has suggested that the acquisition of specific skills in each language depends greatly on social context, particularly the degree of experiences in each language that the child receives (Hoff et al., 2012; Wu, DeTemple, Herman, & Snow, 1994). De Houwer (2007) surveyed bilingual families on parental language input patterns and found a relationship between differences in parental language input patterns and children's use of the language. Specifically, being raised in a home in which both parents spoke the minority language and where at least one parent spoke the majority language increased the child's utilization of both languages. An investigation of infant development yielded similar findings (e.g., Song, Tamis-LeMonda, Yoshikawa, Kahana-Kalman, & Wu, 2012). Latino parents' bilingual background and use in the first few months of life predicted vocabulary skills in each language at 14 months and at 2 years of age. In addition, observed bilingual utterances and reported bilingual parent–child literacy activities longitudinally related to infants' development in the two languages (Song et al., 2012).

Young bilingual children typically reach developmental milestones on time, although whether or not these are met in one or both languages depends on the degree of linguistic input the child receives in each language (De Houwer, 2009). Older children acquiring a second language for the first time (i.e., sequential learners) are likely to have reached the developmental milestones in their home language. For both *sequential* and *simultaneous* learners, bilingual proficiency will depend on the linguistic experiences they receive in both languages throughout the course of their lives (Paradis et al., 2011).

Investigations comparing simultaneous and sequential bilinguals have rarely found evidence to support the advantageous nature of one over the other. In comparison to sequential learners, young children learning two languages simultaneously have not been found to significantly differ in oral language abilities or emergent literacy skills (Hammer, Miccio, & Wagstaff, 2003; Miccio et al., 2006). Furthermore, simultaneous and sequential learners make similar gains over time in the majority language so long as linguistic input remains strong and constant (Lesaux & Siegel, 2003). However, when Kovelman, Baker, and Petitto (2008) studied the relationship between age of first bilingual language exposure and bilingual reading development, they found simultaneous Spanish–English bilinguals (children first exposed to both languages between birth and 3 years of age) perform better on reading, phonological awareness, and language competence in both languages in comparison to sequential bilinguals (children first exposed to both languages between the ages of 3 and 6). Before implications can be drawn from this study, it should be replicated. Indeed, the age cutoff to distinguish sequential from simultaneous bilinguals is neither clear nor consistent across the field and might explain the varying patterns in findings evidenced to date (Paradis, Genesee, & Crago, 2011).

Evidence suggests that although increased early exposure to the majority language does not cause home language loss (Winsler, Diaz, Espinosa, & Rodriguez, 1999), high-quality ongoing exposure to the home language is necessary to avoid this from occurring (Gathercole & Thomas, 2009). Continuous development of the home language is particularly important, since it has been found to support the development of analogous skills in the other language children are developing (Cárdenas-Hagan et al., 2007; Dickinson, McCabe, Clark-Chiarelli, & Wolf, 2004; Hammer, Lawrence, & Miccio, 2007; Lindsey, Manis, & Bailey, 2003; Manis, Lindsey, & Bailey, 2004). Consequently, parents or caregivers in the home environment are encouraged to speak to their children in their native language (López; 2013; McCabe et al., 2013; Paradis et al., 2011).

Child Factors

Finally, children's own characteristics should be considered within the context of early multilingual comprehension. Children's broader cognitive skills in domains such as attention and nonverbal reasoning interplay with their linguistic skills, particularly among younger children (Lightfoot, Cole, & Cole, 2013). Furthermore, *socioemotional functioning* and temperament can influence multilingual development (e.g., Paradis et al., 2011; Strand, Pula, & Parks, & Cerna, 2011; Tabors, 2008). In addition, health and well-being are important considerations in the early trajectories of multilingual children, with some communities experiencing detrimental conditions in the home and/or work environments (Barrueco & O'Brien, 2011).

One of the most frequent concerns about young multilingual children is how multilingualism relates to typical and atypical development. Language development occurs through separate yet connected linguistic systems, preventing the acquisition of one language from hindering the development of the other (Genesee, Paradis, & Crago, 2004). Despite this, uneven linguistic and literacy performance across and within the two languages is common in bilingual children. A child who receives more linguistic input in one language will develop greater proficiency in that language. Similarly, different experiences in each language will result in proficiency for some skills in one language and other skills in the other language (Peña, Bedore, & Zlatic-Giunta, 2002). This unevenness has stirred concerns over the effects of bilingual acquisition, specifically whether it exacerbates impairments in children with disorders such as autism spectrum disorder (ASD) or in children with language impairments (see Chapter 7 by Gear).

To explore this relationship, Hambly and Fombonne (2012) compared the language development of bilingual and monolingual children with ASD and differentiated between simultaneous and sequential learners. They did not find the groups to differ in language development. More important, the evidence did not support the presence of additional language delay among bilingual children. Valicenti-McDermot et al. (2013) compared bilingual and monolingual children with ASD on their expressive and receptive language skills. The two groups, which were comparable in autistic features and cognitive functioning, were not found to differ in all but one feature of expressive language. Specifically, bilingual children were found to vocalize and utilize gestures more often than the monolingual children.

Among children with language impairments, bilingualism has also not been found to be detrimental (see Goldstein, 2012). Furthermore, indicators of language impairment among bilingual children have begun to be identified. Morgan, Restrepo, and Auza (2013) identified that grammatical errors can differentiate bilingual children with and without language impairments if comparisons are made within language groupings; however, some caution must be taken when utilizing this approach to identify bilingual children with language impairments, since bilingual children can generally score lower on morphology tasks when compared with monolinguals. Thus it may be necessary to utilize separate norms for monolingual and bilingual children. The assessment of clitics (object and indirect object pronouns such as *lo* or *la* in Spanish) may provide additional accuracy in identifying language impairment among bilingual children (Jacobson & Schwartz, 2002). See Chapter 10 by Lynch and Lepola for further assessment methods of comprehension skills.

Taken together, the studies of bilingual children with and without impairments carry implications. They serve to rebuff concerns surrounding the effects of bilingualism in children with language impairment, such as that the acquisition of two or more languages causes or exacerbates existing language impairment. Furthermore, they suggest notable distinctions between bilingual children with and without language impairment; these differences can help parents and educators increase their sensitivity in differentiating between a bilingual child with protracted language development due to minimal exposure to one or both languages and a bilingual child with language impairment due to organic factors.

ASSESSMENTS AND INTERVENTIONS

In Figure 8.1, the base of the conceptual model highlights the role that assessments and interventions in addition play in the lives of young multilingual children. Unfortunately, this area is the most underdeveloped in the empirical literature and in critical need of attention. With few measures and interventions available with a specific focus on multilingual comprehension, limitations abound for the science, practice, and policy fields.

Assessments

Awareness and recognition of developmental patterns are particularly important for assessing the linguistic abilities of multilingual children. The rate of development during the *interlanguage* (period of time between first exposure to languages and the achievement of native-like proficiency level) varies greatly among multilingual children and can relate to individual factors such as personality/social style, language aptitude, age, and structure of the languages, as well as quality and quantity of exposure to the languages (Paradis et al., 2011). During the interlanguage, several developmental patterns, consisting of both developmental and transfer-based patterns, are common and often incorrectly perceived as errors (Paradis et al., 2011). Such findings underscore the importance of parents, teachers, and health professionals to be considerate of monolingual and bilingual comparisons, primarily in the early years of school.

This is especially critical, considering that young children who are first exposed to the majority language in a preschool or other educational setting may be at risk of being diagnosed with language delays and impairments when only assessed in English and when compared with monolingual norms (Morgan, Restrepo, & Auza, 2013). In contrast, when Hoff et al. (2012) assessed the total vocabulary and grammatical abilities of bilingual children across both languages and compared it to that of monolingual children, they did not find the two groups to differ. As such, DLLs should be assessed on language and literacy abilities across both languages to obtain a valid representation of full competencies (Barrueco, López, Ong, & Lozano, 2012; De Houwer, 2009; Gutiérrez-Clellen, 2002; Hammer & Miccio, 2006; NAEYC, 2009; Winskel, 2010; Zurer Pearson, Fernandez, & Oller, 1993). In addition, a range of internal and external factors, including socioeconomic status, parental education level, immigration experience, generational status, access to resources, and cultural factors, influence language and emergent literacy development and thus are important to obtaining an understanding of the different levels of proficiency observed among children (López, 2013). See Chapter 2 by Coyne, Neugebauer, Ware, McCoach, and Madura for additional studies on external factors specifically related to maternal educational level and child language.

The availability of measures to directly assess multilingual comprehension skills has progressed steadily, with important implications for research, educational, and clinical practices with young children. A few measures are available to examine general receptive linguistic skills among young multilingual children, particularly Spanish speakers. These include the Battelle Developmental Inventory (Newborg, 2005), Clinical Evaluation of Language Fundamentals (Wiig, Secord, & Semel, 2009), and Preschool Language Scale (Zimmerman, Steiner, & Pond, 2002). More measures have been developed that examine subcomponents of oral comprehension, particularly vocabulary development: Bilingual Vocabulary Assessment Measure (Mattes, 1995), the Spanish version of the Peabody Picture Vocabulary Test (Dunn, Padilla, Lugo, & Dunn, 1986), the preLAS 2000 (Duncan & De Avila, 1998), Receptive and Expressive One-Word Picture Vocabulary Tests, Spanish–Bilingual Edition (Brownell, 2001), and the Woodcock-Muñoz Language Survey (Alvarado, Ruef, & Schrank, 2005). Within the area of the assessment of early literacy comprehension across languages, the Early Literacy Skills Assessment (DeBruin-Parecki, 2005) is one of the few measures developed to date in English and Spanish.

With the advent of measures available in multiple languages, some caution must be taken. Barrueco, López, Ong, and Lozano (2012) identified significant variation in the psychometric, linguistic, and cultural properties of early childhood measures developed in Spanish and English. Attention needs to be paid to not only the strength of each measure under consideration but also the language versions of the same measure, as they may not be equivalent to each other. This undermines attempts to examine multilingual development reliably or validly for important purposes such as special needs identification, program evaluation, and general research. The selection of measures also necessitates attention to the purpose of the assessment (e.g., screening versus full examination; to examine comprehension *within* an individual language or *across* multiple languages). Finally, dialectical considerations are needed. Although some measures have been developed across dialects of a language, others have not and are thus more appropriate for one community over another (e.g., an assessment for young children of Mexican heritage versus Cuban heritage). Distinct words may describe the same object or concept between countries and even across regions of the same country. The word *straw*, for example, has more than 10 translations in Spanish, including *sorbete, pitillo, popote,* and *caña.* Such dialectical variation carries implications for assessing multilingual children in both oral language and early literacy.

Interventions

Within the intervention realm, early childhood care and education have been found effective for improving receptive abilities among low-income multilingual children (for a review, see Buysse et al., 2013). Furthermore, professional development that augments teachers' knowledge and pedagogical skills with multilingual children improves their pupils' phonological awareness (Buysse, Castro, & Peisner-Feinberg, 2010). Similarly, professional development focused on literacy practices improves the emergent skills of ELL preschoolers in this domain (Jackson et al., 2006).

The empirical evidence regarding early intervention is most pronounced in specific oral and preliteracy domains such as vocabulary, phonological awareness, and letter knowledge. In one of the few studies examining comprehension among young multilingual children, Wilson, Dickinson, and Rowe (2012) found that a well-developed preschool program improved vocabulary skills among ELLs but not oral comprehension skills.

Interventions explicitly targeting comprehension with young multilingual children are needed. Such interventions have yielded positive results in other areas, such as in elaborative book reading and vocabulary skills among typically developing ELL children (Collins, 2010) and bilingual dialogic reading with young children experiencing language delays (Tsybina & Eriks-Brophy, 2010).

Similarly, interventions for monolingual and bilingual children with early signs of reading difficulties may respond well to a short program emphasizing early phonemic skills (Koutsoffas, Harmon, & Gray, 2009). One known intervention study with multilingual preschoolers included an explicit focus on comprehension (Roberts & Neal, 2004). This small clinical trial demonstrated that comprehension-oriented small group instruction yields vocabulary and print knowledge improvements among multilingual preschoolers, whereas instruction emphasizing alphabetic and phonological abilities produces increased letter knowledge (Roberts & Neal, 2004).

There is a fair body of evidence supporting the use of multilingual children's home languages in early intervention. Randomized trials of children in bilingual or English-only preschool classrooms showed positive results in improved home language development and comparable English language development (Barnett, Yarosz, Thomas, Jung, & Blanco, 2007; Durán, Roseth, & Hoffman, 2010; Farver, Lonigan, & Eppe, 2009). Similarly, Restrepo et al. (2010) found that a supplemental Spanish oral language program improved preschoolers' Spanish expressive language development. Furthermore, bilingual vocabulary interventions for DLLs with language impairments improved lexical development in Spanish (Restrepo, Morgan, & Thompson, 2013).

CONCLUSION

Among monolingual children, phonological awareness, articulation, receptive vocabulary, narrative skills, concepts and knowledge, and print concepts and awareness have been found to be essential in the development of emergent reading abilities (Whitehurst & Lonigan, 1998). These are acquired informally in the early years of life, and their mastery is greatly dependent on the amount of language and literacy exposure that the child obtains in the home and preschool environments. Whitehurst and Lonigan (1998) conceptualized the development of emergent literacy as consisting of two distinct sets of abilities: inside-out skills and outside-in skills. Whereas the former encompasses phonological awareness and letter knowledge, the latter includes language and understanding of concept (Bialystok & Herman, 1999; Speece, Ritchey, Cooper, Roth, & Schatschneider, 2004; Whitehurst & Lonigan, 1998). As described earlier, the acquisition of these skills in one language has been found to facilitate the development of literacy skills in the second language; this cross-linguistic transfer effect was deemed a bilingual advantage by Bialystok and Herman (1999).

The research on the development of emergent literacy abilities, particularly in the domain of comprehension, in multilingual children has been relatively scarce. Most investigations have focused on the early acquisition of reading abilities in monolingual children, raising concerns of whether or not the findings are applicable to multilingual children. As described in this chapter, differences and similarities exist between the two groups. Undoubtedly, the use of two linguistic systems by multilingual children contributes to differences in how the two groups develop and experience language and literacy (Bialystok, 1997, 2007b; Bialystok & Hakuta, 1999; Campbell & Sais, 1995).

Given these considerations, the chapter reviewed a myriad of factors contributing to comprehension skills among young multilingual children in both the oral and early literacy domains. It is patently clear that comprehension among young multilingual children is a multifaceted process in of itself, with solid development needed within and across the lexical, semantic, syntactic, and pragmatic language systems; environments, multilingual influences, and personal characteristics are all critical agents in early childhood multilingual development; close attention is warranted to both the development and utilization of assessment measures with young multilingual children, particularly in the area of comprehension (Buysse et al., 2010); and prevention and intervention efforts with young multilingual children can yield quite promising results, especially when taking home language into account.

A variety of recommendations for research, practice, and policy emanate from the empirical base. Investigations are sorely needed that examine normative and nonnormative processes related to multilingual oral and emergent literacy comprehension. This includes studies of the developmental sequences themselves, as well as analyses of facilitating and deterring elements in the processes. The multilingual literature is predominately composed of lexical research for both evident reasons (i.e., a core manner in which languages differ from one another is in vocabulary) and pragmatic reasons (i.e., most multilingual measures developed and validated to date are lexical in nature). Although lexical development is undeniably a critical aspect of multilingual children's development, it is important to more fully develop our scientific understanding of adjunctive forms and functions of language—namely, the ability to understand the meaning of speech and text.

Within the practice and policy domains, individuals charged and invested in the care and development of young multilingual children can be guided in their decision making by empirical findings rather than myths that can potentially have detrimental effects. Although there is limited research in the comprehension domain, much has been elucidated in concomitant areas of early childhood multilingualism. Namely, multilingualism is not detrimental to typically or atypically developing children; proficiencies are developed within each language with some degree of reciprocity; contextual influences at home, at school, and in society play key roles in early multilingualism; the home language can be used to facilitate growth in multiple manners; and not only is bilingualism on the rise in the United States, but there may also be a growing cohort of children developing in the context of more than two languages. Disseminating such empirically based information to parents, teachers, health care professionals, and policy makers will likely improve present practices and long-term outcomes for young multilingual children, who continue to constitute an ever-increasing proportion of young children. Thankfully, such effects have already begun (Castro et al., 2013).

REFERENCES

Administration for Children and Families. (2006). *FACES 2003 research brief: Children's outcomes and program quality in Head Start.* Washington, DC: Author.

Administration for Children and Families. (2008). *Dual language learning: What does it take? Head Start dual language report.* Washington, DC: Office of Head Start.

Administration for Children and Families. (2009, April). *Recognizing language diversity in large-scale assessments: Approaches and evidence from FACES 2006.* Presentation at the Society for Research in Child Development Biennial Meeting, Denver, CO.

Alvarado, C.G., Ruef, M.L., & Schrank, F.A. (2005). *Woodcock-Muñoz Language Survey—Revised: Comprehensive manual.* Itasca, IL: Riverside Publishing.

Barnett, W.S., Yarosz, D.J., Thomas, J., Jung, K., & Blanco, D. (2007). Two-way and monolingual English immersion in preschool education: An experimental comparison. *Early Childhood Research Quarterly, 22,* 277–293. doi:10.1016/j.ecresq.2007.03.003

Barrueco, S., López, M., Ong, C.A., & Lozano, P. (2012). *Assessing Spanish–English Bilingual Preschoolers.* Baltimore, MD: Paul H. Brookes Publishing Co.

Barrueco, S., & O'Brien, R. (2011). Latino agricultural families and their young children: Advancing theoretical and empirical conceptualizations. In J. Kromkowski (Ed.), *Annual editions: Race and ethnic relations* (pp. 168–175). New York, NY: McGraw-Hill.

Bialystok, E. (1997). Effects of bilingualism and biliteracy on children's emerging concepts of print. *Developmental Psychology, 33,* 429–440. doi:10.1037/0012-1649.33.3.429

Bialystok, E. (2001). *Bilingualism in development: Language, literacy and cognition.* Cambridge, UK: Cambridge University Press.

Bialystok, E. (2007a). Acquisition of literacy in multilingual children: A framework for research. *Language Learning, 57*(1), 45–77. doi:10.1111/j.1467-9922.2007.00412.x

Bialystok, E. (2007b). Language acquisition and bilingualism: Consequences for a multilingual society. *Applied Psycholinguistics, 28,* 393–397. doi:10.1017.S0142716407070208

Bialystok, E., & Hakuta, K. (1999). Cofounded age: Linguistic and cognitive factors in age differences for second language acquisition. In D. Birdsong (Ed.), *Second language acquisition and the critical period hypothesis* (pp. 161–181). Mahwah, NJ: Erlbaum.

Bialystok, E., & Herman, J. (1999). Does bilingualism matter for early literacy? *Language and Cognition, 2,* 35–44.

Bloomfield, L. (1933). *Language.* New York, NY: Henry Holt.

Bornstein, M.H. (2013). The Specificity Principle (SP) in multiple language learning. *Social Policy Report, 27*(4), 1–37.

Brownell, R. (2001). *Expressive One-Word Picture Vocabulary Test—Spanish-bilingual edition.* Novato, CA: Academic Therapy Publications.

Burchinal, M., Field, S., López, M.L., Howes, C., & Pianta, R. (2012). Instruction in Spanish in prekindergarten classrooms and child outcomes for English language learners. *Early Childhood Research Quarterly, 27,* 188–197. doi:10.1016/j.ecresq.2011.11.003

Butler, Y.G., & Hakuta, K. (2004). Bilingualism and second language acquisition. In T.K. Bhatia & W.C. Ritchie (Eds.), *The handbook of bilingualism* (pp. 114–144). Malden, MA: Blackwell Publishing.

Buysse, V., Castro, D.C., & Peisner-Feinberg, E. (2010). Effects of a professional development program on classroom practices and outcomes for Latino dual language learners. *Early Childhood Research Quarterly, 25,* 194–206. doi:10.1016/j.ecresq.2009.10.001

Buysse, V., Peisner-Feinberg, E., Páez, M., Hammer, C., & Knowles, M. (2013). Effects of early education programs and practices on the development and learning of dual language learners: A review of the literature. *Early Childhood Research Quarterly, 29,* 765–785. doi:10.1016/j.ecresq.2013.08.004

Campbell, R., & Sais, E. (1995). Accelerated metalinguistic (phonological) awareness in bilingual children. *British Journal of Developmental Psychology, 13*(1), 61–68. doi:10.1111/j.2044-835X.1995.tb00664.x

Cárdenas-Hagan, E., Carlson, C.D., & Pollard-Durodola, S.D. (2007). The cross-linguistic transfer of early literacy skills: The role of Initial L1 and L2 skills and language of instruction. *Language, Speech, and Hearing Services in Schools, 38,* 249–259. doi:10.1044/0161-1461(2007/026)

Caspe, M. (2009). Low-income Latino mothers' booksharing styles and children's emergent literacy development. *Early Childhood Research Quarterly, 24*(3), 306–324.

Castro, D.C., García, E.E., & Markos, A.M. (2013). *Dual language learners: Research informing policy.* Chapel Hill: University of North Carolina, Frank Porter Graham Child Development Institute, Center for Early Care and Education—Dual Language Learners.

Chaudry, A., Capps, R., Pedroza, J.M., Castañeda, R.M., Santos, R., & Scott, M. (2010). *Facing our future: Children in the aftermath of immigration enforcement.* Washington, DC: Urban Institute.

Collins, M.F. (2010). ELL preschoolers' English vocabulary acquisition from storybook reading. *Early Childhood Research Quarterly, 25,* 84–97. doi:10.1016/j.ecresq.2009.07.009

Cummins, J. (1979). Linguistic interdependence and the educational development of bilingual children. *Review of Educational Research, 49,* 222–251.

Cummins, J. (1981). The role of primary language development in promoting educational success for language minority students. In California State Department of Education (Ed.), *Schooling and language minority students: A theoretical framework* (pp. 3–49). Los Angeles, CA: California State Department of Education, Evaluation, Dissemination, and Assessment Center.

Cummins, J. (2008). Teaching for transfer: Challenging the two solitudes assumption in bilingual education. In J. Cummins & N.H. Hornberger (Eds.), *Encyclopedia of language and education: Vol. 5. Bilingual education* (2nd ed., pp. 65–75). New York, NY: Springer Science.

De Houwer, A. (2007). Parental language input patterns and children's bilingual use. *Applied Psycholinguistics, 28,* 411–424. doi:10.1017.S0142716407070221

De Houwer, A. (2009). *Bilingual first language acquisition.* Clevedon, UK: Multilingual Matters.

DeBruin-Parecki, A. (2005). *Early Literacy Skills Assessment user guide.* Ypsilanti, MI: High/Scope Press.

Dickinson, D.K., McCabe, A., Clark-Chiarelli, N., & Wolf, A. (2004). Cross-language transfer of phonological awareness in low-income Spanish and English bilingual preschool children. *Applied Psycholinguistics, 25,* 323–347. doi:10.1017.S0142716404001158

Dopke, S. (1992). *One parent one language: An interactional approach.* Amsterdam, Netherlands: John Benjamins.

Duncan, S.E., & De Avila, E.A. (1998). *preLAS 2000: Manual para examinadores. Español Forma C.* Monterey, CA: CTB/McGraw-Hill.

Dunn, L.M., Padilla, E.R., Lugo, D.E., & Dunn, L.M. (1986). *Test de vocabulario en imágenes Peabody: Examiner's manual.* Circle Pines, MI: American Guidance Systems.

Durán, L.K., Roseth, C.J., & Hoffman, P. (2010). An experimental study comparing English-only and Transitional Bilingual Education on Spanish-speaking preschoolers' early literacy development. *Early Childhood Research Quarterly, 25,* 207–217. doi:10.1016/j.ecresq.2009.10.002

Espinosa, L.M. (2013). *Early education for dual language learners: Promoting school readiness and early school success.* Washington, DC: Migration Policy Institute.

Farver, J.M., Lonigan, C.J., & Eppe, S. (2009). Effective early literacy skill development for young Spanish-speaking English language learners: An experimental study of two methods. *Child Development, 80,* 703–719.

Farver, J.M., Xu, Y., Eppe, S., & Lonigan, C.J. (2006). Home environments and young Latino children's school readiness. *Early Childhood Research Quarterly, 21,* 196–212.

Gathercole, V.C.M., & Thomas, E.M. (2009). Bilingual first-language development: Dominant language takeover, threatened minority language take-up. *Bilingualism: Language and Cognition, 12*(2), 213–237. doi:10.1017/S1366728909004015

Genesee, F., Paradis, J., & Crago, M.B. (2004). *Dual language development and disorders: A handbook on bilingualism and second language learning.* Baltimore, MD: Paul H. Brookes Publishing Co.

Goldstein, B.A. (2012). *Bilingual language development and disorders in Spanish-English speakers* (2nd ed.). Baltimore, MD: Paul H. Brookes Publishing Co.

Goodrich, J.M., Lonigan, C.J., & Farver, J.M. (2013). Do early literacy skills in children's first language promote development of skills in their second language? An experimental evaluation of transfer. *Journal of Educational Psychology, 105,* 414–426. doi:10.1037/a0031780

Gottardo, A., & Mueller, J. (2009). Are first- and second-language factors related in predicting second-language reading comprehension? A study of Spanish-speaking children acquiring English as a second language from first to second grade. *Journal of Educational Psychology, 101,* 330–344. doi:10.1037/a0014320

Grosjean, F. (1989). Neurolinguists beware! The bilingual is not two monolinguals in one person. *Brain and Language, 36,* 3–15. doi:10.1016/0093-934X(89)90048-5

Grosjean, F. (2010). *Bilingual: Life and reality.* Cambridge, MA: Harvard University Press.

Gutiérrez-Clellen, V.F. (2002). Narratives in two languages: Assessing performance of bilingual children. *Linguistics and Education, 13*(2), 175–197. doi:10.1016/S0898–5898(01)00061-4

Hakuta, K., Butler, Y.G., & Witt, D. (2000). *How long does it take English learners to attain proficiency?* The University of California Linguistic Minority Research Institute (Policy Reports). Santa Barbara, CA: Linguistic Minority Research Institute.

Hambly, C., & Fombonne, E. (2012). The impact of bilingual environments on language development in children with autism spectrum disorders. *Journal of Autism and Developmental Disorders, 42,* 1342–1352. doi:10.1007/s10803-011-1365-z

Hammer, C.S., Lawrence, F.R., & Miccio, A.W. (2006). *Bilingual children's emergent literacy development during Head Start and kindergarten.* Manuscript submitted for publication.

Hammer, C.S., Lawrence, F.R., & Miccio, A.W. (2007). Bilingual children's language abilities and early reading outcomes in Head Start and kindergarten. *Language, Speech, and Hearing Services in Schools, 38,* 237–248. doi:10.1044/0161-1461(2007/025)

Hammer, C.S., & Miccio, A.W. (2006). Early language and reading development of bilingual preschoolers from low-income families. *Topics in Language Disorders, 26,* 322–337.

Hammer, C.S., Miccio, A.W., & Wagstaff, D.A. (2003). Home literacy experiences and their relationship to bilingual preschoolers' developing English literacy abilities: An initial investigation. *Language, Speech & Hearing Services in Schools, 34*(1), 20–30.

Hammer, C.S., & Rodríguez, B. (2012). Bilingual language acquisition and the child socialization process. In B. Goldstein (Ed.), *Bilingual language development and disorders in Spanish-English speakers* (2nd ed., pp. 31–46). Baltimore, MD: Paul H. Brookes Publishing Co.

Haugen, E. (1953). *The Norwegian language in America: The bilingual community.* Philadelphia: University of Pennsylvania Press.

Hoff, E., Core, C., Place, S., Rumiche, R., Señor, M., & Parra, M. (2012). Dual language exposure and early bilingual development. *Journal of Child Language, 39,* 1–27. doi:10.1017/S0305000910000759

Iglesias, A., & Rojas, R. (2012). Bilingual language development of English language learners: Modeling the growth of two languages. In B.A. Goldstein (Ed.), *Bilingual language development and disorders in Spanish-English speakers* (2nd ed., pp. 3–30). Baltimore, MD: Paul H. Brookes Publishing Co.

Jackson, B., Larzelere, R., St. Clair, L., Corr, M., Fichter, C., & Egertson, H. (2006). The impact of Heads Up! Reading on early childhood educators' literacy practices and preschool children's literacy skills. *Early Childhood Research Quarterly, 21,* 213–226. doi:10.1016/j.ecresq.2006.04.005

Jacobson, P.F., & Schwartz, R.G. (2002). Morphology in incipient bilingual Spanish-speaking preschool children with specific language impairment. *Applied Psycholinguistics, 23,* 23–41. doi:10.1017.S0142716402000024

Kelley, A., & Kohnert, K. (2012). Is there a cognate advantage for typically developing Spanish-speaking English-language learners? *Language, Speech, and Hearing Services in Schools, 43,* 191–204.

Koutsoffas, A.D., Harmon, M.T., & Gray, S. (2009). The effect of Tier 2 intervention for phonemic awareness in a Response-to-Intervention Model for low-income preschool classrooms. *Language, Speech & Hearing Services in Schools, 40,* 116–130.

Kovelman, I., Baker, S.A., & Petitto, L. (2008). Age of first bilingual language exposure as a new window into bilingual reading development. *Bilingualism: Language and Cognition, 11*(2), 203–223. doi:10.1017/S1366728908003386

Leos, K. (2014). What are the nationally accepted terms used to describe young children who speak different languages? In K.N. Nemeth (Ed.), *Young dual language learners: A guide for PreK–3 leaders* (pp. 7–8). Philadelphia, PA: Carlson Publishing.

Lesaux, N.K., & Siegel, L.S. (2003). The development of reading in children who speak English as a second language. *Developmental Psychology, 39*(6), 1005–1019. doi:10.1037/0012-1649.39.6.1005

Lightfoot, C., Cole, M., & Cole, S.R. (2013). *The development of children* (7th ed.). New York, NY: Worth Publishers.

Lindsey, K., Manis, F., & Bailey, C. (2003). Prediction of first-grade reading in Spanish-speaking English language learners. *Journal of Educational Psychology, 95,* 482–494. doi:10.1037/0022-0663.95.3.482

López, L.M. (2013). Promoting positive development among young multilingual learners. *Social Policy Report, 27,* 22–23.

MacLeod, A.A., Fabiano-Smith, L., Boegner-Page, S., & Salome Fontolliet, S. (2013). Simultaneous bilingual language acquisition: The role of parental input on receptive vocabulary development. *Child Language Teaching and Therapy, 29,* 131–142. doi:10.1177/0265659012466862

Manis, F., Lindsey, K.A., & Bailey, C.E. (2004). Development of reading in Grades K–2 in Spanish-speaking English-language learners. *Learning Disabilities Research & Practice, 19,* 214–224. doi:10.1111/j.1540-5826.2004.00107.x

Mattes, L.J. (1995). *Bilingual vocabulary assessment measure.* Oceanside, CA: Academic Communication Associates.

McCabe, A., Tamis-LeMonda, C.S., Bornstein, M.H., Cates, C.B., Golinkoff, R., Guerra, A.W., . . . Song, L. (2013). Multilingual children beyond myths and toward best practices (Social Policy Report). *Sharing child and youth development knowledge, 27*(4), 1–37.

Miccio, A.W., Hammer, C.S., Davison, M.D., & Scarpino, S.E. (2006). *Phonological awareness abilities of bilingual Spanish and English speaking children in Head Start.* Manuscript submitted for publication.

Montrul, S. (2006). Incomplete acquisition as a feature of L2 and bilingual grammars. In R. Slabakova, S. Montrul, & P. Prevost (Eds.), *Inquiries in language development: Studies in honor of Lydia White* (pp. 335–359). Amsterdam, Netherlands: John Benjamins.

Montrul, S. (2008). *Incomplete acquisition in bilingualism: Re-examining the age factor.* Amsterdam, Netherlands: John Benjamins.

Morgan, G.P., Restrepo, M.A., & Auza, A. (2013). Comparison of Spanish morphology in monolingual and Spanish-English bilingual children with and without language impairment. *Bilingualism: Language and Cognition, 16*(3), 578–596. doi:10.1017/S1366728912000697

National Association for the Education of Young Children. (2009). *Developmentally appropriate practice in early childhood programs serving children from birth through age 8.* Washington, DC: Author.

Nemeth, K.N. (2014). What terms do states and practitioners use to describe young children who speak different languages? In K.N. Nemeth (Ed.), *Young dual language learners: A guide for PreK–3 leaders* (pp. 9–11). Philadelphia, PA: Carlson Publishing.

Newborg, J. (2005). *Battelle Developmental Inventory–Second Edition, Spanish.* Itasca, IL: Riverside.

Páez, M.M., Tabors, P.O., & López, M.M. (2007). Dual language and literacy development of Spanish-speaking preschool children. *Journal of Applied Developmental Psychology, 28*(2), 85–102. doi:10.1016/j.appdev.2006.12.007

Paradis, J., Genesee, F., & Crago, M.B. (2011). *Dual language development and disorders: A handbook on bilangualism and second language learning* (2nd ed.). Baltimore, MD: Paul H. Brookes Publishing Co.

Peña, E.D., Bedore, L.M., & Zlatic-Giunta, R. (2002). Category-generation performance of bilingual children. *Journal of Speech, Language, and Hearing Research, 45*, 938–947. doi:10.1044/1092-4388(2002/076)

Restrepo, M.A., Castilla, A.P., Schwanenflugel, P.J., Neuharth-Pritchett, S., Hamilton, C.E., & Arboleda, A. (2010). Effects of a supplemental Spanish oral language program on sentence length, complexity, and grammaticality in Spanish-speaking children attending English-only preschools. *Language, Speech & Hearing Services in Schools, 41*, 3–13.

Restrepo, M.A., Morgan, G.P., & Thompson, M.S. (2013). The efficacy of a vocabulary intervention for dual-language learners with language impairment. *Journal of Speech, Language, and Hearing Research, 56*, 748–765.

Roberts, T., & Neal, H. (2004). Relationships among preschool English language learner's oral proficiency in English, instructional experience and literacy development. *Contemporary Educational Psychology, 29*, 283–311. doi:10.1016/j.cedpsych.2003.08.001

Romaine, S. (1999). Bilingual language development. In M. Barrett (Ed.), *The development of language (Studies in developmental psychology)* (pp. 251–276). Hove, UK: Psychology Press.

Ryan, C. (2013). *Language use in the United States: 2011. American Community Survey Reports.* Washington, DC: U.S. Census Bureau.

Song, L., Tamis-LeMonda, C., Yoshikawa, H., Kahana-Kalman, R., & Wu, I. (2012). Language experiences and vocabulary development in Dominican and Mexican infants across the first 2 years. *Developmental Psychology, 48*(4), 1106–1123. doi:10.1037/a0026401

Speece, D.L., Ritchey, K.D., Cooper, D.H., Roth, F.P., & Schatschneider, C. (2004). Growth in early reading skills from kindergarten to third grade. *Contemporary Educational Psychology, 29*, 312–332. doi:10.1016/j.cedpsych.2003.07.001

Strand, P.S., Pula, K., & Parks, C.G., & Cerna, S. (2011). Shyness–anxiousness and receptive language skills development in Spanish- and English-speaking preschoolers. *Journal of Applied Developmental Psychology, 32*, 363–368. doi:10.1016/j.appdev.2011.06.002

Tabors, P.O. (2008). *One child, two languages: A guide for early childhood educators of children learning English as a second language* (2nd ed.). Baltimore, MD: Paul H. Brookes Publishing Co.

Tabors, P., Páez, M., & López, L. (2003). Dual language abilities of bilingual four-year olds: Initial findings from the Early Childhood Study of Language and Literacy Development of Spanish-Speaking Children. *NABE Journal of Research and Practice,* Winter, 70–91. doi:10.1016/j.appdev.2006.12.007

Tsybina, I., & Eriks-Brophy, A. (2010). Bilingual dialogic book-reading intervention for preschoolers with slow expressive vocabulary development. *Journal of Communication Disorders, 43*, 538–556. doi:10.1016/j.jcomdis.2010.05.006

U.S. Department of Health and Human Services. (2003). *Head Start FACES 2000: A whole-child perspective on program performance.* Washington, DC: U.S. Department of Health and Human Services.

U.S. Department of Labor. (2005). *Findings from the National Agricultural Workers Survey (NAWS) 2001–2002: A demographic and employment profile of United States farm workers.* Washington, DC: U.S. Department of Labor.

Valicenti-McDermott, M., Tarshis, N., Schouls, M., Galdston, M., Hottinger, K., Seijo, R. . . . Shinnar, S. (2013). Language differences between monolingual English and bilingual English-Spanish young children with autism spectrum disorders. *Journal of Child Neurology, 28,* 945–948. doi:10.1177/0883073812453204

Whitehurst, G.J., & Lonigan, C.J. (1998). Child development and emergent literacy. *Child Development, 69*(3), 848–872. doi:10.2307/1132208

Wiig, E.H., Secord, W.A., & Semel, E. (2009). *Clinical Evaluation of Language Fundamentals–Preschool–2 Spanish (CELF-Preschool-2 Spanish).* San Antonio, TX: Pearson.

Wilson, S.J., Dickinson, D.K., & Rowe, D.W. (2012). Impact of an Early Reading First program on the language and literacy achievement of children from diverse language backgrounds. *Early Childhood Research Quarterly, 28,* 578–592. doi:10.1016/j.ecresq.2013.03.006

Winskel, H. (2010). Learning to read in multilingual contexts. In M. Cruz-Ferreira (Ed.), *Multilingual norms* (pp. 237–250). Frankfurt, Germany: Peter Lang International Academic Publishers.

Winsler, A., Díaz, R.M., Espinosa, L., & Rodríguez, J.L. (1999). When learning a second language does not mean losing the first: Bilingual language development in low-income, Spanish-speaking children attending bilingual preschool. *Child Development, 70*(2), 349–362. Retrieved from http://www.ncbi.nlm.nih.gov/pubmed/10218259

Wu, H.S., DeTemple, J.M., Herman, J., & Snow, C.E. (1994). L'animal qui fait oink! Oink!: Bilingual children's oral and written picture descriptions in English and French under varying conditions. *Discourse Processes, 18,* 141–164. doi:10.1080/01638539409544889

Zimmerman, I.L., Steiner, V.G., & Pond, R.E. (2002). Preschool Language Scale, Fourth Edition, Spanish: Examiner's manual. San Antonio, TX: Psychological Corporation.

Zurer Pearson, B., Fernández, S.C., & Oller, D.K. (1993). Lexical development in bilingual infants and toddlers: Comparison to monolingual norms. *Language Learning, 43,* 93–120. doi:10.1111/j.1467-1770.1993.tb00174.x

9

The Role of Hot and Cool Executive Functions in Prereader Comprehension

KELLY B. CARTWRIGHT AND NICOLE RUTHER GUAJARDO

A wonderful process, by which our thoughts and thought-wanderings to the finest shades of detail, the play of our inmost feelings and desires and will, the subtle image of the very innermost that we are, are reflected from us to another soul who reads us through our book . . . And so, to completely understand what we do when we read would almost be the acme of a psychologist's achievements, for it would be to describe very many of the most intricate workings of the human mind, as well as to unravel the tangled story of the most remarkable specific performance that civilization has learned in all its history.

—HUEY (1908, PP. 5–6)

Why, you might ask, would we begin a chapter about prereaders' comprehension with a quote about the wonder and complexity of reading? As Huey (1908) noted, the comprehension of printed text is one of the most complex human accomplishments. To understand the nature of this (or any) achievement, we cannot simply examine its end product: the skilled adult. Rather, we must trace reading comprehension to its roots to see how it develops from an early age in order to better understand successful reading comprehension and the reasons why comprehension processes might go awry. Huey's description also highlights another important feature of comprehension: Skilled readers (as well as listeners) do not simply apprehend objective facts. We make inferences. We deal with multiple sources of information at once. We monitor our thought processes and understanding. We interpret and react to intentions, feelings, and desires of individual characters or authors whose perspectives may differ considerably from our own. These kinds of behaviors—making inferences based on others' thoughts and feelings, mentally juggling multiple perspectives and sources of information—require cognitive self-regulatory abilities (i.e., traditional, cool executive skills), such as cognitive flexibility, working memory, and inhibition (for a review, see Cartwright, 2012), as well as *emotional self-regulatory abilities* (i.e., hot executive skills), such as when a child applies his or her theory of mind (i.e., the ability to consider one's own and others' mental states; Miller, 2012) to understanding a text. The development of these complex mental activities begins long before individuals learn to read, and, as shown in this chapter, these abilities affect prereaders' narrative comprehension in important ways.

Since the start of the 21st century, research has emerged that indicates executive functions play a critical role in the development of reading comprehension (e.g., Borella, Carretti, & Pelegrina, 2010; Cartwright, 2002, 2007, 2012; Cartwright, Marshall, Dandy, & Isaac, 2010; Locascio, Mahone, Eason, & Cutting, 2010; Sesma, Mahone, Levine, Eason, & Cutting, 2009). Much of this work has focused on the traditionally "cool" executive functions (i.e., those that are purely cognitive), such as planning, working memory, inhibition, and cognitive flexibility; however, other "hot" executive skills (i.e., those with a social, motivational, or emotional component; Brock, Rimm-Kaufman, Nathanson, & Grimm, 2009; Zelazo & Carlson, 2012; Zelazo & Müller, 2002; Zelazo, Qu, & Müller, 2005), such as theory of mind, also have been implicated in the development of reading comprehension (e.g., Lecce, Zocchi, Pagnin, Palladino, & Taumoepeau, 2010; Lysaker, Tonge, Gauson, & Miller, 2011). A related skill is counterfactual reasoning, which requires that individuals make inferences about the causes and consequences of characters' behaviors. For example, in reading a book about a boy named Henry who lost his dog, a reader could consider how Henry might have prevented his dog from escaping (Guajardo & Turley-Ames, 2004; Guajardo, Parker, & Turley-Ames, 2009; Hutto, 2007; Roese, 1997). Counterfactual reasoning is related to the development of theory of mind and executive skills (Guajardo & Turley-Ames, 2004; Guajardo et al., 2009), as well as to reading comprehension (Cartwright & Guajardo, 2011; Trabasso & Bartolone, 2003).

Traditional views of reading development suggest reading instruction should focus on word-reading processes in early grades, turning to comprehension instruction in later elementary school (e.g., Chall, 1996). However, a report from the Institute of Education Sciences (Shanahan et al., 2010) highlights the importance of teaching reading comprehension as early as kindergarten, when children are still learning to read, which necessarily involves fostering prereaders' narrative comprehension. Indeed, the comprehension of oral language is an essential component of developing literacy skill (Nation, Cocksey, Taylor, & Bishop, 2010; Whitehurst & Lonigan, 1998).

Work examining the role of executive skills, both hot and cool, in prereaders' comprehension is beginning to emerge and suggests positive connections that can support comprehension development. For example, theory of mind is related to preschoolers' oral language skill (Astington & Jenkins, 1999) and narrative comprehension (see Guajardo & Watson, 2002) and is amenable to training in preschool (Slaughter & Gopnik, 1996), especially when the training involves oral language activities that expand children's abilities to talk about individuals' mental states (Guajardo, Petersen, & Marshall, 2013; Hale & Tager-Flusberg, 2003; Lohmann & Tomasello, 2003). In the Vygotskian tradition, it makes sense that oral language and executive functions would be related because oral language provides children an important means for regulating their own behavior, which is the primary function of executive skills (Bodrova, Leong, & Akhutina, 2011). In fact, preschool children's self-regulatory private speech is related to the development of cognitive flexibility, one of the core cool executive skills (Alarcón-Rubio, Sánchez-Medina, & Prieto-García, 2014); furthermore, oral language predicts hot executive skills, such as theory of mind (Guajardo et al., 2013; Hale & Tager-Flusberg, 2003; Lohmann & Tomasello, 2003).

This chapter is thus designed to provide essential background information on the development of hot and cool executive skills, their relations to reading comprehension development and prereaders' literacy and comprehension development, and recommendations for future work and practice.

COOL AND HOT EXECUTIVE FUNCTIONS:
DEFINITIONS, RELATIONS, AND DEVELOPMENT

As noted previously, traditionally cool executive skills are those purely cognitive skills that are useful for supporting and regulating goal-directed thoughts and behaviors (see Table 9.1 for definitions); the successful deployment of these skills might be described as cognitive regulation (Dawson & Guare, 2010). For the purposes of this chapter, one such goal might be to understand a story. To do so, a preschooler must hold various story elements in mind while actively listening to the story (working memory); refrain from considering irrelevant ideas or thoughts that would disrupt comprehension (inhibition); switch among multiple perspectives, ideas, or sources of information to understand the storyline (cognitive flexibility); and track whether the ongoing text interpretation is consistent with what has been previously heard and understood (monitoring and working memory; for a review of cool executive skills and their relations to reading, see Cartwright, 2012). Story comprehension also recruits processes that involve social and emotion regulation and understanding (i.e., hot executive skills; Brock et al., 2009; Zelazo & Carlson, 2012; Zelazo & Müller, 2002; Zelazo et al., 2005), such as inferring the impact of characters' beliefs, motivations, or feelings on their behavior (theory of mind); understanding authors' intentions in writing the story in particular ways (another example of theory of mind); reflecting on one's own thoughts and feelings about the story as well as their impact on one's interpretation (metacognition and theory of mind); considering or predicting potential events and outcomes that could occur (counterfactual reasoning); or regulating one's own emotional reactions, needs, and impulses in order to focus on the story (self-regulation). See Table 9.1 for additional examples of cool and hot executive skills.

Table 9.1. Definitions and examples of cool and hot executive functions

Process	Definition
Cool executive functions	
Cognitive flexibility	The ability to consider multiple bits of information or ideas at one time and actively switch between them when engaging in a task; this is related to *switching*, also called *shifting*, which is the ability to change one's focus from an initial idea to a new one, also called *attentional control* (see Zhou, Chen, & Main, 2012). *The ability to think of words two ways—as collections of sounds and as representations of meanings—requires cognitive flexibility.*
Inhibition	The ability to restrain one's typical or habitual responses (also called *response inhibition* or *inhibitory control*); sometimes considered a hot skill because it can involve a motivational or emotional component. *A preschooler who resists the impulse to look at a rambunctious classmate while listening to a read-aloud is exhibiting inhibition.*

(continued)

Table 9.1.   *(continued)*

Process	Definition
Metacognition	The ability to take a step back and reflect on thoughts, perspectives, and mental processes and assess their effectiveness. *A reader—or listener—who is able to reflect on his or her own understanding of a story as it is being read (by him or her or to him or her) is exhibiting metacognition.*
Planning	The ability to decide what tasks are necessary to complete a goal, including understanding which ones are most important and the order in which tasks should be completed to most effectively reach the goal. *A reader who scans headings of a book chapter or a preschooler who scans pictures of a book prior to reading is exhibiting planning.*
Working memory	The ability to hold information in mind to support completion of tasks. *A preschooler who can hold in mind characters' names and prior actions while hearing a story read aloud and continuing to construct an interpretation of the story is exhibiting working memory skills.*
Hot executive functions	
Counterfactual thinking	The ability to consider alternatives to an existing situation. *A preschooler who can make predictions about future events in a story's plot is demonstrating counterfactual thinking, as is a child who can generate explanations for what a character might have done differently to avoid a particular outcome.*
Self-regulation	The ability to control one's own behavior and emotions in order to achieve goals. *The preschooler who can sit at circle time without disrupting classmates, raise his or her hand when he or she has a question, or use his or her words when a friend takes a toy is exhibiting self-regulation.*
Theory of mind	The ability to consider one's own and others' mental states, such as thoughts, beliefs, or feelings. *A preschooler with a well-developed theory of mind who knows a story character's dog is asleep under the bed will infer that the character is wandering up and down his or her street calling the dog because the character has a mistaken belief that the dog is lost; the preschooler may also infer that the story character is sad or scared because of the mistaken belief, demonstrating an understanding that characters' mental states can affect actions and feelings, even when those mental states do not match reality.*

Source: Cartwright (2012).

Cool and hot executive skills are related in preschool (Carlson, Moses, & Claxton, 2004; Drayton et al., 2011; Frye, Zelazo, & Palfai, 1995; Guajardo et al., 2009), even when age, temperament, parent education, and verbal comprehension are controlled (Henning, Spinath, & Aschersleben, 2011). There are many possible explanations for the relation between cool and hot executive skills; for example, hot skills may develop before and support cool skills (or vice versa), these classes of skills might be unrelated, or both classes of skills may recruit the same underlying processes or brain regions (for a discussion of possibilities, see Perner & Lang, 1999). Generally, conceptions of the relations between traditionally cool executive skills and relations of those skills to other cognitive skills depend on disciplinary frame. In experimental psychology, executive skills such as inhibition and cognitive flexibility have traditionally been seen as parts of an overall working memory system, whereas in contemporary neuropsychology, working memory is seen as one of an array of executive skills individuals employ to achieve goals

(Schneider, Schumann-Hengsteler, & Sodian, 2005). In this view, hot skills are seen as expressions of the basic ability to control one's cognitions in "the content domain of self and social understanding" (Zelazo et al., 2005, p. 86; also see Miller & Marcovitch, 2012).

Evidence has supported this latter interpretation. For example, in some studies using factor analysis, hot and cool skills are statistically indistinguishable and part of the same overall construct (e.g., Allan & Lonigan, 2011; Prencipe et al., 2011; see Rueda, Posner, & Rothbart, 2005, for a review), and they appear to develop together (Hong-wanishkul, Happeney, Lee, & Zelazo, 2005; Miller & Marcovitch, 2012). Furthermore, cool and hot skills recruit adjacent, sometimes overlapping brain regions (Ardilla, 2013; Blakemore & Choudhury, 2006; Rueda et al., 2005; Saxe, Schulz, & Jiang, 2006; Stone, Baron-Cohen, & Knight, 1998; Zelazo et al., 2005); both types of skills are impaired in individuals on the autism spectrum, though each can be selectively impaired in these individuals (Ozonoff, Pennington, & Rogers, 1991; Pellicano, 2007). Finally, some data suggest cool skills may precede hot skills in development. For example, Benson, Sab-bagh, Carlson, and Zelazo (2013) demonstrated that preschoolers high in cool execu-tive skills experienced significant improvement in response to theory of mind training, whereas children low in cool executive skills did not (also see Carlson, Claxton, & Moses, 2013; Hughes & Ensor, 2007; Prencipe et al., 2011, for more work that suggests cool skills might precede hot skills developmentally). However, other studies suggest hot skills pre-cede cool skills in development. For example, emotion self-regulation in infancy predicts performance on a battery of cool skills at 4 years old (Ursache, Blair, Stifter, Voegtline, & the Family Life Project Investigators, 2013), and infant self-restraint predicts perfor-mance on a battery of cool executive skills at 14 years old (Friedman, Miyake, Robinson, & Hewitt, 2011; also see Miranda, Presentación, Siegenthaler, & Jara, 2011, who trained hot skills in children with attention-deficit/hyperactivity disorder, resulting in improved performance on cool tasks). Clearly, cool and hot executive skills are related in important ways and seem to be expressions of the same kinds of cognitive skills in cognitive and social-emotional contexts, respectively. As Liew (2012) noted, we need to view these as compatible or complementary processes in educational contexts, as both cognitive and social-emotional control contribute to academic success.

Cool and hot executive skills develop considerably during the preschool years and continue to develop across the lifespan (Best & Miller, 2010; Best, Miller, & Jones, 2009; Davidson, Amso, Anderson, & Diamond, 2006; De Luca et al., 2003; Henning et al., 2011; Hughes & Ensor, 2007; Rueda et al., 2005; Wellman & Liu, 2004). In addition, children's cool executive skills become more differentiated from preschool to adolescence (Lee, Bull, & Ho, 2013). According to Munakata, Snyder, and Chatham (2012), the development of children's cognitive control (cool executive function) occurs in three stages across child-hood. Each is characterized by important developmental shifts in self-directed behav-ior and the ability to hold goals in mind, with rapid changes occurring in the preschool period. In the first stage, children's actions are governed by habitual responses that eventually can be overpowered with explicit instruction from others. For example, pre-schoolers may naturally sort pictures of objects by type and eventually gain the ability to overpower this habitual response by re-sorting the same pictures by beginning sound (or some other characteristic) when told to do so, thus demonstrating the ability to inhibit a habitual response and shift flexibly in response to feedback. Before they are able to shift this way, however, young preschoolers will continue to exhibit habitual responses, even when it seems that they understand explicit instructions to change their behavior. In the preceding example, they may express clear understanding of the new sort rule but continue to sort by the first rule anyway!

In the second stage, children shift from being reactive and changing behavior in response to instructions from others to being proactive and engaging in goal-directed behavior that they initiate; however, their goals are often those that were externally generated (e.g., picking up toys when finished with them, reading stories in a certain way). For example, young preschoolers may need to be shown how to hold a book and turn its pages when first exposed to picture books. But before long they will be "reading" (i.e., turning pages, holding the book in the appropriate orientation, constructing a narrative in response to the pictures) to themselves or others in purposeful ways, demonstrating planning, flexibility in managing multiple types of information, and memory for the narrative and conventions of book reading. In this stage, however, their goals are generally externally constructed or guided (e.g., "I am going to read this book like Mommy and my teacher do it").

Finally, in the third stage, Munakata et al. (2012) suggest children move from striving to meet externally guided goals to generating goals of their own, which they can hold in mind while they engage in the behaviors necessary for goal attainment, such as when a child decides to create a book to give as a gift to someone else. Because children vary with respect to the ages at which they achieve these milestones, there are no particular age ranges attached to these stages. In fact, even adults vary in their abilities to represent abstract goals (Sinnott, 1998). Moreover, consistent with this developmental frame, specific executive skills emerge at different points in development: Inhibition and working memory appear to develop early, even in infancy, whereas cognitive flexibility and planning continue to develop into adolescence and beyond (Best & Miller, 2010; Clark et al., 2013; Cartwright, Isaac, & Dandy, 2006; Davidson et al., 2006).

The development of hot executive skills follows a similar trajectory in parallel with cool skills (Zelazo & Carlson, 2012; Zelazo & Müller, 2002). For example, children gain increasing sophistication in theory of mind across the preschool years (Wellman & Liu, 2004). Theory of mind involves reasoning in social, affectively motivated interactions with others (Zelazo & Carlson, 2012; Zelazo & Müller, 2002; Zelazo et al., 2005) and refers to a cluster of skills that involve an understanding of the representational nature of the mind (Whiten, 1994). Broadly, children who comprehend theory of mind concepts understand that people have mental states (e.g., beliefs, desires), that such mental states do not have to be accurate (i.e., false beliefs), that different people can hold varying beliefs about the same situation, and that such knowledge is related to perception (e.g., hearing, seeing). For example, once a child understands these concepts, he or she realizes that his or her mother does not know what happened at preschool unless the child tells her and that his or her mother may think the child behaved well all day when in fact he or she got in trouble several times. Children have a reasonable understanding of these concepts by 4 years of age (Wellman, Cross, & Watson, 2000), though an understanding of more complex concepts (e.g., forgetting, attention, faux pas) comes later (Miller, 2012; Pillow & Lovett, 1998).

Another aspect of social cognition that potentially fits within the definition of "hot" executive functions is counterfactual reasoning, or the ability to consider alternatives to reality and what could have caused situations to be different (Kahneman & Miller, 1986; Kahneman & Tversky, 1982). Such thinking often includes phrases such as "what if" and "if only" and can motivate behavior (Roese, 1994). Considering what one could have done differently to avoid an unfavorable outcome can lead a person to act differently in the future. In fact, parents and teachers may encourage such thinking for this very reason. If a child realizes he or she could have asked the teacher for help when a friend took a book away, he or she might not hit the friend the next time something similar occurs. As with the work on theory of mind, preschool-age children demonstrate an early understanding of counterfactual thinking (Beck, Riggs, & Gorniak, 2009; Drayton, Turley-Ames, & Guajardo, 2011; German & Nichols, 2003; Guajardo & Turley-Ames, 2004; Harris, German, & Mills, 1996), with more complex concepts developing in later childhood (Rafetseder, Schwitalla, & Perner, 2013). We should note that counterfactual thinking is essential for making predictions while reading, an important component of strategic (i.e., self-directed) text comprehension (for a review, see Almasi & Fullerton, 2012), because predicting necessarily involves thinking about potential alternative events that could occur in the text.

Several studies have demonstrated a link between theory of mind understanding, specifically the understanding that people can hold false beliefs that contrast with what a child already knows to be true, and counterfactual reasoning (e.g., Guajardo & Turley-Ames, 2004; Müller, Miller, Michalczyk, & Karapinka, 2007; Riggs, Peterson, Robinson, & Mitchell, 1998). One explanation for this relationship is that both involve consideration of alternatives to reality—thinking concurrently about the real situation and how it could be different. In false belief scenarios, children typically have to consider where an object really is and where a character thinks it is; when reasoning counterfactually, individuals think about how a situation turned out while also considering what could have led to a different outcome. Another explanation is that theory of mind understanding and counterfactual reasoning both rely on other (i.e., "cool") aspects of executive function (German & Nichols, 2003; Guajardo et al., 2009; Guajardo & Turley-Ames, 2004; Müller et al., 2007). Indeed, counterfactual reasoning and false belief understanding rely on inhibition (e.g., Beck et al., 2009; Carlson & Moses, 2001; Drayton et al., 2011; Carlson, Moses, & Breton, 2002; Carlson, Moses, & Hix, 1998), cognitive flexibility (Guajardo et al., 2009; Frye et al., 1995), and working memory (e.g., Davis & Pratt, 1995; Drayton et al., 2011). And like theory of mind, counterfactual reasoning is related to preschoolers' developing oral language skills (Beck et al., 2009; Drayton et al., 2011; Guajardo et al., 2009), an essential component of early literacy development.

Executive skills can be cool (purely cognitive) or hot (having a social, emotional, or motivational component) and become more differentiated with age and development. Some scholars suggest hot skills precede cool skills in development, whereas other scholars suggest cool skills precede hot ones. In addition, hot and cool executive skills appear to be expressions of the same underlying abilities in preschoolers because hot and cool executive skills are related, develop together across the preschool years, recruit overlapping brain regions, and load on the same factors in some studies. Because both cool and hot executive skills in preschool are related to future academic success, we should view them as complementary processes in education contexts. See Table 9.1 for descriptions of hot and cool executive skills.

RELATIONS OF EXECUTIVE SKILLS TO READING COMPREHENSION

Executive skills are differentially related to word reading and reading comprehension abilities, with stronger relations between executive skills and reading comprehension (Sesma et al., 2009). Most research investigating the role of executive skills in reading ability, though, has focused on word-reading skills. (For a review of research in this area, see a meta-analysis by Booth, Boyle, & Kelly, 2010, who found that only 6 of 48 studies focused on reading comprehension difficulties.) Nevertheless, in the past few years, a number of studies have focused specifically on the role of executive skills in reading comprehension. Executive skills including cognitive flexibility (Altemeier, Abbot, & Berninger, 2008; Cartwright, 2002, 2007; Cartwright et al., 2010), attentional control (Conners, 2009; McVay & Kane, 2012), inhibition (Kieffer, Vukovic, & Berry, 2013), monitoring (Best et al., 2011; Oakhill & Cain, 2012), working memory (Cain, 2006; Seigneuric & Ehrlich, 2005), and planning (Sesma et al., 2009) have been found to contribute uniquely to reading comprehension, often beyond traditional predictors such as decoding ability and verbal ability. In addition, students with specific reading comprehension difficulties, despite adequate word-reading ability, have significantly lower cognitive flexibility (Best, Miller, & Naglieri, 2011; Cartwright & Coppage, 2009), inhibition (Borella et al., 2010; Cain, 2006), working memory (Cain, 2006; Carretti, Cornoldi, De Beni, & Romanò, 2005), monitoring (Best et al., 2011), and planning (Best et al., 2011; Locascio et al., 2010) than peers with better comprehension. Furthermore, teaching executive skills results in improvements in reading comprehension for typically developing students (e.g., Cartwright, 2002) and those with low comprehension or other learning difficulties (Cartwright, Guiffré, Bock, & Coppage, 2011; Cartwright, Lane, & Singleton, 2012; Dahlin, 2011; García-Madruga et al., 2013).

Research with elementary-age readers also has shown the importance of hot executive functions for reading comprehension, specifically with respect to the ability to infer characters' mental states to support comprehension. Some elementary-age children may dismiss characters' perspectives in stories; thus, researchers have used character story mapping to help students attend to characters' mental states (i.e., thoughts, motives). Story mapping involves having children read a story, list the key components of the story (e.g., events, problems, resolution), and then engage in discussion about characters' perspectives during the events listed on the map (Emery, 1996; see also Chapter 4 by van Kleeck). The use of character mapping enhances children's story comprehension because it forces them to consider characters' mental states and how different characters may have varying perspectives of the same situation, including how those viewpoints may differ from their own (Emery, 1996; Shanahan & Shanahan, 1997). In the end, children have a more complex understanding of the story (Shanahan & Shanahan, 1997). Given these findings and the fact that preschool, elementary, and college students prefer social stories over nonsocial ones (Barnes, 2012; Barnes & Bloom, 2013), book reading may provide an ideal context for teaching theory of mind, which would then support future reading comprehension. In support of this notion, recent work indicates reading fiction supports theory of mind development in adults (Kidd & Castano, 2013), and Lysaker et al. (2011) showed that when second and third graders were provided relationally oriented reading instruction, their theory of mind (what these authors called "social imagination") and reading comprehension both improved. Thus reading comprehension and theory of mind appear to have a reciprocal relationship (see also Lysaker & Tonge, 2013), which is not surprising given evidence that story comprehension and theory of mind recruit overlapping brain regions to support thinking about others' perspectives (Mar, 2011).

In addition, individuals on the autism spectrum who typically have impairments in theory of mind also demonstrate a preference for nonfiction over social narratives and lower comprehension of social narratives than typically developing peers (Barnes, 2012; Brown, Oram-Cardy, & Johnson, 2013). Finally, although theory of mind is most frequently discussed with respect to understanding others' mental states, it also involves understanding one's own mental states (Astington, Harris, & Olson, 1988). Not surprisingly, students' understanding of their own mental states, specifically with respect to reading processes, is related to their developing reading comprehension. Poor comprehenders are significantly less aware of their own reading processes (Dermitzaki, Andreou, & Paraskeva, 2008; Jacobs & Paris, 1987; Lecce et al., 2010; Paris & Myers, 1981; Vidal-Abarca, Mañá, & Gil, 2010).

In addition to theory of mind, other hot executive skills seem to support reading comprehension, though more work is needed in this area. One skill is counterfactual reasoning. Because generating counterfactuals requires knowledge-based or elaborative inference making (e.g., thinking about what Henry might have done to prevent his dog from escaping requires the use of extratextual knowledge about dogs, reasons why dogs should be prevented from escaping, and ways to keep dogs from escaping), it seems likely that such reasoning would be related to reading comprehension; these kinds of thoughts seem to require the same reasoning as gap-filling inferences (Baker & Stein, 1981). Such inference making supports reading comprehension (Cain & Oakhill, 1999), and poor comprehenders are significantly less skilled at making inferences than peers with better comprehension (Bowyer-Crane & Snowling, 2005; Laing & Kamhi, 2002). There is little work, though, specifically investigating the role of counterfactual thinking in children's reading comprehension (yet see our study, described in the following text). An additional hot skill is self-regulation. There is a good deal of evidence that self-regulation supports reading comprehension: Children who are taught to regulate their own reading comprehension processes through self-directed strategies perform significantly better on assessments of reading comprehension (for reviews, see Pressley, 2002; Gaskins, Satlow, & Pressley, 2007). Taken together, this work indicates that both cool and hot executive functions play significant roles in developing reading comprehension.

Both hot and cool executive skills are related to reading comprehension, though far more work has examined the contributions of cool skills to reading comprehension. For example, cognitive flexibility, working memory, inhibition, attentional control, monitoring, and planning all make independent contributions to reading comprehension. In addition, though very few studies have focused on executive skill interventions, emerging work has demonstrated that teaching cool executive skills such as cognitive flexibility and working memory results in improvements in reading comprehension. Another area that deserves additional attention is the role of hot executive skills in reading comprehension. We know that theory of mind, a hot executive skill involving knowledge of others' thoughts, feelings, and perspectives, appears to have a reciprocal relationship with reading comprehension: Reading fiction improves adults' theory of mind, and teaching theory of mind improves elementary students' reading comprehension. Finally, counterfactual reasoning, a hot executive skill that involves considering alternatives to a situation, also appears to be related to reading comprehension. Future work should focus on the relative roles of hot and cool skills in reading comprehension as well as executive skill–based interventions for improving reading comprehension.

RELATIONS OF EXECUTIVE SKILLS TO PREREADERS' LITERACY SKILLS AND NARRATIVE COMPREHENSION

Executive skills play an important role in skilled reading comprehension. Thus researchers have begun to focus on ways that executive skills, both cool and hot, might support literacy development even before children learn to read. As is typical for work on prereaders' literacy development (and also work on readers' development, as previously discussed), much of this research focuses on word-reading skills, such as letter recognition, phonological awareness, and letter-sound knowledge; however, some work does explore relations of executive skills to meaning-focused emergent literacy skills, such as preschoolers' developing oral language vocabulary and narrative comprehension. As you might expect, preschool literacy and language skills are differentially related to comprehension and word-reading outcomes; for example, expressive vocabulary is specifically related to narrative comprehension, whereas phonological awareness and letter knowledge are related to word-reading skills (Kendeou, van den Broek, White, & Lynch, 2009).

In fact, vocabulary is associated with developing narrative comprehension across the preschool years (Lynch et al., 2008). For further discussion about the role of vocabulary on comprehension, see Chapter 2 by Coyne, Neugebauer, Ware, McCoach, and Madura. Along with preschool narrative comprehension, preschool vocabulary predicts kindergarten oral language skills, including vocabulary, listening comprehension, and television-viewing comprehension (Kendeou et al., 2009). Not surprisingly, vocabulary is also related to reading comprehension across the elementary school years and beyond (Kendeou et al., 2009; Ouellette, 2006; Verhoeven, van Leeuwe, & Vermeer, 2011). Given its importance to the development of reading comprehension and its consistent relations to narrative comprehension, vocabulary is often explored as an outcome measure in studies of children's narrative comprehension; thus, we attend to vocabulary in the review that follows to provide a context for the studies we describe in the next section and to provide a foundation for our recommendations for practice, provided at the end of the chapter.

As noted earlier, preschoolers' executive functions are less differentiated than those of older children and adults. Consequently, there is considerable overlap in relations of hot and cool executive skills to preschoolers' literacy development. Furthermore, executive skills are related to both word-level and meaning-focused aspects of emergent literacy. For example, Allan and Lonigan (2011) found in a factor analysis that hot and cool executive functions were part of the same construct that was related to preschoolers' print knowledge, phonological awareness, and expressive vocabulary. With respect to word-level skills, preschool attentional control contributes unique variance to preschoolers' letter and word identification (Lan, Legare, Ponitz, Li, & Morrison, 2011), and working memory makes a significant unique contribution to 4- to 6-year-olds' letter knowledge over inhibition, social understanding, age, and vocabulary (Miller, Müller, Giesbrecht, Carpendale, & Kerns, 2013). In addition, preschool inhibition predicts unique variance in phonological awareness and letter knowledge, whereas teacher-rated self-regulation and theory of mind predict unique variance only in letter knowledge in kindergarten (Blair & Razza, 2007).

Furthermore, behavioral self-regulation predicts growth in letter and word identification across the prekindergarten year (McClelland et al., 2007). Taken together, these findings indicate that both cool and hot executive skills are important contributors to the development of preschool letter and word knowledge. However, we should note that a study by Willoughby, Kupersmidt, Vogler-Lee, and Bryant (2011) indicated only cognitive regulation (cool skills)—not behavioral regulation (hot skills)—contributed to preschoolers' letter knowledge and phonological awareness.

Van de Sande, Segers, and Verhoeven (2013) extended work on phonological awareness, finding that both cool (attentional control) and hot (behavioral control) skills in kindergarten support the development of phonological awareness and indirectly support first-grade decoding. Consistent with this notion, Farrar and Ashwell (2008, 2012) found that theory of mind is significantly related to preschoolers' phonological awareness. These findings make sense: In order for preschoolers to think of words in multiple ways—as both collections of sounds and as meaningful units—they must develop awareness of their own thinking about words as well as flexibly consider words' multiple features. Awareness of one's own and others' thinking is central to theory of mind development (Astington et al., 1988), which is significantly related to preschoolers' developing cognitive flexibility (Guajardo et al., 2009).

Both cool and hot executive skills also have been implicated in the development of meaning-focused emergent literacy skills, such as vocabulary and narrative comprehension. As noted earlier, Allan and Lonigan (2011) found that hot and cool executive function tasks predicted preschoolers' vocabulary. Behavioral self-regulation (a hot skill) also predicts significant unique variance in preschoolers' vocabulary across cultures (Germany and Iceland; von Suchodoletz et al., 2013), as well as growth in vocabulary from fall to spring across the prekindergarten year (McClelland et al., 2007). Welsh, Nix, Blair, Bierman, and Nelson (2010) demonstrated that preschoolers' cool executive skills (working memory and attentional control) predicted unique variance in kindergarten reading achievement beyond the effects of preschool emergent literacy skills, such as print knowledge and phonological processing. Reading achievement in this study included both word reading and story comprehension measures; thus these findings suggest preschool cool executive skills predict kindergarten narrative comprehension. However, these findings should be interpreted with caution because kindergarten (prereader) story comprehension measures were not reported separately from word-level skills.

Few studies have been conducted to assess directly the relations of cool executive skills to preschoolers' narrative comprehension. Florit, Roch, and Levorato (2011), for example, included working memory as a control variable in their study of contributors to preschool narrative comprehension, finding that working memory was significantly related to both literal and inferential comprehension in their sample. Potocki, Ecalle, and Magnan (2013) confirmed the significant contribution of working memory to preschoolers' narrative comprehension and also found significant relations of working memory to sentence comprehension in these young students.

Although goal-directed planning, another cool executive skill, is not typically assessed in studies of preschool literacy, 4-year-olds are capable of inferring goals in stories and are sensitive to causal relations of story subevents to overall goals, such that stories with more causal connections to the overall goal better support preschoolers' narrative comprehension (Wenner, 2004). In addition, 3-year-olds' sequential reasoning abilities, an important component of planning, are significantly related to their narrative comprehension (Zampini, Suttora, D'Odorico, & Zanchi, 2013). A study expanded on the notion of preschoolers' awareness of causal connections in story narratives and examined the contributions of cool skills (monitoring, inhibition, working memory, and attention control) as well as theory of mind to preschoolers' narrative comprehension using two types of measures: one that required recall of separate story elements and another that required children to be aware of causal connections in the narratives (Strasser & del Río, 2014). As would be expected from prior work, executive skills contributed more unique variance to narrative comprehension of texts that preserve causal coherence; inhibition, monitoring, attentional control, and working memory were implicated in such complex comprehension, but not theory of mind. When narrative comprehension required recall of separate story elements, only working memory made a unique contribution. These findings suggest cool skills may be more important than hot skills for preschoolers' narrative comprehension. However, a substantial body of work on theory of mind development suggests this hot skill also contributes in important ways to preschoolers' narrative comprehension development.

To consider the role of theory of mind understanding in narrative comprehension, particularly at the level of the prereader, it is helpful to think about what a child needs to do or understand to grasp a story. According to Feldman, Bruner, Renderer, and Spitzer (1996), there are two landscapes within a story: landscape of action and landscape of consciousness. Landscape of action refers to the events in the story, whereas the landscape of consciousness includes characters' thoughts, perceptions, and motives (i.e., theory of mind concepts). Comprehension of both landscapes is essential (Bruner, 1988, 1990; Emery, 1996). Understanding the landscape of action seems to be the first step for children, with an understanding of the landscape of consciousness following. One reason for this might be that the landscape of consciousness needs to be inferred, as the characters' thoughts often are not explicitly stated. The final step would be to integrate information from the two landscapes. A child is not able to understand or integrate both landscapes until he or she understands theory of mind concepts (Astington, 1990).

The importance of being able to infer another's thoughts and/or beliefs for story comprehension has been supported with work with prereaders. As early as 4 years of age, children's abilities to infer characters' goals, the actions needed to meet those goals, and their mental states predict their story comprehension skills (Tompkins, Guo, & Justice, 2013). Such inference making supports narrative comprehension directly as well as indirectly through vocabulary development (Lepola, Lynch, Laakkonen, Silvén, & Niemi, 2012).

Furthermore, direct instruction in inferential comprehension, as opposed to literal comprehension, improves preschoolers' narrative comprehension (DeBruin-Parecki & Squibb, 2011; Roberts, 2013; van Kleeck, 2008).

Children who do not understand false belief concepts are more likely to focus only on the landscape of action when retelling a story (the literal features of the story). Those who understand false belief concepts can articulate false beliefs and other mental content in a story, thus comprehending the story at a higher level because they can make deeper inferences about story content (Riggio & Cassidy, 2009). Similarly, 4- and 5-year-old kindergartners who succeed at false belief tasks are more likely to integrate the landscapes of action and of consciousness when they retell a story (Pelletier & Astington, 2004). Rather than only focusing on what happened in a story, these children can consider and connect events with characters' thoughts and motivations. Pelletier and Astington (2004) proposed that children must be able to understand the physical and the mental aspects of stories, as well as make connections between the two, to fully comprehend narrative. Indeed, Lysaker and Miller (2012) demonstrated that theory of mind—which these authors call "social imagination"—plays a significant role in narrative comprehension of wordless picture books.

Other work highlighting a connection between mental state understanding and story comprehension in prereaders has focused on parent–child discourse and narrative. Children's books are a rich source of mental state information (Dyer, Shatz, & Wellman, 2000; Dyer, Shatz, Wellman, & Saito, 2004), and they may serve as important vehicles for teaching children, directly or indirectly, about mental states (Donahue, 2013; Guajardo & Watson, 2002); how to attend to story vocabulary, plot, and sequence (landscape of action); and causal connections of characters' thoughts, feelings, and motivations to the story plot (landscape of consciousness), resulting in richer retellings of stories that preserve more sociocognitive themes and causal story elements (Aram, Fine, & Ziv, 2013). Thus preschoolers' theory of mind understanding can be taught in storybook reading contexts with positive implications for their narrative comprehension development.

Several studies have used storybook reading as a context for examining associations between discourse about mental states and theory of mind understanding (e.g., Adrian, Clemente, & Villanueva, 2007; Adrian, Clemente, Villanueva, & Rieffe, 2005; Guajardo & Watson, 2002; Ruffman, Slade, & Crow, 2002; Sabbagh & Callanan, 1998; Slaughter, Peterson, & Mackintosh, 2007; Symons, Peterson, Slaughter, Roche, & Doyle, 2005). See also Chapter 11 by Enz and Stamm for additional discussion about the role of the parent in shared storybook reading. Frequency of book reading (Adrian et al., 2005) and parental usage of mental state language when discussing stories are correlated with children's understanding of theory of mind concepts both concurrently (e.g., Adrian et al., 2005; Slaughter et al., 2007; Symons et al., 2005) and longitudinally (Adrian et al., 2007). In particular, parents who frequently expand upon mental state content by explaining the events that led to a thought or misperception or by discussing contrasts between characters' thoughts have children who perform well on false belief tasks (Slaughter et al., 2007).

Consideration of this work suggests an interesting developmental process by which children develop skill in narrative comprehension. Children's storybooks often focus on themes that include mental references (i.e., false beliefs, deception), and they provide a natural context in which parents or teachers talk to children about such concepts. These interactions foster theory of mind development, which in turn enhances children's story comprehension. Children who understand the representational nature of the mind are equipped to focus on the landscapes of action and consciousness simultaneously and comprehend stories at a higher level as a result. It is logical to go the next step and propose that these early story comprehension skills in prereaders set the foundation for later reading comprehension. The studies on theory of mind discussed thus far have implications for children's narrative comprehension, yet narrative comprehension was not examined specifically. Two studies that did assess the relation of theory of mind to narrative comprehension will be discussed in the next section.

Both hot and cool executive skills are related to prereaders' literacy development. With respect to word-level skills, attentional control, cognitive and behavioral regulation, inhibition, theory of mind, and working memory are related to preschoolers' letter knowledge. Attentional control, behavioral self-regulation, inhibition, and theory of mind are related to phonological awareness, and attentional control, behavioral self-regulation, and working memory are related to word identification skills. With respect to meaning-focused literacy skills, behavioral self-regulation and cognitive flexibility contribute to vocabulary development, and cognitive flexibility, theory of mind, and working memory contribute to sentence comprehension. Finally, attentional control, cognitive flexibility, skills related to planning (goal inferencing and sequential reasoning), inhibition, monitoring, and theory of mind are related to prereaders' narrative comprehension.

Research investigating the role of hot and cool executive functions in prereaders' literacy development is in its infancy; thus, this summary of findings does not provide a complete picture of the relations of these skills to prereaders' word- and meaning-focused skills. Much research is needed to provide a complete picture of the developmental contributions of hot and cool executive functions to prereaders' literacy development, and virtually no work has yet emerged to target executive skill interventions in support of prereaders' comprehension, despite indications that such work would provide valuable benefits for young learners. (See Table 9.2 for a summary of findings regarding relations of executive skills to prereaders' word- and meaning-focused literacy skills.)

PROMISING QUASI-EXPERIMENTAL AND LONGITUDINAL DATA

Although work in reading comprehension suggests executive skills may play an important role in the development of prereaders' narrative comprehension, little work has examined this question or the impact of executive skills on preschoolers' responsiveness to comprehension interventions. Cartwright, DeBruin-Parecki, Vaughn, Badalis, and Orelski (2014) conducted a study with 3- to 5-year-old preschoolers (n = 49; mean age = 4 years, 7 months; 35.8% minority students, 41.5% girls) to assess the contributions of hot and cool executive skills to these children's expressive vocabulary and narrative comprehension. In addition, they compared the effects of inferential, literal, and typical comprehension instruction on expressive vocabulary and narrative comprehension and assessed the influence of hot and cool executive skills on children's comprehension growth in response to the various comprehension instruction types. Children were pretested on cognitive flexibility, inhibition, working memory, theory of mind, receptive

Table 9.2. Relations of executive functions to prereaders' word- and meaning-focused literacy skills

Literacy skill	Executive skill	Citations
Word-focused skills		
Letter knowledge	Attentional control	Lan, Legare, Ponitz, Li, & Morrison (2011)
	Behavioral self-regulation	Blair & Razza (2007); McClelland et al. (2007)
	Cognitive regulation	Willoughby, Kupersmidt, Vogler-Lee, & Bryant (2011)
	Inhibition	Blair & Razza (2007)
	Theory of mind	Blair & Razza (2007)
	Working memory	Miller, Müller, Giesbrecht, Carpendale, & Kerns (2013)
Print knowledge[a]	Combined hot and cool measures	Allan & Lonigan (2011)[b]
Phonological awareness	Attentional control	Van de Sande, Segers, & Verhoeven (2013)
	Behavioral self-regulation	Van de Sande et al. (2013)
	Combined hot and cool measures	Allan & Lonigan (2011)[b]
	Inhibition	Blair & Razza (2007)
	Theory of mind	Farrar & Ashwell (2008, 2012)
Word identification	Attentional control	Lan et al. (2011); Welsh, Nix, Blair, Bierman, & Nelson (2010)
	Behavioral self-regulation	McClelland et al. (2007)
	Working memory	Welsh, Nix, Blair, Bierman, & Nelson (2010)[b]
Meaning-focused skills		
Vocabulary	Behavioral self-regulation	McClelland et al. (2007); von Suchodoletz et al. (2013)
	Cognitive flexibility	Cartwright, DeBruin-Parecki, Vaughn, Badalis, & Orelski (2014)
	Combined hot and cool measures	Allan & Lonigan (2011)[b]
Sentence comprehension	Cognitive flexibility	Guajardo & Cartwright (2014)
	Theory of mind	Guajardo & Cartwright (2014)
	Working memory	Potocki, Ecalle, & Magnan (2013)

(continued)

Table 9.2.   *(continued)*

Literacy skill	Executive skill	Citations
Narrative comprehension	Attentional control	Strasser & del Río (2014); Welsh et al. (2010)[c]
	Cognitive flexibility	Cartwright et al. (2014)
	Goal inferencing (planning)	Wenner (2004)
	Inhibition	Strasser & del Río (2014)
	Monitoring	Strasser & del Río (2014)
	Sequential reasoning (planning)	Zampini, Suttora, D'Odorico, & Zanchi (2013)
	Theory of mind	Aram, Fine, & Ziv (2013); Astington (1990); Cartwright et al. (2014); Guajardo & Watson (2002); Lysaker & Miller (2012); Pelletier & Astington (2004); Riggio & Cassidy (2009); Tompkins, Guo, & Justice (2013)
	Working memory	Florit, Roch, & Levorato (2011); Potocki, Ecalle, & Magnan (2013); Strasser & del Río (2014); Welsh et al. (2010)[c]

[a] Print knowledge included print concepts, letter discrimination, word discrimination, and letter–name and sound discrimination (Allan & Lonigan, 2011).

[b] Allan and Lonigan (2011) assessed executive functions (EFs) with a battery of hot and cool tasks that involved both behavioral and cognitive skills and tapped such EFs as inhibition, delay of gratification in a behavioral self-regulation task, and deception (a theory of mind task); all eight tasks in the battery loaded onto one factor in factor analysis, which was significantly related to literacy skills.

[c] Welsh et al. (2010) examined the relations of executive functions to literacy skills with a measure that combined both word identification and comprehension skills.

vocabulary, expressive vocabulary, and narrative comprehension. Expressive vocabulary and narrative comprehension were assessed again after the interventions were complete. All cool and hot executive skills were significantly, positively related to preschoolers' narrative comprehension, as expected. Cognitive flexibility predicted significant variance in expressive vocabulary beyond all other pretest variables, consistent with findings for reading comprehension in older children and adults (Cartwright, 2002, 2007; Cartwright et al., 2010). Inferential comprehension instruction produced significant gains in expressive vocabulary and narrative comprehension, even when all pretest variables were controlled. However, findings varied depending on children's pretest levels of executive skills. Specifically, children in the inferential comprehension condition who were high on cognitive flexibility at pretest made significantly greater gains in narrative comprehension than those low on cognitive flexibility (who made no significant comprehension gains); similar significant findings emerged for theory of mind, suggesting that these cool and hot executive skills may provide important cognitive foundations for successful comprehension development. These findings are consistent with the work described earlier in our chapter, yet the sample in this study was small; thus, effects of executive skills on responsiveness to comprehension intervention should be explored in future research.

In addition, we conducted a longitudinal study to examine the relations of hot and cool executive skills to preschoolers' sentence and phrase comprehension as well as to their reading comprehension and metacognitive awareness of reading processes 3.5 years later (Guajardo & Cartwright, 2014). As noted earlier, theory of mind involves awareness of an individual's own mental processes; thus we hypothesized that theory of mind may be related to metacognitive awareness of reading processes (reading awareness; Jacobs & Paris, 1987) and to reading comprehension. To date, no work has examined whether children's theory of mind predicts reading awareness (though Lecce et al., 2010, did show that mental state knowledge was related to metacognitive knowledge about reading) or whether preschool theory of mind predicts later reading comprehension. Furthermore, counterfactual reasoning, likely a hot executive skill because it involves socially and emotionally motivated reasoning, is significantly related to theory of mind and cool executive skills (Guajardo & Turley-Ames, 2004; Guajardo et al., 2009), and it involves the kind of inference making important to successful reading comprehension (Cain & Oakhill, 1999; Roese, 1994, 1997). However, no study has examined the role of counterfactual reasoning in developing narrative or reading comprehension.

Thus the purpose of this study was to examine these questions by testing children's hot and cool executive skills, reading awareness, and comprehension in a sample of 35 preschoolers who were pretested on first-order theory of mind (the ability to think about one's own thoughts as well as another person's thoughts; e.g., *My mother thinks her purse is on the kitchen counter, but I know she really left it on the couch*), counterfactual thinking (both hot executive function skills), color–shape cognitive flexibility, working memory (both of which are cool executive functions), vocabulary, and sentence and phrase comprehension in preschool. We tested these children 3.5 years later on second-order theory of mind, a more advanced form of theory of mind that involves thinking about an individual's thoughts about someone else's thoughts (e.g., *Mom thinks that I think I'm getting clothes for my birthday, but I know I'm getting a bike because I saw it in the garage*); reading-specific cognitive flexibility; decoding ability; reading comprehension; and reading awareness. As would be expected from the results of the preschool study described earlier (Cartwright et al., 2014), cognitive flexibility and theory of mind contributed unique variance to preschool children's sentence and phrase comprehension beyond vocabulary, working memory, and counterfactual thinking, even when preschool income and age were controlled.

As expected, first-order theory of mind in preschool was related to reading awareness in elementary school, whereas preschool counterfactual thinking was related to reading comprehension in elementary school. Furthermore, second-order theory of mind (assessed in elementary school) was significantly related to elementary students' reading awareness and reading comprehension. Regression analyses indicated preschool counterfactual thinking made a unique contribution to reading comprehension in elementary school beyond all other variables. In elementary school, reading-specific cognitive flexibility accuracy and speed each contributed unique variance to reading comprehension beyond other variables, consistent with prior work (Cartwright, 2002, 2007; Cartwright et al., 2010). Decoding skill also was included as a control variable in this analysis because reading-specific cognitive flexibility assessment requires word reading. Second-order theory of mind (assessed in elementary school) also contributed marginally significant variance ($p = .053$) to students' reading comprehension beyond preschool variables, but that variance was mediated by reading-specific cognitive flexibility. Finally, second-order theory of mind contributed to elementary students' reading awareness even when other variables were controlled.

Consistent with the findings of Cartwright et al. (2014), our results indicate both hot and cool executive skills are important components of children's developing comprehension skill—both sentence comprehension in preschool and reading comprehension in elementary school. In particular, both studies demonstrated the importance of cognitive flexibility and theory of mind (both first and second order) for early comprehension. Our study also suggests that early counterfactual thinking facilitates comprehension. Theory of mind may contribute to developing comprehension because of its relation to metacognition. Alternatively, the perspective-taking ability that characterizes theory of mind may contribute to comprehension by enabling children to understand the varied perspectives of authors and characters in text, permitting the inference making that is essential for successful comprehension. Finally, the finding that counterfactual reasoning contributes uniquely to reading comprehension is intriguing, given the limited work in this area. Because these hot executive skills have the potential to be improved through instruction (e.g., see Lysaker et al., 2011), our findings have important implications for education contexts.

RECOMMENDATIONS FOR PRACTICE

As can be seen from the preceding review, work examining the role of hot and cool executive skills in reading comprehension is in its infancy. By analogy, work examining the role of these skills in prereaders' comprehension is in the prenatal period. Thus much remains to be done to fully understand the varied ways preschoolers' developing executive skills, both hot and cool, shape, support, or benefit from their developing narrative comprehension. Yet the work that does exist provides interesting findings with real-world applications for those of us interacting with young children. In this section, we will draw on the existing empirical work to make recommendations for classroom practice. What is clear from our review is that hot and cool executive skills vary considerably in preschoolers, they matter for preschoolers' developing vocabulary and narrative comprehension, and they can be improved with interventions. Thus practice in this area holds great promise for enhancing preschoolers' narrative comprehension.

Executive function skills can be trained, which leads to several implications for teachers. For example, Cartwright (2002, 2010) engaged elementary students in cognitive flexibility training by having them think about words' sounds and meanings simultaneously, which resulted in improved reading comprehension. In fact, cognitive flexibility contributes significantly to beginning readers' (Cartwright et al., 2010), second- to fourth-grade readers' (Cartwright, 2002), and adults' (Cartwright, 2007) reading comprehension, as well as to preschoolers' expressive vocabulary and response to inferential comprehension instruction (Cartwright et al., 2014). Thus it is reasonable to assume that improving prereaders' cognitive flexibility would support their developing narrative comprehension.

The work summarized in this chapter leads to several suggestions for ways in which teachers can facilitate children's comprehension skills through intentional discussions in the context of book reading as well. Executive skills, both cool and hot, can be enhanced through social interaction during book reading. For example, preschool teachers can foster children's awareness of their own comprehension processes through discussions of the purposes and goals of book reading as well as discussions of what good readers and listeners do when they hear stories (e.g., DeBruin-Parecki & Squibb, 2011; Lecce et al., 2010; Roberts, 2013; van Kleeck, 2008). Furthermore, teachers can foster planning by supporting sensitivity to goal structure in stories. This might be accomplished by discussing causal connections of subevents in stories or by teaching children to arrange pictures of story components into sequential, causal order, thus supporting their ability to reason about causal connections between story events (Wenner, 2004; Zampini et al., 2013). Finally, instructors can teach inferential comprehension processes directly, such as predicting, inferring, and making connections between the content of stories and the child's own experiences, resulting in improved narrative comprehension (Cartwright et al., 2014; DeBruin-Parecki & Squibb, 2011; Roberts, 2013). For an extended discussion of comprehension strategies that teachers should use to help promote children's prereader comprehension, see Chapter 1 by DeBruin-Parecki and Pribesh.

Hot executive functions also can be enhanced during story reading. Inference making distinguishes skilled comprehenders (Bowyer-Crane & Snowling, 2005; Laing & Kamhi, 2002), but mental state inferences are more difficult for preschoolers than action-based inferences (Pelletier & Astington, 2004). Preschool teachers should thus highlight characters' mental states when reading to their students. In particular, they can discuss characters' false beliefs and mistaken perceptions to support children's inference making and understanding of mental causes of story events (Riggio & Cassidy, 2009; Tompkins et al., 2013). Character story mapping is one way that students can learn to track what characters are thinking and how those thoughts might influence the actions in a story (Emery, 1996; Shanahan & Shanahan, 1997). In addition, teachers might consider explicitly highlighting the differences between "actions" and "thinking" in stories to support children's awareness that there are two landscapes in stories: action and consciousness (Astington, 1990; Bruner, 1988, 1990). Discussions that purposefully guide students to awareness of both landscapes result in improvements in students' narrative comprehension (Aram et al., 2013). Counterfactual thinking also might be improved through discussion, though empirical exploration of this question is still needed. When reading books to children, teachers could guide discussions about alternative endings to the story or what else characters could have done to change story outcomes in order to foster the inferential thinking that characterizes counterfactual reasoning.

Work on executive skills and narrative comprehension also has implications for text choice. Children and adults prefer social stories (Barnes, 2012; Barnes & Bloom, 2013)—though individuals on the autism spectrum demonstrate a preference for nonfiction over social narratives and lower comprehension of social narratives than typically developing peers (Barnes, 2012; Brown et al., 2012)—and social stories are more likely to afford opportunities to discuss mental states in support of theory of mind development and mental state–based inferences (Dyer et al., 2000; Dyer et al., 2004). Furthermore, for prereaders (or even readers), wordless picture books afford rich opportunities for discussions of characters' mental states (Lysaker & Miller, 2012). Thus teachers can capture children's attention with fiction while also facilitating several skills that will foster reading comprehension.

Finally, hot executive skills also can be enhanced during social interaction beyond storybook reading. Teachers should engage children in discussions about mental states and the fact that different children's viewpoints may vary. If one child takes a toy from another, the teacher can ask questions such as "How do you think that made her feel?" to help children recognize that their peers have mental states that may differ from their own. These discussions enhance theory of mind development (e.g., Ruffman, Perner, & Parkin, 1999), which supports narrative comprehension (Pelletier & Astington, 2004). Such situations also can be used to enhance counterfactual reasoning. Teachers can ask, "What else could you have done to get your toy back rather than grabbing it?" Over time, such conversations are likely to help students consider alternatives to reality, which may support such thinking in story comprehension (Guajardo & Turley-Ames, 2004; Guajardo et al., 2009).

CONCLUSION

As Liew (2012) noted, both hot and cool executive skills are important for academic success, and our review demonstrates that prereader comprehension is no exception. Reading and narrative comprehension are complex tasks that involve processing and manipulating multiple sources of information (cool executive skills); monitoring one's own knowledge; and inferring characters' thoughts, feelings, and intentions (hot executive skills). Critical changes occur in all of these skills during the preschool and early school years, an optimal time to support narrative comprehension development and ultimately reading comprehension. The connections among cool executive skills and hot executive skills also suggest multiple pathways to reading comprehension. If a child is struggling with comprehension, then teachers and parents can engage in interactions to enhance understanding in any of these areas to facilitate comprehension.

REFERENCES

Adrian, J.E., Clemente, R.A., & Villanueva, L. (2007). Mothers' use of cognitive state verbs in picture-book reading and the development of children's understanding of mind: A longitudinal study. *Child Development, 78,* 1052–1067.

Adrian, J.E., Clemente, R.A., Villanueva, L., & Rieffe, C. (2005). Parent-child picture-book reading, mothers' mental state language and children's theory of mind. *Journal of Child Language, 32,* 673–686.

Alarcón-Rubio, Sánchez-Medina, J.A., & Prieto-García, J.R. (2014). Executive function and verbal self-regulation in childhood: Developmental linkages between partially internalized private speech and cognitive flexibility. *Early Childhood Research Quarterly, 29,* 95–105.

Allan, N.P., & Lonigan, C.J. (2011). Examining the dimensionality of effortful control in preschool children and its relation to academic and socio-emotional indicators. *Developmental Psychology, 47,* 905–915.

Almasi, J.F., & Fullerton, S.K. (2012). *Teaching strategic processes in reading* (2nd ed.). New York, NY: Guilford Press.

Altemeier, L.E., Abbott, R.D., & Berninger, V.W. (2008). Executive functions for reading and writing in typical literacy development and dyslexia. *Journal of Clinical and Experimental Neuropsychology, 30,* 588–606.

Aram, D., Fine, Y., & Ziv, M. (2013). Enhancing parent-child shared book reading interactions: Promoting references to the book's plot and socio-cognitive themes. *Early Childhood Research Quarterly, 28,* 111–122.

Ardilla, A. (2013). Development of metacognitive and emotional executive functions in children. *Applied Neuropsychology Child, 2,* 82–87.

Astington, J.W. (1990). Narrative and the child's theory of mind. In B.K. Britton & A.D. Pellegrini (Eds.), *Narrative thought and narrative language* (pp. 151–171). Hillsdale, NJ: Erlbaum.

Astington, J.W., Harris, P.L., & Olson, D.R. (Eds.). (1988). *Developing theories of mind.* New York, NY: Cambridge University Press.

Astington, J.W., & Jenkins, J.M. (1999). A longitudinal study of the relation between language and theory-of-mind development. *Developmental Psychology, 35,* 1311–1320.

Baker, L., & Stein, N. (1981). The development of prose comprehension skills. In C.M. Santa & B.L. Hayes (Eds.), *Children's prose comprehension: Research and practice* (pp. 7–43). Newark, DE: International Reading Association.

Barnes, J.L. (2012). Fiction, imagination, and social cognition: Insights from autism. *Poetics, 40,* 299–316.

Barnes, J.L., & Bloom, P. (2013). Children's preference for social stories. *Developmental Psychology.* Advance online publication. doi:10.1037/a0033613

Beck, S.R., Riggs, K.J., & Gorniak, S.L. (2009). Relating developments in children's counterfactual thinking and executive functions. *Thinking and Reasoning, 15,* 337–354.

Benson, J.E., Sabbagh, M.A., Carlson, S.M., & Zelazo, P.D. (2013). Individual differences in executive functioning predict improvement from theory-of-mind training. *Developmental Psychology, 49,* 1615–1627.

Best, J.R., & Miller, P.H. (2010). A developmental perspective on executive function. *Child Development, 81,* 1641–1660.

Best, J.R., Miller, P.H., & Jones, L.L. (2009). Executive functions after age 5: Changes and correlates. *Developmental Review, 29,* 180–200.

Best, J.R., Miller, P.H., & Naglieri, J.A. (2011). Relations between executive function and academic achievement from ages 15 to 17 in a large, representative national sample. *Learning and Individual Differences, 21,* 327–336.

Blair, C., & Razza, R.P. (2007). Relating effortful control, executive function, and false belief understanding to emerging math and literacy ability in kindergarten. *Child Development, 78,* 647–663.

Blakemore, S., & Choudhury, S. (2006). Development of the adolescent brain: Implications for executive function and social cognition. *Journal of Child Psychology and Psychiatry, 47,* 296–312.

Bodrova, E., Leong, D.J., & Akhutina, T.V. (2011). When everything new is well-forgotten old: Vygotsky/Luria insights in the development of executive functions. *New Directions for Child and Adolescent Development, 133,* 11–28.

Booth, J.N., Boyle, J.M.E., & Kelly, S.W. (2010). Do tasks make a difference? Accounting for heterogeneity of performance of children with reading difficulties on tasks of executive function: Findings from a meta-analysis. *British Journal of Developmental Psychology, 28,* 133–176.

Borella, E., Carretti, B., & Pelegrina, S. (2010). The specific role of inhibition in reading comprehension in good and poor comprehenders. *Journal of Learning Disabilities, 43,* 541–552.

Bowyer-Crane, C., & Snowling, M.J. (2005). Assessing children's inference generation: What do tests of reading comprehension measure? *British Journal of Educational Psychology, 75,* 189–201.

Brock, L.L., Rimm-Kaufman, S.E., Nathanson, L., & Grimm, K.J. (2009). The contributions of "hot" and "cool" executive function to children's academic achievement, learning-related behaviors, and engagement in kindergarten. *Early Childhood Research Quarterly, 24,* 337–349.

Brown, H.M., Oram-Cardy, J., & Johnson, A. (2013). A meta-analysis of the reading comprehension skills of individuals on the autism spectrum. *Journal of Autism and Developmental Disorders, 43,* 932–955.

Bruner, J. (1988). *Actual minds, possible worlds.* Cambridge, MA: Harvard University Press.

Bruner, J. (1990). *Acts of meaning.* Cambridge, MA: Harvard University Press.

Cain, K. (2006). Individual differences in children's memory and reading comprehension: An investigation of semantic and inhibitory deficits. *Memory, 14,* 553–569.

Cain, K., & Oakhill, J.V. (1999). Inference making ability and its relation to comprehension failure in young children. *Reading and Writing, 11,* 489–503.

Carlson, S.M., Claxton, L.J., & Moses, L.J. (2013). The relation between executive function and theory of mind is more than skin deep. *Journal of Cognition and Development.* Advance online publication. doi:10.1080/15248372.2013.824883

Carlson, S.M., & Moses, L.J. (2001). Individual differences in inhibitory control and children's theory of mind. *Child Development, 74*(4), 1032–1053.

Carlson, S.M., Moses, L.J., & Breton, C. (2002). How specific is the relation between executive function and theory of mind? Contributions of inhibitory control and working memory. *Infant and Child Development, 11,* 73–92.

Carlson, S.M., Moses, L.J., & Claxton, L.J. (2004). Individual differences in executive functioning and theory of mind: An investigation of inhibitory control and planning ability. *Journal of Experimental Child Psychology, 87,* 299–319.

Carlson, S.M., Moses, L.J., & Hix, H.R. (1998). The role of inhibitory processes in young children's difficulties with deception and false belief. *Child Development, 69*(3), 672–691.

Carretti, B., Cornoldi, C., De Beni, R., & Romanò, M. (2005). Updating in working memory: A comparison of good and poor comprehenders. *Journal of Experimental Child Psychology, 91,* 45–66.

Cartwright, K.B. (2002). Cognitive development and reading: The relation of reading-specific multiple classification skill to reading comprehension in elementary school children. *Journal of Educational Psychology, 94,* 56–63.

Cartwright, K.B. (2007). The contribution of graphophonological-semantic flexibility to reading comprehension in college students: Implications for a less simple view of reading. *Journal of Literacy Research,
39,* 173–193.

Cartwright, K.B. (2010). *Word callers: Small-group and one-to-one interventions for children who "read" but
don't comprehend.* Portsmouth, NH: Heinemann.

Cartwright, K.B. (2012). Insights from cognitive neuroscience: The importance of executive function for
early reading development and education. *Special Issue on Neuroscience Perspectives—Early Education
and Development, 23,* 34–36.

Cartwright, K.B., & Coppage, E.A. (2009, December). *Cognitive profiles of word callers: Cognitive flexibility,
vocabulary, and word identification in elementary school-aged good and poor comprehenders.* Paper presented at the 59th annual meeting of the Literacy Research Association (formerly the National Reading
Conference), Albuquerque, NM.

Cartwright, K.B., Coppage, E.A., Guiffré, H., & Strube, L. (2008, July). *A comparison of metacognitive skills
and cognitive flexibility in good and poor comprehenders.* Poster presented at the annual meeting of the
Society for the Scientific Study of Reading, Asheville, NC.

Cartwright, K.B., DeBruin-Parecki, A., Vaughn, S., Badalis, J., & Orelski, J. (2014). *Relations of theory of
mind and executive skills to preschoolers' story comprehension and response to comprehension intervention.* Poster to be presented at the Society for Research in Child Development Special Topic Meeting:
Strengthening Connections Among Child and Family Research, Policy and Practice, Alexandria, VA.

Cartwright, K.B., & Guajardo, N.R. (2011, March). *A longitudinal study of the role of theory of mind in elementary students' metacognition and reading comprehension.* Poster presented at the Biennial Meeting of
the Society for Research in Child Development, Montreal, CA.

Cartwright, K.B., Guiffré, H., Bock, A., & Coppage, E.A. (2011, October). *Effects of executive function training on reading comprehension and cognitive flexibility in second to fifth grade struggling readers.* Poster
presented at the biennial meeting of the Cognitive Development Society, Philadelphia, PA.

Cartwright, K.B., Isaac, M., & Dandy, K. (2006). The development of reading-specific representational flexibility: A cross-sectional comparison of second graders, fourth graders, and college students. In A.V. Mit-
tel (Ed.), *Focus on educational psychology* (pp. 173–194). New York, NY: Nova Science Publishers.

Cartwright, K.B., Lane, A.B., & Singleton, T.S. (2012, December). *Effects of an executive skills intervention
for reading comprehension in an RTI framework.* Paper presented at the Annual Meeting of the Literacy
Research Association, San Diego, CA.

Cartwright, K.B., Marshall, T.R., Dandy, K., & Isaac, M.C. (2010). The development of graphophonological-
semantic cognitive flexibility and its contribution to reading comprehension in beginning readers. *Journal of Cognition and Development, 11,* 61–85.

Chall, J.S. (1996). *Stages of reading development* (2nd ed.). Fort Worth, TX: Harcourt Brace.

Clark, C.A.C., Sheffield, T.D., Chevalier, N., Nelson, J.M., Wiebe, S.A., & Espy, K.A. (2013). Charting early
trajectories of executive control with the shape school. *Developmental Psychology, 49,* 1481–1493.

Conners, F.A. (2009). Attentional control and the simple view of reading. *Reading and Writing, 22,* 591–613.

Dahlin, K.I.E. (2011). Effects of working memory training on reading in children with special needs. *Reading and Writing, 24,* 479–491.

Davidson, M.C., Amso, D., Anderson, L.C., & Diamond, A. (2006). Development of cognitive control and
executive functions from 4 to 13 years: Evidence from manipulations of memory, inhibition, and task
switching. *Neuropsychologia, 44,* 2037–2078.

Davis, H.L., & Pratt, C. (1995). The development of children's theory of mind: The working memory explanation. *Australian Journal of Psychology, 47,* 25–31.

Dawson, P., & Guare, R. (2010). *Executive skills in children and adolescents: A practical guide to assessment
and intervention* (2nd ed.). New York, NY: Guilford Press.

De Luca, C.R., Wood, S.J., Anderson, V., Buchanan, J., Proffitt, T.M., Mahony, K., & Pantelis, C. (2003). Normative data from the CANTAB I: Development of executive function over the lifespan. *Journal of Clinical
and Experimental Neuropsychology, 25,* 242–254.

DeBruin-Parecki, A., & Squibb, K. (2011). Promoting at-risk preschool children's comprehension through
research-based strategy instruction. *Reading Horizons, 51,* 41–62.

Dermitzaki, I., Andreou, G., & Paraskeva, V. (2008). High and low reading comprehension achievers' strategic behaviors and their relation to performance in a reading comprehension situation. *Reading Psychology, 29,* 471–492.

Donahue, M.L. (2013). Perspective-taking and comprehension of narratives: Lessons learned from "The Bean." In C.A. Stone, E.R. Silliman, B.J. Ehren, & G.P. Wallach (Eds.), *Handbook of language & literacy: Development and disorders* (2nd ed., pp. 323–338). New York, NY: Guilford Press.

Drayton, S., Turley-Ames, K.J., & Guajardo, N.R. (2011). Counterfactual thinking and false belief: The role of executive function. *Journal of Experimental Child Psychology, 108,* 532–548.

Dyer, J.R., Shatz, M., & Wellman, H. (2000). Young children's storybooks as a source of mental state information. *Cognitive Development, 15,* 17–37.

Dyer, J.R., Shatz, M., Wellman, H., & Saito, M.T. (2004). Mental state expressions in US and Japanese children's books. *International Journal of Behavioral Development, 28,* 546–552.

Emery, D.W. (1996). Helping readers comprehend stories from the characters' perspective. *The Reading Teacher, 49,* 534–541.

Farrar, M.J., & Ashwell, S. (2008). The role of representational ability in the development of phonological awareness in preschool children. In K.B. Cartwright (Ed.), *Literacy processes: Cognitive flexibility in learning and teaching.* New York, NY: Guilford Press.

Farrar, M.J., & Ashwell, S. (2012). Phonological awareness, executive functioning, and theory of mind. *Cognitive Development, 27,* 77–89.

Feldman, C.F., Bruner, J., Renderer, B., & Spitzer, S. (1990). Narrative comprehension. In B.K. Britton & A.D. Pellegrini (Eds.), *Narrative thought and narrative language* (pp. 1–78). Hillsdale, NJ: Erlbaum.

Florit, E., Roch, M., & Levorato, M.C. (2011). Listening text comprehension of explicit and implicit information in preschoolers: The role of verbal and inferential skills. *Discourse Processes, 48,* 119–138.

Friedman, N.P., Miyake, A., Robinson, J.L., & Hewitt, J.K. (2011). Developmental trajectories in toddlers' self-restraint predict individual differences in executive functions 14 years later: A behavioral genetic analysis. *Developmental Psychology, 47,* 1410–1430.

Frye, D., Zelazo, P.D., & Palfai, T. (1995). Theory of mind and rule-based reasoning. *Cognitive Development, 10,* 483–527.

García-Madruga, J.A., Elosúa, M.R., Gil, L., Gómez-Veiga, I., Vila, J.O., Orjales, I., . . . & Rodríguez, R. (2013). Reading comprehension and working memory's executive processes: An intervention study in primary school students. *Reading Research Quarterly, 48,* 155–174.

Gaskins, I.W., Satlow, E., & Pressley, M. (2007). Executive control of reading comprehension in the elementary school. In L. Meltzer (Ed.), *Executive function in education: From theory to practice.* New York, NY: Guilford Press.

German, T.P., & Nichols, S. (2003). Children's counterfactual inferences about long and short causal chains. *Developmental Science, 6*(5), 514–523.

Guajardo, N.R., & Cartwright, K.B. (2014). *A longitudinal study of the role of false belief understanding in elementary students' reading awareness and reading comprehension.* Manuscript in preparation.

Guajardo, N.R., Parker, J., & Turley-Ames, K.J. (2009). Associations among false belief understanding, counterfactual reasoning, and executive function. *British Journal of Developmental Psychology, 27,* 681–702.

Guajardo, N.R., Petersen, R., & Marshall, T.R. (2013). The roles of explanation and feedback in false belief understanding: A microgenetic analysis. *Journal of Genetic Psychology, 174,* 225–252.

Guajardo, N.R., & Turley-Ames, K.J. (2004). Preschoolers' generation of different types of counterfactual statements and theory of mind understanding. *Cognitive Development, 19,* 53–80.

Guajardo, N.R., & Watson, A.C. (2002). Narrative discourse and theory of mind development. *Journal of Genetic Psychology, 163,* 305–325.

Hale, C.M., & Tager-Flusberg, H. (2003). The influence of language on theory of mind: A training study. *Developmental Science, 6,* 346–359.

Harris, P.L., German, T., & Mills, P. (1996). Children's use of counterfactual thinking in causal reasoning. *Cognition, 61,* 233–259.

Henning, A., Spinath, F.M., & Aschersleben, G. (2011). The link between preschoolers' executive function and theory of mind and the role of epistemic states. *Journal of Experimental Child Psychology, 108,* 513–531.

Hongwanishkul, D., Happaney, K.R., Lee, W.S.C., & Zelazo, P.D. (2005). Assessment of hot and cool executive function in young children: Age-related changes and individual differences. *Developmental Neuropsychology, 28,* 617–644.

Huey, E.B. (1908). *The psychology and pedagogy of reading.* New York, NY: Macmillan.

Hughes, C., & Ensor, R. (2007). Executive function and theory of mind: Predictive relations from ages 2 to 4. *Developmental Psychology, 43*, 1447–1459.

Hutto, D.D. (2007). The narrative practice hypothesis: Origins and applications of folk psychology. *Royal Institute of Philosophy Supplement, 60*, 43–68.

Jacobs, J.E., & Paris, S.G. (1987). Children's metacognition about reading: Issues in definition, measurement, and instruction. *Educational Psychologist, 22*, 255–278.

Kahneman, D., & Miller, D.T. (1986). Norm theory: Comparing reality to its alternatives. *Psychological Review, 93*, 136–153.

Kahneman, D., & Tversky, A. (1982). The simulation heuristic. In D. Kahneman, P. Slovic, & A. Tversky (Eds.), *Judgment under uncertainty: Heuristics and biases* (pp. 201–208). New York, NY: Cambridge University Press.

Kendeou, P., van den Broek, P., White, M.J., & Lynch, J.S. (2009). Predicting reading comprehension in early elementary school: The independent contributions of oral language and decoding skills. *Journal of Educational Psychology, 101*, 765–778.

Kidd, D.C., & Castano, E. (2013). Reading literary fiction improves theory of mind. *Science, 342*(6156), 377–380.

Kieffer, M.J., Vukovic, R.K., & Berry, D. (2013, July). Roles of attention shifting and inhibitory control in fourth-grade reading comprehension. *Reading Research Quarterly.* doi:10.1002/rrq.54

Laing, S.P., & Kamhi, A.G. (2002). The use of think-aloud protocols to compare inferencing abilities in average and below-average readers. *Journal of Learning Disabilities, 5*, 436–447.

Lan, X., Legare, C.H., Ponitz, C.C., Li, S., & Morrison, F.J. (2011). Investigating the links between the subcomponents of executive function and academic achievement: A cross-cultural analysis of Chinese and American preschoolers. *Journal of Experimental Child Psychology, 108*, 677–692.

Lecce, S., Zocchi, S., Pagnin, A., Palladino, P., & Taumoepeau, M. (2010). Reading minds: The relation between children's mental state knowledge and their metaknowledge about reading. *Child Development, 81*, 1876–1893.

Lee, K., Bull, R., & Ho, R.M.H. (2013). Developmental changes in executive functioning. *Child Development, 84*, 1933–1953.

Lepola, J., Lynch, J., Laakkonen, E., Silvén, M., & Niemi, P. (2012). The role of inference making and other language skills in the development of narrative listening comprehension in 4–6-year-old children. *Reading Research Quarterly, 47*, 259–282.

Liew, J. (2012). Effortful control, executive functions, and education: Bringing self-regulatory and social-emotional competencies to the table. *Child Development Perspectives, 6*, 105–111.

Locascio, G., Mahone, E.M., Eason, S.H., & Cutting, L.E. (2010). Executive dysfunction among children with reading comprehension deficits. *Journal of Learning Disabilities, 43*, 441–454.

Lohmann, H., & Tomasello, M. (2003). The role of language in the development of false belief understanding: A training study. *Child Development, 74*, 1130–1144.

Lynch, J.S., van den Broek, P., Kremer, K.E., Kendeou, P., White, M.J., & Lorch, E.P. (2008). The development of narrative comprehension and its relation to other early reading skills. *Reading Psychology, 29*, 327–365.

Lysaker, J.T., & Miller, A. (2012). Engaging social imagination: The developmental work of wordless picture book reading. *Journal of Early Childhood Literacy, 13*, 147–174.

Lysaker, J., & Tonge, C. (2013). Learning to understand others through relationally oriented reading. *The Reading Teacher, 66*, 632–641.

Lysaker, J.T., Tonge, C., Gauson, D., & Miller, A. (2011). Reading and social imagination: What relationally oriented reading instruction can do for children. *Reading Psychology, 32*, 520–566.

Mar, R.A. (2011). The neural bases of social cognition and story comprehension. *Annual Review of Psychology, 62*, 103–134.

McClelland, M.M., Cameron, C.E., Connor, C.M., Farris, C.L., Jewkes, A.M., & Morrison, F.J. (2007). Links between behavioral regulation and preschoolers' literacy, vocabulary, and math skills. *Developmental Psychology, 43*, 947–959.

McVay, J.C., & Kane, M.J. (2012). Why does working memory capacity predict variation in reading comprehension? On the influence of mind wandering and executive attention. *Journal of Experimental Psychology: General, 141*, 302–320.

Miller, M.R., Müller, U., Giesbrecht, G.F., Carpendale, J.I.M., & Kerns, K.A. (2013). The contribution of executive function and social understanding to preschoolers' letter and math skills. *Cognitive Development, 28*, 331–349.

Miller, S.A. (2012). *Theory of mind: Beyond the preschool years.* New York, NY: Psychology Press.

Miller, S.E., & Marcovitch, S. (2012). How theory of mind and executive function codevelop. *Review of Philosophical Psychology, 3*, 597–625.

Miranda, A., Presentación, J., Siegenthaler, R., & Jara, P. (2011). Effects of a psychosocial intervention on the executive functioning in children with ADHD. *Journal of Learning Disabilities, 46*, 363–376.

Müller, U., Miller, M.R., Michalczyk, K., & Karapinka, A. (2007). False belief understanding: The influence of person, grammatical mood, counterfactual reasoning and working memory. *British Journal of Developmental Psychology, 25*, 615–632.

Munakata, Y., Snyder, H.R., & Chatham, C.H. (2012). Developing cognitive control: Three key transitions. *Current Directions in Psychological Science, 21*, 71–77.

Nation, K., Cocksey, J., Taylor, J.S.H., & Bishop, D.V.M. (2010). A longitudinal investigation of early reading and language skills in children with poor reading comprehension. *Journal of Child Psychology and Psychiatry, 51*, 1031–1039.

Oakhill, J.V., & Cain, K. (2012). The precursors of reading ability in young readers: Evidence from a four-year longitudinal study. *Scientific Studies of Reading, 16*, 91–121.

Ouellette, G.P. (2006). What's meaning got to do with it: The role of vocabulary in word reading and reading comprehension. *Journal of Educational Psychology, 98*, 554–566.

Ozonoff, S., Pennington, B.F., & Rogers, S.J. (1991). Executive function deficits in high-functioning autistic individuals: Relationship to theory of mind. *Journal of Child Psychology & Psychiatry, 32*, 1081–1105.

Paris, S.G., & Myers, M. (1981). Comprehension monitoring, memory, and study strategies of good and poor readers. *Journal of Reading Behavior, 13*, 5–22.

Pelletier, J., & Astington, J.W. (2004). Action, consciousness, and theory of mind: Children's ability to coordinate story characters' actions and thoughts. *Early Education & Development, 15*, 5–22.

Pellicano, E. (2007). Links between theory of mind and executive function in young children with autism: Clues to developmental primacy. *Developmental Psychology, 43*, 974–990.

Perner, J., & Lang, B. (1999). Development of theory of mind and executive control. *Trends in Cognitive Sciences, 3*, 337–344.

Pillow, B.H., & Lovett, S.B. (1998). "He forgot": Young children's use of cognitive explanations for another person's mistakes. *Merrill-Palmer Quarterly, 44*, 378–403.

Potocki, A., Ecalle, J., & Magnan, A. (2013). Narrative comprehension skills in 5-year-old children: Correlational analysis and comprehender profiles. *Journal of Educational Research, 106*, 14–26.

Prencipe, A., Kesek, A., Cohen, J., Lamm, C., Lewis, M.D., & Zelazo, P.D. (2011). Development of hot and cool executive function during the transition to adolescence. *Journal of Experimental Child Psychology, 108*, 621–637.

Pressley, M. (2002). Metacognition and self-regulated comprehension. In A.E. Farstrup & S.J. Samuels (Eds.), *What research has to say about reading instruction* (3rd ed., pp. 291–309). Newark, DE: International Reading Association.

Rafetseder, E., Schwitalla, M., & Perner, J. (2013). Counterfactual reasoning: From childhood to adulthood. *Journal of Child Experimental Psychology, 114*, 389–404.

Riggio, M.M., & Cassidy, K.W. (2009). Preschoolers' processing of false beliefs within the context of picture book reading. *Early Education & Development, 20*, 992–1015.

Riggs, K.J., Peterson, D.M., Robinson, E.J., & Mitchell, P. (1998). Are errors in false belief tasks symptomatic of a broader difficulty with counterfactuality? *Cognitive Development, 13*, 73–90.

Roberts, K.L. (2013). Comprehension strategy instruction during parent-child shared reading: An intervention study. *Literacy Research and Instruction, 52*, 106–129.

Roese, N.J. (1994). The functional basis of counterfactual thinking. *Journal of Personality and Social Psychology, 66*, 805–818.

Roese, N.J. (1997). Counterfactual thinking. *Psychological Bulletin, 121*, 133–148.

Rueda, M.R,, Posner, M.I., & Rothbart, M.K. (2005). The development of executive attention: Contributions to the emergence of self-regulation. *Developmental Neuropsychology, 28*, 573–594.

Ruffman, T., Perner, J., & Parkin, L. (1999). How parenting style affects false belief understanding. *Social Development, 8*, 395–411.

Ruffman, T., Slade, L., & Crowe, E. (2002). The relation between children's and mothers' mental state language and theory-of-mind understanding. *Child Development, 73*, 734–751.

Sabbagh, M.A., & Callanan, M.A. (1998). Metarepresentation in action: 3, 4, and 5-year-olds' developing theories of mind in parent-child conversations. *Developmental Psychology, 34*, 491–502.

Saxe, R., Schulz, L.E., & Jiang, Y.V. (2006). Reading minds versus following rules: Dissociating theory of mind and executive control in the brain. *Social Neuroscience, 1*, 284–298.

Schneider, W., Schumann-Hengsteler, R., & Sodian, B. (2005). *Young children's cognitive development: Inter-relations among executive functioning, working memory, verbal ability, and theory of mind.* Mahwah, NJ: Erlbaum.

Seigneuric, A., & Ehrlich, M. (2005). Contribution of working memory capacity to children's reading comprehension: A longitudinal investigation. *Reading and Writing, 18,* 617–656.

Sesma, H.W., Mahone, E.M., Levine, T., Eason, S.H., & Cutting, L.E. (2009). The contribution of executive skills to reading comprehension. *Child Neuropsychology, 15,* 232–246.

Shanahan, T., Callison, K., Carriere, C., Duke, N.K., Pearson, P.D., Schatschneider, C., & Torgesen, J. (2010). *Improving reading comprehension in kindergarten through 3rd grade: A practice guide* (NCEE 2010-038). Washington, DC: National Center for Education Evaluation and Regional Assistance, Institute of Education Sciences, U.S. Department of Education. Retrieved from whatworks.ed.gov/publications/practiceguides

Shanahan, T., & Shanahan, S. (1997). Character perspective charting: Helping children to develop a more complete conception of story. *The Reading Teacher, 50,* 668–677.

Sinnott, J.D. (1998). *The development of logic in adulthood: Postformal thought and its applications.* New York, NY: Plenum Press.

Slaughter, V., & Gopnik, A. (1996). Conceptual coherence in the child's theory of mind: Training children to understand belief. *Child Development, 67,* 2967–2988.

Slaughter, V.A., Peterson, C.C., & Mackintosh, E. (2007). Mind what mother says: Narrative input and theory of mind in typical children and those on the Autism spectrum. *Child Development, 78,* 839–858.

Stone, V.E., Baron-Cohen, S., & Knight, R.T. (1998). Frontal lobe contributions to theory of mind. *Journal of Cognitive Neuroscience, 10,* 640–656.

Strasser, K., & del Río, F. (2014). The role of comprehension monitoring, theory of mind, and vocabulary depth in predicting story comprehension and recall of kindergarten children. *Reading Research Quarterly, 49,* 169–187.

Symons, D., Peterson, C., Slaughter, V., Roche, J., & Doyle, E. (2005). Theory of mind and mental state discourse during book reading and story-telling tasks. *British Journal of Developmental Psychology, 23,* 81–102.

Tompkins, V., Guo, Y., & Justice, L.M. (2013). Inference generation, story comprehension, and language skills in the preschool years. *Reading and Writing, 26,* 403–429.

Trabasso, T., & Bartolone, J. (2003). Story understanding and counterfactual reasoning. *Journal of Experimental Psychology: Learning, Memory and Cognition, 29,* 904–923.

Ursache, A., Blair, C., Stifter, C., Voegtline, K., & the Family Life Project Investigators. (2013). Emotional reactivity and regulation in infancy interact to predict executive functioning in early childhood. *Developmental Psychology, 49,* 127–137.

van de Sande, E., Segers, E., & Verhoeven, L. (2013). How phonological awareness mediates the relation between children's self-control and word decoding. *Learning and Individual Differences, 26,* 112–118.

van Kleeck, A. (2008). Providing preschool foundations for later reading comprehension: The importance of and ideas for targeting inferencing in storybook-sharing interventions. *Psychology in the Schools, 45*(7), 627–643.

Verhoeven, L., van Leeuwe, J., & Vermeer, A. (2011). Vocabulary growth and reading development across the elementary school years. *Scientific Studies of Reading, 15,* 8–25.

Vidal-Abarca, E., Mañá, A., & Gil, L. (2010). Individual differences for self-regulating task-oriented reading activities. *Journal of Educational Psychology, 102,* 817–826.

von Suchodoletz, A., Gestsdottir, S., Wanless, S.B., McClelland, M.M., Birgisdottir, F., Gunzenhauser, C., & Ragnarsdottir, H. (2013). Behavioral self-regulation and relations to emergent academic skills among children in German and Iceland. *Early Childhood Research Quarterly, 28,* 62–73.

Wellman, H.M., Cross, D., & Watson, J. (2000). A meta-analysis of theory of mind development: The truth about false-belief. *Child Development, 72,* 655–684.

Wellman, H.M., & Liu, D. (2004). Scaling of theory-of-mind tasks. *Child Development, 75,* 523–541.

Welsh, J.A., Nix, R.L., Blair, C., Bierman, K.L., & Nelson, K.E. (2010). The development of cognitive skills and gains in academic school readiness for children from low-income families. *Journal of Educational Psychology, 102,* 45–53.

Wenner, J.A. (2004). Preschoolers' comprehension of goal structure in narratives. *Memory, 12,* 193–202.

Whitehurst, G.J., & Lonigan, C.J. (1998). Child development and emergent literacy. *Child Development, 69,* 848–872.

Whiten, A. (1994). Grades of mindreading. In C. Lewis & P. Mitchell (Eds.), *Children's early understanding of mind* (pp. 47–70). Mahwah, NJ: Erlbaum.

Willoughby, M., Kupersmidt, J., Voegler-Lee, M., & Bryant, D. (2011). Contributions of hot and cool self-regulation to preschool disruptive behavior and academic achievement. *Developmental Neuropsychology, 36,* 162–180.

Zampini, L., Suttora, C., D'Odorico, L., & Zanchi, P. (2013). Sequential reasoning and listening text comprehension in preschool children. *European Journal of Developmental Psychology, 10,* 563–579.

Zelazo, P.D., & Carlson, S.M. (2012). Hot and cool executive function in childhood and adolescence: Development and plasticity. *Child Development Perspectives, 6,* 354–360.

Zelazo, P.D., & Müller, U. (2002). Executive function in typical and atypical development. In U. Goswami (Ed.), *Blackwell handbook of childhood cognitive development* (pp. 445–469). Malden, MA: Blackwell Publishers.

Zelazo, P.D., Qu, L., & Müller, U. (2005). Hot and cool aspects of executive function: Relations in early development. In W. Schneider, R. Schumann-Hengsteler, & B. Sodian (Eds.), *Young children's cognitive development* (pp. 71–93). Mahwah, NJ: Erlbaum.

Zhou, Q., Chen, S.H., & Main, A. (2012). Commonalities and differences in the research on children's effortful control and executive function: A call for an integrated model of self-regulation. *Child Development Perspectives, 6,* 112–121.

10

Assessment of
Comprehension Skills in Prereaders

Theoretical Foundations,
Methods, Challenges, and Opportunities

JULIE S. LYNCH AND JANNE LEPOLA

A growing body of research is showing that reading comprehension has its foundation in oral language skills that develop well before a child enters school (e.g., Dufya, Niemi, & Voeten, 2001; Kendeou, van den Broek, White, & Lynch, 2009; Lepola, Niemi, Kuikka, & Hannula, 2005; National Institute of Child Health and Human Development [NICHD], 2005; Storch & Whitehurst, 2002). Within the contexts of oral language in general and storytelling in particular, young children develop essential skills and knowledge. They learn vocabulary, morphology, syntax, and inference making, among other skills that will contribute to their understanding of the written texts they will eventually read themselves.

Researchers have made great progress uncovering the developmental paths that lead from oral language competency to success in listening and reading comprehension (e.g., Kendeou et al., 2009; Kendeou, Savage, & van den Broek, 2009; Lepola, Lynch, Laakkonen, Silvén, & Niemi, 2012). Although this area of research has lagged behind the research on the skills that contribute to word decoding (e.g., phonological awareness, letter knowledge), researchers now have a fairly comprehensive view of the development of different language comprehension skills and their relative contribution to reading. The picture that emerges is that oral language skills (such as inference making) develop largely separately from word-decoding skills. Whereas word-decoding skills contribute to reading fluency, oral language skills contribute directly to meaning making important for text comprehension (e.g., Kendeou, Savage, & van den Broek, 2009). These empirical results fit well with theoretical views of text processing, in which the underlying cognitive processes of comprehension, particularly narrative comprehension, are largely the same regardless of the medium in which the information is presented (van den Broek, Lorch, & Thurlow, 1996). Thus comprehension skills learned in the context of oral, audiovisual, or pictorial media can transfer to texts children will eventually read themselves (e.g., Kendeou, Bohn-Gettler, White, & van den Broek, 2008). In short, both research and theory validate efforts to foster oral language skills in the preschool years in order to give children a strong basis in the cognitive skills needed for later reading comprehension.

A logical next step in this area is to develop valid and reliable assessments of comprehension skills in young children. Early childhood educators as well as researchers would benefit greatly from assessments that could accurately measure developing comprehension skills and, importantly, identify children who may be struggling with these skills. However, just as research on early language comprehension skills has trailed behind research on word-decoding skills, the development of measures of these skills has lagged behind those that measure vocabulary, letter identification, and phonological processing (Paris & Paris, 2003). Language comprehension is not one straightforward ability but rather involves an array of skills that gradually become integrated through development. Its multifaceted nature has been a challenge to those developing assessments. However, as we will emphasize, this provides interesting opportunities for the development of assessments as well.

Our purpose in this chapter is to explore important issues to consider when developing, using, and interpreting comprehension measures for young children. Thus we provide an overview of existing assessment methods leading to an agenda for further research in the field. More specifically, we first explain in more depth the theoretical and empirical work that underlies comprehension assessments. Second, we lay out challenges faced when assessing these complex cognitive processes in young children. Third, we explore a number of different methods of assessment: those that have been used by researchers and have the potential to be used in practical settings as well as those that are commercially available to educators. Finally, we explore areas of further research and development within this field.

RESEARCH AND THEORETICAL FOUNDATIONS

Theoretical Views of Discourse and Text Comprehension

Comprehension of texts is theorized to take place simultaneously on several different levels (e.g., Graesser, Millis, & Zwaan, 1997; van Dijk & Kintsch, 1983). The surface code level is the exact wording of the text and usually fades from memory quickly. At deeper levels, comprehension involves making meaningful connections between ideas presented in the text. Comprehenders must make inferences, drawing on information from the text and their prior knowledge to mentally fill in ideas that are not explicitly stated. At the *textbase* level, individuals comprehend the meanings of words and sentences, and they make some local inferences: those involving connections between ideas that are close together in the text. At the situation model level, individuals form a coherent understanding of the text, including its personal importance and connection to their world knowledge (Kintsch & Kintsch, 2005; Graesser et al., 1997).

This view emphasizes that comprehension is not a unitary concept. Therefore, when developing and examining comprehension assessments, it is essential to clearly define what level of comprehension is being assessed or more generally how comprehension is defined within the assessment's context. One definition of assessment may vary widely from the next.

When comprehension is assessed at the level of the textbase or situation model, we look to the structure of the text. By analyzing the text structure, it is possible to predict what inferences comprehenders may make and, more generally, how they may form a textbase or situation model. This analysis can be done in several ways. For instance, texts may be analyzed in terms of their causal structure (e.g., van den Broek, 1990)—that is, the way in which the events or facts in a text lead to or bring about others. The links between causal antecedents and consequences may be based on physical forces as well as less tangible forces such as a character's psychological state or motives. Particularly in narrative contexts, there is evidence that successful comprehenders make mental connections between events based on causality, and this forms an important basis for their textbase or situation model (e.g., Graesser, Singer, & Trabasso, 1994; van den Broek, 1990). Narrative texts may also be analyzed in terms of story grammar categories (Mandler & Johnson, 1977). Statements or propositions within a narrative can be categorized as pertaining to settings, initiating events, characters' goals, attempts toward the goals, and outcomes. The understanding of these categories plays a potentially important role in forming a complete mental representation of a narrative.

Development of Inference-Making Skills

Because inference making is essential to forming a coherent mental representation of a text or narrative, it is important for those assessing comprehension to understand how this ability develops. Previous research has shown that prereaders are able to generate a variety of inferences after listening to a narrative and viewing television or a picture book, as well as in other experimental tasks (Hannon & Frias, 2012; Kendeou et al., 2008; Paris & Paris, 2003). However, studies also show systematic age differences in children's ability to infer meaningful relations in a text. Younger children and those with comprehension difficulties make fewer spontaneous inferences than older children or children with adequate comprehension skills (Cain & Oakhill, 1999; Trabasso & Nickels, 1992). However, younger children and children with comprehension problems are able to make inferences when asked the type of question that challenges them to bridge or connect information (Goldman & Varnhagen, 1986; Kendeou et al., 2008; McKeown & Beck, 2006). When inferences are necessary to establish coherence (Casteel, 1993) or when the assessment of narrative comprehension is based on the child's own language and experiences (Allen, 1985), younger or less-skilled comprehenders are also more likely to make inferences.

Van den Broek et al. (2005) outline suggestive but not definitive age trends in the type of inferences children make in narrative comprehension. Preschoolers are more limited to the relations that refer to concrete objects, whereas older children are sensitive to the abstract ones. In other words, preschoolers focus on external events in a narrative, whereas older children tend to identify internal relations of the events reflecting character's desires, motives, and goals (van den Broek et al., 2005). Younger children's inferences are more bound to individual, picture-level events, whereas older children are also able to recognize the thematic relations between clusters of events or episodes (Lepola et al., 2012; van den Broek et al., 2005). Although already some 4-year-old children are able to understand the overall plot and the theme of a narrative by inferring the moral or the lesson of a story (Lepola, Peltonen, & Korpilahti, 2009), this kind of higher-level inference is more common among older children (van den Broek, Lynch, Naslund, Ivers, & Verduin, 2003). In sum, younger children do have the ability to make inferences and form coherent mental representations of text (i.e., a textbase and situation model) but generally need more support than older children. That support may come through direct questions or texts that are relatively concrete or familiar to them.

Overall, work on young children's language comprehension skills provides an important basis for the development and evaluation of assessment methods. Successful assessments must be rooted in a theoretical view or definition of comprehension. A theoretical view, along with research on the development of comprehension skills, should guide the selection or development of appropriate materials and tasks as well as the analysis of results. For further discussion related to children's abilities to make inferences, see Chapter 4 by van Kleeck.

ASSESSMENT OF COMPREHENSION: CHALLENGES AND OPPORTUNITIES

Despite a strong theoretical and empirical foundation for the development of comprehension assessments, there are still significant challenges in this area. Assessing complex skills, such as language comprehension, is difficult regardless of the developmental level of the students. Assessing preschool-age children's comprehension skills poses particular challenges and opportunities. Educators and researchers must carefully consider both the assessment *context* (i.e., the narratives or other materials used as a basis for comprehension) and the assessment *tasks* (e.g., answering questions, retelling narratives). Both the context and tasks must be appropriate for the child's developmental level.

One potential challenge lies in constructing an appropriate assessment context. Different media must be used other than texts students read themselves. This actually provides a number of opportunities. As explained previously, both theoretical models and empirical evidence support the idea that underlying comprehension processes are largely the same regardless of the media in which they are presented. Therefore, researchers and practitioners can choose among a number of other media for assessment. Preschoolers' comprehension has been successfully assessed via picture sequences (i.e., Paris & Paris, 2003), oral stories, and audiovisual media (i.e., Kendeou et al., 2009; Lynch et al., 2008), for example. Moreover, these media are often familiar and entertaining for young children. There are challenges to using different media, however. Although there is evidence of the generality of comprehension processes, we cannot discount the possibility that there are factors that differ across media that will affect comprehension. Some of these factors may be, for instance, the support of visual images in some media, the familiarity of the media, and how engaging or motivating it is for children who increasingly interact with digital media.

Other possible challenges in assessment are rooted in children's developing verbal and cognitive skills. It is well established that children's receptive vocabulary develops faster than their expressive vocabulary (e.g., Schafer & Plunkett, 1998; Torppa et al., 2007). Thus preschool-age children may well understand more of a text than they are able to express. Open-ended questions, in particular, may be difficult for young children or children with depressed expressive language. Although open-ended questions and other tasks in which the child constructs more lengthy responses are used often in the field, they may not fully capture a younger child's comprehension. Carefully and sensitively adjusted prompts, specific questions, or other supports to aid children's verbal and non-verbal communication are often beneficial. However, an opportunity for researchers lies in developing means of assessment that do not rely as heavily on productive language, such as cloze procedures (Dempsey & Skarakis-Doyle, 2001; Skarakis-Doyle & Dempsey, 2008) or pictures to aid children's answers to questions (e.g., Florit, Roch, & Levorato, 2014; MacGinitie, MacGinitie, Maria, & Dreyer, 2000).

Young children's limited working memory may pose other challenges. Working memory is called upon for all comprehension processes. Specifically, inference making requires keeping at least two separate facts or events in memory at once and then doing the mental work of connecting those events (van Dijk & Kintsch, 1983). Those developing assessments for preschoolers must keep in mind these children's limited working memory (Dempster, 1981) when choosing appropriate texts as well as tasks for assessment. For instance, it may be difficult for children to understand stories or answer questions that require connections to be made between events that are distant from each other in the text (van den Broek, 1989). Similarly, those developing assessments must be aware of preschoolers' limited attention span (e.g., Ruff, Capozzoli, & Weisberg, 1998). However, comprehension assessments can be developed that are adapted to young children's developing working memory and attention skills. Some of the methods used to accommodate children's developing verbal skills may also be useful in this respect. For instance, providing pictures or audiovisual material may help support working memory. Also, breaking up assessment tasks into smaller units is helpful, so as to not overly tax young children's attention span. In short, it is important to choose or to make assessments that will appropriately challenge young children's skills. See Chapter 9 by Cartwright and Guajardo for a discussion of the relations among comprehension, executive function, and theory of mind.

Another important aspect of young children's cognitive development involves their prior knowledge and experiences. Young children's understanding in some assessment contexts may be limited by a lack of background knowledge. Background knowledge is generally necessary not only to understand vocabulary and individual events but also to make inferences and form a situation model of the text (e.g., van Dijk & Kintsch, 1983). In light of preschool children's varying (and often limited) world knowledge, careful consideration should be made when choosing materials to be included in the assessment context. When analyzing the structure of texts (or even pictorial materials), researchers and educators should consider what type of knowledge would be necessary to make key inferences.

Because of their level of social and emotional development as well as their limited experience with formal education, young children may not show what they know when being assessed. They may lack motivation to answer questions or finish other tasks. Why would they answer questions if the narrative or task is not interesting to them? They also may show anxiety when being tested, especially in a context that is not familiar to them. They may not answer or they may respond with one-word or very short answers. Culture may also play a role, in terms of both differences in narrative style between cultures (Gutiérrez-Clellen, Pena, & Quinn, 1995) and the types of questions generally asked of children (e.g., Heath, 1989). Again, the children's social and emotional development as well as their culture may also provide opportunities in developing assessment contexts and tasks. Assessments can be engaging for young children. Those developing assessments can be aware of children's interests and backgrounds when choosing materials. Children should also be assessed, whenever possible, in a familiar and comfortable environment, ideally with someone they know and trust (Hirsh-Pasek, Kochanoff, Newcombe, & de Villiers, 2005).

Although there are obviously no assessments that can completely overcome these challenges, researchers have capitalized on the opportunities for assessing young children's comprehension. Next, we explore the major methods that have been used, particularly focusing on how these methods can be adapted for different purposes as well as on evidence for their validity.

METHODS OF ASSESSMENT

General Approaches to Assessments

There are several dimensions on which assessments may be classified. As dimensions rather than black-and-white categories, it is important to note that assessments can, and often do, fall somewhere between the two ends of the continuum. It is also important to note that one method of assessment is generally not preferable to another. Those developing and using assessments must be aware of the different alternatives to match the purposes of the assessment.

One example is the classification of either online or offline assessment. In research on text comprehension, this distinction relates to the timing of the assessment tasks and what aspects of cognition it captures. In contrast to the more common use of the terms, *online* and *offline* in this literature do not relate to the medium in which the assessment task is presented. In general, online assessments portray comprehension processes while they are happening, whereas offline assessments measure comprehension after the text has been processed. In other words, online assessments reflect the process and offline assessments reflect the product (Graesser et al., 1997). Another dimension is static versus dynamic assessments. Static assessments generally assess comprehension skills at one point in time and are administered in the same manner to all children and across situations. These types of assessments are often seen as conventional or traditional compared with dynamic assessments. Dynamic assessments, on the other hand, are designed to measure potential growth and are often responsive to the individual children's answers (Grigorenko & Sternberg, 1998). In some aspects, dynamic assessments are similar to online assessments in that they generally assess cognitive processes rather than products. Assessments may also be categorized as quantitative, producing numerical results, or qualitative, producing results that are more narrative or descriptive. Practically all the assessments we review in this chapter are quantitative. However, in some cases (such as the case of narrative retellings or answers to open-ended questions), results of the assessments could also be examined in a qualitative manner.

With these general approaches to assessment in mind, we will explore a number of methods of comprehension assessment that have been used for research purposes and in educational settings.

Story Retelling Tasks

A common method of assessment is asking individuals to retell narratives after they are presented. These tasks are sometimes presented as free recall of narratives (i.e., the child is prompted to say everything he or she remembers from the story) and sometimes as retelling the story (i.e., the child is prompted to retell the story to the assessor or sometimes to a puppet; Lynch et al., 2008). Regardless of the way in which the task is explained, the same general cognitive processes are captured. Therefore, we will address these tasks and refer to them as retelling tasks. After being asked to retell the story, those being assessed are provided with only nondirective prompts (e.g., "What else happened?") until they cannot or will not produce any more information.

The results of retelling tasks can be analyzed in a number of ways. The most straightforward way is to simply determine the number of events or facts recalled from the text. However, this provides little depth in understanding how comprehension has taken place. One way to examine the completeness and coherence of understanding is the extent to which individuals retell events that are central to the causal structure of the narrative relative to events that are not causally central. This is an index of how sensitive an individual is to the causal structure and, indirectly, how likely he or she is to make causal inferences (Lynch et al., 2008). Another common way to view story retelling tasks is to examine the story grammar categories individuals are most likely to remember (Lepola et al., 2012; Mandler & Johnson, 1977). Consequently, information about the setting, initiating events, goals of the characters, reactions of characters, or solutions/resolutions is scored. This type of analysis provides insight into how comprehensive the child's mental representation of the narrative is.

In general, retelling tasks are considered offline. They are, by definition, done after the individual has initially processed the text. Also, generally, these assessments are completed in a static manner without changes to the types of questions or prompts provided. However, these measures could be adapted to be more dynamic in nature by assessors providing varying levels of support for children as they recall or retell.

Story retelling tasks are generally a straightforward way to assess comprehension. They are nondirective, so children's responses are not unduly influenced by specific adult prompts. Also, how children choose to structure their responses can provide insight into their comprehension process (Paris & Paris, 2003). As described previously, retelling tasks can be analyzed in various ways and therefore are quite flexible.

However, story retelling tasks can be challenging for preschoolers. Young children may not express all that they comprehend. This is due to limited productive language skills, lack of familiarity with this type of questioning that is often present in test-like settings, and possibly a lack of motivation or interest. Also, the task is taxing on a young child's working memory. Caution must also be used when interpreting the results of children from diverse cultures, as they may have been exposed to different conventions for telling stories (Gutiérrez-Clellen et al., 1995).

In sum, story retelling tasks can play an important role in the assessment of preschooler's narrative or text comprehension. However, because of the challenges they pose for young children, these tasks are often complemented with other methods that provide more support for children to express their comprehension.

Story Generation Tasks with Wordless Picture Books

A method of assessment that has been verified is storybook or picture narrations (e.g., Berman & Slobin, 1994). These procedures employ a series of pictures that tell a coherent story without words. Children are asked to tell the story or tell what they are thinking as they look through the pictures. Some examples of materials used in this assessment context are a series of books by Mayer—namely, *A Boy, a Dog, and a Frog* (Mayer, 1967) and *Frog Where Are You?* (Mayer, 1969)—as well as *Robot-Bot-Bot* (Krahn, 1979; see Paris & Paris, 2003).

Story generation tasks can be quantified along several dimensions. For instance, Paris and Paris (2003) examined children's book-handling skills, engagement, comments on pictures, comments on the storyline, and comprehension strategies while initially reviewing the book. Trabasso and Nickels (1992) examined preschoolers' narrations for evidence of goal-based episodes, an indication of their understanding of narrative structure. Furthermore, Tompkins, Guo, and Justice (2013) examined generated narratives for evidence of different types of inferences young children generated. Wenner, Burch, Lynch, and Bauer (2008) rated the narrations in terms of their global quality, which was defined in terms of coherence and completeness.

Story generation tasks are most often considered online procedures, as they attempt to assess children's comprehension processes in the midst of task performance. However, many researchers have complemented the online generation tasks with offline methods. After giving their initial narrations or thoughts on the pictures, children may be asked to retell the story or answer questions regarding the storyline (Lepola et al., 2012; Paris & Paris, 2003). Although dynamic assessments could be used for story generation tasks, most of these procedures are conducted in a fixed way, making them static in nature.

Researchers have found evidence that these tasks have internal validity, and interrater reliability is strong. In addition, these measures are sensitive to developmental changes in comprehension (Paris & Paris, 2003). For many preschoolers, looking through picture books is a familiar task, and it is common for preschools to focus on storytelling in their curricula (Paris & Paris, 2003), thus contributing to its pedagogical validity. The variety of different ways that the generated stories can be analyzed can also be considered as a strength of this type of assessment. However, this method of assessment relies heavily on children's expressive language skills. Although the pictures certainly support children as they generate stories, the rather cognitively complex task of telling a narrative may tax children's limited working memory abilities as well. Also, findings are somewhat mixed on how sensitive the procedures are to developmental changes (Tompkins et al., 2013) and how well they relate to other measures of literacy (Paris & Paris, 2003). Still, story generation tasks hold much promise as means of assessment for both research and pedagogical purposes.

Questioning

A common method of assessing children's (as well as adults') comprehension is questioning them after they are exposed to the text or narrative. Questions are used within a variety of assessment contexts, including oral narratives (e.g., Tompkins et al., 2013), wordless picture books (e.g., Lepola et al., 2012), and audiovisual narratives (e.g., Kendeou et al., 2008). Comprehension questions should be written based on a view or theory of comprehension. There are a number of ways that this can be done. For instance, children can be asked inferential questions, which are questions about information that was not explicitly stated in the text (e.g., Paris & Paris, 2003; Tompkins, Guo, & Justice, 2013). Children's answers to these types of questions can be contrasted with their answers to questions about information that was explicitly stated in the text, providing insight into children's surface code comprehension versus their ability to form situation models (e.g., Florit, Roch, & Levorato, 2011; Lepola et al., 2012). Similarly, questions can also be written to assess children's memory of events that are central to the causal structure of a narrative as opposed to those that are not (Lynch et al., 2008). Children's differing answers to these questions reflect their ability to identify and integrate information across narrative events and generally reveal children's sensitivity to the causal structure of the narrative.

Questions can also be used to assess the particular type of inferences that children make in comprehending a text/narrative. For instance, questions may address the causal inferences that are particularly important to understanding the plot of a narrative. For a fine-grained assessment of the type of causal inferences children make, questions may be written to differentiate children's ability to answer questions regarding physical causality versus causality based on psychological or other intangible forces (Thompson & Myers, 1985). Questions may also contrast children's ability to make inferences connecting statements that are close together in a text as opposed to those that are farther apart in the text. This assesses children's ability to integrate information at a local level and their ability to form a global situation model of the text. When assessing narrative comprehension, questions that address the connections between characters' goals and their actions may be particularly important, as this is a key aspect of narrative structure (Lynch & van den Broek, 2007; Wenner, 1999). Although certainly challenging for most young children, questions may also focus on inferences that connect individual events or facts to an overall theme.

Most of the time, questioning procedures are done after a child has listened to or experienced a text and are presented in a uniform manner for all children. Therefore, generally, these assessments are considered both offline and static. However, questioning procedures may take on other qualities. For instance, questions may be asked while the child is experiencing the text, which may be considered an online measure. Also, questioning procedures may be dynamic in nature, with increasingly supportive prompts given in order to aid the child in answering. In such dynamic assessments, scores are based, at least in part, on the number of prompts needed to answer correctly (e.g., Elleman, Compton, Fuchs, Fuchs, & Bouton, 2011).

Questioning procedures have the advantage of being a direct way to assess children's understanding of texts. Questioning procedures are also flexible, as they can be used within either online or offline as well as static or dynamic assessments. As with all the other methods, some cautions need to be taken when implementing these methods. Questions must be carefully written (and piloted) to ensure they are not leading or suggestive. Young children may also be limited by their expressive vocabulary. Thus careful prompts are often needed to encourage children to fully explain their ideas. Pictures could also be used to support children as they answer questions (e.g., MacGinitie et al., 2000).

Although online questioning is common and often found to be useful, there is also some evidence that questioning during a text or narrative may actually interfere with children's comprehension (van den Broek, Tzeng, Risden, Trabasso, & Basche, 2001). Also, although dynamic questioning methods hold much promise, more research is needed to determine their validity and reliability, particularly with preschool children.

Evidence of Validity of Story Retelling, Story Generation, and Questioning Tasks

Convergent Validity   Story retelling, story generation, and questioning tasks are the most common ways of assessing preschoolers' comprehension skills. Often multiple measures are employed and their intercorrelations provide information on the convergent validity of these measures—that is, the extent to which these measures yield comparable scores. Because these assessments are designed to capture the same general psychological construct (oral and/or narrative language comprehension), their intercorrelations are expected to be high. For instance, Paris and Paris (2003) examined whether picture-based retelling and inferential questioning tasks are related to text-based retelling and inferential questioning assessment tasks. Their findings show the consistency of these narrative comprehension measures among kindergartners as well as the first and second graders. Similarly, in a longitudinal study of Finnish-speaking children, Lepola (2014) found strong correlations between retelling and questioning tasks following an orally presented story and questioning tasks following a story generation task. These correlations were found at all ages examined: 4, 5, 6, and 9 years old. Examining specifically the relations among comprehension assessments using different media, Kendeou et al. (2008) and Lynch et al. (2008) found that retelling and questioning tasks following both aural narratives and television narratives were highly interrelated. A variety of other studies examining the development of children's narrative comprehension skills have found similar results (e.g., Hannon & Frias, 2012; van Kraayenrood & Paris, 1996). Thus there is convincing evidence that retelling, story generation, and questioning assessments are tapping related underlying comprehension processes.

Predictive Validity   The predictive validity of these measures has also been established in a number of longitudinal studies. In other words, children's scores on these measures do predict later literacy and language outcomes. Preschool-age children's performance on retelling, story generation, and questioning tasks predicts their performance on similar tasks given in kindergarten or even later in elementary school. For instance, the study by Lepola et al. (2012) revealed that answers to questions in response to pictorial narratives at ages 4 and 5 contributed both directly and indirectly, via vocabulary, to later performance on retelling and questioning tasks in response to orally presented narratives. Similarly, retellings and inference-based questions in response to both oral and audiovisual narratives at age 4 predicted performance on similar comprehension measures at age 6 (Kendeou, 2008).

There is also convincing evidence that these assessments of preschool comprehension predict later reading comprehension skill. Lepola (2014) found that when measured at both ages 4 and 6, children's answers to inferential questions are significant predictors of their reading comprehension skill at age 9, when the children were in third grade. Furthermore, even when statistically controlling for individual differences in vocabulary and letter knowledge, answers to questions at age 6 were significantly related to reading comprehension at age 9. Similarly, Kendeou et al. (2009) showed that sensitivity to the causal structure of a narrative (as assessed through retelling tasks) at age 6 was a unique predictor of reading comprehension in the second grade.

Discriminant Validity   There is also evidence of the discriminant validity of these comprehension measures—that is, the measures' ability to differentiate separate skills or psychological constructs. Although inference making should be connected to text recall, as theoretical models would predict, these constructs are not the same. In fact, based on confirmatory factor analysis, the study by Lepola et al. (2009) revealed that among 4-year-old children, inferential questions measured an inference-making component that correlated with, but was independent of, a language factor including vocabulary, verbal memory, and overall listening comprehension. Similarly, although vocabulary is related to narrative recall and inference making, these skills cannot be reduced to just vocabulary skill (Lynch et al., 2008). Furthermore, story retelling and questioning assessments generally do not have a strong association with assessments that predict later word reading skills, such as letter knowledge or phonological awareness (i.e., Kendeou et al., 2008; Lynch et al., 2008). In addition, these assessments of early comprehension skills generally do not predict later text reading speed, a skill that is better predicted by early letter knowledge (Lepola, 2014).

Whereas retelling, story generation, and questioning tasks are the most common ways of assessing preschoolers' comprehension in research and educational settings, there are other innovative methods that hold promise for both researchers and educators, such as cloze procedures and comprehension monitoring, which we review next.

Cloze Procedures

In assessments that use cloze procedures, children are prompted to fill in words or, perhaps, larger parts of the story after listening to the story once before. One specific assessment that uses a cloze procedure is the joint story retelling task (Dempsey & Skarakis-Doyle, 2001; Skarakis-Doyle & Dempsey, 2008). This procedure uses a relatively short story based on events that are familiar to most young children (such as getting ready for bed). After reading the story, the assessor asks for the child's "help" to retell the story, pausing a number of times for the child to fill in individual words. Most cloze procedures fall into the categories of offline and static assessments, as they are generally done after listening to a text and when the items and procedures do not vary with the child's responses.

Cloze procedures have the advantage of providing support or scaffolding for young children, being less taxing on their expressive language skills and working memory. They have been shown to have strong or moderately strong correlations to other measures of comprehension (Dempsey & Skarakis-Doyle, 2001). However, it is difficult to construct an effective cloze task. The possible answers to fill in must be sufficiently constrained so a child who did thoroughly comprehend the story will be able to answer clearly. However, if the items are too constrained, then there is a danger that the procedure will assess only surface-level (or surface code) comprehension. It may also just measure how sensitive a child is to grammatical morphemes denoting to the semantic relations of words and the sentence structure (Hagtvet, 2003; Skarakis-Doyle & Dempsey, 2008).

Comprehension Monitoring

An aspect of comprehension that has received less attention in early childhood research is comprehension monitoring. Comprehension monitoring is an important aspect of comprehension, particularly as children progress through the school years (McKeown & Beck, 2009), and it can be assessed during early childhood. Particularly, Skarakis-Doyle (2002) developed the expectancy violation detection task in which young children listen to a story once and then are asked to listen for the assessor's mistakes in a second reading. These "mistakes" can include changing the character performing the action or introducing events that are inconsistent with the overarching goal of the main character. If the child indicates verbally or nonverbally that they caught the mistake, it is an indication that he or she is actively attempting to integrate information in the story and understand the general structure.

This measure of comprehension is considered online, as it is done as children are listening to a narrative (although it is their second exposure to the narrative). As the procedure has been used to date, it is also static. The expectancy violation detection task has been shown to be both valid and reliable (Skarakis-Doyle, 2002). However, in general, little developmental research has been conducted validating comprehension-monitoring assessments among young children (Kinnunen, Vauras, & Niemi, 1998).

Standardized Measures

There are a number of standardized measures of early comprehension skills available. Some of the most commonly cited are the listening comprehension subtests of the Woodcock-Johnson IV (Woodcock, McGrew, & Mather, 2014), the Gates-MacGinitie Reading Tests (MacGinitie et al., 2000), Oral and Written Language Scales (OWLS; Carrow-Woolfolk, 1995), Early Literacy Skills Assessment (ELSA; DeBruin-Parecki, 2007), and the Bus Story Test (Renfrew, 1969). These tests draw upon different assessment contexts (e.g., oral passages, pictures, or a combination) and tasks (e.g., questioning, retelling) to assess comprehension. Therefore, many of the same considerations should be made when choosing one of these measures as outlined in the previous sections. In particular, it is important for those using these tests to examine the data on the reliability as well as the convergent, predictive, and discriminate validity of these measures that are available from the developers.

In addition to the data provided by the publishers of these tests, we advise that researchers and educators closely examine the theoretical underpinnings of these assessments. Do they assess the children's abilities to form a textbase or situation model of a passage? Some standardized assessments do tap these levels, such as those that involve inferential questioning (such as the Gates-MacGinitie Reading Tests) as well as those that ask children to make predictions or connections to their own lives (such as the ELSA). Other standardized measures may instead assess comprehension at the sentence level rather than the text level (e.g., some subtests of the OWLS) or the sophistication of children's expressive language (e.g., the Sentence Length and Complexity Scales of the Bus Story Test). Although these abilities are certainly a prerequisite skill for understanding an entire passage or narrative, these assessments do not directly tap children's abilities to mentally connect ideas and ultimately form a situation model. Similarly, tests of vocabulary or comprehension at the word level assess abilities that are necessary but not sufficient alone for narrative or text comprehension (see, e.g., Lynch et al., 2008).

AREAS OF FUTURE RESEARCH

A growing body of evidence is supporting the validity of a variety of prereading assessment methods. However, research on methods of assessment for preschoolers' comprehension is relatively new, particularly compared with assessments of other preliteracy skills such as vocabulary, phonological awareness, or letter knowledge. Therefore, much more research is needed to establish both the validity and reliability of comprehension measures in general. Specifically, we need data on some of the relatively new methods of assessment, such as dynamic assessments and measures of comprehension monitoring. More information on different types of reliability and validity would also be beneficial. For instance, we do not have enough information on factorial validity and factorial invariance on the reviewed measures.

Many of the assessments reviewed in this chapter have been used primarily for research purposes. Although there is reason to believe they could be used in the classroom, as they are modified, many of the assessments reviewed have not been tested in educational or other practical settings. Furthermore, research is needed in order to determine how these assessments can be used by preschool teachers in their own classrooms.

Practically all the assessments we have reviewed are based on narratives. There is good reason for this, as preschoolers generally have a great deal of exposure to narratives through oral stories, pictorial storybooks, television, and other audiovisual media. Also, in elementary school, narratives are often used as instructional materials. For theoretical purposes, the structure of narratives, at least within Western culture, is well understood, as are the cognitive processes used to comprehend them. This provides a sound basis on which to develop valid assessments. An important area of future research is developing assessments that measure children's comprehension of expository texts. Hannon and Frias (2012) have developed an assessment of inference making using short, nonnarrative materials, but this is one of the few assessments of its type. Children's access to prior knowledge and ability to extract meaning from nonnarrative texts are important for their future academic success as well.

The studies reviewed in this chapter, to our knowledge, were conducted in Western cultures. Furthermore, most included largely Caucasian, middle-class samples. There is a need in this area of research to study more diverse populations. We should not take for granted that the results of studies reviewed in this chapter will apply to those with different ethnic or socioeconomic backgrounds. It is particularly important to look at diverse populations when establishing the reliability and validity of assessments. It is possible that current (or future) assessment methods in the field of comprehension may underestimate the skills of children from minority populations (see Hirsh-Pasek et al., 2005). For instance, many current methods of assessment rely heavily on children's productive language skills, thus potentially discriminating against children who grow up in homes where English (or the dominant language of the culture) is not spoken. Also, the "standard" narrative structure varies between and within cultures (Gutiérrez-Clellen et al., 1995). For additional information on multilingualism and comprehension, see Chapter 8 by Barrueco and Fernández.

Researchers also need to investigate the validity of these methods of assessment among children with atypical development, as assessing children with special needs may be an area of concern for many preschool educators who teach in inclusive classrooms. See Chapter 7 by Gear for a discussion of authentic assessments embedded in classroom routines to support included preschoolers with special needs. The measures reviewed in this chapter hold promise for use with special needs populations. Studies have shown, for instance, that individuals with Down syndrome are sensitive to the causal structure of narratives, their comprehension skills generalize across media (Kim, Kendeou, van den Broek, White, & Kremer, 2008), and their oral memory explains success in listening comprehension (Roch, Florit, & Levorato, 2012). Skaradis-Doyle and Dempsey (2008) have shown the sensitivity of certain measures (such as cloze procedures) among children with language impairments. However, much more research is needed to test the validity of these and other assessment methods among special needs populations.

CONCLUSION

As reviewed in this and the other chapters in the volume, there is a strong foundation in theory and research for the further development of comprehension assessments in prereaders. This work leads to a number of questions those developing and using assessments should consider:

- *How is comprehension defined?* Particularly given the complex, multidimensional nature of comprehension, researchers, educators, and other professionals need to be clear about how comprehension is defined in the assessment context. Is it defined in terms of memory for individual words or events, the completeness or coherency of the individual's mental representation of the text, or the individual's ability to connect the text to other knowledge? In other words, does the assessment tap the level of the surface code, textbase, or situation model?

- *What general type of assessment best fits the purpose?* Is the purpose of the assessment to gain insight into comprehension processes, thus calling for online assessments that could be either static or dynamic? Or is the focus on the products of comprehension, thus calling for offline and likely static assessments? Alternatively, will both the processes and the products be assessed?

- *What is the assessment context? What specific materials should be used?* The texts or narratives to be used must be considered carefully. They should be analyzed, for instance, based on length, complexity of the causal structure, types of inferences elicited, and the amount of background knowledge needed to make those inferences, among other factors. Research on the development of comprehension can be a guide to choosing materials that are developmentally sensitive. Although more research is needed, considerations should also be made for children's cultural background. Also, the medium in which the material is presented is a key. We have noted that deeper-level comprehension processes are not medium specific. However, different media may be more or less motivating, leading to differing levels of ecological validity and providing different amounts of support for children's comprehension processes.

- *What assessment tasks should be employed?* We have outlined the benefits as well as disadvantages to the main tasks used to assess preschooler's comprehension (e.g., retelling, story generation, questioning, cloze procedures). The developmental level of the students is also important to consider. The students' level of expressive language skills and working or verbal memory is important, as well as their comfort with test-taking situations.

- *What evidence is there regarding the assessment's reliability and validity?* We have reviewed evidence of different assessments' convergent and predictive validity. Although those developing assessments gather more data on their psychometric properties, those using these methods should be aware of the current research.

Clearly, there is no "right" way to assess comprehension in young children. This is definitely not a limitation or problem for researchers, early childhood educators, and other practitioners. Comprehension and the minds of young children in general are too complex to be captured with one measure. Reflection on the general assessment context, purposes of the assessment, and characteristics of the students can guide researchers and practitioners as they choose an assessment method or a combination of methods that are effective.

REFERENCES

Allen, J. (1985). Inferential comprehension: The effects of text source, decoding ability, and mode. *Reading Research Quarterly, 20*(5), 603–615. doi:10.2307/747946

Berman, R.A., & Slobin, D.I. (1994). Narrative structure. In R.A. Berman & D.I. Slobin (Eds.), *Relating events in narrative: A crosslinguistic developmental study* (pp. 39–82). Hillsdale, NJ: Erlbaum.

Cain, K., & Oakhill, J.V. (1999). Inference making ability and its relation to comprehension failure in young children. *Reading and Writing, 11,* 489–503.

Carrow-Woolfolk, E. (1995). *Oral and Written Language Scales.* Los Angeles, CA: Western Psychological Services.

Casteel, M.A. (1993). Effects of inference necessity and reading goal on children's inferential generation. *Developmental Psychology, 29,* 346–357.

DeBruin-Parkcki, A. (2007). *Early Literacy Skills Assessment.* Ypsilanti, MI: High/Scope Educational Research Foundation.

Dempsey, L., & Skarakis-Doyle, E. (2001). The validity of the joint story retell as a measure of young children's comprehension of familiar stories. *Journal of Speech-Language Pathology and Audiology, 25,* 201–211.

Dempster, F.M. (1981). Memory span: Sources for individual and developmental differences. *Psychological Bulletin, 89,* 63–100.

Dufya, M., Niemi, P., & Voeten, M.J.M. (2001). The role of phonological memory, word recognition, and comprehension skills in reading development: From preschool to grade 2. *Reading and Writing, 14*(1/2), 91–117. doi:10.1023/A: 1008186801932

Elleman, A.M., Compton, D.L., Fuchs, D., Fuchs, L.S., & Bouton, B. (2011). Exploring dynamic assessment as a means of identifying children at risk of developing comprehension difficulties. *Journal of Learning Disabilities, 44*(4), 348–357. doi:10.1177/0022219411407865

Florit, E., Roch, M., & Levorato, M.C. (2011). Listening text comprehension of explicit and implicit information in preschoolers: The role of verbal and inferential skills. *Discourse Processes, 48,* 119–138.

Florit, E., Roch, M., & Levorato, M.C. (2014). Listening text comprehension in preschoolers: A longitudinal study on the role of semantic components. *Reading and Writing, 27,* 793–817. doi:10.1007/s11145-013-9464-1

Goldman, S., & Varnhagen, C.K. (1986). Memory for embedded and sequential story structure. *Journal of Memory and Language, 25,* 401–418.

Graesser, A.C., Millis, K.K., & Zwaan, R.A. (1997). Discourse comprehension. *Annual Review of Psychology, 48,* 163–189.

Graesser, A.C., Singer, M., & Trabasso, T. (1994). Constructing inferences during narrative text comprehension. *Psychological Review, 101,* 371–395.

Grigorenko, E.L., & Sternberg, R.J. (1998). Dynamic testing. *Psychological Bulletin, 124*(1), 75–111.

Gutiérrez-Clellen, V.F., Pena, E.D., & Quinn, R. (1995). Accommodating cultural differences in narrative style: A multicultural perspective. *Topics in Language Disorders, 15,* 54–67.

Hagtvet, B.E. (2003). Listening comprehension and reading comprehension in poor decoders: Evidence for the importance of syntactic and semantic skills as well as phonological skills. *Reading and Writing: An Interdisciplinary Journal, 16,* 505–539.

Hannon, B., & Frias, S. (2012). A new measure of assessing the contributions of higher level processes to language comprehension performance in preschoolers. *Journal of Educational Psychology, 104,* 897–921. doi:10.1037/a0029156

Heath, S.B. (1989). Oral and literate traditions among Black Americans living in poverty. *American Psychologist, 44,* 367–373.

Hirsh-Pasek, K., Kochanoff, A., Newcombe, N.S., & de Villiers, J. (2005). Using scientific knowledge to inform preschool assessment: Making a case for "empirical validity." *Social Policy Report of the SRCD, 19*(1).

Kendeou, P., Bohn-Gettler, C., White, M.J., & van den Broek, P. (2008). Children's inference generation across different media. *Journal of Research in Reading, 31*(3), 259–272. doi:10.1111/j.1467-9817.2008.00370.x

Kendeou, P., Savage, R., & van den Broek, P. (2009). Revisiting the simple view of reading. *British Journal of Educational Psychology, 79,* 353–370.

Kendeou, P., van den Broek, P., White, M.J., & Lynch, J.S. (2009). Predicting reading comprehension in early elementary school: The independent contributions of oral language and decoding skills. *Journal of Educational Psychology, 101,* 765–778.

Kim, O., Kendeou, P., van den Broek, P., White, M.J., & Kremer, K. (2008). Cat, rat and rugrats: Narrative comprehension in young children with Down syndrome. *Journal of Developmental Physical Disabilities, 20,* 337–351. doi:10.1007/s10882-008-9101-0

Kinnunen, R., Vauras, M., & Niemi, P. (1998). Comprehension monitoring in beginning readers. *Scientific Studies of Reading, 2,* 353–375.

Kintsch, W., & Kintsch, E. (2005). Comprehension. In S. Stahl & S. Paris (Eds.), *Children's reading comprehension and assessment* (pp. 71–92). Mahwah, NJ: Erlbaum.

Krahn, F. (1979). *Robot-bot-bot.* New York, NY: Dutton.

Lepola, J. (2014). *Continuity and developmental associations among oral language comprehension, decoding, motivation and reading skills: A longitudinal study from preschool to Grade 3.* Manuscript in preparation.

Lepola, J., Lynch, J.S., Laakkonen, E., Silvén, M., & Niemi, P. (2012). The role of inference making and other language skills in the development of narrative listening comprehension in 4–6-year-old children. *Reading Research Quarterly, 47*(3), 259–282.

Lepola, J., Niemi, P., Kuikka, M., & Hannula, M.M. (2005). Cognitive-linguistic skills and motivation as longitudinal predictors of reading and arithmetical achievement: A follow-up study from kindergarten to Grade 2. *International Journal of Educational Research, 43*(4/5), 250–271. doi:10.1016/j.ijer.2006.06.005

Lepola, J., Peltonen, M., & Korpilahti, P. (2009). Kuvanarratiivi neljävuotiaiden tarinan ymmärtämisen arvioinnissa [Pictorial narrative as a tool for the assessment of narrative comprehension among 4-year-old children]. *Puhe ja Kieli, 29,* 121–143.

Lynch, J.S., & van den Broek, P.W. (2007). The development of goal-based inference making. *Cognitive Development, 22,* 323–340.

Lynch, J.S., van den Broek, P., Kremer, K.E., Kendeou, P., White, M.J., & Lorch, E.P. (2008). The role of narrative comprehension in early literacy. *Reading Psychology, 29,* 327–365.

MacGinitie, W., MacGinitie, R., Maria, K., & Dreyer, L. (2000). *Gates-MacGinitie Reading Tests.* Chicago, IL: Riverside.

Mandler, J.M., & Johnson, N.S. (1977). Remembrance of things parsed: Story structure and recall. *Cognitive Psychology, 9,* 111–151.

Mayer, M. (1967). *A boy, a dog and a frog.* New York, NY: Dial Books for Young Readers.

Mayer, M. (1969). *Frog where are you?* New York, NY: Dial Books for Young Readers.

McKeown, M., & Beck, I. (2006). Encouraging young children's language interactions with stories. In D. Dickinson & S. Neuman (Eds.), *Handbook of early literacy research* (pp. 281–294). New York, NY: Guilford Press.

McKeown, M., & Beck, I. (2009). The role of metacognition in understanding and supporting reading comprehension. In D.J. Hacker, J. Dunlosky, & A.C. Graesser (Eds.), *Handbook of metacognition in education* (pp. 7–25). New York, NY: Routledge.

National Institute of Child Health and Human Development (NICHD) Early Child Care Research Network. (2005). Pathways to reading: The role of oral language in the transition to reading. *Developmental Psychology, 41*(2), 428–442. doi:10.1037/0012-1649.41.2.428

Paris, A.H., & Paris, S.G. (2003). Assessing narrative comprehension in young children. *Reading Research Quarterly, 38*(1), 36–76.

Renfrew, C.E. (1969). *The bus story: A test of continuous speech.* Old Headington, UK: Oxford University Press.

Roch, M., Florit, E., & Levorato, M.C. (2012). The advantage of reading over listening comprehension in Down syndrome: What is the role of verbal memory? *Research in Developmental Disabilities, 33,* 890–899.Ruff, H., Capozzoli, M., & Weisberg, G. (1998). Age, individuality, and context as factors in sustained visual attention during the preschool years. *Developmental Psychology, 34,* 454–464.

Schafer, G., & Plunkett, K. (1998). Rapid word learning by fifteen-month-olds under tightly controlled conditions. *Child Development, 69,* 309–320.

Skarakis-Doyle, E. (2002). Young children's detections of violations in familiar stories and emerging comprehension monitoring. *Discourse Processes, 33,* 175–197.

Skarakis-Doyle, E., & Dempsey, L. (2008). Assessing story comprehension in preschool children. *Topics in Language Disorders, 28*(2), 131–148.

Storch, S.A., & Whitehurst, G.J. (2002). Oral language and code-related precursors to reading: Evidence from a longitudinal structural model. *Developmental Psychology, 38,* 934–947.

Thompson, J.G., & Myers, N.A. (1985). Inferences and recall at ages four and seven. *Child Development, 56,* 1134–1144.

Tompkins, V., Guo, Y., & Justice, L.M. (2013). Inference generation, story comprehension, and language skills in the preschool years. *Reading and Writing, 26,* 403–429.

Torppa, M., Tolvanen, A., Poikkcus, A., Ekiund, K., Lcrkkanen, M., Leskinen, E., & Lyytinen, H. (2007). Reading development subtypes and their early characteristics. *Annals of Dyslexia, 57,* 3–32. doi:10.1007/S11881-007-0003-0

Trabasso, T., & Nickels, M. (1992). The development of goal plans of action in the narration of a picture story. *Discourse Processes, 15,* 249–275.

van den Broek, P. (1989). Causal reasoning and inference making in judging the importance of story statements. *Child Development, 60,* 286–297.

van den Broek, P. (1990). The causal inference maker: Towards a process model of inference generation in text comprehension. In D.A. Balota, G.B. Flores d'Arcais, & K. Rayner (Eds.), *Comprehension in Reading* (pp. 423–446). Hillsdale, NJ: Erlbaum.

van den Broek, P., Kendeou, P., Kremer, K.E., Lynch, J.S., Butler, J., White, M.J., & Lorch, E.P. (2005). Assessment of comprehension abilities in young children. In S. Stahl & S. Paris (Eds.), *Children's reading comprehension and assessment* (pp. 107–130). Mahwah, NJ: Erlbaum.

van den Broek, P., Lorch, E.P., & Thurlow, R. (1996). Children's and adults' memory for television stories: The role of causal factors, story-grammar categories, and hierarchical level. *Child Development, 67,* 3010–3028.

van den Broek, P., Lynch, J.S., Naslund, J., Ivers, C., & Verduin, K. (2003). Children's comprehension of main ideas in narratives: Evidence from the selection of titles. *Journal of Educational Psychology, 95,* 707–718.

van den Broek, P., Tzeng, Y., Risden, K., Trabasso, T., & Basche, P. (2001). Inferential questioning: Effects on comprehension of narrative texts as a function of grading and timing. *Journal of Educational Psychology, 93,* 521–529.

van Dijk, T.A., & Kintsch, W. (1983). *Strategies of discourse comprehension.* New York, NY: Academic.

van Kraayenrood, C.E., & Paris, S. (1996). Story construction from a picture book: An assessment activity for young learners. *Early Childhood Research Quarterly, 11,* 41–61.

Wenner, J.A. (1999). *Panning for goals: Preschoolers' comprehension of goal structure in narratives* (Unpublished doctoral dissertation). University of Minnesota, Minneapolis.

Wenner, J.A., Burch, M., Lynch, J.S., & Bauer, P. (2008). Becoming a teller of tales: Predicting qualities of children's fictional narratives from parent-child reminiscence about the past. *Journal of Experimental Child Psychology, 101,* 1–19.

Woodcock, R.W., McGrew, K.S., & Mather, N. (2014). *The Woodcock-Johnson IV.* Rolling Meadows, IL: Riverside Publishing.

11

The Parent's Role in Developing Children's Comprehension

BILLIE J. ENZ AND JILL STAMM

Five-day-old Robbie begins to cry. Quickly, his mom responds, her high-pitch, exaggerated sing-song speech called parentese *is music and comfort to his ears. He has been listening to her voice since he was 6 months in utero. Her voice is something he knows, something he understands. As he looks into her face, he begins to recognize her features and will soon automatically recognize her face.*

Robbie, as young as he is, comprehends. He is learning that when he cries, his family will respond to his needs. This cause-and-effect relationship is the start of the many facets of comprehension. He and his family have begun a remarkable journey together. So we begin our discussion of the parent's role in supporting children's prereading comprehension.

Comprehension is not a unitary activity. Rather, it is a set of complex and interrelated skills and actions (Kintsch & Kintsch, 2005) that begin to develop prior to birth (Tsao, Liu, & Kuhl, 2004). For comprehension/learning to occur, a child's brain has to develop multiple concurrent and hierarchical functions, such as the following: perceiving and integrating sensory information, learning and interpreting new information and connecting to prior knowledge, and adapting behavior and/or changing the environment. This cycle is constant; learning and behavior are refined continuously and almost instantaneously (Liston, McEwen, & Casey, 2009).

Parents are their child's first teachers. Beginning at birth, parents help to provide the support and stimuli that children need to begin to make sense of the world. By talking to and interacting with their children and by labeling the thousands of objects in the home with words, parents help them build the uniquely human gift and cognitive tool of language. This chapter will explore several aspects of parental support of comprehension in prereaders by intertwining child language and literacy development with research regarding the following:

- The results of a national survey regarding parental involvement in storybook reading

- The impact of shared reading on children's language, literacy skills, and comprehension

- The research regarding the content and impact of parent literacy programs
- Conditions that affect access to age-appropriate books

LANGUAGE: THE FOUNDATION FOR COMPREHENSION

We define prereading comprehension as the process of simultaneously extracting and constructing meaning through interaction and involvement with "text." We broadly describe text as verbal conversation or printed texts such as books, magazines, and newspapers. We also include electronic tools such as computers, notebooks, pads, and smartphones (see Chapter 5 by Dooley and Welch). In addition, we extend text to include illustrations, pictures, television, videos, and music. We also base our definition of the word *literate* on its Latin origin: the pursuit of information and knowledge, not simply decoding symbols. With these clarifications, we begin our discussion of the parent's role in helping to support children's prereading comprehension.

During the first month of an infant's life, most of oral communication consists of crying. The greatest challenge parents face is interpreting the subtle variations in their child's cries. During the second to third months after birth, infants begin to respond to their parents' voices nonverbally with coy smiles and body wiggles. From 4 to 6 months, infants mimic the facial movements of their parents. Delighting in the sound of their own voice, most developing infants can make almost all the vowel and consonant sounds. Infants coo and gurgle endlessly, joyfully experimenting with phonemic variations, pitch, and volume. When spoken to, most infants begin a stream of conversation—called *sound play*—that parallels the adult speaker.

From 6 to 9 months, infants' muscle strength, balance, and coordination allow them to have greater independent control over the environment as they master the fine art of crawling and stumble-walking around furniture. These physical accomplishments stimulate further cognitive development, as infants now have the ability to explore the world under their own power (Glenberg & Gallese, 2012). At the same time, infants' babbling increases dramatically. However, the sounds they produce begin to resemble words. Called *echolalia*, these repeated sounds are still not words with a cognitive connection or meaning. Around the seventh month, most children begin to distinguish syllables, which enable them to detect word boundaries. Prior to this, "whereisyourtoy?" is a pleasant tune but not explicit communication. After auditory boundaries become apparent, infants will hear distinct words: "Where / is / your / toy?" As sounds become words that are frequently used in context to label a specific object, the acquisition of word meaning and comprehension begins (Thiessen & Saffran, 2003). Reading storybooks with simple illustrations appears to help infants hear the word boundaries through repeated reading (Karrass & Braungart-Rieker, 2005; Trivette, Dunst, & Gorman, 2010).

Soon after, babbling begins to exhibit conversation-like tones and behaviors. This pattern of speech is called *vocables*. This form of prelanguage is play-like in nature and not a deliberate use of language to communicate a need or accomplish a goal.

Between 9 months to 1 year, most children use real, goal-oriented language as they speak their first word. During this time, expressive and receptive vocabularies grow rapidly. In addition, infants' command of nonverbal gestures and facial expressions expand from waving. *Holophrastic words,* in which one word carries the semantic burden for a whole sentence or phrase, begin to emerge, as the following example illustrates:

Eleven-month-old Briar pats the garage door, garnering her mom's attention.

> Briar: Ide.
>
> Mom: *Do you want to go outside?*
>
> Briar: *[shaking her head] Ide!*
>
> Mom: *[opening the garage door] Ide?*
>
> Briar: *[pointing at the stroller] Ide.*
>
> Mom: *Stroller! You want to go for ride in the stroller?*
>
> Briar: *[raising her arms, nodding her head vigorously] Ide!*

As Briar's mother (and most mothers) begins to make sense of her child's speech, she also begins to comprehend her child's meaning and/or intent. Malloch and Trevarthen (2010) studied these interactions between parents and infants who were too young to speak. They concluded that the turn-taking structure of conversation is developed through games and nonverbal communications long before actual words are uttered. In the preceding example, the mother's questions supported and enabled Briar to successfully communicate her intentions using a one-word sentence, something she could not have done on her own.

By the time most children are crawling/walking, they begin pointing at new and unfamiliar objects; "Dat?" is a common question. As parents follow their child's pointing gesture, they share a moment of joint attention, and the goal of pointing is to learn the name of the object (Butterworth, 2003). Pointing things out for other people seems like a very simple act, but it turns out that this is a uniquely human form of communication. Important skills in joint attention are following eye gaze and identifying intention, as the two communicators must interpret the goal or purpose of pointing. The ability to identify intention is important for many aspects of language development including comprehension, production, and word learning (Tomasello, Carpenter, & Lizskowski, 2007). Shared attention with another person allows a young child to either request information or offer information, depending on the communication context. Take the following as an example:

Nolan (11 months): Reading with his mother, Nolan points to a large, gray creature with a great hose of a nose. Mom interprets his pointing as wanting to know the name of the large creature. "That's an elephant, Nolan." Mom infers Nolan's pointing as a request for information—the animal's name.

Nora (12 months): Grandma has folded Nora's clothes and is walking into Nora's bedroom. Nora, who is playing on the floor, observes her grandma and points to the chest of drawers to indicate where the clothes should go. Nora correctly interprets her grandma's intentions.

With the support of parents and family members, a child's linguistic abilities undergo rapid changes during the second year of life. By 16 months, his or her production vocabulary is more than 50 words, and by 24 months, most children are typically combining words to make small sentences. Most of their words identify or label the people, pets, and objects that are familiar and meaningful to them. Research suggests that young children will learn and remember approximately nine new words a day (Sabbagh & Baldwin, 2005). This amazing comprehension ability to relate new words to preexisting internalized concepts and then remember and use them after only one exposure is called *fast mapping* (Golinkoff & Hirsh-Pasek, 1999). Research also suggests storybook reading facilitates this process (Hepburn, Egan, & Flynn, 2010).

Comprehension also requires the activation of prior knowledge. The parent often serves as a bridge to help create the connection between the new and the known (Enz & Foley, 2009). When new information enters a child's working memory, it sets off a search throughout the brain's memories for related patterns or information including images or content (Fuster, 2003). Parents can enhance this process by providing their child with multiple forms of information, such as expository and/or storybooks, videos, television, movies, and photos (Christakis & Zimmerman, 2013). See Chapter 5 by Dooley and Welch for an excellent discussion on comprehension in the digital world. The following example illustrates of how several forms of information are integrated in the mind of a young learner.

Annie, 30 months, has been watching a science television show with her father. During the program, Annie watches a sequence where a chick hatches from an egg. Annie, thinking for a moment, goes to her bookshelf and finds two books she has seen previously, The Egg *(Jeunesse & de Bourgoing, 1989) and* A Nest Full of Eggs *(Jenkins, 1995). The expository texts provide more information about how chicks and birds develop in the egg. Over the next few days, Annie requests these books to be read again and again.*

Later in the week, in the middle of the night, Annie's parents awake to sounds in the kitchen. When they investigate, they find Annie sitting on the floor, surrounded by nearly a dozen cracked eggs. With a look of puzzlement, Annie asks, "Daddy, where are the chicks?"

Annie comprehended a number of concepts from watching television and reading books with her parents. Her inferences and new mental connections inspired her to conduct her own scientific investigation. Annie's hypothesis, though disproved this time, was a masterpiece of connecting old information with new. To learn more about informational texts and comprehension, see Chapter 6 by Hall-Kenyon, Culatta, and Duke.

By the time most children enter preschool, they are fairly competent language users, able to use language to accomplish personal goals and able to listen to language to learn new information, as the following vignette illustrates:

On a very warm afternoon, 40-month-old Bree and Gigi (her grandmother) are snuggled together in a comfortable rocking chair reading Leo Lionni's A Color of His Own *(1975) for the first time.*

> Gigi: *Bree, look at the special animal. [pointing to the cover illustration] What do you think it is?*

Bree: *It's a lizard.*

Gigi: *Yes, you are right, but he is a special lizard called a chameleon. A chameleon can change colors. What colors does he have?*

Bree: *He is lots of colors, yelloo, burple, boo, red. He looks mad. Gi, why he mad?*

Gigi: *I don't know, but the title says* A Color of His Own—*maybe the chameleon wants . . . ?*

Bree: *His own color?*

Gigi: *That is a great guess. But I wonder what color that would be? Can you turn the page, Bree? We can start to read to find out what is going on.*

Sharing books aloud with children is a wonderful activity for both the adult and child. In that quick interaction, Bree continues her apprenticeship with text as a source of entertainment, enjoyment, and new knowledge. Children develop literacy skills and an awareness of language long before they are able to read. Because language development is fundamental to all areas of learning, skills developed early in life can help set the stage for later school success. See Chapter 4 by van Kleeck for an excellent review on academic talk. By reading aloud to their young children, parents help them acquire the skills they will need to be ready for school (Bus, van IJzendoorn, & Pellegrini, 1995; Dickinson, Griffith, Michnick-Golinsk, & Hirsh-Pasek, 2012; Duursma, Augustyn, & Zuckerman, 2008; Stamm, 2007). However, shared reading is not an activity that has the same expectations or dimensions for all families. To better understand how families engage in literacy practices in the home, we review national survey research.

HOME LITERACY PRACTICES: A NATIONAL SURVEY

The National Center for Education Statistics (NCES) is the primary federal entity for collecting, analyzing, and reporting data related to education in the United States and other nations. It fulfills a congressional mandate to collect, collate, analyze, and report full and complete statistics on the condition of education in the United States. In 2007, NCES conducted a phone survey to determine the literacy practices conducted in the home. The survey, called the National Household Education Surveys Program (NHES), used a random, stratified sample and collected data from parents of 2,633 children ages 3 to 6. The NHES provided national cross-sectional estimates for the 50 states and the District of Columbia. The design also yielded estimates for subgroups of interest, including the child's age, parents' socioeconomic status, parental education, and ethnicity. In addition to providing cross-sectional estimates, the NHES also provides estimates of change over time in key statistics. The survey (Herrold & O'Donnell, 2008) revealed the following results:

- The percentage of young children who are read aloud to every day by a family member has shown little change between 1993 and 2007. In 2007, 55% of 3- to 5-year-old children (who had not yet entered kindergarten) were read to every day, compared with 53% in 1993.

- Young children who are Caucasian or Asian are more likely to be read to than children who are either Hispanic or African American. In 2007, 67% of Caucasian and 60% of Asian 3- to 5-year-olds were read to every day by a family member, compared with 35% of African American children and 37% of Hispanic children.

- Young children are more likely to be read to if their mothers have completed higher levels of education. In 2007, 74% of young children whose mothers had graduated from college were read to every day by a family member. In contrast, 55% of children whose mothers had some college education were read to every day, compared with 39% whose mothers had only finished high school and 31% whose mothers had not finished high school.

- Young children living in poverty are less likely to be read to every day by a family member than are children living at or above the poverty line. In 2007, 40% of poor 3- to 5-year-olds were read to every day, compared with 50% of children in families at 100%–199% of poverty and 64% of children in families at 200% of poverty and above. As of 2012, in the United States, the poverty threshold for a family of four, including two children, was $23,550 (Adamson, 2012).

- Children living with two married parents are more likely to be read to every day than children with one or two unmarried parents. In 2007, 62% of children with two married parents were read to every day versus 43% of children with one unmarried parent and 24% of children with two unmarried parents.

- Children with mothers working part time (fewer than 35 hours a week) or not in the labor force are more likely than other children to be read to every day. In 2007, 63% of children with mothers working part time and 58% of children with mothers not in the labor force were read to every day, compared with 51% of children with mothers who worked full time and 40% of children with mothers looking for work.

In terms of accumulated amount of exposure, researchers Hart and Risley (1996) discovered that this means the average child growing up in a low-income family has only been exposed to 25 hours of one-to-one reading, whereas the average child growing up in a middle-class family has been exposed to 1,000 to 1,700 hours of one-to-one picture book reading. Beyond entertainment, what effect does shared reading have on preschool children's literacy development, including vocabulary, early literacy skills, and comprehension?

IMPACT OF SHARED READING: A REVIEW OF META-ANALYSIS RESEARCH STUDIES

Since the mid-1980s, a tremendous amount of research has been conducted regarding the impact of shared reading on children's language and literacy. These studies most often include the following:

- Qualitative studies that explore and document the interactions between a parent and child during shared reading time. Often, the investigators observe specific populations, such as families from different educational, cultural, or socioeconomic backgrounds (e.g., Heath, 1982).

- National surveys using telephones or mail to collect data from a random stratified population, such as the NCES (2007, 2012).

- Experimental intervention studies where parents are *randomly* assigned to either a control or intervention group. The intervention group learns and then applies specific shared reading strategies (Hargrave & Sénéchal, 2000; Whitehurst & Lonigan, 1998).

- Quasi-experimental studies involving *intact groups,* such as parents of children in a preschool classroom or parent-education group. These participants are taught shared reading strategies. In these studies, it is common for Group A to receive Treatment 1, whereas Group B might receive Treatment 2 (see Valdez-Menchaca & Whitehurst, 1992).

The children involved in these studies are typically evaluated using multiple measures of standardized emergent literacy assessments, including vocabulary, concepts of print, and comprehension measures. The outcomes of the experimental groups are compared with the control group, or the outcomes of different treatments are compared.

To help understand the outcomes of the thousands of shared reading interventions, we have chosen to review several meta-analysis studies that looked at the impact of shared reading on vocabulary, early literacy skills, and comprehension. Meta-analysis studies statistically combine all the relevant research on a given person in order to determine the aggregated results of the selected research, identifying patterns among study results, sources of disagreement among those results, or other interesting relationships that may emerge in the context of multiple studies. In its simplest form, meta-analysis is normally done by identification of a common measure of effect size. A weighted average of that common measure is the output of a meta-analysis. The weighting is related to sample sizes within the individual studies and provides the reader with extensive information on whether a treatment effect exists (Glass, McGaw, & Smith, 1981).

A review of the meta-analysis research on the impact of shared reading revealed several facts about shared reading with young children from birth to preschool, which we discuss in the following sections.

Develops Vocabulary, Expanding Both Expressive and Receptive Language

The effects of reading to infants and toddlers were examined in a meta-analysis conducted by Dunst, Simkus, and Hamby (2012a) of six intervention studies using experimental and quasi-experimental designs and involving 408 participants. Results indicated that interventions were effective in promoting the children's expressive and receptive language.

Another meta-analysis conducted in 2008 used 16 studies, of which 8 studies reported measures of both receptive and expressive vocabulary. Of the remaining studies, seven tested only receptive vocabulary, whereas one focused solely on expressive vocabulary. A total of 626 parent–child dyads were included. Researchers found the benefits of the vocabulary interventions increased when interventions began sooner and were implemented over longer durations (Mol, Bus, de Jong, & Smeets, 2008).

One reason researchers offered for the finding relates to the nature of children's books. Books contain many words, especially the more sophisticated words that children are unlikely to encounter frequently in daily spoken language. For example, children's books contain 50% more rare words than prime-time television or most adult conversation (Dunst, Simkus, & Hamby, 2012b). Furthermore, qualitative studies have consistently observed parents, typically mothers, pointing to and labeling illustrations/pictures while reading to their young children. These activities greatly increase children's expressive and receptive vocabularies (DeLoache & DeMendoza, 1987; Shapiro, Anderson, & Anderson, 1997).

"Shared Reading Does Not Always Translate into Explicit Improvement in Letter–Sound Knowledge or Concepts of Print"?

Meta-analysis studies about the impact of shared reading on early reading readiness skills such as the development of phonological awareness and letter/sound recognition show less positive results. A meta-analysis conducted by Scarborough and Dobrich (1994) was based on 30 years of research. Using 20 correlational and 11 experimental studies, the investigators found that although shared story reading positively influenced language, it had a limited effect on the development of early literacy skills. This finding could be explained by subsequent qualitative studies (Shapiro et al., 1997) that used videotape data on 12 middle-class mothers interacting with their children during shared read-alouds. For content consistency, each mother read the same two books. Over 24 videotaped sessions, researchers found that "scant attention, either verbally or by gesture, was paid to print or print concepts in this study" (p. 52). Furthermore, in a subsequent study, Phillips, Norris, and Anderson (2008) analyzed the findings of several meta-analyses and qualitative studies. Phillips et al. concluded that adults without specific training typically did not draw the children's attention to the features of the print, and children most often attended to the illustrations. Therefore, it appears that when parents engage in shared reading activities with their young children, they do not automatically teach letter–sound relationships or concepts about print.

Specific Interactions During Shared Reading Time Have Positive Outcomes on Comprehension Skills

The effects of children's story retelling on early literacy and language development were examined in a meta-analysis conducted by Dunst et al. (2012a). The researchers reviewed 11 studies including 687 toddlers and preschoolers. Results indicated that children's story retelling influenced story-related comprehension and expressive vocabulary, as well as nonstory-related receptive language and early literacy development. However, the studies under review used specific interactive storybook reading techniques for parents as part of the treatment.

Nearly all studies reviewed for this chapter found shared reading to have a significant effect on both receptive and expressive language (Bus et al., 1995; Dunst et al., 2012b; Shapiro et al., 1997). These findings may be due to the fact that in nearly all cases, parents discuss the illustrations as they read the story, introducing and reinforcing new vocabulary. In most situations, unless parents had explicit training with interactive, shared book practices, they rarely included a focus on letters, sounds, or concepts about print or spent a great deal of time asking questions that would prompt or teach comprehension (Phillips et al., 2008). However, researchers found parent training in dialogic reading techniques, which teaches adults how to prompt children with questions and engage them in discussions while reading to them, can have a significant impact on the ways that parents conduct shared book time.

By expanding on the child's responses, encouraging children to retell stories, and reiterating the names, objects, and events in the book, dialogic reading helps young children build and reinforce the basic language and literacy skills that will make them successful readers (Lonigan & Whitehurst, 1998; DeBruin-Parecki & Gear, 2013; Lever & Sénéchal, 2011). Therefore, we will review the impact of parent literacy programs and their impact on children's outcomes.

IMPACT OF FAMILY LITERACY AND PARENT EDUCATION PROGRAMS

The meta-analysis conducted by Jeynes (2012) included 51 studies of school-based parental involvement programs, serving students from prekindergarten through 12th grade and comprising approximately 15,000 students. The study included analyses of the effects of all the parental involvement programs combined and of each type of parental involvement program. The purpose was to determine whether certain types of programs had greater effects on student achievement. A review of the 51 studies allowed for six distinct types of parental involvement program:

1. *Shared reading program:* Programs that encourage parents and their children to read together

2. *Emphasized partnership program:* Efforts designed to help parents and teachers collaborate with one another as equal partners in improving children's academic and/ or behavior outcomes

3. *Checking homework program:* School-based parental involvement initiatives that encourage parents to make daily checks on whether their children have completed their homework

4. *Communication between parents and teachers program:* Programs incorporating efforts by schools to foster increased communication between parents and teachers

5. *Head Start program:* Head Start programs that place a special emphasis on parental involvement

6. *English as a second language (ESL) teaching program:* School-based efforts to raise parental involvement levels by teaching parents English via ESL programs

The key findings of the meta-analysis are as follows.

Parental Involvement Programs Are Associated with Higher Student Academic Outcomes

The results of the meta-analysis indicate that school-based parental involvement programs are associated with higher student achievement outcomes. There is a positive relationship between parental involvement programs *overall* and student outcomes, as well as between most of the specific program types included in the analysis and student outcomes. Overall, parental involvement programs yielded a statistically significant effect size of .30 of a standard deviation, which is equivalent to approximately .35–.40 of a grade point on student outcomes (e.g., the difference between a grade of B to a grade of A). The effect sizes were quite similar for the studies in the meta-analysis that used control variables, such as race, socioeconomic status (SES), and gender, and those that did not. What this means is that the academic achievement of children whose schools had parental involvement programs was substantially higher than that of their counterparts whose schools did not, even controlling for factors such as race, SES, and gender. Therefore it appears that when parents know how to explicitly support children's efforts in school, children's learning is enhanced.

Programs that Require Parental Involvement Actions Had Statistically Significant, Positive Effects on Student Outcomes

This meta-analysis found that there were statistically significant, positive effects on student outcomes for those school-based programs that emphasized parental involvement actions such as shared reading (.51), teacher–parent partnership (.35), checking homework (.27), and teacher–parent communication (.28).

The effect for school-based programs may have been due to the benefit of parents' receiving guidance from teachers about reading strategies, book selection, and so forth, which may have enhanced the benefit of parent–child shared reading practices.

School-based programs are just one way parent educational programs are delivered. Programs may be offered in libraries, community centers, book stores, churches, and online. Regardless of the place, a goal of most family literacy intervention programs includes teaching parents to use dialogic/interactive strategies through using age-appropriate books (DeBruin-Parecki, 2007; DeTemple & Snow, 2003; Jay & Rohl, 2005; Paratore, 2005; van Kleeck, 2006). Table 11.1 provides a brief overview of the most successful read-aloud strategies.

Outcomes of these programs have revealed generally positive results. Parents and caregivers of all socioeconomic levels are able to learn new strategies and engage their children more successfully during read-alouds (Roberts, Jurgens, & Burchinal, 2005; Sénéchal & Young, 2008). A study conducted by Blom-Hoffman, O'Neil-Pirozzi, and Cutting (2006) also found that parents could successfully learn to use dialogic strategies via videotape instruction. Likewise, DeBruin-Parecki and Gear (2013) found parents to be highly responsive to observational assessment and specific coaching using the Adult–Child Interactive Reading Inventory (ACIRI).

It is important to remember that children arrive in our classroom with different individual language and literacy experiences (Hart & Risley, 1996; Heath, 1982). Family conceptions of literacy learning and practices vary widely, and given our increasingly diverse communities, composed of many different cultures, languages, religions, races, and complex family systems, teachers are more challenged than ever before to understand what this diversity means for supporting children's learning (Vukelich, Christie, & Enz, 2011). Since the mid-1980s, research has consistently determined that teachers who use culturally sensitive pedagogy, teaching in ways that allow their students to work to

Table 11.1. Description of three shared reading strategies

The basic components of shared reading strategies involve teaching parents to converse by listening and responding to children during read-alouds, whether the text is narrative or expository. The outcomes of shared reading are active engagement, extended learning opportunities, and increased vocabulary and background knowledge (Bowman, Donovan, & Burns, 2001; DeBruin-Parecki & Gear, 2013; Wasik & Bond, 2001; Whitehurst et al., 1994).

Dialogic reading is an interactive, sustained conversation between an adult and a child about the content of a storybook. The fundamental reading technique in dialogic reading is the **PEER** sequence. This is a short interaction between a parent and child. The adult does the following:
- **P**rompts the child to say something about the book
- **E**valuates the child's response
- **E**xpands the child's response by rephrasing and adding information to it
- **R**epeats the prompt to make sure the child has learned from the expansion

Imagine that the parent and child are looking at the page of a book that has a picture of a dog on it. The parent says, "What is this?" (prompt) while pointing to the dog. The child says, "Dog," and the parent follows with, "That's right (evaluation). It's a shaggy brown dog (expansion). Can you say shaggy dog (repetition)?"

In **dialogic reading**, the adult helps the child become the teller of the story. The adult becomes the listener, the questioner, and the audience for the child. To ensure a rich exchange, adults should use the following prompts, referred to as **CROWD:**
- **C**ompletion prompts: Leave a blank at the end of a sentence for children to fill in. For example, "Mary had a little lamb, his fleece was white as _____." This prompt uses a child's sensitivity to the structure of language.
- **R**ecall prompts: These prompts encourage children to remember what happened in the book. For example, you say, "The first little pig made his house of hay. Do you remember what happened when he finished his house?" Use this prompt to help children organize the story and remember its sequence.
- **O**pen-ended prompts: These prompts focus on the pictures in books. You might say, "It's your turn to read the story. What is happening on this page?" When you encourage children to help tell the story, you provide practice in expressive fluency and attention to detail in illustrations.
- **W**hat, where, when, and why prompts: These questions also focus on the pictures in books. When you ask, "What's this?" you are teaching children new words. When you ask, "Why do you think the snail was being silly?" you are encouraging them to retrieve words from their own vocabulary store to express their opinions.
- **D**istancing prompts: These prompts guide children to make connections between the book and their experience. For example, reading *Goldilocks and the Three Bears,* you ask, "Have you ever had someone break one of your toys?" Distancing allows children to practice their conversational and storytelling skills.

The goal of **interactive reading,** such as dialogic reading, is for parents to engage together with the child by sharing a book. One of the many interactive strategies is Before, During, and After (BDA).

Before strategies activate children's prior knowledge and set a purpose for reading.
- Read an age-appropriate book that the child selected (see Table 11.2).
- Encourage children's understanding of concepts of print by allowing them to hold the book and turn the pages.
- Activate children's interest by posing open-ended questions about the title and front cover illustration.
- Introduce any new or interesting vocabulary words.

During strategies help children make connections, monitor their understanding, generate questions, and stay focused.
- Help relate the book's content to the child's real-life experiences.
- Prompt questions and predictions using visual/picture cues.
- Pause and listen as the child answers questions.
- Confirm and expand the child's answers.
- Insert brief definitions for new vocabulary—for example, "Pram is another name for a stroller."

After strategies provide children the opportunity to summarize, question, reflect, discuss, and respond to text.
- Review the story by asking the child to retell the story: "What happened first?" "Then what?" "How did it end?"
- Ask open-ended questions that encourage the child to share opinions: "What was your favorite part of the story?" "Who was your favorite character?" "Why?"
- When the child is interested, identify a letter or word to talk about.
- Invite the child to dramatize stories with simple props.

their strengths—and these strengths are going to be related to children's cultural backgrounds—achieve better academic results (Gay, 2010).

At their best, parent education programs are an extension of classroom literacy instruction. The same respect and understanding teachers offer their young students should be given to their families. Establishing meaningful, positive relationships with parents and teaching them how to integrate research-based practices into their home environment will positively affect children's learning (Paratore, 2005; Sénéchal & Young, 2008).

ACCESS TO AGE-APPROPRIATE BOOKS

Another feature of parent educational programs is enhancing family access to age-appropriate books. Researchers Smith, Constantino, and Krashen (1997) found significant differences in children's access to books in different socioeconomic communities. They studied three neighboring communities in Southern California:

- Beverly Hills, with a median income of $83,000 (family of four), had an average of 199 age-appropriate books in the home.

- Compton, with a median income of $20,000 (family of four), had 2.7 age-appropriate books in the home.

- Watts, with a median income of $15,000 (family of four), had only 0.04 age-appropriate books available in the home.

These findings suggest that in addition to knowing how to read to children, families must also have access to age-appropriate books to read. In fact, it appears that the home environment, specifically the availability of reading material, is a stronger predictor of later academic achievement than socioeconomic status (Britto, Brooks-Gunn, & Griffin, 2006).

Likewise, a multivariate study by McQuillan (1998) and a replication study by Krashen and McQuillan (2012) examined the relation between access to reading material and scores on the 1992 NAEP reading test, given to samples of fourth graders in the United States. The measure of access was a combination of three measures of access to reading material at home, two measures of access to reading in school, and three measures of access to reading in the community library. Their findings revealed that even after controlling for the effect of poverty, access to print was a significant and strong predictor of performance on the NAEP reading test: Children with more access to reading material scored higher. Table 11.2 presents a guideline for selecting age-appropriate books and a synthesis of parental support by child's age.

CONCLUSION

A review of recent research that synthesizes the impact of parental interactive reading with young children found that this activity, done frequently, interactively, and consistently, enhances the concurrent development of language and the multifaceted aspects of comprehension (Baumann, 2005; Hannon, Morgan, & Nutbrown, 2006; Nyhout & O'Neill, 2013). The most effective read-alouds are those in which children are actively

Table 11.2. Parental support and best books by age

Age	Key features	Book examples	Adult support
0–6 months	Are made of sturdy cardboard or cloth or soft plastic, as first books will need to withstand a great deal of love and chewing Feature simple pictures so infants may focus their eyes on the object and examine the illustration closely Have high contrasting colors such as black/white or red/yellow, as infants' vision is not fully developed; therefore, they respond best to bold contrasting colors	Hoban, T. (1993). White on black. New York, NY: Greenwillow Books. Priddy, R. (2003). Fuzzy bee and friends. New York, NY: Macmillan/Priddy Books. Priddy, R. (2013). Hello baby: Faces. New York, NY: Macmillan/Priddy Books.	Hold books 10–12 inches from the infant's face, as initially an infant's' vision and focus is best at this distance. By 4 months the infants' vision has nearly adult acuity. Infants are hardwired to focus on faces and will study real faces and pictures and drawings of faces. Point to and label objects using parentese, the exaggerated, drawn-out form of speech that people use to communicate with infants. The use of parentese plays a vital role in helping infants to analyze and absorb the phonetic elements of their parents' language. Read and reread books for 5–10 minutes, at least daily.
6–12 months	Have simple illustrations and bold colors to stimulate infant's vision and focus infant's interest Encourage infants to reach out and touch the pages and enjoy reading as a tactile experience; textures allow infants to build on their sensory exploratory approach to objects around them	Carle, E. (1992). Brown bear, brown bear, what do you see? New York, NY: Henry Holt. Kindersley, D. (1999). Touch and feel: Baby animals. New York, NY: Dorling Kindersley Publishing. Kunhardt, D. (1940). Pat the bunny. New York, NY: Golden Books.	Point to and label objects. After several readings, ask the infant to point to familiar objects—for example, Can you point to the ladybug? This activity, called rehearsal, strengthens short-term memory. Use descriptive language to describe the textures they are feeling—for example, The blue blanket is so soft and fuzzy. Joint attention between the child and adult helps to develop the child's vocabulary. Read and reread books for 5–15 minutes (depending on the child's engaged attention span), at least daily.
12–24 months	Develop children's understanding of story—a beginning, middle, and end with interesting characters who are trying to solve a problem that young children can relate to; story/narrative books have illustrations that help tell the story Provide children with a deeper understanding about the world; expository (fact or nonfiction) texts for young children often describe plants, animals, and cars/trucks/trains/planes/ships and may use detailed, realistic photos or illustrations Have opportunities to directly interact with the pages—for example, sturdy lift-the-flap books and texture books	London, J. (1992). Froggy gets dressed. New York, NY: Scholastic. Boynton, S. (2007). Bathtime. New York, NY: Workman Publishing. Carle, E. (1969). The very hungry caterpillar. New York, NY: Penguin Books. Stanley, M. (2002). The wheels on the bus. Bristol, PA: Baby's First Book Club. Bauer, M.D. (2003). Toes, ears, & nose! New York, NY: Little Simon.	Children begin to experience a language explosion at this time as short- and long-term memory begins to develop; therefore, parents can begin to ask the child to name the familiar objects on the page—for example, [point to an object] What is this? Encourage the child to hold the book and turn pages as this allows the child to be in charge of the book during storytime, which facilitates interest and attention span. Read and reread books for 10–15 minutes (depending on the child's engaged attention span), at least daily or as often as the child is interested. Remember, children love their books and want to read them over and over again.

(continued)

Table 11.2. *(continued)*

Age	Key features	Book examples	Adult support
24–36 months	Encourage children to label/discuss emotions Have story plots that reflect real-life events that children often experience—for example, sibling rivalry, getting into trouble, being fearful Offer opportunities to learn about colors and shapes Provide occasions to count and begin to learn to recognize numbers	Henkes, K. (1990). *Julius, the baby of the world.* New York, NY: HarperCollins. Sendak, M. (1988). *Where the wild things are.* New York, NY: HarperTrophy. Shannon, D. (1998). *No David!* New York, NY: Scholastic Trade. Mayer, M. (1968). *There's a nightmare in my closet.* New York, NY: Dial Books. Carle, E. (2011). *The artist who painted the blue horse.* New York, NY: Penguin Books. Lionni, L. (1959). *Little blue and little yellow.* New York, NY: Random House. Gerth, M. (2000). *Ten little ladybugs.* Franklin, TN: Dalmatian Press.	Comprehension, at its most basic, relies on a child's interest, attention, and memory. To help stimulate all three, parents need to engage children with interactive questions before, during, and after reading. *Literal/fact questions* ask the child to locate, remember, and/or recognize key facts about the story that can be found in the text: *What is the name of this character?* *What happened first in the story?* *Where do penguins lay their eggs?* *Inferential and interpretative questions* ask the child to draw on prior knowledge and experience and the hints in the text to make sense of the story: *Why do you think he _____?* *What do you think will happen next? Why?* *How do you think that character felt? Why?* *Application questions* ask children to connect the story to their own experiences. Application questions help children to transfer knowledge learned in one context to another: *What other book talks about this?* *Is there another character who acted this way?* *Have you ever had an experience like this? Tell me about it!* *Analysis and evaluation questions* allow children to offer their own opinion, make judgments, compare and contrast, and develop reasoning skills. *What is your favorite wild thing? Why?* *If you could change one thing in the story, what would it be? Why?*
36–60 months	Teach information and basic skills—for example, teaching the alphabet (books that teach the alphabet in joyful rhymes are a favorite) Offer time to sing and move, including fingerplays Continue to teach about science, nature, and math Talk about feelings and behavior; these stories also encourage dramatic play, which allows children to practice emotional responses	Ehlert, L. (2007). *Eating the alphabet: Fruits and vegetables from A to Z.* New York, NY: Houghton, Mifflin, Harcourt. Trapani, I. (1993). *The itsy bitsy spider.* Watertown, MA: Charlesbridge Publishing. Carle, E. (2004). *Mister seahorse.* New York, NY: Penguin Books. Henkes, K. (1996). *Lilly's purple plastic purse.* New York, NY: HarperCollins.	
Additional advice			
Shared reading time should be fun and relaxed. Children will remember these happy moments with love and joy, and it sets the stage for later learning!			Read and reread books for 10–20 minutes (depending on the child's engaged attention span), at least daily or as often as the child is interested.

involved, by both asking and answering questions and making predictions rather than passively listening (Dickinson et al., 2012; Duke, Pearson, Strachan, & Billman, 2011; Lennox, 2013). Essentially, reading becomes a shared, social experience with rich opportunities for learning about language and literacy. Regardless of SES, race, education, or culture, most parents do not apply these interactive reading techniques spontaneously (Britto et al., 2006). Therefore, the need for parental training is essential for all parents, regardless of SES, culture, or ethnicity. Programs should focus on teaching strategies that increase children's understanding about book concepts and comprehension methods, such as open- versus close-ended questions and predicting and confirming procedures— all of which help to maintain child engagement. Parents also need support in knowing how to introduce letter–sound relationships as well as vocabulary. Parents should also learn more about how to select age-appropriate books and how to read texts multiple times with their children.

REFERENCES

Adamson, P. (2012). *Measuring child poverty: New league tables of child poverty in the world's rich countries* (Innocenti Report Card 10). Florence, Italy: UNICEF Innocenti Research Centre.

Bauer, M.D. (2003). *Toes, ears, & nose!* New York, NY: Little Simon.

Baumann, J.F. (2005). Vocabulary-comprehension relationships. In B. Maloch, J.V. Hoffman, D.L. Schallert, C.M. Fairbanks, & J. Worthy (Eds.), *Fourth yearbook of the national reading conference* (pp. 117–131). Oak Creek, WI: National Reading Conference.

Behne, T., Carpenter, M., & Tomasello, M. (2005). One-year-olds comprehend the communicative intentions behind gestures in a hiding game. *Developmental Science, 8*(6), 492–499.

Blom-Hoffman, J., O'Neil-Pirozzi, T.M., & Cutting, J. (2006). Read together, talk together: The acceptability of teaching parents to use dialogic reading strategies via videotaped instruction. *Psychology in the Schools, 43*(1), 71–78.

Bowman, B., Donovan, M., & Burns, M. (2001). *Eager to learn: Education our preschoolers.* Washington, DC: National Academy Press.

Boynton, S. (2007). *Bathtime.* New York, NY: Workman Publishing.

Britto, P., Brooks-Gunn, J., & Griffin, T. (2006). Maternal reading and teaching patterns: Associations with school readiness in low income African American families. *Reading Research Quarterly, 41*(1), 68–89.

Bus, A.G., van IJzendoorn, M.H., & Pellegrini, A.D. (1995). Joint book reading makes for success in learning to read: A meta-analysis on intergenerational transmission of literacy. *Review of Educational Research, 65*(1), 1–21.

Butterworth, G. (2003). Pointing is the royal road to language for babies. In K. Sotaro (Ed.), *Pointing: Where language, culture, and cognition meet* (pp. 9–33). Mahwah, NJ: Erlbaum.

Carle, E. (1969). *The very hungry caterpillar.* New York, NY: Penguin Books.

Carle, E. (1992). *Brown bear, brown bear, what do you see?* New York, NY: Henry Holt.

Carle, E. (2004). *Mister seahorse.* New York, NY: Penguin Books.

Carle, E. (2011). *The artist who painted the blue horse.* New York, NY: Penguin Books.

Christakis, D.A., & Zimmerman, F.J. (2013). *The elephant in the living room: Make television work for your children.* Emmaus, PA: Rodale.

DeBruin-Parecki, A. (2007). *Let's read together: Improving literacy outcomes with the Adult–Child Interactive Reading Inventory (ACIRI).* Baltimore, MD: Paul H. Brookes Publishing Co.

DeBruin-Parecki, A., & Gear, S.B. (2013). Parent participation in family programs: Involvement in literacy interactions, adult and child instruction, and assessment. *Dialogue, 16*(1), 236–252.

DeLoache, J.S., & DeMendoza, O.A.P. (1987). Joint picturebook interactions of mothers and 1-year-old children. *British Journal of Developmental Psychology, 5*(2), 111–123.

DeTemple, J.M., & Snow, C.E. (2003). Learning words from books. In A. van Kleeck, S.A. Stahl, & E.B. Bauer (Eds.), *On reading books to children: Parents and teachers.* (pp. 16–36). Mahwah, NJ: Erlbaum.

Dickinson, D.K., Griffith, J.A., Michnick-Golinkoff, R., & Hirsh-Pasek, K. (2012). How reading books fosters language development around the world. *Child Development Research,* 1–15. doi:10.1155/2012/602807

Duke, N.K., Pearson, P.D., Strachan, S.L., & Billman, A.K. (2011). Essential elements of fostering and teaching reading comprehension. In S.J. Samuels & A.E. Farstrup (Eds.), *What research has to say about reading instruction* (4th ed., pp. 51–93). Newark, DE: International Reading Association.

Dunst, C., Simkus, A., & Hamby, D. (2012a). Children's story retelling as a literacy and language enhancement strategy. *CELLreviews, 5*(2). 1–14. Retrieved from http://www.earlyliteracylearning.org/cellreviews/cellreviews_v5_n2.pdf

Dunst, C.J., Simkus, A., & Hamby, D.W. (2012b). Effects of reading to infants and toddlers on their early language development. *CELLreviews, 5*(4), 1–7. Retrieved from http://www.earlyliteracylearning.org/cellreviews/cellreviews_v5_n4.pdf

Duursma, E., Augustyn, M., & Zuckerman, B. (2008). Reading aloud to children: The evidence. *Archives of Disease in Childhood, 93*(7), 554–557.

Ehlert, L. (2007). *Eating the alphabet: Fruits and vegetables from A to Z.* New York, NY: Houghton, Mifflin Harcourt.

Enz, B.J., & Foley, D. (2009). Sharing a language and literacy legacy—a middle-class family's experience. In G. Li (Ed.), *Multicultural families, home literacies, and mainstream schooling* (pp. 153–174). Charlotte, NC: New Age Information.

Fuster, J.M. (2003). *Cortex and mind: Unifying cognition.* New York, NY: Oxford University Press.

Gay, G. (2010). Culturally responsive teaching: Research, theory and practice (2nd ed.). New York, NY: Teachers College Press.

Gerth, M. (2000). *Ten little ladybugs.* Franklin, TN: Dalmatian Press.

Glass, G.V., McGaw, B., & Smith, M.L. (1981). *Meta-analysis in social research.* Beverly Hills, CA: Sage.

Glenberg, A.M., & Gallese, V. (2012). Action-based language: A theory of language acquisition, comprehension, and production. *Cortex, 48*(7), 905–922.

Golinkoff, R.M., & Hirsh-Pasek, K. (1999). *How babies talk: The magic and mystery of language in the first three years of life.* New York, NY: Dutton Publishers.

Hannon, P., Morgan, A., & Nutbrown, C. (2006). Parents' experiences of a family literacy programme. *Journal of Early Childhood Research, 3*(3), 19–44.

Hargrave, A.C., & Sénéchal, M. (2000). A book reading intervention with preschool children who have limited vocabularies: The benefits of regular reading and dialogic reading. *Early Childhood Research Quarterly, 15*(1), 75–90.

Hart, B., & Risley, T. (1996). *Meaningful differences in the everyday experience of young American children.* Baltimore, MD: Paul H. Brookes Publishing Co.

Heath, S. (1982). What no bedtime story means: Narrative skills at home and school. *Language in Society, 11,* 49–76.

Henkes, K. (1990). *Julius, the baby of the world.* New York, NY: HarperCollins.

Henkes, K. (1996). *Lilly's purple plastic purse.* New York, NY: HarperCollins.

Hepburn, E., Egan, B., & Flynn, N. (2010). Vocabulary acquisition in young children: The role of the story. *Journal of Early Childhood Literacy, 10*(2), 159–182.

Herrold, K., & O'Donnell, K. (2008). *Parent and family involvement in education, 2006–07 school year, from the national household education surveys program of 2007* (NCES 2008-050). Washington, DC: U.S. Department of Education.

Hoban, T. (1993). *White on black.* New York, NY: Greenwillow Books.

Jay, J., & Rohl, M. (2005). Constructing a family literacy program: Challenges and successes. *International Journal of Early Childhood, 37*(1), 57–78.

Jenkins, P.B. (1995). *A nest full of eggs.* New York, NY: Scholastic.

Jeunesse, G., & de Bourgoing, P. (1989). *The egg.* New York, NY: Scholastic.

Jeynes, W. (2012). A meta-analysis of the efficacy of different types of parental involvement programs for urban students. *Urban Education, 47*(4), 706–742.

Karrass, J., & Braungart-Rieker, J. (2005). Effects of shared parent-infant book reading on early language acquisition. *Applied Developmental Psychology, 26*(2), 133–114.

Kindersley, D. (1999). *Touch and feel: Baby animals.* New York, NY: Dorling Kindersley Publishing.

Kintsch, W., & Kintsch, E. (2005). Comprehension. In S.G. Paris & S.A. Stahl (Eds.), *Current issues in reading comprehension and assessment* (pp. 71–92). Mahwah, NJ: Erlbaum.

Krashen, S., Lee, S., & McQuillan, J. (2012). Is the library important? Multivariate studies at the national and international level. *Journal of Language and Literacy Education, 8*(1), 26–36.

Kunhardt, D. (1940). *Pat the bunny.* New York, NY: Golden Books.

Lennox, S. (2013). Interactive read-alouds—an avenue for enhancing children's language for thinking and understanding: A review of recent research. *Early Childhood Education Journal, 41*(5), 381–389. doi:10.1007/s10643-013-0578-5

Lever, R., & Sénéchal, M. (2011). Discussing stories: How a dialogic reading intervention improves kindergarteners' oral narrative construction. *Journal of Experimental Child Psychology, 108*(1), 1–24. doi:10.1016/j.jecp.2010.07.002

Lionni, L. (1959). *Little blue and little yellow.* New York, NY: Random House.

Lionni, L. (1975). *A color of his own.* New York, NY: Scholastic.

Liston, C., McEwen, B.S., & Casey, B.J. (2009). Psychosocial stress reversibly disrupts prefrontal processing and attentional control. *Proceeding of the National Academy of Sciences of the United States of America, 106*(3), 912–917.

Liszkowski, U., & Tomasello, M. (2011). Individual differences in social, cognitive, and morphological aspects of infant pointing. *Cognitive Development, 26,* 16–29.

London, J. (1992). *Froggy gets dressed.* New York, NY: Scholastic.

Lonigan, C.J., & Whitehurst, G.J. (1998). Relative efficacy of parent and teacher involvement in a shared-reading intervention for preschool children from low-income backgrounds. *Early Childhood Research Quarterly, 13*(2), 263–290.

Malloch, S., & Trevarthen, C. (2010). *Communicative musicality: Exploring the basis of human companionship.* Oxford, UK: Oxford University Press.

Martini, F., & Sénéchal, M. (2012). Learning literacy skills at home: Parent teaching, expectations and child interest. *Canadian Journal of Behavioral Sciences, 44,* 210–221. doi:10.1037/a0026758

Mayer, M. (1968). *There's a nightmare in my closet.* New York, NY: Dial Books.

McQuillan, J. (1998). *The literacy crisis: False claims real solutions.* Portsmouth, NH: Heinemann.

Mol, S., Bus, A., de Jong, M., & Smeets, D. (2008). Added value of dialogic parent-child book readings: A meta-analysis. *Early Education and Development, 19*(1), 7–26.

National Center for Educational Statistics, Institute of Educational Sciences, National Household Education Surveys. (2007). *Parent and family involvement in education and early childhood program participation* (NCES Report No. 2013028). Retrieved from http://nces.ed.gov/pubsearch/pubsinfo.asp?pubid=2013028

National Center for Educational Statistics, Institute of Educational Sciences, National Household Education Surveys. (2012). *Parent and family involvement in education and early childhood program participation* (NCES Report No. 2008050). Retrieved from http://nces.ed.gov/pubsearch/pubsinfo.asp?pubid=2008050

Nyhout, A., & O'Neill, D.K. (2013). Mothers' complex talk when sharing books with their toddlers: Book genre matters. *First Language, 33*(2), 115–131.

Paratore, J.R. (2005). Approaches to family literacy: Exploring the possibilities. *The Reading Teacher, 56,* 394–396.

Phillips, L.M., Norris, S.P., & Anderson, J. (2008). Unlocking the door: Is parents' reading to children the key to early literacy development? *Canadian Psychology. 49*(2), 82–88.

Priddy, R. (2003). *Fuzzy bee and friends.* New York, NY: Macmillan/Priddy Books.

Priddy, R. (2013). *Hello baby: Faces.* New York, NY: Macmillan/Priddy Books.

Roberts, J., Jurgens, J., & Burchinal, M. (2005) The role of home literacy practices in preschool children's language and emergent literacy skills. *Journal of Speech, Language, and Hearing Research, 48,* 345–359.

Sabbagh, M.A., & Baldwin, D. (2005). Understanding the role of communicative intentions in word learning. In N. Eilan, C. Hoerl, T. McCormack, & J. Roessler (Eds.), *Joint attention: Communication and other minds: Issues in philosophy and psychology* (pp. 167–201). New York, NY: Clarendon/Oxford University Press.

Scarborough, H.S., & Dobrich, W. (1994). On the efficacy of reading to preschoolers. *Developmental Review, 14,* 145–302.

Sendak, M. (1988). *Where the wild things are.* New York, NY: HarperTrophy.

Sénéchal, M., & Young, L. (2008). The effect of family literacy interventions on children's acquisition of reading from kindergarten to Grade 3: A meta-analytic review. *Review of Educational Research, 78,* 880–907. doi:10.3102/0034654308320319

Shannon, D. (1998). *No David!* New York, NY: Scholastic.

Shapiro, J., Anderson, J., & Anderson, A. (1997). Diversity in parental storybook reading. *Early Child Development and Care, 127–128,* 47–59.

Smith, C., Constantino, R., & Krashen, S. (1997). Access to books in Watts, Compton and Beverly Hills. *Emergency Librarian, 24*(40), 8–10.

Stamm, J. (2007). *Bright from the start.* New York, NY: Penguin Press.

Stanley, M. (2002). *The wheels on the bus.* Bristol, PA: Baby's First Book Club.

Thiessen, E.D., & Saffran, J.R. (2003). When cues collide: Use of statistical and stress cues to word boundaries by 7- and 9-month-old infants. *Developmental Psychology, 39,* 706–716.

Tomasello, M., Carpenter, M., & Lizskowski, U. (2007). A new look at infant pointing. *Child Development, 78*(3), 705–722.

Trapani, I. (1993). *The itsy bitsy spider.* Watertown, MA: Charlesbridge Publishing.

Trivette, C.M., Dunst, C.J., & Gorman, E. (2010). Effects of parent-mediated joint book reading on the early language development of toddlers and preschoolers. *CELLreviews,3*(2), 1–15.

Tsao, F.M., Liu, H.M., & Kuhl, P.K. (2004). Speech perception in infancy predicts language development in the second year of life: A longitudinal study. *Child Development, 75*(4), 1067–1084.

Valdez-Menchaca, M.C., & Whitehurst, G.J. (1992). Accelerating language development through picture book reading: A systematic extension to Mexican child care. *Developmental Psychology, 28*(6), 1106–1114.

van Kleeck, A. (2006). *Sharing books and stories to promote language and literacy (emergent and early literacy).* San Diego, CA. Plural Publishing.

Vukelich, C., Christie, J., & Enz, B.J. (2011). *Helping young children learn language and literacy* (3rd ed.). New York, NY: Allyn-Bacon.

Wasik, B.A., & Bond, M.A. (2001). Beyond the pages of a book: Interactive book reading in preschool classrooms. *Journal of Educational Psychology, 93,* 43–50.

Whitehurst, G.J., Epstein, J.N., Angell, A.L., Payne, A.C., Crone, D.A., & Fischel, J.E. (1994). Outcomes of an emergent literacy intervention in Head Start. *Journal of Educational Psychology, 86,* 542–555.

Whitehurst, G.J., & Lonigan, C.J. (1998). Child development and emergent literacy. *Child Development, 69*(3), 848–872.

Zevenbergen, A.A., & Whitehurst, G.J. (2003). Dialogic reading: A shared picture book reading intervention for preschoolers. In A. van Kleeck, S.A. Stahl, & E.B. Bauer (Eds.), *On reading books to children: Parents and teachers* (pp. 177–200). Mahwah, NJ: Erlbaum.

12

It Takes Two

How Parents and Teachers Bridge the Gap Between Listening and Reading Comprehension

JAMIE ZIBULSKY AND ANNE E. CUNNINGHAM

Learning to read is the most consequential task of children's school careers, because the capacity to decipher and understand text allows students to access information about many academic subjects. However, the process of reading development unfolds over the course of many years, and multiple and interactive skills need to be activated and integrated for a child to become a successful reader (Scarborough, 2001). Most adults are generally aware of the developmental nature of reading and language development. Yet to fully support children throughout this process, attention must be given to a central component underlying the developmental nature of reading: how prereading comprehension transitions to reading comprehension.

During the process of reading acquisition, distinctions are often made between the time period that facilitates learning to read and the time period that facilitates reading to learn (Chall, 1993). Reading comprehension is often considered the final stage in the process of reading acquisition, yet the prerequisite skills for comprehension develop when children are quite young (e.g., Kendeou, van den Broek, White, & Lynch, 2007). In this chapter we focus on linkages between children's early language and listening skills and their later reading comprehension skills in third grade and beyond. We will argue that during children's early years, a focus on the shared and interactive nature of comprehension development and its relationship to oral language skills serves to enrich the skills children must build to become successful readers. Furthermore, in order for children to truly become competent readers, it is necessary for policy makers, researchers, educators, and parents to better understand the research and practices that allow prereaders to build strong comprehension skills. To further this goal, we first highlight many of the important skills that contribute to successful reading comprehension and then describe the developmental progression of these skills over the course of the preschool and elementary school years.

COMPONENTS OF COMPREHENSION

Comprehension is "the process of simultaneously extracting and constructing meaning through interaction and involvement with written language," whether the child is listening to a book being read or reading on his or her own (RAND Reading Study Group, 2002, p. 11). This is the ultimate goal of the reading experience, whether a child is reading poetry, a scientific text, a to-do list, or a storybook. A discussion of how young children develop comprehension skills must take into account a broad definition of comprehension, as well as a more specific focus on both listening comprehension and reading comprehension.

Relationship Between Listening and Reading Comprehension

It is important to consider the various component skills and abilities that children need to acquire as they learn to read. Reading researcher Gough and his colleagues described what they termed the *simple view of reading*, which states that a person's reading comprehension develops to the level of his or her listening comprehension but does not surpass it (Hoover & Gough, 1990). The implication of this model is that listening comprehension, or the ability to understand and process spoken language, is a foundational component of reading comprehension. Research has demonstrated that listening comprehension begins when children are very young and predicts later reading success (Perfetti, Landi, & Oakhill, 2005). For this reason, it is important to explore the similarities between oral and written comprehension, as well as how language and listening comprehension facilitates future reading development.

Reading comprehension involves the joint processes of word recognition and listening comprehension; that is, it involves being able to decode words in text and derive meaning from what is being read (Hoover & Gough, 1990; Snow, 2002). Children's ability to decode develops relatively independently from their capacity for listening comprehension, and there is a significant body of work demonstrating this difference: Some children possess strong decoding skills but struggle with text comprehension and others struggle with decoding but possess strong comprehension skills (e.g., Catts, Hogan, & Fey, 2003). Longitudinal evidence supports the distinction between decoding and comprehension, which remains stable over time (Catts et al., 2003; Oakhill, Cain, & Bryant, 2003).

Role of Vocabulary

Oral language skills underlie children's decoding ability because children need a repository of words for written language to be meaningful. Thus for the decoding process to be truly successful, the sounds that constitute oral language must be familiar as well. Furthermore, being familiar with words in their oral form—that is, having a large vocabulary—increases children's capacity to decode text. Possessing a large vocabulary allows children to store words in memory based on their component sounds rather than simply recalling words as units (Metsala & Wally, 1998). Children are then increasingly able to categorize and recall words using component sounds, which leads to even greater vocabulary size. See Chapter 2 by Coyne, Neugebauer, Ware, McCoach, and Madura for their work on vocabulary and its role in early comprehension.

As children become more sophisticated readers and learn to decode with fluency, vocabulary size continues to contribute to reading comprehension (e.g., Sénéchal, Ouellette, & Rodney, 2006; Stanovich, 1986). Possessing the language skills to understand information that is presented orally is the foundation of listening comprehension and essential for later reading comprehension. However, reading comprehension also requires a child to translate text back into speech. As a result, reading comprehension skills often lag behind listening comprehension skills when the child is still developing the ability to decode text (Sticht & James, 1984). When a child can understand language equally well in verbal or written form, the distinction between listening and reading comprehension ceases to be important (Snow, Burns, & Griffin, 1998). Yet research suggests that most children do not reach this point until seventh or eighth grade (Diakidoy, Stylianou, Karefillidou, & Papageorgiou, 2004; Hoover & Gough, 1990).

Given these findings, it is important to account for the developments that occur in the years that listening comprehension abilities are more developed than reading comprehension abilities. Researchers have posited that during preschool and elementary school, comprehension abilities develop largely through "interactive experiences during which children learn to use and understand decontextualized language" that describes objects and events removed from their present setting (Snow, 1991, p. 8). Thus for preschool- and elementary-age children, the conversations they have with adults may be one of the most effective ways for them to be exposed to and understand new information (Kendeou et al., 2007; Price, van Kleeck, & Huberty, 2009; Snow, 1991). For further discussion on the parent's role in developing their children's comprehension abilities, see Chapter 11 by Enz and Stamm.

Oral Language versus Text

Despite the close association between listening and reading comprehension, there are some important differences to note between spoken and written language. The way people write differs from the way they talk (Hayes & Ahrens, 1988), including the fact that written sentences tend to be more complex and formal and require a more sophisticated understanding of semantic and pragmatic language (Perfetti, 1994). For this reason, when parents and teachers provide children with access to the decontextualized language often found in print, they help children move from understanding everyday spoken language to acquiring the comprehension skills required for interpreting texts (Price et al., 2009; Zucker, Cabell, Justice, Pentimonti, & Kadaraek, 2013).

Moreover, there are many comprehension processes (such as making causal connections between events or inferring a character's motivation) that develop before children become independent readers but facilitate later reading development (Kendeou et al., 2005). The processes are fostered through conversation about events and situations depicted not only in print but also in other media, such as television programs and puppet shows (Kendeou et al., 2005). When communicating about these events, children get the opportunity to think about cause and effect and draw links between events. The ability to make such connections facilitates the development of a *construction–integration model* of comprehension, which requires a child to construct knowledge by integrating his or her background knowledge with information presented in books or other sources of information and stories (Kintsch, 1998). These comprehension processes are also facilitated through interactions with parents and teachers who can help children consider and elaborate on the nuances of stories they hear (Garner & Bochna, 2004; Price et al., 2009; Roberts, 2013; Zucker et al., 2013).

However, for many children, the adjustment from everyday conversations to academic discourse is challenging (Beck, McKeown, & Kucan, 2002; Snow, 1991), as is the process of learning to make connections between multiple events in a story (e.g., Kendeou et al., 2007). Yet dialogue with adults—particularly within the context of shared reading—fosters several skills that are linked to comprehension of complex text (Dickinson & Smith, 1994; Lawrence & Snow, 2011). Several researchers have suggested that the questions and comments that adults make during shared reading time do more than just facilitate receptive and expressive language development; in fact, they contribute to children's ability to use language to reason about situations and experiences (Kintsch, 2005; Makdissi & Boisclair, 2006; van Kleeck, 2008). The capacity for deep comprehension of text develops over many years and requires the integration of these skills. See Chapter 4 by van Kleeck for a comprehensive discussion on academic talk and children's language and comprehension development.

CONNECTIONS BETWEEN SKILLS THAT SUPPORT COMPREHENSION

We have already discussed the strong relationship between early language comprehension and later reading comprehension, but it is important to acknowledge as well the many other skills that facilitate reading success. Scarborough (2001) elegantly describes the component skill that fosters reading development as individual threads that are woven together to become a stronger and more cohesive rope over the course of elementary school (see Figure 12.1). Initially, there are two clusters of threads that operate largely in isolation from one another: The first cluster includes threads that represent language

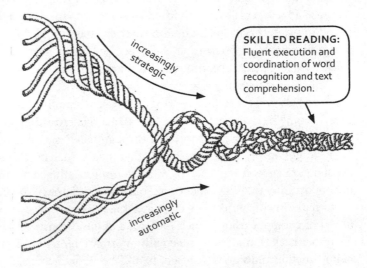

LANGUAGE COMPREHENSION

BACKGROUND KNOWLEDGE
(facts, concepts, etc.)

VOCABULARY
(breadth, precision, links, etc.)

LANGUAGE STRUCTURES
(syntax, semantics, etc.)

VERBAL REASONING
(inference, metaphor, etc.)

LITERACY KNOWLEDGE
(print concepts, genres, etc.)

WORD RECOGNITION

PHONOLOGICAL AWARENESS
(syllables, phonemes, etc.)

DECODING (alphabetic
principle, spelling-sound
correspondences)

SIGHT RECOGNITION
(of familiar words)

increasingly strategic

increasingly automatic

SKILLED READING: Fluent execution and coordination of word recognition and text comprehension.

Figure 12.1.   The many strands that are woven into skilled reading. (Republished with permission of Guilford Press, from Scarborough, H. [2001]. Connecting early language and literacy to later reading [dis]abilities: Evidence, theory, and practice. In S.B. Neuman & D.K. Dickinson [Eds.], *Handbook of early literacy research* [Vol. 1, pp. 97–110]. New York, NY: Guilford Press; permission conveyed through Copyright Clearance Center, Inc.)

comprehension skills, including prerequisite skills such as background knowledge, vocabulary, language structures, verbal reasoning, and literacy knowledge. The second cluster includes threads that represent *word recognition* skills, including phonological awareness, decoding, and sight recognition (Scarborough, 2001).

These two skill sets merge over time, and even skilled decoders—who have mastered the skills of the word recognition strand—will experience reading difficulties if they have not developed commensurate language comprehension skills (Adlof, Perfetti, & Catts, 2011). As Scarborough explains, for children who do not know the meaning of the words they decode or how these words relate semantically and syntactically to other words, or for children who lack background knowledge and the ability to make inferences about a text, "'reading comprehension' deficits are essentially *oral* language limitations" (2001, p. 98). This point is important because the developmental trajectory of reading is often thought to proceed in a linear fashion from word recognition skills to reading comprehension skills. However, language comprehension is a critical and early component of reading development (Scarborough, 2005). If parents and teachers overlook the importance of language comprehension for reading success, children may miss out on opportunities to develop the skills and comprehension processes that predict academic success in later years. In addition, there are also many other variables that play a role in determining future comprehension skills.

Cognitive Abilities

Each child's cognitive abilities and processing skills help shape his or her development as a reader, and these variables can influence multiple strands of the reading braid. For example, working memory skills facilitate vocabulary learning and allow children to engage in important reading comprehension strategies such as inference generation and comprehension monitoring (Cain, Oakhill, & Bryant, 2004). Processing speed, or the ability to quickly and accurately complete basic tasks, is implicated in reading fluency and bottlenecks in automatic processing of text at the word level. This means that children with slow processing speed have fewer cognitive resources available for engaging in comprehension strategies (Wolf & Katzir-Cohen, 2001). Thus the reasons for any one child's reading success or lack thereof cannot be determined solely by examining performance on measures of word recognition and language comprehension. One must also consider this broader constellation of variables that are associated with cognition. For example, see Chapter 9 by Cartwright and Guajardo for an in-depth perspective of the hot and cool executive functions. Later in this chapter, we will discuss the growth of specific thinking abilities—causal reasoning and inferential thinking—that are implicated in reading comprehension.

Reading-Specific Factors

Although cognitive abilities are, arguably, not particularly malleable to change, there are several factors that influence the transition from prereading comprehension to successful reading comprehension. Both the *environment* and the *support* that children receive from parents and teachers help shape the development of reading-specific factors, including the possession of background knowledge, vocabulary development, print exposure, and reading motivation.

Background Knowledge   Background knowledge is critically important for both oral and written language comprehension (Cunningham & Stanovich, 1997; Snow, 1991), although it is not required for the development of the word recognition skills that children develop in early elementary school. For that reason, we often see the effects of background knowledge on reading development emerge in later elementary school when children become fluent readers (Adlof et al., 2011; Chall, 1993). However, studies focused on story comprehension demonstrate that background knowledge supports comprehension development even in the preschool years (Neuman, Newman & Dwyer, 2011). Without a clear understanding of story elements such as the characters and their motivations, the setting, and the events that take place, children will not be able to interpret, recall, and react to what is happening in a narrative. Parents and teachers help children build background knowledge by providing an expansive running narrative about daily events, including providing information about the reasons people chose to behave in certain ways and labeling and explaining the new vocabulary and ideas in unfamiliar books and other media. See Chapter 3 by Newman, Dickinson, Hirsh-Pasek, and Golinkoff for an excellent discussion of using play to foster children's deeper knowledge of vocabulary and comprehension of narratives.

As important as background knowledge is for comprehension of narrative texts, some researchers have demonstrated that it is even more important for comprehension of expository or informational texts (Best, Floyd, & McNamara, 2008). In order to integrate new information into their existing knowledge base, readers must rely on their prior knowledge as a foundation and point of reference. Students who lack sufficient background knowledge or who are unable to appropriately activate this knowledge often have difficulty making sense of the information presented in school across multiple subject areas. Indeed, research indicates that prior knowledge has a strong influence on reading comprehension, which explains the significant variance in standardized test scores of reading comprehension (Dochy, Segers, & Buehl, 1999; Best et al., 2008). The ability to comprehend informational texts is central to the Common Core State Standards (CCSS) for teaching English language arts in elementary school and beyond. For this reason, early childhood educators must begin to develop this repository of knowledge in children at a young age to support future success in reading comprehension. Just as parents and teachers can expand on details of stories with young children to build background knowledge related to narrative texts, they can also expand on facts related to the world around them to build background knowledge in this domain. For example, when visiting the zoo, parents can point out the placards that accompany each animal's habitat, explain the goal of the author in sharing that information, and discuss some of the language and concepts relevant to understanding that particular habitat. For a detailed discussion of using informational texts to build comprehension, see Chapter 6 by Hall-Kenyon, Culatta, and Duke.

Vocabulary Knowledge   There is a great deal of research to suggest that vocabulary knowledge is strongly associated with reading comprehension (Oakhill & Cain, 2012) and that this association persists over time. For example, in a 10-year longitudinal study, Cunningham and Stanovich (1997) found that children's first-grade vocabulary predicted 11th-grade reading comprehension. Although some vocabulary growth occurs as a result of structured language experiences, such as explicitly teaching new vocabulary words (Beck, Perfetti, & McKeown, 1982), the majority of children's encounters with new words occur within the context of their daily experiences, like reading (Cunningham & Stanovich, 1991, 1998; Hayes & Ahrens, 1988; Nagy, Herman, & Anderson, 1985). In fact, many researchers believe that it is reading volume that explains most of the differences over time in children's vocabulary knowledge (Nagy et al., 1985; Stanovich & Cunningham, 1992).

Exposure to Text   Reading volume, or print exposure, aids reading comprehension by expanding on background and vocabulary knowledge, as well as in other ways. Children who are familiar with text structure, through either shared or independent reading activities, are more easily able to relate to, recall, and organize the ideas conveyed in a new text. In fact, these skills often begin to develop outside of a book-reading context through conversations with parents that include key words for sequencing like *first* and *then* and highlight why events occurred using words like *because* (Fivush, Reese, & Haden, 2006; Lange & Carroll, 2003). A child who has a well-developed sense of story schema will be better equipped to develop comprehension skills through identifying and interpreting important information within a story (Anderson & Pearson, 1984). An awareness of how stories are generally structured frees a child's cognitive resources to focus on the content of the particular story he or she is reading or hearing. In contrast, children with limited exposure to books and stories—and therefore a poorer understanding of story structure—may struggle with comprehension (Perfetti, 1994). Modeling enthusiasm for reading, providing easy access to varied and high-interest reading materials, and praising children's effort rather than ability during reading time are all strategies that parents and teachers can use to promote avid reading.

Dispositional Factors   It is also important to recognize that variables as diverse as child motivation and temperament may influence the duration, frequency, and quality of children's conversational and reading time with parents (e.g., Bus & van IJzendoorn, 1997; Clingenpeel & Pianta, 2007), as well as their exposure to information about particular topics. For example, some children may be particularly interested in the natural world and animals and will often request a visit to the zoo. Some of these children may also be able to sit and focus more readily than others, frequently requesting to read books about animals. Those children would likely acquire the background knowledge required to learn about different species at a much younger age than other children with equally intact cognitive and reading skills who expressed less interest in that topic or displayed less capacity to jointly engage in a task.

Interaction Effects   Just as the strands of reading development become interconnected with one another, the variables discussed here are also not wholly separable from one another. For instance, even after accounting for factors such as general intelligence and reading ability, reading volume significantly contributes to verbal skills (Cunningham & Stanovich, 1991; Stanovich & Cunningham, 1992, 1993). In turn, reading volume is partially dependent on parent and child motivation to engage in reading tasks (e.g., Clingenpeel & Pianta, 2007; Wigfield & Guthrie, 1997). This constellation of variables is dynamically connected, demonstrating why it is important to consider reading development from a sociocultural perspective. Many of these skills are reciprocally facilitative and spurred on by parent and teacher interactions. Although it is beyond the scope of this chapter to explore how sociodemographic variables like family income and parental education affect reading development, examining reading development from a sociocultural perspective highlights the many ways environmental variables and interactions with caregivers influence the quality and quantity of a child's experiences. The disparities in educational outcomes between children who have frequent, high-quality interactions and those who do not tend to increase over time: another reason it is important to support prereaders before these gaps in achievement emerge and widen (Stanovich, 1986).

ENVIRONMENTAL INFLUENCES: A SOCIOCULTURAL PERSPECTIVE

Although there are many variables that affect reading comprehension, the importance of oral language development is quite apparent, and thus it is necessary for educators who want to support prereaders to consider the context in which language skills develop. The language experiences of a toddler and young preschool child are largely social in nature, and both the environment and human facilitators of knowledge initially guide children's development (Rogoff, 2003; Vygotsky, 1978). Vygotsky (1978) posited that language development occurs first as a social act between people (at an interpsychological level) and then as an intrapsychological act, as we gradually internalize directions, strategies, and advice by verbalizing them (first aloud and then internally) to ourselves.

When applied to comprehension, this theory implies that the thinking a child does about a story—whether that story is delivered orally or read from a book—begins as a collaboration. In conversation about events, adults define unfamiliar words, ask questions about situations that arise, and muse about why people behaved in particular ways. Adult interaction can help or hinder the process of producing and internalizing speech and speech structures.

Parent–child and teacher–child interactions are crucial to the development of language abilities, as well as the self-regulatory abilities that govern later metacognitive strategies implicated in reading comprehension (Roberts, 2013). For this reason, helping parents and teachers understand how to use questions and comments to facilitate language development generally, and the development of vocabulary and inferential thinking more specifically, may be mechanisms by which reading comprehension can be developed (Lawrence & Snow, 2011; van Kleeck, 2008; Whitehurst et al., 1988). Over time, children will internalize the same strategies that adults model for them and develop the ability to comprehend text more independently.

Dickinson and Smith built on this Vygotskian idea that parent and teacher language use can support skill development and reading comprehension, suggesting that shared book reading time can serve as a "potentially supportive setting [for] . . . cognitively challenging talk" (1994, p. 29). Other researchers have characterized the dialogue that occurs during this time as extratextual talk, which may focus on either the words on the page or their meaning (Price et al., 2009; Zucker et al., 2013). Indeed, interactions with adults or more skilled others—whether generated by book reading or other situations—allow for children to have necessary interpsychological experiences that are precursors to developing strategies for reading comprehension.

For example, there is a considerable body of research demonstrating that a particular form of shared reading—dialogic reading—may be a powerful mechanism in the development of children's comprehension skills (see also Chapter 7 by Gear and Chapter 11 by Enz and Stamm). Dialogic reading—in which an adult serves as the guide through a book but allows the child to take a leadership role in the reading process—fosters the development of language skills in preschoolers (e.g., Hargrave & Sénéchal, 2000; Justice, 2002; Lever & Sénéchal, 2011; Whitehurst et al., 1988). Creating opportunities for peer interaction in elementary school also helps children make deep analogies when reading informational texts (e.g., Brown, 1997). Taken together, these lines of research help reinforce that literacy development is dependent on language development and that literacy development is social in nature.

To illustrate that children need adult support and guidance to strengthen reading skills throughout the course of development and that the type of support and guidance they need changes over time, the following section highlights the comprehension skills of preschoolers and third graders. Considering the skills that directly and indirectly contribute to comprehension development at these different points in time may help policy makers, researchers, educators, and parents determine how to foster environments and programs that facilitate comprehension development.

COMPREHENSION AT DIFFERENT AGES

To explore the ways that comprehension skills unfold over the preschool and elementary school years is a difficult feat because there are many commonalities between listening comprehension and reading comprehension. There are also differences that make assessing the comprehension abilities of prereaders challenging. Examining comprehension in prereaders requires thinking about language and story comprehension rather than the comprehension of written materials. However, parents and educators can use written materials to facilitate the development of these skills. Reading aloud to young children provides the early exposure to text structure and written language that eases the transition from oral to written stories and sets the stage for successful comprehension of text (Roberts, 2013).

Many of the language comprehension skills we discuss in this chapter *appear* to lie dormant during the kindergarten through second grade period, when children are learning to decode text with speed and accuracy. During that time, reading success is assessed largely using measures of fluency, to which language comprehension skills contribute minimally. However, these language comprehension skills become critically important for reading comprehension in middle to late elementary school and begin to contribute considerable variance to reading success (Sénéchal et al., 2006). One might think of them as having a "sleeper effect": Even though these skills do not account for much variance in early elementary reading skills, their lack will be felt once children read to learn. The same skills that were important for earlier listening and story comprehension across different formats and media remain as important for successful independent reading comprehension. For that reason, we will detail in the following sections how several of the important skill sets discussed earlier first develop in early childhood and become stronger over time with the assistance of parents and teachers. These skill sets may look very different when observed in a preschooler and a third grader, but it is important for parents and educators to understand the connection between early and later manifestations of these skills.

Prerequisite Knowledge Development over Time

Research has shown the volume and diversity of language that a child hears at home during these early years predict a child's vocabulary size very well and better than school experiences do (Biemiller, 2006; Hirsch, 2003). By the time a child is 3 years old, the amount that he or she speaks tends to match the amount that his or her parents spoke to the child when he or she was first learning to talk, highlighting the primary importance of the home environment for the development of vocabulary skills (Hart & Risley, 1999). But a shift takes place around the middle of elementary school, at which point children have generally acquired most of the words that they can learn through oral language. The language used in texts, including and particularly children's books, exceeds the variety and complexity of language used in many other contexts (Hayes & Ahrens, 1988). For this reason, by third or fourth grade, children need to turn to the printed page as their primary source of word learning (Beck, McKeown, & Kucan, 2002). Although vocabulary gains often still arise through social interactions, children are increasingly able to reason about unfamiliar words and print somewhat independently, using the units of speech they do know to approximate the meaning of new words (Anglin, 1993). It stands to reason then that successful readers are those children who already use the words learned through oral language with facility and can dedicate their conscious attention to making sense of novel words read in context.

Similarly, an understanding of story schema first begins to develop through interactions with parents (Fivush, Reese, & Haden, 2006; Lange & Carroll, 2003). By the age of 3, children are able to provide general accounts of events in an appropriate sequence (Nelson, 1986); by age 5, children usually include information about main events, characters, settings, and problems and talk about the order of events in stories and the relationship between cause and effect (Trabasso & Stein, 1997). See Chapter 3 by Newman, Dickinson, Hirsh-Pasek, and Golinkoff and Chapter 5 by Dooley and Welch, both of which also address children's narrative and text structures. By age 9, children structure stories in a similar way to adults, including information on characters' goals, attempts to reach those goals, and the outcomes of their actions; their knowledge of story schema becomes increasingly sophisticated and refined into adolescence (Trabasso & Stein, 1997).

Children's general knowledge about the world around them increases during this time period as well through exposure to new ideas and experiences. This is especially important because building young children's knowledge about the world provides a strong basis for text comprehension (Hirsch, 2006; Simmons, Pollard-Durodola, Gonzalez, Davis, & Simmons, 2008). It is not just that these skills facilitate book reading but also that book reading facilitates these skills—third and fourth graders who read more acquire larger vocabularies and more general knowledge than their peers who read less, even when their cognitive skills are taken into account (Stanovich & Cunningham, 1992).

Each of these skills is developed first at what Vygotsky would call the interpsychological level, through interactions with more skilled others. Adults mediate learning experiences for young children and can cultivate the growth of these skills (Roberts, 2013). Moreover, these skills are necessary precursors to thinking processes such as causal reasoning and inferential thinking (Cain, Oakhill, Barnes, & Bryant, 2001), higher-order aspects of reading comprehension.

The Development of Thinking Abilities over Time

We expect that preschoolers will require guidance and support to understand text structure and, at an even more sophisticated level, infer why events happened and why people behaved in particular ways. In turn, we assume that older elementary school children are on their way to developing metacognitive and comprehension-monitoring strategies to reason about text more independently. It is notable, though, that the development of these strategies often proceeds slowly and requires teachers to create interactive learning environments where identifying main ideas, summarizing, predicting, and reflecting are strategies that are modeled and practiced (Palincsar & Brown, 1984; Paris, Wasik, & Turner, 1996). Many of the strategies utilized with elementary school readers continue to rely on the Vygotskian notion that knowledge is acquired across, rather than within, people. Deep comprehension, throughout preschool and elementary school, requires the support of a more skilled other.

Causal Reasoning   Causal reasoning is the ability to think logically as well as to order facts, understand how people affect one another, and identify causes and consequences of events. This type of reasoning helps the reader or listener understand what made certain events happen, anticipate future consequences, and weave together a cohesive picture of a series of events (van den Broek, 1997). Research suggests that events that are causally connected are much more likely to be remembered than are isolated events or even events that are temporally related but not necessarily causally connected (Trabasso & Stein, 1997). Causal reasoning skills generally tend to emerge around age 4 and continue to grow increasingly advanced until around age 9 when development begins to plateau (Brown, 2008).

Research demonstrates that 4-year-olds can engage in basic causal reasoning when provided with an appropriate level of support (Poulsen, Kintsch, Kintsch, & Premack, 1979). Furthermore, 4-year-olds are more likely to identify reasons for characters' actions when adults use dialogic reading questions and prompts (Zevenbergen, Whitehurst, & Zevenbergen, 2003). Finally, studies have found that parents who use more explanations when they talk to their children and discuss causality more often when their children are 2 1/2 years old have children who talk more about causality when they are 5 years old (Haden, Haine, & Fivush, 1997).

By the middle of elementary school, cause-and-effect relationships are easier for children to detect independently, allowing them to allocate more resources to making inferences and predictions. However, as the length and complexity of the texts children read increases, the demands of comprehension increase as well. The further events are separated in a text, the more difficult it is for children to notice the causal relationships between them (van den Broek et al., 2005). And as texts become denser, the connections between events may not be as proximal, requiring readers to do more reasoning. In elementary school, children also become more aware of the internal events occurring in a story—characters' motivations and feelings—and develop the ability to reason about them as well rather than focusing solely on the physical actions that happen. This growth in causal reasoning skills primes children to make inferences about text.

Inferential Thinking   The ability to make inferences or to go beyond the pictures and text to interpret what the author is saying is deeply connected with comprehension skills, and the two are reciprocally related. In fact, some research demonstrates that inferential thinking abilities may be causally related to comprehension skills (Cain & Oakhill, 1999). Making inferences allows children to string together disparate aspects of a narrative and to fill in any gaps. Children who are less-skilled comprehenders are often unable to make appropriate inferences when they read. Instead, they tend to interpret text literally, not because of a lack of relevant knowledge, but rather because they are unsure of when to use relevant knowledge to make appropriate inferences (Oakhill, 1993; Perfetti et al., 2005). Yet with appropriate supports, even preschoolers are capable of making inferences (van den Broek et al., 2005; van Kleeck, 2008).

Children's abilities to make inferences follow a developmental progression. Using their budding causal reasoning skills, children are first able to make inferences about relationships between physical events (van den Broek et al., 2005). As children get older, their capacity to make inferences regarding physical relationships grows, and they also develop the ability to make inferences about internal states, such as characters' feelings, goals, and desires. Not all inferences are equally difficult for young children; events that occur closer together in time are easier for children to link inferentially than are distant events (Schmidt, Paris, & Stober, 1979).

It is important for adults to help preschoolers make these connections in order to provide the base for later fluent reading comprehension. Adults can do so by asking questions and making comments that draw children's attention to how events in the story are connected (Makdissi & Boisclair, 2006; van den Broek et al., 2005; van Kleeck, 2008). Thinking back to one of the basic tenets of sociocultural theory—that all thinking first occurs across people and then internally—young children may initially need help connecting two pictures or ideas that are proximally connected and then later need scaffolding to connect more distal ideas. Van Kleeck (2008) suggests focusing 40% of shared book reading questions on inferencing rather than literal aspects of a text and asking preschoolers three types of inferencing questions: 1) causal questions that help elucidate the story schema, 2) informational questions about the text and background knowledge that can aid in interpretation, and 3) evaluative questions about the outcome of story situations. To further the discussion that addresses inferencing, see Chapter 4 by van Kleeck and Chapter 10 by Lynch and Lepola.

As children get older, though, they become more able to make complex inferences as well as inferences that are less reliant on the text or the child's background knowledge (van den Broek et al., 2005). Elementary school–age students are increasingly prepared to make deeper connections to the texts they read. At this point, adults can ask inferential questions more of the time and concentrate on the literal aspects of the text with less frequency. The goal of comprehension instruction in middle elementary school is—through strategies such as reciprocal teaching, think-alouds, and peer-assisted learning—to encourage children to ask and answer these questions in ways that will eventually allow them to internalize them at an intrapsychological level (Brown, 1997; Duke & Pearson, 2002; Fuchs & Fuchs, 2007; Kintsch, 1998). Although it is beyond the scope of this chapter to address comprehension strategies at the elementary level in any depth, it is worth noting that the demands on elementary school students continue to increase in this regard as states begin to provide instruction aligned with the CCSS (Shanahan, 2013).

The Influence of Dispositional Factors over Time

Dispositional factors, such as motivation, temperament, and attention span, are important to mention as well. Because comprehension is an interactive experience for beginning readers, factors related to parental disposition—such as knowledge and interest in reading—are also important to consider (Bennett, Weigel, & Martin, 2002; Curenton & Justice, 2008). Noncognitive skills, such as persistence, have been implicated in the reading success of young children (Newman, Noel, Chen, & Matsopoulos, 1998). Similarly, maternal beliefs and practices regarding shared reading time have been demonstrated to influence preschool children's interest in reading (DeBaryshe, 1995). The benefits of cultivating enthusiasm for reading at a young age should not be underestimated, as preschoolers whose parents viewed reading as pleasurable reported reading more frequently and achieved higher scores on tests of reading achievement when in third grade (Sonnenschein, Baker, Serpell, & Schmidt, 2000). These findings help illustrate the truly dynamic nature of reading development.

As the reading demands placed upon children increase, it stands to reason that their motivation to engage in reading continues to play a role in successful comprehension. The relationship among skill, reading volume, and reading engagement is cyclical, and the idea of the Matthew effect in reading (an allusion to a passage from the book of Matthew stating that the rich become richer while the poor become poorer) highlights the dynamic way these variables lead to an increasing gap between those students who read more and get better over time and those students who lack both skills and reading motivation (Stanovich, 1986). This feedback loop begins early, and many studies have shown that enthusiasm for reading drops upon entry into formal schooling and continues to drop over time (Eccles & Wigfield, 2002; Gottfried, Fleming, & Gottfried, 2001). For these reasons, it is even more essential to consider how adults can support precomprehension abilities in young children.

CONCLUSION

It is important to understand that comprehension skills start to develop long before children begin their formal education and that there are many similarities between listening and reading comprehension. At the same time, however, it is essential to recognize that significant differences exist between the comprehension demands placed on prereaders and readers. As discussed, written language differs from spoken language in many ways, with differences in formal, semantic, and pragmatic dimensions of text. Adults can serve as facilitators and guides throughout the process of reading development. Still, children are increasingly expected to activate their own background knowledge, draw upon their repository of vocabulary words, and make connections between disparate sections of text as they progress through elementary school. The removal of scaffolds—visual supports, text laid out in small chunks, and adult guides—constitutes a considerable shift in the world of young readers.

However, the cognitive consequences of engaging with text are the same for both prereaders and mid-elementary school readers. Reading comprehension requires the possession of many component skills, several of which are acquired through oral or written exposure to texts. The reciprocal relationship among general knowledge, vocabulary, and reading volume highlights the importance of sharing books with children early and often. When these skills are present at a young age, children have access to increasingly more sophisticated ideas and texts, making the long road to reading comprehension one that is relatively free of obstacles.

Although the focus of reading instruction in the primary grades is generally on word analysis and reading fluency, it is important to remember that these skills are necessary precursors to reading comprehension but by no means the only skills required. Parents and educators need to build the important skills discussed throughout this volume even during the years that their importance may seem secondary. Scarborough's analogy of component reading skills as individual threads in a braided rope is a powerful one because it highlights the need to strengthen all skills that are important for later reading comprehension. For many years, comprehension instruction has been an overlooked area of focus in preschool and early elementary education. In order for this skill set to be developed as strongly as those areas that receive more attention—phonemic awareness, letter recognition, and reading fluency—it is important to embed the strategies discussed in this volume into early childhood education.

Finally, it is important to consider what future work should be done to advance our understanding of prereaders' comprehension and its progression into text comprehension. This development is challenging to quantify because comprehension is a complex task that draws on many different cognitive skills and processes. Moreover, different skills and processes become particularly important for comprehension success as children become skilled readers and conversationalists (Cain, Oakhill, & Bryant, 2004). See Chapter 1 by DeBruin-Parecki and Pribesh for research on teachers' use of comprehension strategies to help prepare children for reading success in school. Young children's reading comprehension is strongly predicted by prerequisite language skills such as word recognition skills and verbal ability. Older children begin to use comprehension processes such as inference generation with increasing frequency and are better equipped to construct an integrated and coherent model of a text's meaning. We have not determined, at a granular level, the unique contribution made by each of these skills at different times in child development. Thus a fully integrated model of comprehension across the age span—one that mirrors Scarborough's braid—is needed and is a necessary area of exploration for future research. The research contained in this volume contributes greatly to the burgeoning work conducted in this area.

REFERENCES

Adlof, S., Catts, H., & Little, T. (2006). Should the simple view of reading include a fluency component? *Reading and Writing, 19,* 933–958.

Adlof, S.M., Perfetti, C.A., & Catts, H.W. (2011). Developmental changes in reading comprehension: Implications for assessment and instruction. In S.J. Samuels & A.E. Farstrup (Eds.), *What research has to say about reading instruction* (pp. 186–214). Newark, DE: International Reading Association.

Anderson, R.C., & Pearson, P.D. (1984). A schema-theoretic view of basic processes in reading comprehension. In P.D. Pearson, R. Barr, M.L. Kamil, P. Mosenthal, & R. Dykstra (Eds.), *Handbook of reading research* (pp. 255–291). New York, NY: Longman.

Anglin, J.M. (1993). Vocabulary development: A morphological analysis. *Monographs of the Society for Research in Child Development, 28,* 58.

Beck, I.L., McKeown, M.G., & Kucan, L. (2002). *Bringing words to life: Robust vocabulary instruction.* New York, NY: Guilford Press.

Beck, I.L., Perfetti, C.A., & McKeown, M.G. (1982). Effects of long-term vocabulary instruction on lexical access and reading comprehension. *Journal of Educational Psychology, 74,* 506–521. doi:10.1037/0022-0663.74.4.506

Bennett, K.K., Weigel, D.J., & Martin, S.S. (2002). Children's acquisition of early literacy skills: Examining family contributions. *Early Childhood Research Quarterly, 17,* 295–317.

Best, R.M., Floyd, R.G., & McNamara, D.S. (2008). Differential competencies contributing to children's comprehension of narrative and expository texts. *Reading Psychology, 29,* 137–164.

Biemiller, A. (2006). Vocabulary development and instruction: A prerequisite for school learning. In D. Dickinson & S.B. Neuman (Eds.), *Handbook of early literacy research* (Vol. 2, pp. 41–51). New York, NY: Guilford Press.

Brown, A.L. (1997). Transforming schools into communities of thinking and learning about serious matters. *American Psychologist, 52*(4), 399–413.

Brown, D.D. (2008). The use of causal connections by young children: Implications for school readiness. *NHSA Dialogue, 11*(1), 44–53.

Bus, A.G., & van IJzendoorn, M.H. (1997). Affective dimension of mother-infant picturebook reading. *Journal of School Psychology, 35,* 46–61.

Cain, K., & Oakhill, J.V. (1999). Inference making ability and its relation to comprehension failure in young children. *Reading and Writing, 11,* 489–503.

Cain, K., Oakhill, J.V., Barnes, M.A., & Bryant, P.E. (2001). Comprehension skill, inference making ability, and the relation to knowledge. *Memory and Cognition, 29,* 850–859.

Cain, K., Oakhill, J.V., & Bryant, P.E. (2004). Children's reading comprehension ability: Concurrent prediction by working memory, verbal ability, and component skills. *Journal of Educational Psychology, 96*(1), 31–42.

Catts, H.W., Hogan, T.P., & Fey, M.E. (2003). Subgrouping poor readers on the basis of individual differences in reading-related abilities. *Journal of Learning Disabilities, 36*(3), 151–164.

Chall, J.S. (1993). *Stages of reading development.* New York, NY: McGraw-Hill.

Clingenpeel, B.T., & Pianta, R.C. (2007). Mothers' sensitivity and book-reading interactions with first graders. *Early Education & Development, 18*(1), 1–22.

Cunningham, A.E., & Stanovich, K.E. (1991). Tracking the unique effects of print exposure in children: Associations with vocabulary, general knowledge, and spelling. *Journal of Educational Psychology, 83*(2), 264–274.

Cunningham, A.E., & Stanovich, K.E. (1997). Early reading acquisition and its relation to reading experience and ability 10 years later. *Developmental Psychology, 33*(6), 934–945.

Cunningham, A.E., & Stanovich, K.E. (1998). What reading does for the mind. *American Educator, 22*(1–2), 8–15.

Curenton, S., & Justice, L.M. (2008). Children's preliteracy skills: Influence of maternal education and mothers' beliefs about shared-reading interactions. *Early Education and Development, 19,* 261–283.

DeBaryshe, B.D. (1995). Maternal belief systems: Linchpin in the home reading process. *Journal of Applied Developmental Psychology, 16,* 1–20.

Diakidoy, I., Stylianou, P., Karefillidou, C., & Papageorgiou, P. (2004, January–March). The relationship between listening and reading comprehension of different types of text at increasing grade levels. *Reading Psychology: An International Quarterly, 26*(1), 55–80.

Dickinson, D.K., & Smith, M.W. (1994). Long term effects of preschool teachers' book readings on low-income children's vocabulary and story comprehension. *Reading Research Quarterly, 29*(2), 104–122.

Dochy, F., Segers, M., & Buehl, M. (1999). The relation between assessment practices and outcomes of studies: The case of research on prior knowledge. *Review of Educational Research, 69*(2), 147–188.

Duke, N.K., & Pearson, D. (2002). Effective practices for developing reading comprehension. In A.E. Farstrup & S.J. Samuels (Eds.), *What research has to say about reading instruction* (3rd ed., pp. 205–242). Newark, DE: International Reading Association.

Eccles, J.S., & Wigfield, A. (2002). Motivational beliefs, values and goals. *Annual Review of Psychology, 53,* 109–132.

Fivush, R., Reese, E., & Haden, C.A. (2006). Elaborating on elaborations: Role of maternal reminiscing style in cognitive and socioemotional development. *Child Development, 77*(6), 1568–1588. doi:10.1111/j.1467-8624.2006.00960.x

Fuchs, D., & Fuchs, L.S. (2007). Increasing strategic reading comprehension with peer-assisted learning strategies. In D.S. McNamara (Ed.), *Reading comprehension strategies: Theories, interventions, and technologies* (pp. 175–197). Mahwah, NJ: Erlbaum.

Garner, J.K., & Bochna, C.R. (2004). Transfer of a listening comprehension strategy to independent reading in first-grade students. *Early Childhood Education Journal, 32*(2), 69–74.

Gottfried, A.E., Fleming, J.S., & Gottfried, A.W. (2001). Continuity of academic intrinsic motivation from childhood through late adolescence: A longitudinal study. *Journal of Educational Psychology, 93,* 3–13.

Haden, C.A., Haine, R.A., & Fivush, R. (1997). Developing narrative structure in parent-child reminiscing across the preschool years. *Developmental Psychology, 33,* 295–307.

Hargrave, A.C., & Sénéchal, M. (2000). A book reading intervention with preschool children who have limited vocabularies: The benefits of regular reading and dialogic reading. *Early Childhood Research Quarterly, 15*(1), 75–90.

Hart, B., & Risley, T.R. (1999). *The social world of children learning to talk.* Baltimore, MD: Paul H. Brookes Publishing Co.

Hayes, D.P., & Ahrens, M.G. (1988). Vocabulary simplification for children: A special case of "motherese"? *Journal of Child Language, 15,* 395–410.

Hirsch, E.D., Jr. (2003). Reading comprehension requires knowledge—of words and the world. *American Educator, 27*(1), 10–29.

Hirsch, E.D., Jr. (2006). *The knowledge deficit: Closing the shocking education gap for American children.* New York, NY: Houghton-Mifflin Company.

Hoover, W.A., & Gough, P.B. (1990). The simple view of reading. *Reading and Writing: An Interdisciplinary Journal, 2,* 127–160.

Joshi, R.M., Williams, K.A., & Wood, J.R. (1998). Predicting reading comprehension from listening comprehension: Is this the answer to the I.Q. debate? In C. Hulme & R.M. Joshi (Eds.), *Reading and spelling development and disorders* (pp. 319–327). Mahwah, NJ: Erlbaum.

Justice, L.M. (2002). Influences on preschoolers' novel word learning during shared storybook reading. *Reading Psychology, 23,* 87–106.

Karrass, J., VanDeventer, M.C., & Braungart-Rieker, J.M. (2003). Predicting shared parent-child book reading in infancy. *Journal of Family Psychology, 17,* 134–146.

Kendeou, P., Lynch, J.S., van den Broek, P., Espin, C.A., White, M.J., & Kremer, K.E. (2005). Developing successful readers: Building early comprehension skills through television viewing and listening. *Early Childhood Education Journal, 33,* 91–98. doi:10.1007/s10643-005-0030-6

Kendeou, P., van den Broek, P., White, M.J., & Lynch, J. (2007). Comprehension in preschool and early elementary children: Skill development and strategy interventions. In D.S. McNamara (Ed.), *Reading comprehension strategies: Theories, interventions, and technologies* (pp. 27–45). Mahwah, NJ: Erlbaum.

Kintsch, E. (2005). Comprehension theory as a guide for the design of thoughtful questions. *Topics in Language Disorders, 25*(1), 51–64.

Kintsch, W. (1998). *Comprehension: A paradigm for cognition.* Cambridge, UK: Cambridge University Press.

Lange, G., & Carroll, D.E. (2003). Mother-child conversation styles and children's laboratory memory for narrative and nonnarrative materials. *Journal of Cognition and Development, 4*(4), 435–457. doi:10.1207/S15327647JCD0404_03

Lawrence, J.F., & Snow, C. (2011). Oral discourse and reading. In M. Kamil, P.D. Pearson, E.B. Moje, & P. Afflerbach (Eds.), *Handbook of reading research* (Vol. 4, pp. 320–338). Mahwah, NJ: Erlbaum.

Lever, R., & Sénéchal, M. (2011). Discussing stories: On how a dialogic reading intervention improves kindergartners' oral narrative construction. *Journal of Experimental Child Psychology, 108,* 1–24.

Makdissi, H., & Boisclair, A. (2006). Interactive reading: A context for expanding the expressions of causal relations in preschoolers. *Written Language and Literacy, 9*(2), 177–211.

Metsala, J.L., & Wally, A.C. (1998). Spoken vocabulary growth and the segmental restructuring of lexical representations: Precursors to phonemic awareness and early reading ability. In J. Metsala & L. Ehri (Eds.), *Word recognition in beginning reading* (pp. 89–120). Hillsdale, NJ: Erlbaum.

Nagy, W.E., Herman, P.A., & Anderson, R.C. (1985). Learning words from context. *Reading Research Quarterly, 20,* 233–253. doi:10.2307/747758

Nelson, K. (1986). *Event knowledge: Structure and function in development.* Hillsdale, NJ: Erlbaum.

Neuman, S.B., Newman, E.H., & Dwyer, J. (2011). Educational effects of a vocabulary intervention on preschoolers' word knowledge and conceptual development: A cluster-randomized trial. *Reading Research Quarterly, 46,* 249–272. doi:10.1598/RRQ.46.3.3

Newman, J., Noel, A., Chen, R., & Matsopoulos, A.S. (1998). Temperament, selected moderating variables and early reading achievement. *Journal of School Psychology, 36*(2), 215–232.

Oakhill, J. (1993). Children's difficulties in reading comprehension. *Educational Psychology Review, 5*(3), 223–237.

Oakhill, J.V., & Cain, K. (2012). The precursors of reading ability in young readers: Evidence from a four-year longitudinal study. *Scientific Studies of Reading, 16*(2), 91–121.

Oakhill, J.V., Cain, K., & Bryant, P.E. (2003). The dissociation of word reading and text comprehension: Evidence from component skills. *Language and Cognitive Processes, 18,* 443–468.

Palincsar, A.S., & Brown, A.L. (1984). Reciprocal teaching of comprehension-fostering and comprehension-monitoring activities. *Cognition and Instruction, 1*(2), 117–175.

Paris, S.G., Wasik, B.A., & Turner, J.C. (1996). The development of strategic readers. In R. Barr, M.L. Kamil, P.B. Mosenthal, & P.D. Pearson (Eds.), *Handbook of reading research* (Vol. 2, pp. 609–640). New York, NY: Longman.

Perfetti, C.A. (1994). Psycholinguistics and reading ability. In M.A. Gernsbacher (Ed.), *Handbook of psycholinguistics* (pp. 849–894). San Diego, CA: Academic Press.

Perfetti, C.A., Landi, N., & Oakhill, J. (2005). The acquisition of reading comprehension skill. In M.J. Snowling & C. Hulme (Eds.), *The science of reading: A handbook* (pp. 227–247). Oxford, UK: Blackwell.

Poulsen, D., Kintsch, E., Kintsch, W., & Premack, D. (1979). Children's comprehension and memory for stories. *Journal of Experimental Child Psychology, 28,* 379–403.

Price, L.H., van Kleeck, A., & Huberty, C.J. (2009). Talk during book sharing between parents and preschool children: A comparison between storybook and expository book conditions. *Reading Research Quarterly, 44*(2), 171–194.

RAND Reading Study Group. (2002). *Reading for understanding: Toward a research and development program in reading comprehension.* Santa Monica, CA: Office of Education Research and Improvement.

Roberts, K.L. (2013). Comprehension strategy instruction during parent-child shared reading: An intervention study. *Literacy Research and Instruction, 52*(2), 106–129.

Rogoff, B. (2003). *The cultural nature of human development.* Oxford, UK: Oxford University Press.

Scarborough, H. (2001). Connecting early language and literacy to later reading (dis)abilities: Evidence, theory, and practice. In S.B. Neuman & D.K. Dickinson (Eds.), *Handbook of early literacy research* (Vol. 1, pp. 97–110). New York, NY: Guilford Press.

Scarborough, H. (2005). Developmental relationships between language and reading: Reconciling a beautiful hypothesis with some ugly facts. In H.W. Catts & A.G. Kamhi (Eds.), *The connections between language and reading disabilities* (pp. 3–24). Mahwah, NJ: Erlbaum.

Schmidt, C.R., Paris, S.G., & Stober, S. (1979). Inferential distance and children's memory for pictorial sequences. *Developmental Psychology, 15*(4), 396–406.

Sénéchal, M., & LeFevre, J. (2001). Storybook reading and parent teaching: Links to language and literacy development. In P. Rebello Britto & J. Brooks-Gunn (Eds.), *The role of family literacy environments in promoting young children's emerging literacy skills* (pp. 53–71). New York, NY: Jossey-Bass.

Sénéchal, M., Ouellette, G., & Rodney, D. (2006). The misunderstood giant: On the predictive role of early vocabulary in future reading. In D.K. Dickinson & S.B. Neuman (Eds.), *Handbook of early literacy research* (Vol. 2, pp. 173–184). New York, NY: Guilford Press.

Shanahan, T. (2013). Letting the text take center stage: How the common core state standards will transform English language arts instruction. *American Educator, 3,* 4–11, 43.

Share, D.L., & Stanovich, K.E. (1995). Cognitive processes in early reading development: Accommodating individual differences into a model of acquisition. *Issues in Education: Contributions from Educational Psychology, 1,* 1–57.

Simmons, D.C., Pollard- Durodola, S.D., Gonzalez, J.E., Davis, M.J., & Simmons, L.E. (2008). Shared book reading interventions. In. S.B. Neuman (Ed.), *Educating the other America* (pp. 187– 212). Baltimore, MD: Paul H. Brookes Publishing Co.

Snow, C.E. (1991). The theoretical basis for relationships between language and literacy in development. *Journal of Research in Childhood Education, 6*(1), 5–10.

Snow, C. (2002). *Reading for understanding: Toward an R&D program in reading comprehension.* Santa Monica, CA: RAND Corporation.

Snow, C.E., Burns, M.S., & Griffin, P. (1998). *Preventing reading difficulties in young children.* Committee on the Prevention of Reading Difficulties in Young Children. Washington, DC: National Academy Press.

Sonnenschein, S., Baker, L., Serpell, R., & Schmidt, D. (2000). Reading is a source of entertainment: The importance of the home perspective for children's literacy development. In K.A. Roskos & J.F. Christie (Eds.), *Play and literacy in early childhood: Research from multiple perspectives* (pp. 125–137). Mahwah, NJ: Erlbaum.

Stanovich, K.E. (1986). Matthew effect in reading: Some consequences of the individual difference in the acquisition of literacy. *Reading Research Quarterly, 24,* 360–407.

Stanovich, K.E., & Cunningham, A.E. (1992). Studying the consequences of literacy within a literate society: The cognitive correlates of print exposure. *Memory & Cognition, 20*(1), 51–68.

Stanovich, K.E., & Cunningham, A.E. (1993). Where does knowledge come from? Specific associations between print exposure and information acquisition. *Journal of Educational Psychology, 85*(2), 211–229.

Sticht, T.G., & James, J.H. (1984). Listening and reading. In D. Pearson (Ed.), *Handbook of research on reading* (Vol. 1, pp. 293–317). New York, NY: Longman.

Trabasso, T., & Stein, N.L. (1997). Narrating, representing, and remembering event sequences. In P.W. van den Broek, P.J. Bauer, & T. Bourg (Eds.), *Developmental spans in event comprehension and representation* (pp. 237–270). Mahwah, NJ: Erlbaum.

van den Broek, P. (1997). Discovering the cement of the universe: The development of event comprehension from childhood to adulthood. In P.W. van den Broek, P.J. Bauer, & T. Bourg (Eds.), *Developmental spans in event comprehension and representation* (pp. 321–342). Mahwah, NJ: Erlbaum.

van den Broek, P., Kendeou, P., Kremer, K., Lynch, J.S., Butler, J., White, M.J., & Lorch, E.P. (2005). Assessment of comprehension abilities in young children. In S. Paris & S. Stahl (Eds.), *Children's reading comprehension and assessment* (pp. 107–130). Mahwah, NJ: Erlbaum.

van Kleeck, A. (2008). Providing preschool foundations for later reading comprehension: The importance of and ideas for targeting inferencing in storybook-sharing interventions. *Psychology in the Schools, 45*(7), 627–643.

Vygotsky, L.S. (1978). *Mind in society: The development of higher psychological processes.* Cambridge, MA: Harvard University Press.

Whitehurst, G.J., Falco, F.L., Lonigan, C.J., Fischel, J.E., DeBaryshe, B.D., Valdez-Menchaca, M.C., & Caulfield, M. (1988). Accelerating language development through picture book reading. *Developmental Psychology, 24,* 552–559.

Wigfield, A., & Guthrie, J.T. (1997). Motivation for reading: An overview. *Educational Psychologist, 32,* 57–58.

Wolf, M., & Katzir-Cohen, T. (2001). Reading fluency and its intervention. *Scientific Studies of Reading, 5,* 211–238.

Zevenbergen, A.A., Whitehurst, G.J., & Zevenbergen, J.A. (2003). Effects of a shared-reading intervention on the inclusion of evaluative devices in narratives of children from low-income families. *Applied Developmental Psychology, 24,* 1–15.

Zucker, T.A., Cabell, S.Q., Justice, L.M., Pentimonti, J.M., & Kadaraek, J.N. (2013). The role of frequent, interactive prekindergarten shared reading in the longitudinal development of language and literacy skills. *Developmental Psychology, 49*(8), 1425–1439.

Index

Page numbers followed by *f* and *t* indicate figures and tables, respectively.